Applications of Expert Systems

Volume 2

Turing Institute Press

Managing Editor Jon Ritchie
Academic Editor Dr Peter Mowforth

The Turing Institute, located in Glasgow, Scotland, was established in 1983 as a not-for-profit company, named in honour of the late Alan M. Turing, the distinguished British mathematician and logician whose work has had a lasting influence on the foundations of modern computing.

The Institute offers integrated research and teaching programmes in advanced intelligent technologies – in particular, logic programming, computer vision, robotics and expert systems. It derives its income from research and training contracts, both governmental and industrial, and by subscription from its Industrial Affiliates. It assists Affiliates with the transfer of technology from research to application, and provides them with training for their technical staff, a wide range of software tools and a comprehensive library and information service.

The Turing Institute is an Academic Associate of the University of Strathclyde, and its research staff work closely with different departments of the University on a variety of research programmes.

Other titles published in association with the Turing Institute Press

Applications of Expert Systems
J. Ross Quinlan (Ed.)

Structured Induction in Expert Systems
Alen D. Shapiro

Knowledge-Based Programming
Enn Tyugu

Applications of Expert Systems

Volume 2

Based on the Proceedings of the
Third and Fourth Australian
Conferences

Edited by

J. Ross Quinlan
University of Sydney

TURING INSTITUTE PRESS
in association with

ADDISON-WESLEY PUBLISHING COMPANY
Sydney · Wokingham, England · Reading, Massachusetts
Menlo Park, California · New York · Don Mills, Ontario
Amsterdam · Bonn · Singapore
Tokyo · Madrid · San Juan

Cover designed by Crayon Design, Henley-on-Thames
and printed by The Riverside Printing Co. (Reading) Ltd.
Typeset by Columns, Reading.
Printed in Great Britain by Mackays of Chatham PLC, Chatham, Kent.

First printed 1989

British Library Cataloguing in Publication Data
Applications of expert systems—volume 2:
    based on the proceedings of the third and
    fourth Australian conferences.
    1. Expert systems. Applications
    I. Quinlan, J. Ross (John Ross), *1943*–
    006.3'3

    ISBN 0–201–41655–7

Library of Congress Cataloging in Publication Data
(Revised for vol. 2)

Applications of expert systems.

    (Turing Institute Press)
    Papers largely drawn from the proceedings of
the Australian Conferences on Applications of
Expert Systems, held in Sydney in 1987 and 1988.
    Includes bibliographies and index.
    1. Expert systems (Computer science) 2. Artificial
intelligence. I. Quinlan, J. R. (John Ross), 1943– .
II. Australian Conference on Applications of Expert
Systems. III. Turing Institute Press (Series)
QA76.76.E95A66 1987 006.3'3 87–12611
ISBN 0–201–41655–7 (U.S.)

Preface

It is a real pleasure to write a preface for Volume 2 of *Applications of Expert Sy~~~ms*. Someone must have found Volume 1 interesting (or the kind folk at Addison-Wesley would not have suggested a successor) and there is always the possibility that the series could extend further (Volume 5? Volume 27?).

The papers in this collection are largely drawn from the Proceedings of the Third and Fourth Australian Conferences on Applications of Expert Systems, held in Sydney in 1987 and 1988. The purpose of these conferences has always been to stimulate informed use of expert systems technology through exposition of its many advantages, but without ignoring potential hazards and pitfalls. The papers reflect this pragmatic stance, discussing successful implementations alongside gripes about deficiencies of current techniques and tools.

The first group of papers, which I have labelled *Perspectives*, takes a broad look at where expert systems technology is heading and explores its relationship with its parent, artificial intelligence. The group of papers labelled *Applications* is subdivided into four categories: service industries, manufacturing, government and administration, and agriculture. The final group, *Techniques*, examines issues at a more general level than a specific application, with two subheadings: knowledge representation, and knowledge acquisition and maintenance. The boundary between applications and techniques is often fuzzy as some of the former papers also discuss general methods while some of the latter refer to concrete applications, so this division was made on the basis of each paper's emphasis and contribution. The following paragraphs give brief introductory notes on the individual papers.

Edward Feigenbaum sees computing as having reached the beginnings of a new stage in which machines will process knowledge rather than information. After a brief overview of the evolution of expert systems (ES) ideas and applications, he turns to shortcomings characteristic of the field, such as lack of naturalness in user interfaces, brittleness and limited reasoning modes. Feigenbaum then shares his vision of how the technology might develop in the longer term. Bruce Buchanan, another ES pioneer, stresses the need for more scientific method in AI. He sees a deficiency of analysis, the step in which we attempt to understand what we have learned from building a system. Analysis is often the bridge that leads to future advances and Buchanan suggests that ES provides an apparatus for understanding the relevance of different architectures and representations. Douglas Lenat and Edward Feigenbaum return to the fundamental axiom of ES, referred to as the *Knowledge Principle*, namely, knowledge is the primary source of power in intelligent systems. The authors find that current systems are more or less deficient in their implementation of this principle and, expanding on themes raised in Feigenbaum's paper, stress that novel situations are best dealt with by falling back on more general knowledge and the pervasive use of analogy.

The first subgroup of applications concerns the service sector, particularly financial services. On the Australian scene, Sue Zawa describes a system developed by a major bank to assess applications for personal loans. Besides presenting this specific application, the paper gives an inside view of the steps taken by a large corporation in setting up its first ES project, including selection of the task and evaluation of tools. Amanda Crofts, Victor Ciesielski, Wayne Jenkins, Michael Molesworth, Timothy Smith and Richard Lee present another financial services system, this time for underwriting life insurance. The emphasis of the paper is on the lessons learned in moving from a prototype to an industrial-strength system and the evaluation of the product from a management perspective. Nancy Lubich's survey of activity in the USA examines several financial domains, including commercial banking, financial planning and insurance, and applications designed to lower the cost of service provision, provide decision-making support, improve consistency and others. It addresses the question of the requirements for a successful application development.

The second set of applications deals with expert systems in manufacturing. Kim Horn, M. Brown and L. Lo have developed an expert system to diagnose manufacturing faults in cardiac pacemakers. The system currently has a better than 90% success rate and the authors show how the use of causal modelling will allow its coverage to be extended. Laurie Lock Lee, K. Teh and R. Campanini describe an application in process control in which an ES provides guidance to the operator of a complex iron ore sintering plant. This paper also stresses the importance of integration with the existing information system environment. In a similar vein, L.D. Cung and T.S. Ng have developed an operator assistance system for rectifying faults in a plate rolling mill that processes 700 000 tons of steel each year. An ancillary topic of their paper is a methodology for knowledge acquisition from experts with diverse backgrounds and skills.

The three applications in administration and government display the breadth of relevance of expert systems. Robin Stanton and Hugh Mackenzie describe a shell, SPECS, that has been developed to assist spatial planning. The problems that it must cope with include policy formalization and underspecified or conflicting policies. The paper includes a particularly scenic application: development of a zoning plan for the Great Barrier Reef. The second paper, by Stephen Nethercote, concerns a 'demonstrator' project commissioned by the Victorian State Government. The VBARS system refers enquirers seeking commercial assistance to the appropriate agency. The paper also describes TODAY-ES, an inductive tool integrated with a fourth generation language. Peter Cox, Terry White, Andrew Sutcliffe and Chris Liles have developed an expert system to assist experts who assess seasonal adjustments of time series. Like Sue Zawa's paper, this report traces an organization's first ventures into ES technology, and embodies the evaluation of a development methodology and tool.

Two papers focus on expert systems in agriculture, an uncommon domain but one that clearly has great potential. R. Finlayson and Brynn Hibbert describe a system that uses results of spectroscopic analysis and other information to identify problems and suggest remedies for the hydroponic cultivation of strawberries. The authors report that a useable system was developed in only one man-month! Matthew Clarke describes one aspect of SIRATAC, a long-running system to advise farmers on the chemical control of cotton pests. This paper looks at the nature and role of explanations in an ES environment, an essential feature if the systems must establish their credibility.

Leading off the first set of techniques papers, Randall Davis addresses the importance of reasoning from first principles if expert systems are to be robust. He cites an example from the second flight of the Space Shuttle to show that unanticipated events cannot be handled properly by shallow rules. Davis argues that the required deep knowledge should be captured as part of the design process. Raymond Lister examines the general area of fault diagnosis. Two types of fault tree are described and compared, but a need becomes apparent for more complex systems exploiting constraints, frames, and sophisticated inference modes. The paper includes a very useful review of approaches and a comprehensive bibliography. Anthony Grech and Claude Sammut describe the use of an assumption-based truth maintenance system in making sense of conflicting evidence. The application – passive identification of radar transmitters – requires the system to carry out information fusion in order to analyse and rank candidate solutions.

The final three papers concern problems of knowledge acquisition and maintenance of a knowledge base. Donald Michie examines the inductive processes that are used to assist the development of rules. He notes that the knowledge derived in this way should reflect the expert's viewpoint, so that different viewpoints give different encodings. The paper discusses a successful application to credit assessment. John Debenham provides a systematic approach to traditional knowledge acquisition from a human expert. He differentiates between three categories – data, information and knowledge – and suggests how the expert should be guided in the elicitation process. Paul Compton, Kim Horn, Les Lazarus, K. Ho and I take up the issue of maintaining a live knowledge base. The application in question – the provision of interpretive comments on thyroid assays – has been in routine use for nearly four years and has generated 20 000 reports. The paper hypothesizes that knowledge 'debugging' by experts is difficult because an expert rule is not absolute, but rather justifies one hypothesis over others in an established context.

Finally, a word of thanks and appreciation to the overseas keynote speakers who contributed so much to the conferences, and to members of the Sydney Expert Systems Group who helped to make them happen.

Ross Quinlan
Sydney, May 1988

Acknowledgements

The publisher would like to thank the following individuals for giving their permission to reproduce their material:

Brown, M. (Paper 7)
    Telectronics Pty Ltd, 2 Sirius Road, Lane Cove, NSW 2066, Australia.

Buchanan, Bruce G. (Paper 2)
    Knowledge Systems Laboratory, Stanford University, 701 Welch Road, Palo Alto, CA 94304, USA.

Campanini, R. (Paper 8)
    BHP Central Research Laboratories, PO Box 188, Wallsend, NSW 2287, Australia.

Ciesielski, Victor B. (Paper 5)
    Department of Computer Science, Royal Melbourne Institute of Technology, GPO Box 2476U, Melbourne, Victoria 3001, Australia.

Clarke, Matthew (Paper 14)
    Artificial Intelligence Centre South Pacific, Digital Equipment Corporation (Australia) Pty Ltd, PO Box 384, Chatswood, NSW 2067, Australia.

Compton, Paul (Paper 20)
    Garvan Institute of Medical Research, St Vincents Hospital, Darlinghurst, NSW 2010, Australia.

Cox, Peter (Paper 12)
    Australian Bureau of Statistics, PO Box 10, Belconnen, ACT 2600, Australia.

Crofts, Amanda E. (Paper 5)
    McMullan Kilvington Pty Ltd, 1–4 Layfield Street, South Melbourne, Victoria 3205, Australia.

Cung, L.D. (Paper 9)
    Department of Electrical and Computer Engineering, University of Wollongong, Wollongong, NSW 2500, Australia.

Davis, Randall (Paper 15)
Sloan School of Management, Massachusetts Institute of Technology, Cambridge, MA 02139, USA

Debenham, John (Paper 19)
Key Centre for Advanced Computing Sciences, University of Technology (Sydney), Broadway, NSW 2007, Australia.

Feigenbaum, Edward A. (Papers 1 and 3)
Computer Science Department, Stanford University, Stanford, CA 94305, USA.

Finlayson, R. (Paper 13)
Department of Analytical Chemistry, University of NSW, Kensington, NSW 2033, Australia.

Grech, Anthony (Paper 17)
Department of Computer Science, University of New South Wales, PO Box 1, Kensington, NSW 2033, Australia.

Hibbert, D.B. (Paper 13)
Department of Analytical Chemistry, University of NSW, Kensington, NSW 2033, Australia.

Ho, K. (Paper 20)
Garvan Institute of Medical Research, St Vincents Hospital, Darlinghurst, NSW 2010, Australia.

Horn, K. (Papers 7 and 20)
Telectronics Pty Ltd, 2 Sirius Road, Lane Cove, NSW 2066, Australia.

Jenkins, Wayne (Paper 5)
Department of Computer Science, Royal Melbourne Institute of Technology, GPO Box 2476U, Melbourne, Victoria 3001, Australia.

Lazarus, L. (Paper 20)
Garvan Institute of Medical Research, St Vincents Hospital, Darlinghurst, NSW 2010, Australia.

Lee, Richard Y. (Paper 5)
McMullan Kilvington Pty Ltd, 1–4 Layfield Street, South Melbourne, Victoria 3205, Australia.

Lenat, Douglas B. (Paper 3)
Microelectronics and Computer Technology Corporation, 3500 W. Balcones Center, Austin, TX 78759, USA.

Liles, Chris (Paper 12)
Fujitsu Australia Ltd, 7–9 Moore Street, Canberra, ACT 2600, Australia.

Lister, Raymond (Paper 16)
Basser Department of Computer Science, University of Sydney, Sydney, NSW 2006, Australia.

Lo, L. (Paper 7)
Telectronics Pty Ltd, 2 Sirius Road, Lane Cove, NSW 2066, Australia.

Lock Lee, L.G. (Paper 8)
BHP Central Research Laboratories, PO Box 188, Wallsend, NSW 2287,
Australia.

Lubich, Nancy I. (Paper 6)
Management Sciences 3160, BankAmerica Corporation, PO Box 37000,
San Francisco, CA 94127, USA.

Mackenzie, H.G. (Paper 10)
Division of Information Technology, CSIRO, GPO Box 664, Canberra,
ACT 2601, Australia.

Michie, Donald (Paper 18)
Turing Institute, George House, 36 North Hanover Street, Glasgow
G1 2AD, UK.

Molesworth, Michael (Paper 5)
Cologne RE, 9th Floor, 32 Bridge Street, Sydney 2000, Australia.

Nethercote, Stephen (Paper 11)
6 Mayfair Avenue, Lower Templestowe, Victoria 3107, Australia.

Ng, T.S. (Paper 9)
Department of Electrical and Computer Engineering, University of
Wollongong, Wollongong, NSW 2500, Australia.

Quinlan, J.R. (Paper 20)
Basser Department of Computer Science, University of Sydney, Sydney,
NSW 2006, Australia.

Sammut, Claude (Paper 17)
Computer Science Department, University of New South Wales, PO
Box 1, Kensington, NSW 2033, Australia.

Smith, Timothy J. (Paper 5)
McMullan Kilvington Pty Ltd, 1–4 Layfield Street, South Melbourne,
Victoria 3205, Australia.

Stanton, R.B. (Paper 10)
Department of Computer Science, Australian National University,
Canberra, ACT 2601, Australia.

Sutcliffe, Andrew (Paper 12)
Australian Bureau of Statistics, PO Box 10, Belconnen, ACT 2600,
Australia.

Teh, K. (Paper 8)
BHP Central Research Laboratories, PO Box 188, Wallsend, NSW 2287,
Australia.

White, Terry (Paper 12)
> Australian Bureau of Statistics, PO Box 10, Belconnen, ACT 2600, Australia.

Zawa, Sue (Paper 4)
> State Bank of NSW, 223 Liverpool Street, Ashfield, NSW 2131, Australia.

The publisher is also grateful to:

D. Reidel Publishing Company who hold the copyright on 'Artificial Intelligence as an Experimental Science', in *Aspects of Artificial Intelligence*, James Fetzer (ed.), 1988, Kluwer Academic Publishers. Paper 2 in this book is an abridged version of the above.

International Joint Conferences on Artificial Intelligence, Inc. who hold the copyright on Paper 3 in this book. Copies of this and other IJCAI Proceedings are available from Morgan Kaufmann Publishers, Inc., PO Box 50490, Palo Alto, CA 94303, USA.

The State Bank of NSW who hold the copyright on Paper 4 in this book.

The Commonwealth of Australia who hold the copyright on Paper 12 in this book.

Digital Equipment Corporation (Aust.) Pty, Ltd who hold the copyright on Paper 14 in this book.

National Academy Press for permission to quote from *Human Factors in Automated and Robotic Space Systems, Proceedings of a Symposium*, held at the National Academy of Sciences, Washington D.C., January 29–30, 1986, sponsored by the Committee on Human Factors of the National Research Council (Paper 15 in this book.)

Contents

Part One

Perspectives

1
Knowledge Processing: From File Servers To Knowledge Servers

Edward A. Feigenbaum
Stanford University

It has been said that when people make forecasts, they overestimate what can be done in the short run and underestimate what can be achieved in the long run. I have worked in the science and technology of Artificial Intelligence for 20 years and confess to being chronically optimistic about its progress. The gains have been substantial, even impressive. But we have hardly begun, and we must not lose sight of the point to which we are heading, however distant it may seem.

We are beginning the transition from data processing to knowledge processing. The key tool of our specialty is the digital computer, the most complex – and yet the most general – machine ever invented. Though the computer is a universal symbol-processing device, we have exploited, to date, only its mundane capabilities to file and retrieve data (file service) and to do high-speed arithmetic. The researchers in Artificial Intelligence have been studying the techniques for representing human knowledge for computer use and the methods by which that knowledge can be used to reason toward the solution of problems, the formation of hypotheses, and the discovery of new concepts and new knowledge. These researchers have been inventing the knowledge servers of our future.

Scientists and technologists (like all creators) must dream, must put forth a vision, else relegate their work to near-pointless incrementalism. My dream is about the future of Artificial Intelligence research and development over the next several decades, and the knowledge systems that can be produced thereby to assist the modern knowledge worker.

The beginnings of the dream

Fifty years ago, before the modern era of computation began, Turing's theorems and abstract machines gave hint of the fundamental idea that the computer could be used to model the symbol-manipulating processes that make up the most human of all behaviours – thinking. Thirty years ago, the work began in earnest (1986 was the thirtieth anniversary of the Dartmouth Summer Conference on Artificial Intelligence). The founding principle of the AI research area is really an article of faith – that the digital computer has the necessary and sufficient means for intelligent action. This first principle is called the **Physical Symbol System Hypothesis**.

The early dreaming included intelligent behaviour at very high levels of competence. Turing speculated on wide-ranging conversations between people and machines and also on chess playing programs. Later, Newell and Simon wrote about champion-level chess programs, and began their work toward that end. Samuel (checker playing), Gelernter (geometry theorem proving) and others shared the dream.

At Stanford, Lederberg and I chose reasoning in science as our task, and began work with Buchanan and Djerassi on building a program that would solve chemical structure elucidation problems at a high level of competence – the DENDRAL program. What emerged from the many experiments with DENDRAL was an empirical hypothesis that the source of the program's power to solve chemical structure problems from spectral data was its knowledge of basic and spectral chemistry. For DENDRAL, knowledge was power. Obvious? In retrospect, perhaps. But the prevailing view in AI at the time ascribed power to the reasoning processes – in modern terms, to the 'inference engine', not the knowledge base. Thus, in the late 1960s, the *knowledge as power hypothesis* stood as a *contra*-hypothesis, awaiting further test and the accumulation of evidence.

Much evidence came in the 1970s. Medical problem solving provided the springboard. The MYCIN program of Shortliffe and others at Stanford was the prototype of the expert-level advisory (or consultation) system. The core of MYCIN was its knowledge base of rules for infectious disease diagnosis and therapy. Its reasoning process was simple (backward chaining), even *ad hoc* in parts. But MYCIN was built as an integrated package of intellectual abilities. It could interact with a professional in the professional jargon of the specialty. It could explain its line of reasoning. And, it had a subsystem that could aid in the acquisition of new knowledge by guiding an expert to find defects in the stored knowledge. Overall, MYCIN provided strong confirmation to the knowledge as power hypothesis.

At nearly the same time, other efforts in medical problem solving were providing similar results. At the University of Pittsburgh the focus of the INTERNIST project was the construction of an enormous 'electronic textbook' of the knowledge of internal medicine (Pople, Myers and Miller). With its current knowledge base of 572 diseases, nearly 4500 manifestations, and hundreds of thousands of links between them, INTERNIST has provided the strongest confirmation yet of the knowledge as power hypothesis.

In the late 1970s, in fields other than medicine, an explosion of expert systems was taking place: in engineering, in manufacturing, in geology, in molecular biology, in financial services, in diagnostic servicing of machinery, in military signal processing, and many other areas. There is little to tie these areas together other than the fact that, in each, high-quality problem solving is guided by experiential, qualitative, heuristic knowledge. The explosion of applications created a new type of professional, the knowledge engineer (now in extremely short supply) and a new industry, the expert systems industry (now expanding rapidly). The scientific generalization from the frenzy of activity is simply massive additional confirmation of the knowledge as power hypothesis. The reasoning procedures associated with all of these systems are weak. In their knowledge bases lies their power.

Other areas of Artificial Intelligence research made shifts to the knowledge-based viewpoint. It is now commonplace to say that a program for understanding natural language must have extensive knowledge of its domain of discourse. A vision program for image understanding must have knowledge of the 'world' it is intended to see. And even this: learning programs must have a substantial body of knowledge from which to expand (that is, learning takes place at the fringes and interstices of what is already known).

Thus, the dream of the computer that performs at a high level of competence, over a wide variety of tasks that people perform well, seems to rest upon knowledge in the task areas.

The knowledge as power hypothesis has received so much confirmation that we can now assert it as the Knowledge Principle:

> **Knowledge Principle** A system exhibits intelligent understanding and action at a high level of competence primarily because of the specific knowledge that it contains about its domain of endeavour.

A corollary of the Knowledge Principle is that reasoning processes of an intelligent system, being general and therefore weak, are not the source of power that leads to high levels of competence in behaviour.

The Knowledge Principle simply says that if a program is to perform well, it must know a great deal about the 'world' in which it operates. In the absence of knowledge, reasoning will not help.

The Knowledge Principle is the emblem of the first era of Artificial Intelligence, the first part of the dream. It should inform and influence every decision about what is feasible in the AI science and with the AI technology.

The middle of the dream

Today, our intelligent artifacts perform well on specialized tasks within narrowly defined domains. An industry has been formed to put this technological understanding to work and widespread transfer of this technology has been achieved. Although the first era of the intelligent machine is ending, many problems remain to be solved.

One of these is 'naturalness'. The intelligent agent should interact with its human user in a fluid and flexible manner that appears natural to the person. But the systems of the first era share with the majority of computer systems an intolerable rigidity of stylistic expression, vocabulary and concepts. For example, programs rarely accept synonyms, and they cannot interpret and use metaphors. They always interact in a rigid grammatical straitjacket. The need for metaphor to induce in the user a feeling of naturalness seems critical. Metaphorical reference appears to be omnipresent and almost continuous in our use of language. Further, if you believe that our use of language reflects our underlying cognitive processes, then metaphor is a basic ideational process.

In the second era, we will see the evolution of the natural interface. The processes controlling the interaction will make greater use of the domain knowledge of the system, and knowledge of how to conduct fluid discourse. Harbingers of 'naturalness' already exist; they are based, to a large extent, upon pictures. The ONCOCIN project team at Stanford invested a great effort in an 'electronic flow sheet' to provide a seamless transition for the oncologist from paper forms for patient data entry to electronic versions of these forms. The commercially available expert system development software tools sometimes contain elegant and powerful packages for creating pictures that elucidate what the knowledge system is doing, and what its emerging solution 'looks like' (for example, IntelliCorp's KEE Pictures and Active Images). '

'Naturalness', of course, need not rely upon pictures. The advances in natural language understanding have been quite substantial, particularly in the use of knowledge to facilitate understanding. In the second era, it will become commonplace for knowledge systems to interact with users in human language, within the scope of the systems' knowledge.

The interaction systems of the second era will increasingly rely on continuous natural speech. In person-to-person interactions, people generally say what they want rather than type it. Typing is useful but unnatural. Speech understanding systems of wide applicability based on the Knowledge Principle are coming. At Stanford, we are beginning experiments with an experimental commercial system interfaced to the ONCOCIN expert system.

A limitation of first-era systems is their 'brittleness'. To mix metaphors, they operate on a high plateau of knowledge and competence until they reach the extremity of their knowledge; then they fall off precipitously to levels of utter incompetence. People suffer from the same difficulty (they, too, cannot escape the Knowledge Principle), but their fall is more graceful. The cushion for the soft fall is the knowledge and use of weaker, but more general, models that underlie the highly specific and specialized knowledge of the plateau. For example, when diagnosing the failure of an electronic circuit, an engineer with no specific knowledge of the circuit can fall back upon his or her knowledge of electronics, on circuit analysis methods, and on handbook data for the components. The capability for such model-based reasoning by machine is just now under study in many laboratories, and will emerge as an important feature of second-era systems. The capability does not come for free. Knowledge engineers must explicate and codify general models in a wide variety of task areas.

Task areas? But what if there is no 'task'? Can we envisage the intelligent program that behaves with common sense at the interstices between tasks or when 'task knowledge' is completely lacking? 'Common sense' is itself knowledge – an enormous body of knowledge distinguished by its ubiquity, and the circumstance that it is rarely codified and passed on to others, as is more formal knowledge. For example, take the 'common sense' fact that pregnancy is associated with females, not males. The extremely weak, but extremely general, forms of cognitive behaviour implied by common sense reasoning constitute for many the ultimate goal in the quest for machine intelligence. Researchers are now beginning the arduous task of understanding the details of the logic and representation of common sense knowledge: and codifying large bodies of 'common sense' knowledge. The first fruits of this will appear in the later systems of the second era. Common sense reasoning will probably appear as an unexpected naturalness in one's interaction with an intelligent agent. As an example of this in medical consultation advisory systems, if pregnancy is mentioned early in the interaction or can be readily inferred, the interaction shifts seamlessly to understanding that a female is involved. Magnify this example by 100 000 or 1 000 000 unspoken assumptions, and you will understand what I mean by a large knowledge base of common sense knowledge.

As knowledge in systems expands, so does the scope for modes of reasoning that have so far eluded the designers of these systems. Foremost among these are reasoning by analogy and its sibling, metaphorical reasoning. The essence of analogy has been evident for some time, but the details of analogizing have not. An analogy is a partial match of the description of some 'current situation' with stored knowledge. The extent of the match is critical. If the match is too 'partial' then the analogy is seen to be vacuous or far-fetched; if too complete then the 'analogy' is seen as hardly an analogy at all. Analogizing broadens the relevance of the entire knowledge base. It can be used to construct interesting and novel interpretations of situations and data. It can be used to retrieve knowledge that has been stored, but not stored in the 'expected' way. Analogizing can supply default values for attributes not evident in the description of the current situation. Analogizing can provide access to powerful methods that otherwise would not be evoked as 'relevant'. For example, in a famous example from early twentieth century physics, Dirac made the analogy between quantum theory and mathematical group theory that allowed him to use the powerful methods of group theory to solve important problems in quantum physics. We will begin to see reasoning by analogy emerge in knowledge systems of the second era.

Analogizing is seen also as an important process in automatic knowledge acquisition, another name for machine learning. In first-era systems, adding knowledge to knowledge bases has been almost always a manual process: people codify knowledge and place it in knowledge structures. Recent experiments by Douglas Lenat have shown that this laborious process can be 'semi-automated', facilitated by an analogizing program. The program suggests the relevant analogy to a new situation, and the knowledge engineer 'fills in the details'. In the second era, we will see programs that acquire the details with less, or no, human help. Many other techniques for automatic learning will find their way into second-era systems. For example, we are currently seeing the early experiments on 'learning apprentices' that carefully observe people performing complex tasks and infer, thereby, the knowledge needed for competent performance. The second era will also see (I predict) the first successful systems that couple language understanding with learning, so that knowledge bases can be augmented by the reading of text. Quite likely these will be specialized texts in narrow areas at the outset.

To summarize, because of the increasing power of our concepts and our tools, and the advent of the automatic learning methods, we can expect that during the second era the knowledge bases of intelligent systems will become very large, representing therein hundreds of thousands – perhaps millions – of facts, heuristics, concepts, relationships and models. Automatic learning will be facilitated thereby, since, by the Knowledge Principle, the task of adding knowledge is performed more competently the more knowledge is available ('the more we know, the easier it is to know more').

Finally, in the second era we will achieve a broad reconceptualization of what we mean by a knowledge system. In the broader concept, the 'system' will be conceived as the colleagular relationship between an intelligent computer agent and an intelligent person (or persons). Each will perform tasks that it/he/she does best, and the intelligence of the system will be an emergent of the collaboration. If the interaction is, indeed, seamless and natural, then it may hardly matter whether the relevant knowledge or the reasoning skills needed are in the head of the person or in the knowledge structures of the computer.

The far side of the dream: the Library of the Future

Here's a 'view from the future', looking back at our 'present', from Professor Marvin Minsky of MIT:

> 'Can you imagine that they used to have libraries where the books didn't talk to each other?'

The libraries of today are warehouses for passive objects. The books and journals sit on shelves, waiting for us to use our intelligence to find them, read them, interpret them, and cause them finally to divulge their stored knowledge. 'Electronic' libraries of today are no better. Their pages are pages of data files, but the electronic page images are equally passive.

Now imagine the library as an active intelligent knowledge server. It stores the knowledge of the disciplines in complex knowledge structures (perhaps in a knowledge representation formalism yet to be invented). It can reason with this knowledge to satisfy the needs of its users. These needs are expressed naturally, with fluid discourse. The system can, of course, retrieve and exhibit (that is, it can act as an electronic textbook). It can collect relevant information; it can summarize; it can pursue relationships.

It acts as a consultant on specific problems, offering advice on particular solutions, justifying those solutions with citations or with a fabric of general reasoning. If the user can suggest a solution or an hypothesis, it can check this and even suggest extensions. Or it can critique the user viewpoint, with a detailed rationale of its agreement or disagreement.

It pursues relational paths of associations to suggest, to the user, previously unseen connections. Collaborating with the user, it uses its processes of association and analogizing to 'brainstorm' for remote or novel concepts. More autonomously, but with some guidance from the user, it uses criteria of 'interestingness' to discover new concepts, new methods, new theories, new measurements.

The user of the Library of the Future need not be a person. It may be another knowledge system, that is, any intelligent agent with a need for knowledge. Thus the Library of the Future will be a network of knowledge systems, in which people and machines collaborate.

Publishing is an activity transformed. Authors may bypass text, adding their increment to human knowledge directly to the knowledge structures. Since the thread of responsibility must be maintained, and since there may be disagreement as knowledge grows, the contributions are authored (incidentally allowing for the computation of royalties for access and use). Knowledge base maintenance (that is, the 'updating' of knowledge) itself becomes a vigorous part of the new publishing industry.

At the far horizon, the dream can take many forms and dimensions. I have briefly sketched only a few, and I invite you to exercise your imagination to sketch your own. At the far horizon, the question is not 'if' or 'whether', but only 'when'.

Power tools for the mind: a statement of the encompassing vision

The hard work of the farmer was revolutionized by agricultural machinery. The labour of the industrial worker was revolutionized by engines and heavy machinery. As we move toward the post-industrial period of the twenty-first century, as work becomes increasingly the work of professionals and knowledge workers, the power tools are digital computers. The economic and social well-being of the advanced societies increasingly is the result of working 'smarter' rather than working 'harder', and computers are the agents of that change. Knowledge is power in human affairs, and knowledge systems are amplifiers of human thought and action.

'For the first time in the history of mankind, innovation is the fundamental raw material. Real strategic resources are no longer represented by coal, steel or oil but by the cleverness and cognitive capability of man.' (Carlo De Benedetti, Chief Exective of Olivetti)

2
What Do Expert Systems Offer the Science of AI?

Bruce G. Buchanan
Stanford University

1 Introduction

The assertion by Simon (1969) that AI is an experimental science is appealing to those in AI because of the comforting and legitimate sound of the term 'science'. Not all AI research has the form of experimental science, however, especially in its attention – or lack of attention – to data collected through observation and experimentation. Expert systems offer an experimental apparatus that can enhance the scientific nature of investigations in AI. This paper describes that perspective of expert systems, and largely ignores the important contributions that expert systems make in the role as applications.

In calling AI an *experimental* science, we presuppose the ability to perform controlled experiments involving intelligent behaviour, which are much more easily done with computer programs than with people. At the present time, AI has to be more concerned with qualitative statements of regularities rather than statistical statements because the framework for being more precise does not yet exist, as we argue in Sections 2 and 3 of this paper.

AI has both theoretical and experimental concerns. McCarthy (1983) distinguishes basic and applied research in AI and calls for more basic research on the premise that 'reaching human level artificial intelligence will require fundamental conceptual advances.' Nilsson (1983) mentions two different research strategies in AI. The first he calls the 'function-follows-form approach' – more popularly known as creating solutions in search of problems. He admits that 'some of the enthusiasm for the use of logic in AI might also be explained by this function-follows-form approach'. The second he calls the 'form-follows-function approach' – which is the problem-driven approach followed in most AI research. Here, the researcher is motivated by a desire to find a way (any way) of making a computer or computer-controlled device solve some specific problem. What the researcher finds or invents to do then is less

11

determined by enthusiasm for a methodology than by an enthusiasm for making things work.

Instead of a dichotomy of research paradigms, however, AI seems to contain a progression of steps from theorizing to engineering, from engineering to analysis, and from analysis back to theorizing. All seem important for progress. Upon examining individual pieces of research, however, we note that many researchers stop before completing the progression. Most work, to date, falls into either the theoretical or engineering categories. Future progress requires additional work on analysis and generalization that is characteristically scientific.

There are six more or less separate steps in this cycle, as shown below:

Theoretical steps:

1.   Identify the problem.

2.   Design a method for solving it.

Engineering steps:

3.   Implement the method in a computer program.

4.   Demonstrate the power of the program (and thus of the method).

Analytical steps:

5.   Analyse data collected in demonstrations.

6.   Generalize the results of the analysis.

Too many pieces of research, to date, stop after steps 2, 3 or 4; the best experimental research involves all six steps. One of the best and earliest examples of AI as an experimental science, illustrating all six steps, is the research on GPS by Newell and Simon (1972).

The first two steps in the list are termed 'theoretical' because they are often carried out with paper and pencil in the absence of an implemented program. The second two are termed 'engineering' because they involve building an artifact (a program) and observing its performance, perhaps experimenting with it under different conditions. The last two are termed 'analytical' to stand for both analysis of empirical data and formulation of general hypotheses that explain the data. The analysis steps are essential for progress in science. They also allow cycling back to theorizing or engineering with new problems, sometimes with explicit hypotheses to test.

Expert systems fit into this model at every step, but most strongly in the engineering steps. At present, implementers of expert systems in the commercial world are satisfied with a successful step 3. For scientific purposes, however, these systems must become the basis for steps 4–6 as well.

1.1 Theoretical steps in AI

An alternative view to the six-step experimental approach shown in Section 1 – that AI is a theoretical discipline – emphasizes formalism in describing methods, skips the two engineering steps entirely, and formalizes the analysis to proofs about the strengths and limits of the method. The results of the analysis are presumably as general as they can be, so the final step of generalization is not needed. The modified steps 1, 2' and 5' thus constitute the essence of the theoretical approach. It would be naïve to argue that theoretical studies do not advance our understanding of physical phenomena: Einstein's mathematics provide a compelling counterexample to anyone so inclined. While this paper attempts to show that we lack an adequate vocabulary for describing our methods, and argues in favour of the six-step experimental approach in AI, it is not an argument against theoretical methods. When they are successful they can revolutionize a discipline. In the absence of a theoretician to do this, however, the rest of the scientific community can be making advances experimentally (Kuhn, 1970).

Theoretical work in AI is largely pursued in the framework of symbolic logic. Mathematics is the language of choice for theoretical work in the so-called 'hard' sciences of physics and chemistry. However, almost by definition, mathematics is inappropriate for describing the phenomena with which AI is concerned because these include methods of symbolic reasoning, or reasoning without expressing everything numerically. The only candidate for a formal framework suitable for formalizing symbolic reasoning is symbolic logic, but present formulations are still not adequate for describing all the kinds of relations that AI systems need to describe, such as temporal reasoning and non-monotonic reasoning. McCarthy (1983) wrote: 'AI badly needs mathematical and logical theory, but the theory required involves conceptual innovations – not just mathematics.'

Unfortunately, there is considerable work in AI in which the method is designed first and the problems for which the method offers a solution are identified second. This is usually justified as 'pure research', and undoubtedly has an important place in every science. But it is undirected by data and guided by the same notions of simplicity and elegance that brought us windowless monads and other rationalistic constructs. They are not necessarily wrong, but they are speculations about how intelligent programs ought to behave.

There are many successful pieces of theoretical work in AI. One of the more successful was the work by Doyle (1979) on truth maintenance. In the absence of an implemented program, Doyle designed, and argued for, a method for maintaining a true description of the world in the face of new axioms that contradict previous information. McCarthy, Hayes,

Manna, and many others have made other important theoretical contributions.

Theorizing in the absence of data can be successful in AI because AI programs are artifacts, designed to run under the control of man-made languages and operating systems on man-made computers. Insofar as the layers of artifacts – and their interactions – are well understood, it is possible to design programs that behave in specified ways.

In complex problem areas the number of interactions leaves the result of theorizing uncoupled from interesting instantiations of the problem. As Simon (1969) notes, the number of variables in problems of interest is too great to allow us to understand the complexity of the interactions. Another difficulty with theorizing in the absence of data is oversimplification of the initial problem. Bayesians, for instance, believed that MYCIN's one-number calculus of confirmation could be replaced by Bayes' Rule. It had, after all, been used in medical diagnosis programs for years. But MYCIN's calculus was developed partly in response to a need to work with a single number associated with premise–conclusion pairs – a measure of *increased* support of a conclusion (Horvitz *et al.*, 1986) – not with prior and posterior probabilities, because that was the way that our medical collaborators defined the problem. The ideal conditions required by most theories hold only in simplified problems, which are often so unrelated to their complex instantiations that the principles for solving them bear little resemblance to the original theory.

1.2   Engineering steps in AI

Work in building expert systems and other applications programs is very clearly seen as engineering work. As such, it engenders considerable controversy over its part in scientific research because it is seen as stopping with the engineered product. Applications of AI, in addition to expert systems, include robotics and vision, automatic programming, and natural language understanding. In all of these areas, AI ideas and methods have matured enough to be applied outside the research laboratories. There is little controversy about the benefits of transferring and developing research ideas, when they are done well, but there is not universal agreement about the necessity of steps 3 (implementation) and 4 (demonstration) in AI research.

Omitting the implementation certainly saves time and trouble. It often takes graduate students 12–24 months to construct and debug a working prototype, and it requires substantial equipment resources beyond paper and pencil. The running program itself is only an existence proof that a computer program *can* be written to solve a few problems. It does not tell us how well the program works or how much of its performance is due to the design (and how much is a result of the programmer's cleverness or a happy choice of test problems). So why bother with the implementation? Much of the answer lies in the nature of the evidence that compels one to accept the ideas proposed in the design.

As stated above, the complexity of the problems and of the solution methods precludes making a convincing theoretical argument that a designed method is sufficient for solving problems of a type – unless the problems are reduced to trivial proportions. The implementation thus allows demonstrations of the method working (or not) on problems of varying complexity. 'Only when it [a bridge] has been overloaded do we learn the physical properties of the materials from which it is built,' wrote Simon (1969).

The most elementary question to be answered by the demonstration is whether the method works at all. Another question is the scope of problems for which it works. Both the problem description and the design are often open-ended, in the sense that they allow endless argument over these two questions. An implementation provides specifics to argue about: we can examine what the program does and how it does it.

Demonstrations can take many forms and can provide different levels of support for claims about methods. Several fine pieces of AI research culminated in implementations that ran only on single problems. MOLGEN (Stefik, 1981a and 1981b) and TEIRESIAS (Davis, 1982) are two of those. Demonstrations such as these show that the method will work on at least one large problem, more convincingly than if there had been no implementation at all, because of their complexity and the complexity of both the programs and the problems. MYCIN was run on many medical cases and its performance was demonstrated with three formal studies (Shortliffe, 1974; Yu et al., 1979a and 1979b). DENDRAL (Lindsay et al., 1980) analysed molecular structures of many sets of challenging chemical molecules convincingly enough to warrant publication in the chemistry literature. Meta-DENDRAL (Buchanan and Mitchell, 1978) discovered rules of mass spectroscopy for a previously unreported family of chemical structures, and those rules were published (Buchanan et al., 1972) as a contribution to the science of mass spectrometry.

Section 3.2 discusses the question of *what* we demonstrate. As McCarthy (1983) wrote:

'We have to think hard about how to make experiments that are really informative. At present, the failures are more important than the successes, because they often tell us that the intellectual mechanisms we imagined would intelligently solve certain problems are inadequate.'

1.3   Analytical steps in AI

Many experimental researchers stop after the demonstration step in the hope that the power of their ideas is now obvious. This is characteristic of an engineering approach to questions in which the product speaks for itself. However, the needs of science are not met – and progress in AI is impeded – until there is considerable work on steps 5 (analysis) and 6 (generalization) of the process.

Progress in science is only achieved through careful analysis of methods and their power. Designing without analysis is idle speculation. Implementation without analysis is tinkering. Alone they have no research value. All too often we read of major pieces of AI work that stop with the engineering steps. But we need to know how the implemented program embodies the design, and that the program works well because of the design.

Work on the program AM (Lenat, 1976), for example, caused considerable puzzlement among researchers about what and how much Lenat had shown with this program. It had successfully rediscovered some important concepts in mathematics, such as prime numbers, but other researchers were unable to understand well enough why the program worked. A subsequent paper (Lenat and Brown, 1984) analysed AM's methods carefully and provided a better understanding of them than is provided by Lenat's first description of the program with examples.

Writings on scientific method emphasize the importance of analysing data, with the whole weight of mathematical statistics thrown into the task. AI has not taken advantage of these analytical methods for two related reasons: it is tedious to collect data, and it is not obvious what is worth measuring. Data collection in science can be accomplished either by passive observation or by active experimentation, or by variations on both. In AI there has been little effort expended on collecting sets of data points, although considerable expense goes into the construction of each program. Each program can be seen as a single data point, or as the experimental apparatus with which we can generate many data points. Either way, there is little activity that we call active data collection in AI.

Generalization is added as an explicit step, because science progresses beyond the strict boundaries of what has actually been observed with the formulation of general hypotheses. A clearly formulated statement of a claim provides a target for attempts at refutation, which in the view of Popper (1959), at least, is a necessary element of scientific progress. The complexity of interactions within any layer – and across layers – precludes our making predictions with certainty. AI needs, as much as the physical sciences, the insightful – but unproven – generalizations that are based on data, but that cover more than the data.

McDermott (1983) has noted that the increased number of expert systems

'has not been accompanied by even a modest growth in our understanding of the relationship between knowledge and search. The problem is lack of data. Though the number of expert systems that have been developed is now sufficient to allow us to begin to deepen our understanding, the information available about those systems is inadequate.'

Davis (1982), too, recognized early the need for generalization. He states four simple architectural principles for building expert systems which he generalized from the collective literature and experience of early work:

1.   separate the inference engine and knowledge base,
2.   use as uniform a representation as possible,
3.   keep the inference engine simple, and
4.   exploit redundancy.

These remain good, easy-to-remember guiding principles even after some years. But, as Davis pointed out, they are a bit oversimplified. Separating the inference engine and the knowledge base is not always as easy or as desirable as it sounds in cases where the grain size of relevant knowledge is large or where the knowledge encoded in the knowledge base is strongly sequential. Also, there are many instances where one abandons a uniform representation in favour of specialized representations. If specialized representations are employed, however, it is often necessary to abandon the principle of keeping the inference procedure simple.

Davis correctly notes that performance is not the only criterion for measuring the design and implementation of an expert system. In addition, he cites explanation and knowledge acquisition. Criteria such as these are discussed in more detail in Section 3, for these are the kind of terms needed in generalizations.

2   Measurement and comparison

In every science we see measurements of the systems under study, with much of routine science devoted to making increasingly more precise measurements, or at least more detailed qualitative statements. For instance, precise values of theoretical constants, such as the speed of light, are of intense interest – or frequencies of expressed genetic traits in a population, or correlations among proposed chemical causes and biological effects. Sometimes, better measurements provide better understanding. Even before precise measurements are possible, however, qualitative comparisons aid our understanding and predictive power. For example, social scientists can accurately predict voters' behaviour based on preferences, without having precise measures of numerical attributes.

AI, too, has a need for measurement and comparison in order to increase our understanding of the methods we design and the programs we build. We talk about the size and complexity of a program, or about the simplicity and expressive power of a knowledge base representation, but we cannot measure them. And we talk about the efficiency and inferential power of reasoning methods without being at all precise. Even if we never agree on units for absolute measures, we still need a way to place programs on relevant comparative scales.

A theory of AI would allow, among other things, predicting the consequences of modifying a program. It is of extreme interest to know, for example, how a program's execution speed will change as its knowledge base grows.

In a simple production-rule architecture, for example, a program will examine *every* rule in order to determine which rules are applicable and then decide which one to apply (Davis and Buchanan, 1977). That changes the description of the situation, then, and on every reasoning cycle, the same things must happen. As more rules are added, the program has more to do on every cycle. Thus adding knowledge to improve the quality of the answer has a predictable effect on the increased time a program will take, if it is implemented in this simple architecture.

In many, more complex programs we observe the paradox of increased knowledge – a disappointing exponential slow-down as the program's knowledge increases. In other programs, a richer organization of the knowledge base keeps the slow-down linear. In some, however, we see a positive effect of adding more knowledge. The scientific disappointment is that we rarely can predict whether the effect of more knowledge will be positive or negative, let alone predicting the magnitude of the effect.

In MYCIN, for example, Davis and Buchanan (1977) added strategy rules (called meta-rules) to guide MYCIN's reasoning. Our belief at the time was that an additional layer of reasoning about *which* medical rules to invoke, and in which order, would make the domain-level reasoning about the medical problem more efficient. When we tested that hypothesis by implementing a few strategy rules, however, we were surprised. Meta-rules carry an overhead, as does all reasoning about strategy. And we were able to find implementations of our simple strategy considerations in the domain-level rules themselves. Therefore the test showed less efficiency when meta-rules were used in the few situations we tested, than when domain-rules were modified to reflect the same strategies. Although the initial belief still seems reasonable, MYCIN's rule set was not complex enough to justify the extra layer of reasoning about strategy. We are currently examining this belief in a more complex problem area, the determination of molecular structure of proteins (see Section 3.1).

Toulmin (1953) contrasts descriptive and prescriptive phases of science. Biology before Mendel was descriptive, where much effort was expended on collecting specimens and describing them. Until there was an adequate vocabulary for a theory, however, the science remained descriptive. With Mendel's theory of inheritance, and even more with biochemical models of biological processes, biology has entered a prescriptive phase. AI is still in a descriptive phase. Observation of natural objects and phenomena, however, has been replaced in AI by observation of computer programs and their behaviour. We have many specimens and we publish lengthy descriptions of them. Unfortunately, we do not use our descriptive terms consistently, nor do we even know all of the features of a program that are worth noticing.

Pairs of implementations of the same programs can provide interesting data for comparisons. Too seldom are there records of initial implementations that failed to achieve desired performance, and almost never are there records comparing discarded and saved methods, or written notes on why methods were changed. The primary reasons for these lapses are probably the complexity of the methods (and their implementation), and our present inability to sort out essential from non-essential attributes of problems and solution methods. In addition, the process of writing and debugging a large program encourages making hundreds of incremental changes – some small and some large – and using the resulting program to stand as the best – sometimes only – documentation of the details of the method.

Active experimentation in AI is rare. The existence of pairs of observations, such as pairs of implementations of DENDRAL, MOLGEN, and other large programs implemented twice, is mostly accidental. Sometimes researchers construct a second implementation as a way of seeing if a second method will work, or work better, as in the case of DART, MOLGEN and INTERNIST. Sometimes they are responding to fundamental dissatisfactions with the quality or speed of performance from one or another of the versions, as in the case of DENDRAL.

Programs, when compared at all, are usually described without a detailed analysis of the prior version, and without systematic experimentation and measurement. But what do we measure? What are the relevant terms for describing programs and intelligent behaviour? We do not know the answers to these questions, but we can look at some of the attributes that researchers are measuring already and some of the generalizations they are making.

3   Vocabulary

Formulating general hypotheses about AI methods and programs, either theoretically or experimentally, requires a vocabulary containing names of relevant features of those procedures, as well as names of effects we want to predict. That is, a general form of the sort of hypothesis in AI that would be testable is: under background conditions (C), methods or programs with attributes $A_1 \ldots , A_n$ will result in effects (E):

Schema H1: C & A_1 & ... & A_n ---> E

A variation on this form that would be easier to formulate and test is: under background conditions, including specification of many relevant attributes, a change in one or more relevant attributes will result in a change in effect E:

Schema H2: C & ΔA ---> ΔE

In this section, we examine the kinds of terms that have been used in AI to describe effects and those used to describe programs and methods.

Niwa *et al.* (1984) undertook an experimental comparison of four representation schemes for the same task – risk management of large construction projects. The four were: a simple production system, a structured production system, a frame-based system, and a logic-based system. Their careful comparison led to many interesting observations, which they summarized in three general hypotheses:

1.   'In a poorly understood domain whose knowledge structure cannot be well described, modular knowledge representations, e.g., simple production and logic systems, should be used. However, this causes low run-time efficiency.

2.   The use of structured knowledge representations, e.g., structured production and frame systems, increases run-time efficiency as well as reducing the effect of the knowledge volume on run-time. However, system implementation is more difficult.

3.   Mathematical completeness makes logic systems more difficult to implement and less efficient in run-time. Our problem was too simple to demonstrate adequately the advantages of logic representation.'

These hypotheses represent the kinds of associations that are being made at present, when they are explicitly stated at all. We examine below some of the studies from which generalizations have been formed and examine some of the terms that are used in the formulation of hypotheses.

3.1 Outcome variables

The convincingness of a demonstration depends on stating clearly, in advance, what the demonstration will 'prove'. With AI programs, designers often advance many interdependent claims at once. The most usual claim is an implicit one: that the method, as implemented in the program, is sufficient for solving a class of problems.

Other claims may centre on efficiency because measures of efficiency are the coin of the realm of computing. This assumes that the quality of solutions is so good that we even want to measure efficiency. For example, an extremely fast program with dubious performance for identifying shore birds is the one line program:

```
PRINT 'It is a sandpiper.'
```

Several categories of claims are discussed in this section. Whatever the claim, it is important that it focus on attributes of programs that are well defined and measurable in principle. The capabilities of human problem solvers that lead to intelligent performance are generally capabilities that we want AI programs to have, especially if we cannot reproduce that quality of performance otherwise. Intuitive problem solving is one of those capabilities. But it does not advance the science of AI to argue whether a program has the capability for reasoning intuitively unless we can define what that means. For that reason, measuring quality of performance is likely to tell us more about progress than trying to determine if some *modes* of human thinking are reflected in a program.

Some suggested criteria for evaluating expert systems were discussed in Buchanan (1983). These included: accuracy and reliability, correctness of the lines of reasoning, appropriateness of input–output content, characteristics of the hardware environment, efficiency of the program, and cost-effectiveness of the whole system. This, as other similar sets of suggestions, is a disparate list that can be structured under the four headings suggested below.

3.1.1 Productivity

Expert systems are constructed commercially to provide assistance within an organization but can also serve as data points in our collection of examples that behave more or less intelligently. Their ability to provide assistance can be taken as one measure of how successfully the system designer has captured the important aspects of problem solving in a narrow area. Insofar as an expert system saves time, or money, within the organization it is commercially successful.

This measure of productivity is too gross, however, for the science of AI. It is akin to using volume of traffic over the Golden Gate Bridge as a measure of the builder's design principles. Low volume does not mean the design was faulty, and if volume is high we do not know if it is *because of* a good design or *in spite of* flaws. Nevertheless, the financial success of numerous expert systems constructed on the same design lends some evidence that their design is sound and worth emulating – see Buchanan (1986).

3.1.2 Human factors

Measures of human factors are more important than productivity for judging some aspects of the merit of designs. References to ease-of-use, familiarity, and understandability are sometimes published. Davis (1982) charted the approximate time in person-years that was needed to construct several expert systems. Decreased times were taken to be a measure of increased understanding of design principles, and thus of scientific progress. But they might also reflect better judgement about selecting smaller problems to work on, increased skill of programmers and knowledge engineers, and so forth. In the context of chess, Wilkins (1979) wrote the PARADISE program to examine the strength of some methods of reasoning about plans. One of his claims was that the methods were extensible, that is that new chess knowledge could be given to the system easily when PARADISE stumbled over new problems. He demonstrated this by showing that he could add new chess knowledge within a few minutes to solve failed problems. (The time – about ten minutes – was long enough to allow analysis of what went wrong and to conceptualize the new rule that was needed, but short enough to disallow major changes in representation or inference procedures.) In this way, a claim about ease of modification was quantified.

3.1.3 Computational requirements

Computational requirements are also used as a measure of design principles. We prefer methods that run in time linearly proportional to the number of elements being reasoned about to methods that run in exponential time. We also prefer methods that use less memory in the computer. The unconstrained DENDRAL algorithm generated huge numbers of molecular structure graphs with small chemical compositions of 10–20 atoms (Smith, 1975). With heuristics as constraints on the generator, problems 5–10 times that large could be solved in 'reasonable' amounts of time.

In addition to time and space requirements, two other computational characteristics of AI programs that are of interest are portability and extensibility. **Portability** refers to the technical characteristics that allow a program to run on a variety of different computers. **Extensibility** refers to characteristics that allow the program to grow without severely straining the time and space limits. (Another aspect of extensibility – the ease of making extensions – was discussed in Section 3.1.2.)

3.1.4   Performance

The final set of outcome measures used to substantiate claims about AI methods is the set of performance measures. Performance can be defined in many ways, often including the measures of computational resources mentioned above. It seems informative to separate quality of performance from efficiency, thus we mean here measures of quality. Performance is a fundamental measure: unless two programs are performing at about the same levels of quality, it does not make sense to compare their efficiency. This can be difficult to measure, when problems have no decision procedure for determining, with certainty, whether or not a purported solution is a solution. Also, many problems have more than one correct solution. In MYCIN's problem area – diagnosis and treatment of bacterial infections – the problem was defined to be finding appropriate therapy before all the relevant information was available to identify the bacteria causing the infection.

When there is no easily determined 'correct' solution, performance can be measured against a 'gold standard' (Gaschnig *et al.*, 1983). In the case of MYCIN, the gold standard was the therapy recommendations of Stanford specialists in infectious diseases. With expert systems this kind of comparison is now routinely mentioned (even if not used frequently enough) to validate the strength of the methods. In other contexts outside of expert systems, performance is rarely measured. AM (Lenat, 1976), for example, is cited for its methods of discovering new concepts in mathematics, in the absence of demonstration beyond a few examples. It accomplished something that had not been done before – that was sufficient. Both accuracy and precision are important components of performance. DENDRAL was demonstrated to be accurate by showing, for hundreds of known problems, that the correct solution was contained in DENDRAL's set of best five solutions. Its precision could have been measured by the mean and variance of the rank of the correct solution. The accuracy and precision of PROTEAN's reasoning have been measured (Lichtarge *et al.*, 1986) in the context of using NMR data to determine the three-dimensional structures of proteins. In both cases, analysis shows that precision can be improved with more, or better, chemical data about the problems. That is, imprecision came less from the methods than from the data provided to the programs.

Claims made for AI methods have involved many classes of outcome variables. Only the four mentioned above – productivity, human factors, computational requirements, and performance – are defined precisely enough at this time to be measured, and these only with difficulty. Other capabilities suggested for AI programs, such as reasoning with common sense, intuition, or causal models, are better dealt with as performance at a behavioural level than at a dispositional level.

There is no reason, or desire, to use only a single measure of success; evidence favouring a method can take many forms. Yet if AI is to be seen as an experimental science, the claims must first of all be explicit and clear. Second, the claims must be testable, with reproducible experiments. And third, it is desirable, although not necessary, that the claims be measurable.

3.2   Descriptive attributes

In a predictive theory, outcome variables, such as those just discussed, are predicted from the description of a situation, phenomenon or object. To be meaningful, those descriptions are framed in terms of attributes that are objectively determined. In mathematical expressions of relationships, those attributes are quantitative and measurable; in more qualitative theories, the attributes are at least testable in the sense that objective observers will be able to determine their truth or falsity. What observations can we make about AI programs?

There are many analyses of algorithms that relate attributes of an algorithm to computational resources. Algorithms for sorting have been well analysed (Knuth, 1973), for example. The attributes are simple quantities, such as the number of items in a list to be sorted. The analyses relate these quantities to the time a particular sorting algorithm will take or the amount of computer memory that will be required to store intermediate and final results. Whereas small algorithms can be analysed, complex programs cannot and must be studied empirically.

With AI programs, especially, there are so many potentially relevant variables that attempts to name the one or two *most relevant* ones in simple hypotheses have not been satisfactory. It is also extremely troublesome to argue that two sets of background conditions are the same 'for all practical purposes'. Thus it is necessary to do controlled experiments in which some attributes are held constant and others are varied. The two parts of this section discuss large and small variations. In the former, gross attributes of programs are varied, with qualitative (or sometimes quantitative) observations made on effects. In the latter, considerably more attributes are held constant, with small variations in only a few, carefully-studied attributes.

3.2.1   Observations on large variations

Two classes of attributes of AI programs that are often mentioned are system architecture and task type. Both are abstract concepts that are ill-defined and not measurable. In many pairs of implementations of programs – including pairs of implementations of DENDRAL, MOLGEN, and INTERNIST – architectural attributes were varied while the task (and thus the task type) was held constant. These include primarily the methods for representing knowledge in the system and the methods for

Table 2.1 Some types of large variations from which comparisons of AI methods have been made. (See text for other combinations.)

Task type	Task	Architecture	Examples
constant	constant	vary	Pairs of implementations of DENDRAL, MOLGEN, INTERNIST, and other programs
constant	vary	constant	EMYCIN, other shell systems
constant	vary	vary	MYCIN–PROSPECTOR comparison
vary	vary	constant	PROLOG, other languages providing an architecture

making inferences. (See Buchanan and Duda (1983) for discussion of several major architectural choices.)

Descriptions of task type have been unsatisfactory in that they do not settle the question of when two problems (tasks) are of the *same* type. We distinguish tasks better by the methods that can be used to solve them than by intrinsic features of the tasks themselves. To some extent, it is helpful to view all problem solving as search (Simon, 1969; Newell and Simon, 1976; Buchanan and Duda, 1983) so, to that extent, all tasks fit into a single category. Broadly speaking, we can distinguish construction (or formulation) methods from decomposition methods (Amarel, 1971); that is, methods that successively combine primitives to construct a solution from methods that incrementally decompose or refine a whole into primitive parts. DENDRAL is a prime example of the former, in which descriptions of molecular structures were constructed by systematically adding one chemical atom at a time into partial structure descriptions until all atoms in the specified chemical composition were accounted for. MYCIN is a good example of the latter, in which the final goal of recommending appropriate therapy for a patient with a bacterial infection was decomposed into subgoals. One of the subgoals was to identify, as well as possible on the available evidence, the organism causing the infection. That subgoal, in turn, was decomposed further. At the 'bottom', MYCIN reached sub-subgoals whose truth or falsity, if known at all, could be established by asking questions that were factual and observational.

Two programs may be compared at a gross level if either task type or system architecture is held constant. Additionally, some experiments have varied the task, within the same task type. If all vary, no comparisons can be made. If all are constant, we can compare differences in implentation or other variations at a finer level of detail. The remaining four possibilities are shown in Table 2.1.

In each of four system architectures, Niwa *et al.* (1984) implemented two small prototype expert systems that solved the *same* task. The major architectural classes were: simple production system, structured production system, frame system and logic system. For each they implemented both forward chaining and backward chaining inference procedures. They measured a number of static attributes of each program including the size of the knowledge bases and the size of the inference procedures (for example, in number of characters used to express them). They also measured some dynamic attributes of the programs, including average inference time (in seconds) required to reach (presumably correct) solutions to three problems with three different sizes of knowledge base. One set of results, for example, shows that the run-time of systems decreases with increased structure in the knowledge base.

Some experiments in AI have held a program's architecture and task *type* constant and varied the tasks. EMYCIN's architecture is rule-based backward chaining, with inexact inferences. It was used – with different knowledge bases – to solve many problems of a type we call classification or **evidence-gathering problems**. BB1 (Hayes-Roth *et al.*, 1986) is another framework system for solving many similar problems with the same architecture, which is opportunistic reasoning in what is called the **blackboard architecture**. It has been used to solve several problems of a type we call assembly problems. Other frameworks have been used in similar ways – see, for example, Harmon and King (1985), and Kulikowski and Weiss (1982). Other framework systems make less of an architectural commitment to a class of problems, for example, Brownston *et al.* (1985), Genesereth (1982), Smith (1983), and Stefik *et al.* (1983) and serve more as general system-building environments. By keeping the architecture and task *type* fixed, these systems allow experimentation with different aspects of tasks of the same type. These are closer to controlled trials than the grosser ones in which either task type or architectural attributes vary.

The task of the PROSPECTOR system (Duda *et al.*, 1978) – advising on the likelihood of significant mineral deposits in a geographical area – shares many features with MYCIN's task of medical diagnosis. The designers of PROSPECTOR used an architecture with several differences from MYCIN's: for example, they added more structure to the rule set (linking rules in a network instead of using a hierarchy of rule sets as in MYCIN) and they added capabilities to allow users of PROSPECTOR to guide the line of reasoning. One of the most significant differences is in their calculus for uncertain reasoning, which they analysed and compared to MYCIN's (Duda *et al.*, 1976). Insofar as the tasks are of the same type and the architectures are roughly the same (both are rule-based), their analysis shows a better theoretical grounding for PROSPECTOR's (essentially Bayesian) calculus of confirmation with equal success in building their knowledge base of rules.

In these kinds of gross experiment, with variations in either system architecture or task type, it is extremely difficult to say what has varied and what has remained constant. In most experiments – including those by Niwa, or the PROSPECTOR–MYCIN comparison – new procedures or new knowledge bases are written to make different systems. All who are familiar with computer programming, however, will recognize the difficulty in comparing effects of code written by different persons or in different languages. Or, if the effects can be compared, it is impossible to sort out the contributions of the programmer from those of the method.

3.2.2 Controlled experiments on smaller variations

The gross classes of attributes mentioned in Section 3.2.1 allow qualitative statements about characteristics of programs. Too many things may vary when one is only concerned about holding the architecture of the task type constant. But there is still a hope that quantitative attributes can be found.

There have been many attempts in AI (Gaschnig (1979), for example) to measure smaller, relevant attributes of AI programs, such as the size of their knowledge bases, and make meaningful statements relating these attributes to performance (or another one of the outcome variables). Mostly this search for relationships must take place, as in other disciplines, in very controlled situations in which it is possible to vary one input parameter at a time and measure effects.

Except in very simple situations, controlled experiments in AI are extremely tedious and difficult to interpret. Small problem areas, sometimes called 'micro-worlds', serve as the rat mazes or the Drosophila of AI (McCarthy, 1983). The two most widely used micro-worlds have been board games (specifically chess) and the world of children's blocks. In the latter, programs have been constructed for answering questions, in English, about the arrangements of coloured blocks on a table (Winograd, 1972), for planning the steps involved in arranging blocks into a specified goal state (Sussman, 1973), and learning classification rules for arches (Winston, 1975). In principle, micro-worlds offer the opportunity for controlled experiments; regrettably, the opportunity has seldom been exploited. A primary reason is that we lack a good set of descriptive attributes of methods. That is, we do not know how to simplify our descriptions of methods sufficiently well to identify only a few relevant attributes to vary systematically while holding everything else constant.

Size of solution space From the early days of AI, the sizes of solution spaces provided a measure of how much work a program had to do and the power of its heuristics to do that work. Game playing programs, for example, were frequently characterized by the number of *possible* complete games that could be played from start to finish. This helped differentiate trivially simple tasks, which can often be solved by table

MYCIN: combinations of 1–6 organisms from list of 120 organisms	$= 10^9$
plausible ones	$= 6 \times 10^6$
INTERNIST: combinations of 1–3 diseases from list of 571	$= 31 \times 10^6$
DIPMETER ADVISOR: any one of 65 geological categories for an arbitrary number (around 500) of depth levels	$= 65^{500}$
XCON: a configuration of 50–150 computer system components selected from 20 000 types	$=$ billions

Figure 2.1   The size of the solution spaces for several expert systems. This number is important in describing the complexity of a problem but it must be interpreted carefully since there are so many arbitrary ways to choose the numbers used.

lookup or simple decision trees, from those that required more reasoning power and more knowledge.

The power of an expert system's knowledge and reasoning method is also related to its ability to find correct (or acceptable) solutions to large problems, where the size of the problem is the number of possible solutions in the search space. MYCIN gathered evidence for and against 120 organism identities in its diagnostic procedure and then collected the likely identities. Since there were rarely more than six likely causes of infection in a patient, MYCIN's search space of diagnoses could be said to be all subsets of 120 identities with six or fewer items – a space of millions. The size of DENDRAL's search space was exponentially related to the number of atoms in the chemical compound of interest, and grew to tens of millions with 15–20 atoms. Some other examples are shown in Figure 2.1. These numbers, though, are so large as to be uninformative. There is no longer any question that AI methods can deal with large solution spaces, if constrained by enough knowledge. Therefore, we need to look more finely for relevant descriptive terms of programs and the problems they solve.

Complexity of solution space: number of inferences   Another measure of a problem solving method is the way it organizes its search of the solution space. Exhaustive search requires less intelligence than guided search. Thus the number (or percentage) of nodes in the search space that are *actually* examined is as interesting as the total number. An approximate measure of this is a function b^d, where d is average depth of search and b is the average branching factor. For instance, MYCIN's knowledge base contained chains of at most six rules, with the average length of an inference chain (depth of search) about four. At each intermediate

Table 2.2 Vocabulary sizes of some well-known expert systems. Note, many attributes take continuous numerical values.

	Size	=	Number of objects	+	Number of attributes	+	Number of values
MYCIN	715+	=	(17	+	257	+	441+)
INTERNIST	4674	=	(571	+	4100	+	3)
XCON	934+	=	(94	+	840	+	??)
XSEL	408+	=	(79	+	329	+	??)
XFL	326+	=	(74	+	252	+	??)

conclusion in the inference chains, about 5.5 rules contributed evidence to the conclusion. Thus it actually examined about 1000 (5.5^4) nodes in the search space for a single case – about one millionth of the much larger implicit space of inferences.

Size of knowledge base Simple counts of the number of lines of code in a program are misleading because of the variability of how much goes in a line, what concepts are represented, how efficiently a programmer writes code, and so forth.

Similarly, simple counts of the number of statements in an AI program's knowledge base are unenlightening. A decade ago, rule-based expert systems were compared on the number of rules in their knowledge bases as if the quality of their performance depended more on the number of rules than on their content. Nevertheless, computational requirements are nearly always sensitive to sizes.

Conditional statements are not the only measurable quantity in a knowledge base, however. Each conditional rule mentions objects and their attributes. For example, INTERNIST's knowledge base contains associations among diseases and manifestations. It represents 571 diseases with an average of about 80 relevant manifestations per disease. Another measure of 'how much' a program knows might be the size of the vocabulary. One such measure is a count of objects, attributes and values known to the system – perhaps expressed as the sum shown in Table 2.2. This measure is problematic when it comes to continuous ranges of values and object-types that can be instantiated in arbitrarily many ways. For example, MYCIN used some continuous values of numerical attributes, such as fever, weight, and concentrations. And it used names of object-types, such as Culture and Organism, in rules which were then instantiated for each culture of bacteria growing from specimens taken from a patient and each organism growing in the culture. XCON (McDermott, 1981), XSEL (McDermott, 1982) and XFL are members of

Table 2.3   The number of rules and objects in some rule-based and object-centered expert systems. The ratio of the two separates the two paradigms. This ratio is interesting but not useful for describing the size or complexity of a knowledge base. The DIPMETER ADVISOR system (Smith, 1984) assists in interpretation of data from oil wells; the CAR ADVISOR (Plotkin, private communication) assists in diagnosing automobile problems.

	$\left(\begin{array}{l} Number\ of \\ rules \end{array} \right.$	$\left. \begin{array}{l} Number\ of \\ object\ names \end{array} \right)$
Rule-based systems:		
MYCIN	62.3	= (1059 / 17)
XCON	61.0	= (5739 / 94)
XSEL	27.1	= (2148 / 79)
XFL	21.8	= (1618 / 74)
Object-centered systems:		
INTERNIST	5.2	= (2600 / 500)
Schlumberger DIPMETER ADVISOR	1.4	= (90 / 65)
Teknowledge CAR ADVISOR	0.4	= (1242 / 3317)

the same family of systems designed to assist in configuring computer systems for customers. (Numbers from McDermott (private communication).)

In an object-oriented architecture, such as a frame-based system, the number of objects may be more indicative of the scope of a program's knowledge. Depending on whether a rule-based or object-centered architecture is used, a designer generally increases the number of rules or objects, respectively, with equivalent quality of performance (see Table 2.3). So there is no special significance to these counts.

Contents of knowledge base   Some experiments vary the contents of the program's knowledge base to measure the effects on quality of performance. In these, the semantic force of the elements in the knowledge base is the issue, rather than an objective measurement like the cardinality of a set. All other performances being equal, we may prefer smaller sets to larger ones, but even that is not assured since the understandability of the program's knowledge base is also an issue.

DENDRAL was run many hundreds of times with small changes to a single list, called BADLIST. The intent of these informal experiments was to find the rules of chemical structure that accurately predicted instability of chemical compounds under normal conditions. Peroxides, for example, can be identified in a structural description by the presence of two oxygens covalently bonded. Manual examination of DENDRAL's lists of structures by a chemist revealed structures that were unstable and which should have been excluded by BADLIST (while excluding no stable structures). The rules on BADLIST were formulated gradually through this sequence of controlled trials. When we attempted to vary many things at once (for example, changing the procedures by which structures were generated or filtered), we were easily confused.

Greiner (1985) introduced the term 'ablation experiments' into AI, to describe systematic excision of parts of a program with subsequent analysis of failure (a variation on Mill's Method of Differences). This required careful design of the program so that pieces can be excised with resulting gradual degradation of performance. Usually when we attempt this with programs, we cause catastrophic failures because the relevant pieces are so interdependent. At the time of design, then, the experiments must be envisioned so that the program can be made to be robust enough and the knowledge base made to be modular enough, to avoid the catastrophes.

In many expert systems, knowledge bases are separate from inference procedures and elements of the knowledge base are modular, that is, nearly independent. In these cases, ablation experiments can be easily performed on the knowledge bases to determine how much knowledge is needed for good performance. It is not easy to know which are the meaningful experiments, however, nor how to interpret the results.

The size of the vocabulary used for constructing a knowledge base is an important consideration in comparing AI programs. But it is not unambiguously described, as discussed above, nor is it the only consideration. The complexity of the inference network, including the size of the total space of possible solutions, is equally important. Finally, no comparison of numbers can be as illuminating in comparing AI programs as comparison of the semantic *content* of knowledge bases. The power of a program to reason effectively in a large combinatorial space lies in the knowledge it can use to guide the search and prune implausible solutions.

Both large-scale and small-scale variations in programs can provide meaningful data when extreme care is taken in controlling unwanted variations and in interpreting the results. Some patterns and principles are emerging from the experiments already performed. But they are sparse. Considerably more experimentation is needed to advance the science of AI.

4 Conclusion

AI is a new discipline, so it is unreasonable to expect all the same methodological characteristics found in the more mature disciplines. In looking at research in AI we see theoretical (often mathematical), engineering, and analytical concerns, as in other experimental disciplines. Each has its advantages, but the greatest advantage to AI comes from a coordinated effort in all three styles.

AI's struggle to develop a coordinated, coherent methodology may provide an opportunity for researchers in other empirical disciplines to take stock of their own methods. One important lesson to be learned from the various and many successes of the sciences is that theorizing *after* collecting data has a far better track record than theorizing in the absence of data. But we see in AI, once again, the fundamental difficulty of deciding on the vocabulary of attributes that we *can* measure and that are *worth* measuring.

Expert systems provide the apparatus for making detailed experiments. Because they are often implemented in shell systems that provide constancy in syntax, at least, it is possible to vary, say, the contents of a knowledge base and observe the effects. It is imperative that we use these opportunities.

References

Amarel S. (1971). Representations and modeling in problems of program formation. In *Machine Intelligence 6* (Michie D., ed.), pp. 411–466. New York: American Elsevier

Brownston L., Farrell R., Kant E. and Martin N. (1985). *Programming Expert Systems in OPS5: An Introduction to Rule-Based Programming*. Reading MA: Addison-Wesley

Buchanan B.G. (1983). Constructing an expert system. In *Building Expert Systems* (Hayes-Roth F., Waterman D. and Lenat D., eds.), pp. 127–168. New York: Addison-Wesley

Buchanan B.G. (1986). Expert systems: working systems and the research literature. *Expert Systems*, 3(1) 32–51

Buchanan, B.G. (1988). Artificial intelligence as an experimental science. In *Aspects of Artificial Intelligence* (Fetzer J.H., ed.), pp. 209–250. Boston: Kluwer Academic Publishers

Buchanan B.G., Feigenbaum E.A. and Sridharan N.S. (1972). Heuristic theory formation: data interpretation and rule formation. In *Machine Intelligence 7* (Meltzer B. and Michie D., eds.), pp. 267–290. New York: John Wiley & Sons

Buchanan B.G. and Mitchell T.M. (1978). Model-directed learning of production rules. In *Pattern-Directed Inference Systems* (Waterman D.A. and Hayes-Roth F., eds.), pp. 297–312. New York: Academic Press

Buchanan, B.G. and Duda R.O. (1983). Principles of rule-based expert systems. In *Advances in Computers* (Yovits M., ed.). New York: Academic Press

Davis R. (1982). TEIRESIAS: applications of meta-level knowledge. In *Knowledge-Based Systems in Artificial Intelligence* (Davis R. and Lenat D.B., eds.). New York: McGraw-Hill

Davis R. and Buchanan B.G. (1977). Meta-level knowledge: overview and applications. In *Proc. IJCAI-77*, Cambridge MA, pp. 920–927.

Doyle J. (1979). A truth maintenance system. *Artificial Intelligence*, **12**, 231–272

Duda R.O., Hart P.E. and Nilsson N.J. (1976). Subjective Bayesian methods for rule-based inference systems. In *Proc. 1976 Nat. Computer Conf. (AFIPS Conf. Proc.)*, pp. 1075–1082. June 1976

Duda R.O., Hart P.E., Nilsson, M.J. and Sutherland G.L. (1978). Semantic network representations in rule-based inference systems. In *Pattern-Directed Inference Systems* (Waterman D.A. and Hayes-Roth F., eds.), pp. 203–221. New York: Academic Press

Gaschnig J. (1979). Preliminary performance analysis of the PROSPECTOR consultant system for mineral exploration. In *Proc. IJCAI-79*, Tokyo, Japan, pp. 308–310

Gaschnig J., Klahr P., Pople H. and Shortliffe E. (1983). *Teknowledge Series in Knowledge Engineering. Volume 1: Evaluation of Expert Systems: Issues and Case Studies*. Reading MA: Addison-Wesley

Genesereth M.R. (1982). *An Introduction to MRS for AI Experts*. Technical Report HPP-82-27, Stanford University CA

Greiner R. (1985). Learning by understanding analogies. *PhD Thesis*, Stanford University

Harmon P. and King D. (1985). *Expert Systems: Artificial Intelligence in Business*. New York: John Wiley & Sons

Hayes-Roth B., Buchanan B.G., Lichtarge O., Hewett M., Altman R., Brinkley J., Cornelius C., Duncan B. and Jardetzky O. (1986). PROTEAN: deriving protein structure from constraints. In *Proc. AAAI-86*, pp. 904–909. AAAI, Philadelphia, PA, August

Horvitz E.J., Jeckerman D.E. and Langlotz C.P. (1986). A framework for computing alternative formalisms for plausible reasoning. In *Proc. AAAI-86*, pp. 210–214. AAAI, Philadelphia PA, August, 1986

Knuth D.E. (1973). *The Art of Computer Programming. Volume 3: Sorting and Searching*, Reading MA: Addison-Wesley

Kuhn T.S. (1970). *The Structure of Scientific Revolutions* 2nd edn. Chicago IL: Chicago University Press

Kulikowski C. and Weiss S.M. (1982). Representation of expert knowledge for consultation: the CASNET and EXPERT projects. In *Artificial Intelligence in Medicine* (Szolovits P., ed.), pp. 21–55. Boulder CO: Westview Press

Lenat D.B. (1976) AM: an artificial intelligence approach to discovery in mathematics as heuristic search. *PhD Thesis*, Stanford University. Reprinted with revisions in Davis R. and Lenat D.B. (1982).

Knowledge-Based Systems in Artificial Intelligence. New York:
McGraw-Hill

Lenat D.B. and Brown J.S. (1984). Why AM and EURISKO appear to
work. *Artificial Intelligence* **23**, 269–294

Lichtarge O., Jardetzky O., Cornelius C. and Buchanan B.G. (1986).
Validation of PROTEAN on Myoglobin (in preparation)

Lindsay R.K., Buchanan B.G., Feigenbaum E.A. and Lederberg J.
(1980). *Applications of Artificial Intelligence for Organic Chemistry:
The DENDRAL Project*. New York: McGraw-Hill

McCarthy J. (1983). President's quarterly message: AI needs more
emphasis on basic research. *AI Magazine*, **4**(4) 5

McDermott D.V. (1983). Generalizing problem reduction: a logical
analysis. In *IJCAI-83 Vol. 1*, Karlsruhe, West Germany, August
1983, pp. 302–208

McDermott J. (1981). R1: the formative years. *AI Magazine*, **2**(2), 21–29,
summer

McDermott J. (1982). XSEL: a computer sales person's assistant. In
Machine Intelligence 10 (Hayes J.E., Michie D. and Pao Y-H.,
eds.), pp. 325–337. Chichester: Ellis Horwood Ltd

McDermott J. Private communication. Carnegie–Mellon University

Newell A. and Simon H. (1972). *Human Problem Solving*. Englewood
Cliffs NJ: Prentice-Hall

Newell A. and Simon H.A. (1976). Computer science as empirical inquiry:
symbols and search, the 1976 (ACM) Turing Lecture.
Communications of ACM, **19**(3), 113–126

Nilsson N.J. (1983). Artificial intelligence prepares for 2001. *AI
Magazine*, **4**(4)

Niwa K., Sasaki K. and Ihara H. (1984). An experimental comparison of
knowledge representation schemes. *AI Magazine*, **5**(2), 29–36

Novak G.S. (1981). GLISP: An efficient, English-like programming
language. In *Proc. 3rd Annual Conf. of Cognitive Science Society*,
University of California at Berkeley

Plotkin B. Private communication. Teknowledge Corp.

Popper K.R. (1959). *Logic of Scientific Discovery*. London: Hutchinson

Shortliffe E.H. (1974). MYCIN: a rule-based computer program for
advising physicians regarding antimicrobial therapy selection. *PhD
Thesis*, Stanford University. Reprinted with revisions as Shortliffe
E.H. (1976). *Computer-Based Medical Consultations: MYCIN*. New
York: American Elsevier

Simon H.A. (1969). *Sciences of the Artificial*. Cambridge MA: MIT Press

Smith D.H. (1975). The scope of structural isomerism. *J. Chem. Inf. and
Comp. Sci.*, **15**(4), 203–207

Smith R.G. (1983). STROBE: support for structured object knowledge
representation. In *Proc. IJCAI-83*, pp. 855–858. IJCAI, Karlsruhe,
West Germany, August, 1983

Smith R.G. (1984). On the development of commercial expert systems. *AI Magazine*, **5**(3), 61–73

Stefik M.J. (1981a). Planning with constraints (MOLGEN: part 1). *AI*, **16**(2), 111–140

Stefik M.J. (1981b). Planning and meta-planning (MOLGEN: part 2). *AI*, **16**(2), 141–170

Stefik M., Bobrow D., Mittal S. and Conway L. (1983). Knowledge programming in Loops. *AI Magazine*, **4**(3), 3–13

Sussman G.J. (1973). *A Computer Model of Skill Acquisition*. New York: American Elsevier (based on PhD Thesis, MIT, 1973)

Toulmin S. (1953). *The Philosophy of Science*. London: Hutchinson

Wilkins D.E. (1979). Using patterns and plans to solve problems and control search. *PhD Thesis*, Stanford University

Winograd T. (1972). *Understanding Natural Language*. New York: Academic Press.

Winston P.H. (1975). Learning structural descriptions from examples. In *The Psychology of Computer Vision* (Winston P.H., ed.), pp. 157–209. New York: McGraw-Hill

Yu V.L., Buchanan B.G., Shortliffe E.H., Wraith S.M., Davis R., Scott A.C. and Cohen S.N. (1979a). An evaluation of the performance of a computer-based consultant. *Computer Programs in Biomedicine*, **9**, 95–102

Yu V.L., Fagan L.M., Wraith S.M., Clancey W.J., Scott A.C., Hannigan J., Blum R.L., Buchanan B.G., Cohen S.N., Davis R., Aikins J., van Melle W., Shortliffe E. and Axline S. (1979b). Antimicrobial selection by a computer: a blinded evaluation by infectious disease experts. *JAMA*, **242**(12), 1279–1282. Also in Buchanan B.G. and Shortliffe E. (1984). *Rule-Based Expert Systems* Reading MA: Addison-Wesley

3

On the Thresholds of Knowledge

Douglas B. Lenat

Microelectronics and Computer Technology Corporation

Edward A. Feigenbaum

Stanford University

We articulate the three major findings and hypotheses of AI to date:

1. The Knowledge Principle: if a program is to perform a complex task well, it must know a great deal about the world in which it operates. There are three particular thresholds to cross, each leading to qualitative changes in emergent intelligence.

2. A plausible extension of that principle, called the Breadth Hypothesis: there are two additional abilities necessary for intelligent behaviour in unexpected situations: falling back on increasingly general knowledge, and analogizing to specific but far-flung knowledge.

3. AI as Empirical Inquiry: Premature mathematization, or focusing on toy problems, washes out details from reality that later turn out to be significant. Thus, we must test our ideas experimentally, on large problems, using computers in the way astronomers use telescopes.

We present evidence for these propositions, contrast them with other strategic approaches to AI, point out their scope and limitations, and discuss the future directions they mandate for the main enterprise of AI research – mapping the human memome.

1   Introduction

For over three decades, our field has pursued the dream of the computer that competently performs various difficult cognitive tasks. AI has tried many approaches to this goal, and accumulated much empirical evidence. The evidence suggests the need for the computer to have and use domain-specific knowledge.

Intelligence is the power to find rapidly an adequate solution in what appears *a priori* (to observers) to be an immense search space. So, in those same terms, we can summarize the empirical evidence: 'knowledge is power' or, more cynically 'intelligence is in the eye of the (uninformed) beholder.' The *knowledge as power* hypothesis has received so much confirmation that we now assert it as:

> **The Knowledge Principle (KP)**   A system exhibits intelligent
> understanding and action at a high level of competence primarily because
> of the *specific* knowledge that it can bring to bear: the concepts, facts,
> representations, methods, models, metaphors, and heuristics about its
> domain of endeavour.

The word *specific* in the KP is important. Knowledge is often considered compiled search. Despite this, the KP claims that only a small portion of the knowledge can be generalized so it applies across domains, without sacrificing most of its power. Why? Many searches are costly, and it is *not* costly to preserve the knowledge for future use. We all know about electricity, but few of us have flown kites in thunderstorms. This is an economic argument that *generality is not enough*; if you stop after acquiring only the general methods, your search for solutions to problems will not be constrained adequately.

Section 2 of this paper discusses the Knowledge Principle in more detail, and presents three thresholds that can be crossed as one adds more and more knowledge to a program:

1.   First, enough knowledge is present so that the problem becomes *well-formed*; at this stage, one could, in principle, search for a solution.

2.   As more knowledge is added, the program incrementally attains *competence*, performing at the level of a general practitioner of that task.

3.   Beyond this stage, the knowledge added is occasionally useful, and forms what is usually referred to as expertise; there is a threshold here of the *complete expertise* for performing some task. At that point, additional knowledge is either not yet known by human experts, or not yet recognized as relevant, or so far-flung that it is possibly relevant only as grist for analogies.

Section 2 also discusses *why* the KP works, and Section 3 provides experimental evidence for the KP.

We then discuss, in Section 4, the brittleness of current knowledge based systems. They have a plateau of competence, but the edges of that plateau are steep descents into complete incompetence. Our evidence for how *people* cope with novelty is sparse and unreliable. Still, there is suggestive evidence supporting their reliance on generality and analogy. This leads us to a plausible extension of the Knowledge Principle:

> **The Breadth Hypothesis (BH)**   Intelligent performance often requires the problem solver to fall back on increasingly general knowledge, and/or to analogize to specific knowledge from far-flung domains.

Are we, of all people, advocating the use of general problem solving methods and a breadth of knowledge? Yes! That does not contradict the KP, since most of the power still derives from a large body of specific task-related expertise. But a significant component of intelligence is still due to the way that we cope with novel situations, namely by analogizing, or by drawing on less specific knowledge. Evidence for BH comes from an examination of the limits of what AI can do today. Section 5 presents some of this, drawn from the subfields of natural language understanding and machine learning.

There is an additional element in our paradigm of AI research, which says that intelligence is still so poorly understood that nature still holds most of the important surprises in store for us. This leads to our central *methodological* tenets:

> **Empirical Inquiry Hypothesis (EH)**   The most profitable way to investigate AI is to embody our hypotheses in programs, and gather data by running the programs. The surprises usually suggest revisions that start the cycle over again. Progress depends on these experiments being able to falsify our hypotheses; that is, these programs must be capable of behaviour not expected by the experimenter.
>
> **Difficult Problems Hypothesis**   There are too many ways to solve simple problems. Raising the level and breadth of competence we demand of a system makes it *easier* to test – and raise – its intelligence.

The Knowledge Principle is a mandate for humanity to concretize the knowledge used in solving hard problems in various fields. This *might* lead to faster training based on explicit knowledge rather than apprenticeships. It has *already* led to over 1000 profitable expert systems.

The Breadth Hypothesis is a mandate to spend the resources necessary to construct one immense knowledge base (KB). This map of the human memome should extend horizontally across an encyclopaedic span of human thought and experience, and vertically extend upward from a moderate level of detail all the way up to encompass the most sweeping generalities.

The Empirical Inquiry Hypothesis is a mandate to try to build such systems, rather than theorize about them and about intelligence. Use these systems the way astronomers use telescopes.

In Section 7, the above principles and hypotheses combine to suggest a sweeping three-stage research programme for the main enterprise of AI research:

1. slowly hand-code a large, broad knowledge base;
2. when enough knowledge is present, it will be faster to acquire more from texts, data bases, etc.; and
3. to go beyond the frontier of human knowledge, the system will have to rely on learning by discovery, carrying out research and development projects to expand its knowledge base.

Some evidence is then presented that stages 1 and 2 may be accomplished this century; that is, intelligence is within our grasp. Lenat's current work at MCC, on the CYC program (Lenat, Shepherd and Prakash, 1986), is a serious effort to carry out the first stage by the mid-1990s.

We are betting our professional lives, the few decades of useful research we have left in us, on KP, BH, and EH. That's a scary thought, but one has to place one's bets somewhere in science. It is especially scary because:

1. the hypotheses are not obvious to most AI researchers
2. they are unpalatable even to us, their advocates!

Why are they not obvious? Most AI research focuses on very small problems, attacking them with machinery (both hardware and search methods) that overpower them. The end result is a program that 'succeeds' with very little knowledge, and so KP, BH, and EH are irrelevant. One is led to them only by tackling problems in difficult 'real' areas, with the world able to surprise and falsify.

Why are our three hypotheses (KP, BH, EH) not particularly palatable? Because they are unaesthetic! Until we are forced to them, Occam's Razor encourages us to theorize more elegant solutions.

Section 9 lists several limitations and problems. We do not see any of them as insurmountable. Some of the problems seem, at first blush, to be 'in-principle limitations', and some seem to be pragmatic engineering and usability problems. Yet we lump them side by side, because our methodology says to approach them all as symptoms of gaps in our (and our programs') knowledge, which can be identified and filled in incrementally, by in-context knowledge acquisition.

The biggest hurdle of all has already been put well behind us: the enormous local maximum of building and using *knowledge-free systems*. On the far side of that hill we found a much larger payoff, namely expert systems. We have learned how to build intelligent artifacts that perform well, using knowledge, on specialized tasks within narrowly defined domains. An industry has been formed to put this technological understanding to work, and widespread transfer of this technology has been achieved. Many fields are making that transition, from data processing to knowledge processing.

And yet we see expert systems technology, too, as just a local maximum. AI is finally beginning to move on beyond that threshold. This paper presents what its authors glimpse on the far side of the expert systems hill: the promise of very large scale knowledge bases (VLSK), the promise of analogical reasoning and common sense knowledge.

2 The Knowledge Principle

There is a continuum between the power of already knowing and the power of being able to search for the solution; in between lie, for example, generalizing and analogizing and plain old observing (for instance, noticing that your opponent in chess is castling). Even in the case of having to search for a solution, the *method* to carry out the search may be something that you already know, or partial-match to get, or search for in some other way. This recursion bottoms out in things (facts, methods, etc.) that are *already known*. Though the knowledge/search tradeoff is often used to argue for the primacy of search, we see here that it equally well argues for the primacy of knowledge.

Before you can apply search *or* knowledge to solve some problem, though, you need to know enough, at least, to state the problem in a well-formed fashion:

> **The well-formedness threshold** For each task, there is some minimum knowledge needed for one to even formulate it.

A more positive way to view this threshold is that a large part of solving a problem is accomplished by having a good representation; that determines what distinctions to make explicitly and which ones are irrelevant.

Beyond this bare minimum, today's expert systems (ES) also include enough knowledge to reach the level of a typical practitioner performing the task (Feigenbaum, 1977). Up to that 'competence' level, the knowledge–search tradeoff is strongly tipped in favour of knowledge:

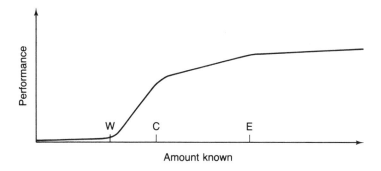

Figure 3.1   The level of performance of a program for some task, as a function of the amount of knowledge it embodies. The thresholds are (W) well-formed, (C) competent, and (E) total expert. To the left of W, not enough is known to even search for a solution; to the right of E lies mastery of 'unrelated' knowledge.

> **The competence threshold**   Difficult tasks succumb non-linearly to knowledge. There is an ever greater 'payoff' to adding each piece of knowledge, up to some level of competence (for example, where an NP complete problem becomes polynomial). Beyond that, additional knowledge is useful but only infrequently needed.

Crossing the competence threshold, one enters the realm of experts. There, the knowledge–search tradeoff is fairly evenly balanced; such knowledge deals, for example, with rare but not unheard-of cases. If the tradeoff was not nearly balanced, if the knowledge was frequently required, then the typical general practitioner would have acquired it. Most currrent ES, in what we would still call the 'first era' of expert systems, incorporate an amount of knowledge greater than that minimal level of competence for a task, yet less than all the existing expert knowledge about that task. That latter level of total expertise forms:

> **The total expert threshold**   Eventually, almost all of the rare cases are handled as well. Continuing to add knowledge beyond this expert level is even *less* useful (per piece of knowledge added).

Human experts in a field are distributed between the competent and total expert levels (see Figure 3.1). This does not mean that all other knowledge is useless to their task, just that it is not already understood to be relevant. For instance, it might not have been discovered yet; or it might be very far-flung specific knowledge that can be analogized to, and which will then lead to a solution in some tough or novel situation.

The above arguments describe how the KP *might* work; but why *does* it work so frequently? Many useful real-world tasks are sufficiently narrow that the competence threshold can be crossed with only 50–1000 if-then rules, and an equal number of additional rules takes one much of the way toward the total expert threshold. Moreover, current experts do not already have all those rules explicitly codified; standard software design methodology cannot build a program 'in one pass' to perform the task. However, as the developing ES makes mistakes, the experts can correct them, and those corrections incrementally accrete the bulk of the hitherto unexplicated rules. In this manner, the system incrementally approaches competence and even expertise.

The newly added rules need to interface seamlessly to the existing ones; to put this the other way, you can never be sure in advance how the knowledge already in the system is going to be used, or added to, in the future. Thus:

> **Explicit Knowledge Principle**   Much of the knowledge in an intelligent system needs to be represented explicitly (although compiled forms of it may also be present).

When knowledge – including procedural knowledge – is represented as explicit objects, meta-rules can apply to it, for example, helping to acquire, check, or debug other rules. Such *knowledge objects* can be more easily analogized to, and enable generalizations to be structurally induced from them.

What about the control structure of an intelligent system? Even granted that lots of knowledge is necessary, might we not need sophisticated – as yet unknown – reasoning methods?

> **Knowledge is All There Is Hypothesis**   No sophisticated, as yet unknown, control structure is required for intelligent behaviour; control strategies are knowledge, and a standard evaluator can apply them.

On the one hand, we already understand deduction, induction, analogy, specialization, generalization, etc., well enough to have knowledge be our bottleneck, not control strategies. On the other hand, all such strategies and methods are themselves just pieces of knowledge. The control structure of the intelligent system can be *opportunistic*: select one strategy, apply it for a while, monitor progress, and perhaps decide to switch to another strategy (when some other piece of knowledge suggests it should do so).

Can we be more specific about the manner in which knowledge boosts competence? Can we give, say, an equation for how to measure the effective power of the knowledge in a system, when it is applied to a problem P? It is premature to even attempt to do so – it may never be possible to do so – though Figure 3.2 speculates on what some of the terms in that equation would be.

Factor 1   Consider a heuristic H, for example, 'Drive carefully late at night'. It has a characteristic curve of how powerful or useful it is, as a function of what problem it's applied to. As detailed in Lenat's *Nature of Heuristics*, the area under this curve is roughly constant. In simpler and more familiar terms, this is just the generality versus power tradeoff: the more powerful a heuristic's 'peak power', the narrower its domain of applicability is likely to be. A heuristic that only applied to driving on Saturday nights, in Austin, might be far more powerful than H, but its range of applicability is correspondingly narrower. As a first approximation to the power of the knowledge in the system, we might simply superpose all the 'power curves' of the heuristic (and algorithms) that comprise the knowledge. That would give us an overall idea of the power of the system as a function of what problem it was applied to. If we are interested in applying the system to a particular problem P, we could then read off the value of this curve at point P. If we are going to apply the system to several problems, so that P is a large distribution, then we would weight the result by that distribution.

Factor 2   As a correction to this first rough guess, we would want to factor out all the redundancy and dependence among the pieces of knowledge.

Factor 3   We would also want to weight each heuristic by how costly it is to run. 'Cost', here, includes literal CPU and memory resources used, and also includes the less tangible cost of asking questions of slow and busy human beings. Also included in this factor would be the down-side risks of what might happen if the heuristic gave incorrect advice.

Factor 4   To be fair to the less knowledge-based approaches, we should also deduct some amount which amortizes the effort we spent acquiring that rule or method.

Figure 3.2   Some of the factors in measuring the effective power of the knowledge in a system.

3   Evidence for the Knowledge Principle

Fifty years ago, before the modern era of computation began, Turing's theorems and abstract machines gave a hint of the fundamental idea that the computer could be used to model the symbol-manipulating processes that make up that most human of all behaviours – thinking.

Thirty years ago, following the 1956 Dartmouth Summer Conference on AI, the work began in earnest. The founding principle of the AI research paradigm is really an article of faith, first concretized by Newell and Simon:

> **The Physical Symbol Hypothesis**   The digital computer has sufficient means for intelligent action, to wit: representing real-world objects, actions and relationships internally as interconnected structures of symbols, and applying symbol manipulation procedures to those structures.

The early dreaming included intelligent behaviour at very high levels of competence. Turing speculated on wide-ranging conversations between people and machines, and also on expert level chess playing programs. Newell and Simon also wrote about champion chess programs, and began working with Cliff Shaw toward that end. Gelernter, Moses, Samuel, and many others shared the dream.

At Stanford, Lederberg and Feigenbaum chose to pursue the AI dream by focusing on scientific reasoning tasks. With Buchanan and Djerassi, they built DENDRAL, a program that solved structure elucidation problems at a high level of competence. Many years of experimenting with DENDRAL led to some hypotheses about what its source of power might be, how it was able to solve chemical structure problems from spectral data. Namely, the program worked because it had enough knowledge of basic and spectral chemistry.

Table 3.1 shows that, as each additional source of chemical knowledge was added, the DENDRAL program proposed fewer and fewer candidates (topologically plausible structures) to consider (see Buchanan *et al.*, 1969). When the rules of thumb for interpreting NMR data were also added to the program, many problems – such as the one illustrated – resulted in only a single candidate isomer being proposed as worth considering! Threatened by an *a priori* huge search space, DENDRAL managed to convert it into a tiny search space. That is, DENDRAL exhibited intelligence.

When searching a space of size 1, it is not crucial in what order you expand the candidate nodes. If you want to speed up a blind search by a factor of 43 million, one could, perhaps, parallelize the problem and (say, by 1995) employ a 43 mega-processor; but even back in 1965 one could, alternatively, talk with the human experts who routinely solve such problems, and then encode the knowledge they bring to bear to avoid searching.

Table 3.1 DENDRAL at work: finding all atom-bond graphs that could have the formula $C_{20}H_{43}N$.

Information source	Number of structures generated
Topology (limits of 3D space)	42 867 912
Chemical topology (valences)	14 715 814
Mass spectrography (heuristics)	1 284 792
Chemistry (first principles)	1 074 648
NMR (interpretation rules)	1

Obvious? Perhaps, in retrospect. But at the time, the prevailing view in AI (for example, the Advice Taker) ascribed power to the reasoning processes, to the inference engine and not to the knowledge base. The *knowledge as power* hypothesis stood as a *contra*-hypothesis. It stood awaiting further empirical testing to either confirm or falsify it.

The 1970s were the time to start gathering evidence for or against the Knowledge Principle. Medical and scientific problem solving provided the springboard. Shortliffe's MYCIN program formed the prototype for a large suite of expert-level advisory systems which we now label 'expert systems' (Feigenbaum, 1977). Its reasoning system was simple (exhaustive backward chaining) and *ad hoc* in parts. DEC has been using and extending McDermott's R1 program since 1981; its control structure is also simple: exhaustive forward chaining. These ES could interact with professionals in the jargon of the specialty; could explain their line of reasoning by displaying annotated traces of rule-firings; had subsystems (TEIRESIAS and SALT, respectively) which aided the acquisition of additional knowledge by guiding the expert to find and fix defects in the knowledge (rule) base.

Pople's INTERNIST program got under way at nearly the same time as MYCIN. By now it has grown to a KB of 572 diseases, 4500 manifestations, and many hundreds of thousands of links between them. In the past decade, thousands of expert systems have mushroomed in engineering, manufacturing, geology, molecular biology, financial services, machinery diagnosis and repair, signal processing, and in many other fields.

Very little ties these areas together, other than the fact that, in each one, some technical problem-solving is going on, guided by heuristics: experiential, qualitative rules of thumb – rules of good guessing. Their reasoning components are weak; in their knowledge bases lies their power. In the details of their design, development, and performance lies the evidence for the various adjunct propositions from Section 2.

Lenat's AM and EURISKO programs, over a decade old by now, demonstrated that several hundred heuristic rules, of varying levels of generality and power, could adequately begin to guide a search for plausible (and often interesting) new concepts in many domains, including set theory, number theory, wargaming tactics, physical device design, evolution, and programming. These experiments showed how scientific discovery – a very different sort of intelligent behaviour from most expert systems' tasks – might be explained as rule-guided, knowledge-guided search. Not all of the AM experiments were successful; indeed, the ultimate limitations of AM, as it was run longer and longer, finally led to EURISKO, whose ultimate empirical limitations led to CYC, of which more later.

In the 1980s, many other areas of AI research began making the shift over to the knowledge-based point of view. It is now common to hear that a program for understanding natural language must have extensive knowledge of its domain of discourse. Or, a vision program must have an understanding of the 'world' it is intended to analyse scenes from. Or even, a machine learning program must start with a significant body of knowledge which it will expand, rather than trying to learn from scratch.

4   The Breadth Hypothesis

A limitation of first-era expert systems is their brittleness. They operate on a high plateau of knowledge and competence until they reach the extremity of their knowledge; then they fall off precipitously to levels of ultimate incompetence. People suffer the same difficulty, too, but their plateau is much broader and their fall is more graceful. Part of what cushions the fall are layer upon layer of weaker, more general models that underlie their specific knowledge.

For example, if an engineer is diagnosing a faulty circuit with which he or she is unfamiliar, he or she can bring to bear general electronics knowledge, circuit analysis techniques, experiences with the other products manufactured by the same company, handbook data for the individual components, common sense familiarity with water circuits (looking for leaks or breaks), electrical devices (turn it off and on a few times), or mechanical devices in general (shake it or smack it a few times.) The engineer might analogize to the last few times that his or her car engine failed, or even to something more distant (for example, a failed love or a broken arm).

Domain-specific knowledge represents the distillation of experience in a field – for example, nuggets of compiled hindsight. In a situation similar to the one in which they crystallized, they can powerfully guide search. But when confronted by a *novel* situation, we turn to generalizing and analogizing. This leads to the Breadth Hypothesis (BH), which we stated in Section 1 as follows:

> intelligent performance often requires the problem solver to fall back on increasingly general knowledge, and/or to analogize to specific knowledge from far-flung domains.

Generalization often involves accessing a body of general knowledge, one that is enormous, largely present in each person, yet rarely passed on explicitly from one person to another. It is *consensus reality*: 'water flows downhill', 'living things get diseases', 'doing work requires energy', 'people live for a single, contiguous, finite interval of time'. Lacking these simple common sense concepts, ES' mistakes often appear ridiculous in human terms: a skin disease diagnosis program might decide that a 10-year-old car with reddish spots on its body had measles.

Analogy involves *partial*-matching from your current situation to another (often simpler) one. Why does it work? There is much common causality in the world; that leads to similar events A and B; people (with our limited perception) then notice a little bit of that shared structure; finally, since we *know* that human perception is *often* limited, people come to rely on the following rule of thumb:

> **Analogical method**   If A and B appear to have some unexplained similarities, then it is worth your time to hunt for additional shared properties.

This rule is general but inefficient. There are many more specialized rules for successful analogizing in various task domains, in various user-modes (for example, by someone in a hurry, or a child), among analogues with various epistemological statuses, depending on how much data there is about A and B, and so on. These are some of the n dimensions of analogy-space; we can conceive having a special body of knowledge – an ES – in each cell of that n-dimensional matrix, to handle just that sort of analogical reasoning.

Why focus on causality? If cause A and cause B have no specific common generalization, then similarities between A and B are more likely to be superficial coincidences, a metaphor useful, perhaps, as a literary device but not as a heuristic one.

The above is really just a rationalization of how analogy *might* work. The reason this *frequently* succeeds has to do with three properties that happen to hold in the real world.

1.   The distribution of causes with respect to effects. If there were a vast number of distinguishable kinds of causes, or if there were only a couple, then analogy would be less useful.

2.   The moderately high frequency with which we must cope with novel situations, and the moderate degree of novelty they present. Lower frequency, or much higher or lower novelty, would decrease the usefulness of analogy.

3.   The obvious metric for locating relevant knowledge – namely, 'closeness of subject matter' – is, at best, an imperfect predictor. Far-flung knowledge *can* be useful.

Analogizing broadens the relevance of the entire knowledge base. It can be used to construct interesting and novel interpretations of situations and data; to retrieve knowledge that has not been stored the way that is now needed; to guess values for attributes; to suggest methods that just might work; and as a device to help students learn and remember. It can provide access to powerful methods that might work in this case, but which might not otherwise be perceived as 'relevant'. For example, Dirac analogized between quantum theory and group theory, and very gingerly brought the group theory results over into physics for the first time, with quite successful results.

Today, we suffer with laborious manual knowledge entry in building an ES, carefully codifying knowledge and placing it in a data structure. Analogizing may be used in the future, not only as an inference method inside a program, but also as an aid to adding new knowledge to it.

When faced with a complex situation, we often analogize to a much simpler one. Simplification is often overdone: 'the stock market is a seesaw'; 'medication is a resource' (this leads many patients to overdose). Cross-field mapping is rarer but can pay off: 'curing a disease is like fighting a battle' helps doctors devise new tactics to try.

Succesful analogizing often involves components of both vertical (simplifying) and horizontal (cross-field) transformation. For instance, consider reifying a country as if it were an individual person: 'Russia is angry'. That accomplishes two things: it simplifies dealing with the other country, and it also enables our vast array of firsthand experiences (and lessons learned) about interpersonal relations to be applied to international relations.

5   Evidence for the Breadth Hypothesis

If we had as much hard evidence about the BH as we do for the KP, we would be calling it the *Breadth Principle*. Still, the evidence is there, if we look closely at the limits of what AI programs can do today. For brevity, we will focus on natural language understanding (NL) and machine learning (ML), but similar results are appearing in most other areas of AI as well. As Mark Stefik recently remarked to us: 'Much current research in AI is stalled. Progress will be held back until a sufficient corpus of knowledge is available on which to base experiments.'

5.1   The limits of natural language understanding

To understand sentences in a natural language, one must be able to disambiguate which meaning of a word is intended, what the referent of a pronoun probably is, what each ellipsis means, . . . These are knowledge-intensive skills. For example, the following sentences presume word knowledge furiously:

1.   I saw the Statue of Liberty flying over New York.

2.   The box is in the pen. The ink is in the pen.

3.   Mary saw a dog in the window. She wanted it.

4.   Napoleon died on St. Helena. Wellington was saddened.

Consider the first sentence. Who is flying – you or the statue? Clearly we are not getting any clues from English to do that disambiguation; we must know about people, statues, passenger air travel, the size of cargo that is shipped by air, the size of the Statue of Liberty, the ease or difficulty of seeing objects from a distance, . . . In sentence 2, one 'pen' is a corral, the other is a writing implement. In sentence 3, does 'it' refer to the dog or the window? What if we said 'She *smashed* it'? A program which *understood* sentence 4 should be able to answer: 'Did Wellington hear of Napoleon's death? Did Wellington outlive Napoleon?'

For any particular sample text, an NL program can incorporate the necessary body of twentieth century Americana, of common sense facts and scripts, that may be required for semantic disambiguation, question answering, anaphoric reference, and so on. But then one turns the page – the new text requires more semantics to be added.

In a sense, the NL researchers *have* cracked the language understanding problem. But to produce a general Turing-testable system, they would have to provide more and more semantic information, and the program's semantic component would more and more resemble the immense KB mandated by the Breadth Hypothesis.

Have we overstated the argument? Hardly, if anything we have drastically *understated* it! Look at almost any newspaper story, for example, and attend to how often a word or concept is used in a clearly metaphorical, non-literal sense. Once every few minutes, you might guess? No! Reality is full of surprises. The surprise here is that almost every sentence is packed with metaphors and analogies (Lakoff and Johnson, 1980). An unbiased sample: here is the first article we saw today (7 April, 1987), the lead story in the *Wall Street Journal*:

'Texaco lost a major ruling in its legal battle with Pennzoil. The Supreme Court dismantled Texaco's protection against having to post a crippling $12 billion appeals bond, pushing Texaco to the brink of a Chapter 11 filing.'

Lost? Major? Battle? Dismantled? Posting? Crippling? Pushing? Brink? The example drives home the point that, far from overinflating the need for real-world knowledge in language understanding, the usual arguments about disambiguation barely scratch the surface. (Drive? Home? The point? Far? Overinflating? Scratch? Surface? Oh no, I can't stop!!!) These layers of analogy and metaphor eventually 'bottom out' at physical – somatic – primitives: up, down, forward, back, pain, cold, inside, see, sleep, taste, growth, containment, movement, birth, death, strain, etc.

NL researchers – and dictionaries – usually get around analogic usage by allowing several meanings to a word. Definition number 1 for 'war' is the literal one, and the other definitions are various common metaphorical uses of 'war.'

There are many hundreds of thousands – perhaps a few million – things that we authors can assume you readers know about the world: the number of tyres on a car; who Reagan is; what happens if you fall asleep when driving – what we called consensus reality. To use language effectively, we select the best consensus image to evoke quickly in your mind the complex thought we want to convey. If our program does not already know most of those million shared concepts (experiences, objects, processes, patterns, . . .), it will be awkward for us to communicate with it in NL.

It is common for NL researchers to acknowledge the need for a large semantic component nowadays; Schank and others were saying similar things a decade ago! But the first serious efforts to build one have only recently begun (CYC (Lenat *et al.*, 1986) and the Japanese Electronic Dictionary Research (EDR) project), so we will have to wait several years until the evidence is in.

5.2   The limits of machine learning (induction)

We will pick on AM and EURISKO because they exemplify the extreme knowledge-rich end of the current ML spectrum. Many experiments in machine learning were performed on them. We had many surprises along the way, and we gained an intuitive feel for how and why heuristics work, for the nature of their power and their brittleness. Lenat and Brown (1983) present many of those surprises, including:

1.   It works. Several thousand concepts, including some novel concepts and heuristics, from several domains, were discovered.

2. Most of the interesting concepts could be discovered in several different ways.

3. Performing the top N tasks on the agenda in simulated-parallel provided only about a factor of 3 speed-up even when N grew as large as 100.

4. Progress slows down unless the program learns new heuristics (compiles its hindsight) often.

5. Similarly, progress slowed down partly because the programs could not learn competently to choose, switch, extend, or invent different representations.

6. These programs are sensitive to the assumptions woven into their representations' semantics; for example, what does it mean for Jane to appear as the value on the spouse slot of the Fred frame?

7. Some of their apparent power is illusory, only present in the mind of the intelligent observer who recognizes concepts which the program defines but does not appreciate properly.

8. Structural mutation works if, and only if, syntax mirrors semantics: represent heuristics using many small if- and many small then-parts, so the results of point mutation can more be meaningful.

9. In each new domain, there would be a flurry of plausible activities, resulting in several unexpected discoveries, followed by a period of decreased productivity, and finally a lapse into useless thrashing. The above techniques (numbers 4, 5, and 8, for example) only delayed this decay.

Despite their relative knowledge-richness, the ultimate limitations of these programs derive from their small size. Not their small number of methods, which were probably adequate, but the small initial knowledge base on which they had to draw. One can analogize to a campfire that dies out because it was too small, and too well isolated from nearby trees, to start a major blaze. As Porter recently remarked to us: 'Nothing new is learned except with respect to what's already known.' Minsky cites a variant of this relationship in his afterword to Vinge (1984): 'The more you know, the more (and faster) you can learn.'

Learning can be considered a task. Like other tasks, it is subject to the Knowledge Principle. The inverse of this enabling relationship is a disabling one, and this is what ultimately doomed AM and EURISKO:

Knowledge facilitates learning (catch 22): If you do not know very much to begin with, do not expect to learn a lot quickly.

This is the standard criticism of pure Baconian induction: 'To get ahead, get a theory.' Without one, you will be lost. It will be difficult (or time-consuming) to determine whether or not each new generalization is going to be useful. This theme is filtering into ML in the form of explanation-based generalization and goal-based learning.

Do human beings not violate this catch 22, starting from nothing? Maybe, but it is not clear what we start with. Evolution has produced not merely physically sophisticated structures, but also brains whose architecture is well suited to learning many of the simple facts that are worth learning about the world. Our senses (vision, for example) are carefully tuned as well, to supply the brain with data that is already filtered for meaning: edges, shapes, motion, etc. The exploration of those issues is beyond the scope of this paper, and probably beyond the scope of twentieth century science, but one thing is clear – neonatal brains are far from *tabulae rasae*.

Besides starting from well-prepared brain structures, humans also have to spend a lot of time learning. It is unclear what processes go on during infancy. Once the child begins to communicate by speaking, *then* we are into the symbolic sort of learning on which AI has traditionally focused.

6   The Empirical Inquiry Hypothesis

We scientists have a view of ourselves as terribly creative, but compared to nature we suffer from a poverty of the imagination; it is thus much easier for us to uncover than to invent. Premature mathematization keeps nature's surprises hidden, washing out details that later turn out to be significant. For example, contrast the astonishing early empirical studies by Piaget (Stages of Development) with his subsequent five decades of barren attempts to mathematize them. This attitude leads to our central methodological hypothesis, our paradigm for AI research: the Empirical Inquiry Hypothesis (EH). We stated it in Section 1, and repeat it here:

> Intelligence is still so poorly understood that nature still holds most of the important surprises in store for us. So the most profitable way to investigate AI is to embody our hypotheses in programs, and gather data by running the programs. The surprises usually suggest revisions that start the cycle over again. Progress depends on these experiments being able to falsify our hypotheses; these programs must be capable of behaviour not expected by the experimenter.

What do we mean by 'a surprise'? Surely we would not want to increase surprises by having more naïve researchers, less careful thought and planning of experiments, sloppier coding, etc. We have in mind astronomers getting surprised by what they see (and hear) through telescopes; that is, things surprising to the professional. Early AI programs often surprised their builders in this fashion; for example, Newell and Simon's LT program and Gelernter's geometry program, circa 1960. Then fascination with axiomatizing and proving set in, and surprises from 'the real world' became rare. The inverse to the EH is cruel:

Inverse to the Empirical Inquiry Hypothesis   If one builds programs which cannot possibly surprise him or her, then one is using the computer either:

1.   as an engineering workhorse, or

2.   as a fancy sort of word processor (to help articulate one's hypothesis), or

3.   as a (self-) deceptive device masquerading as an experiment.

Most expert systems work falls into the former category; DART's use of MRS exemplifies the middle (Genesereth, 1984); PUP5 (by the young Lenat) and HACKER (by the young Sussman) exemplify the latter category.

To illustrate this point, we will use some of our own earlier work. The PUP5 program used a community of about 100 beings (actors, knowledge sources, mini-experts) to cooperate and synthesize a long LISP program, namely a variant of the ARCH-learning program that Winston had written for his thesis several years earlier. That was the program that PUP5 was built to synthesise, the target it was to hit. We chose that target first, and wrote a clean version of the program in INTERLISP. Next, we wrote down an English dialogue in which a user talked to an idealized automatic program synthesis program which then gradually wrote the target program. Next, we analysed the script of that dialogue, writing down the specific knowledge needed on the part of the synthesizer to handle each and every line that the user typed in. Finally, we encoded each of those pieces of knowledge, and bundled up the related ones into little actors or beings.

Given this methodology, it should come as no surprise that PUP5 was then able to carry on that exact dialogue with a user, and synthesize that exact ARCH program. We still firmly believe in the paradigm of multiple cooperating knowledge sources, it is just that our methodology ensured that there would be no surprises when we ran PUP5. Why? All along the way, there were numerous chances to cut corners, to put down knowledge consciously or unconsciously in a very specific form, in just the form that it would be needed during the dialogue we knew was going to be run. There was not much else that PUP5 could do, therefore, besides hit its target, and there was not much that we learned about automatic programming or intelligence from that long exercise.

There was one crucial *meta*-level lesson we did learn: You cannot do science if you just use a computer as a word processor, to illustrate your ideas rather than test them. That is the coarse form of the Empirical

Inquiry Hypothesis. We resolved to choose a task that eliminated or minimized the chance of building a wind-up toy like PUP5. We did not want a program whose target behaviour was so narrow, so precisely defined, that it could 'succeed' and yet teach us nothing. The AM program was the direct result of Lenat's violent recoil from the PUP5 project.

There was no particular target behaviour that AM was designed with; rather, it was an experiment: what would happen if a moderate sized body of a few hundred math heuristics (about what were plausible directions to go in, about when something was and was not interesting) were applied in an agenda-managed best-first search, given an initial body of 100 or so simple math concepts? In this sense, AM's task was less constrained than any program's had ever been: to explore areas of mathematics and do interesting things (gather data, notice regularities, etc.), with no preconceptions about what it might find or by what route it would find it.

Unlike PUP5, AM provided hundreds of surprises, including many experiments that led to the construction of EURISKO. EURISKO ran for several thousand CPU hours, in half a dozen varied domains. And again, the ultimate limitation was not what we expected (CPU time), or hoped for (the need to learn new representations of knowledge), but rather something at once surprising and daunting: the need to have a large fraction of consensus reality already in the machine. In this case, the data led Lenat to the next project to work on – CYC – an undertaking we would have shied away from if the empirical evidence had not forced us to it.

Progress along our path was due to running large experiments. As the Difficult Problems Hypothesis said in Section 1:

> There are too many ways to solve simple problems. Raising the level and breadth of competence we demand of a system makes it easier to test and raise its intelligence.

Cognitive psychology, for example, traditionally sidesteps hard-to-quantify phenomena, such as scientific creativity or reading and comprehending a good book, in favour of very simple tasks, such as remembering nonsense syllables. If a 'messy' task *is* studied, then usually either:

1.   it is abstracted and simplified beyond recognition (for example, BACON), or

2.   the psychologist focuses on (and varies) one specific variable, so 'respectable' statistical tests for significance can be run.

We have an abiding trust in empirical inquiry, in doing science the same way as the early Piaget, Newell, Simon, and Gelernter. The number of states that a brain or a computer can be in is immense; both those numbers are so huge as to be almost unimaginable. Turing's hypothesis likens them to each other; the only other system with which we are familiar and with that degree of complexity is nature itself. Mankind has made progress in studying natural phenomena only after centuries of empirically studying those phenomena; there is no reason to expect intelligence to be exempt.

James Wilkinson was recently asked why he was the first to discover the truncation errors of early twentieth century integration methods. After all, Wilkes at Cambridge, and others, had access to equal or better machines at the same time. He replied that at the National Physical Laboratory, the pilot ACE machine was sitting out, available to all to use and to watch. He was fascinated by the rows of blinking lights, and often stood mesmerized by them while his programs ran. Soon he began to recognize patterns in the lights – patterns where there should *not* have been patterns! By contrast, the Cambridge computer was screened off from its users, who got one-day turnaround on their card decks, but who were denied access to the phenomenon that Wilkinson was allowed to observe.

Much of the confusion about AI methodology may be due to our casual mixing together of two quite different things: AI *goals* and AI *strategies* for achieving those goals. The confusion arises because many entries appear on both lists. But almost any strategy can apply toward any goal. Here we will consider just one example: an *expert system strategy* for a *language understanding goal* might be to build a rule-based system containing rules like 'if a person gets excited, they break more grammatical rules than usual.' By contrast, a *language understanding strategy* for an *expert system goal* might be an English front end that helps an expert enter and edit rules.

All scientific disciplines adopt a paradigm: a list of the problems that are acceptable and worthwhile to tackle, a list of the methods that can and should be tried, and the standards by which the results are judged. Adopting a paradigm is done for reasons of cognitive economy, but each paradigm is one narrow view. Adding to the confusion, some paradigms in AI have grown up both around the various goals *and* around the various strategies! See Appendix 1 for a more detailed look into AI goals and strategies.

Finer distinctions can be drawn, involving the *tactical* choices to be made, but this turns out to be misleading. How? Tactics that appear to be superficially different may share a common source of power (Lenat, 1984); predicate calculus and frames both rely on a judicious dividing up of the world. And some tactics which appear superficially similar to each other may draw on very different sources of power (e.g., if-then rules representing logical assertions, versus if-then rules of good guessing.)

The KP and BH and EH are all *strategic* statements. Each could be prefaced by the phrase '*Whichever of the ultimate goals for AI you are pursuing, . . .'* The strategic level is, apparently, the level where one needs to take a stand. This is rarely stated explicitly, and it is rarely taken into account by news media or by conference organizers.

7   A programme for AI research: mapping the human memome

AI must somehow get to that stage where – as called for by KP and BH – learning begins to accelerate due to the amount already known. Learning will not be an effective means to get to that stage; unfortunately, we shall have to hand-craft that large 'seed' KB one piece at a time. In terms of the graph in Figure 3.3, all the programs that have ever been written, including AM and EURISKO, lie so far toward the left edge of the x-axis that the learning curve is more or less horizontal. Several of the more successful recent additions to the suite of ML techniques can be interpreted as pushes in the direction of adding more knowledge from which to begin the learning.

The graph in Figure 3.3 shows learning by discovery constantly accelerating: the more one knows, the faster one can discover more. Once you speak fluently, learning by talking with other people is more efficient than rediscovery, until you cross the frontier of what humanity already knows (the vertical line at $x = F$), at which point there is no one to tell you the next piece of knowledge. 'Learning by discovery' is meant to include not only scientific research (for example, cancer research), but also the many smaller scale events in which someone formulates a hypothesis, gathers data to test it, and uses the results to adjust their 'theory'. That small scale case can occur in a (good) classroom; or just by driving the same route to work over various different times of the day (and hypothesizing on rush hour patterns.) It involves defining new concepts (at least in principle), formulating new heuristics, and even adjusting or changing one's representation of knowledge. The discovery line in Figure 3.3 illustrates:

1.   it is much *slower* than other forms of learning – such as being told – but,

2.   it is the chief method that extends the boundary F of human knowledge.

By contrast, the rate of hand coding of knowledge is fairly constant, though it, too, drops to zero once we cross the boundary of what is already known by humanity. The hand-coding rate may slope down a bit, since the time to find related concepts will increase, perhaps as the log of the size of the KB. Or, instead, the hand-coding rate may

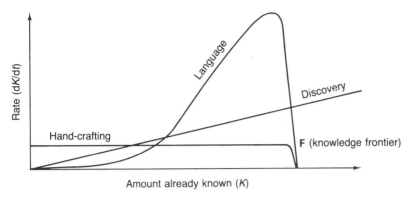

Figure 3.3   The rate at which one can learn new knowledge. One can also integrate these three curves with respect to time, to see how the total amount known might grow over time.

slope *up* a bit, since copy&edit is a powerful technique for knowledge entry, and, as the KB grows, there will be more chance that some very similar concept is already present.

This is an example of EH (the Empirical Inquiry Hypothesis which was presented in Section 1): only by trying to hand-code the KB will we see which of those two counteracting factors outweighs the other, and by how much. Only by continued work on NL and ML will we determine whether or not there is a region, near where all three curves meet, where ML temporarily surpasses NL as a way to grow the KB. And only much farther in the future, after our program crosses the frontier F, will we find out if the discovery curve begins to slope up or down.

Figure 3.3 suggests a sweeping three-stage research programme for the coming three decades of AI research:

1.　slowly hand-code a large, broad knowledge base;
2.　when enough knowledge is present, it will be faster to acquire more through reading, assimilating data bases, etc.; and
3.　to go beyond the frontier of human knowledge, the system will have to rely on learning by discovery, carrying out research and development projects to expand its KB.

Three decades, not three centuries? What are the scales on the axes of Figure 3.3? Why do we think it is not a 30-*century* programme? Even if the vague shapes of the curves are correct, and even if we are near the left edge, how far over to the right is that place where language understanding meets and then surpasses the hand-coding level? Might we need a trillion things in our knowledge base, in order to get analogy and generalization to pay off? The usefulness and timeliness of the Breadth Hypothesis rest on the following quantitative assumption:

Breadth is within our grasp   A KB of under one million frames will provide a significant performance increase, due to generalization and analogy; this will consume about two person-centuries of time, about US$ 50 million, and about one decade. Why such a 'small size'? That is about all that people know!

'Under a million things! What an insult!' you may say. 'You just argued that the world is a complicated place. Surely we human beings each know an effectively infinite number of things! It is hopeless to try to represent an appreciable fraction of that, so we may as well settle on writing programs that know only 10–1000 specific things.'

What goes on during the 200 000 hours between birth and age 21? Certainly most of it is spent gathering experiences, building up long-term memories; some conscious time (and perhaps some sleep time) is spent generalizing and organizing one's memories. Much of what we are learning is quite specific to ourselves, our home, our family, our friends, and our culture. (Humour results from thrusting someone into a different culture; for example, Crocodile Dundee, A Connecticut Yankee, The Beverly Hillbillies, The Gods Must Be Crazy).

Three recent independent estimates of the number of concepts (frames) needed for full breadth of knowledge all came up with a figure of approximately one million:

1.   CYC: 30 000 articles × 30 frames per article,

2.   EDR: 200k words × 1 frame for each of a few languages,

3.   Minsky: 4 long-term memory entries/hour from birth to adulthood.

Two other ways for bounding the 'bits' a human brain can store lead to much larger numbers:

1.   counting neurons and synapses, but it is unclear how memories are stored in them;

2.   counting pixels in our 'mental images', but controversy rages in cognitive psychology over whether mental imagery is just an illusion caused by the consistency and regularity in the world that lets us fill in missing pieces of memories – and of dynamic sensory experiences – with default values.

So it is unclear what those larger numbers signify. (Also, though it is clearly an oversimplification, having a million entries means that there can be a trillion one-step inferences involving pairs of them.)

Here again is a situation in which one should apply the EH. Various theories give various estimates, and the way to settle the issue – and, perhaps, achieve the goal of having the KB we want – is to go off and try to build the large KB. Along the way it will, no doubt, become clear how big it is growing and what the actual obstacles are that must be overcome.

8 Differences with other positions

8.1 Our position regarding the aesthetes

People do – and *should* – prefer the simplest consistent hypothesis about any phenomenon. That does not make them correct, of course. Early astronomers with poor instruments had no problem with a geocentric model. When one friend of Wittgenstein's ridiculed them for making this error, he replied 'Ah, yes, how foolish. But I wonder what it would have looked like if the sun *did* go around the earth?'

Biologists, who are unable to perform experiments on evolution, or even get precise data on it, can still believe it operates so quickly using nothing more than random mutation, random generate-and-test – a simple, elegant, appealing, and (as we in AI found out empirically) woefully inadequate problem solving method. Another example: James Wilkinson, a Fellow of the Royal Society and one of the world's leading numerical analysts, recently spoke about bugs in early twentieth century methods of numerical integration. These algorithms had 'proofs', and were used (to a couple of iterations only) by human beings armed only with pencil and paper. Those people, by the way, were called 'computers'. The introduction of the high-speed electronic digital computer provided the next round of 'criticism' – namely, truncation errors made the algorithms unstable – which led to the next round of improvement in that field. And one final example: Chapter 1 of Lakatos (1976) presents the historical series of mathematicians' retreats from the initial form of the Euler–Descartes conjecture to increasingly longer, less elegant versions, with more and more terms to take obscure cases and exceptions into account.

If only there were a secret ingredient for intelligence – the Maxwell's equations of thought. If only we could axiomatize the world, and deduce everything. If only our learning program could start from scratch. If only our neural net were big enough. If only the world were like that. But it is not. The evidence indicates that almost all the power is in the bulk knowledge. As Whitehead remarked, 'God is in the details'.

A quarter of a century ago, Simon provided the spectacular image of an ant on a beach: though its path is complex, that is due to the complexity of the beach, not the ant. It is a beautiful hypothesis that thinking might be based on such simple mechanisms; that is, that the apparent complexity of the human mind is an illusion, reflecting a very simple, very general problem solver thrust into a complex environment. With apologies to Wittgenstein, we reply, 'Ah, yes, but I wonder what it would look like if the mind *were* filled with – and dependent upon – knowledge?'

This difference of opinion about whether or not the world must admit an elegant and simple formalization of intelligence leads to a deep methodological difference between our 'scruffy' way of doing AI and the aesthetes'. Following the Difficult Problems Hypothesis, we are firmly convinced that the AI researcher must make a major time commitment to the domain(s) in which his or her programs are to be competent; for example, the two years that Stefik and Friedland spent learning about molecular biology before doing MOLGEN; the decade-long time frame for CYC. This is in contrast to, for example, research that uses the 15 puzzle, or cryptarithmetic, as its domain. Even in physics, where nature so far *has* been remarkably elegant, it is still strongly cost-effective to expend the enormous time and money to build and use a SLAC or a CERN.

We may be exhausting the range of potent experimental AI theses that can be carried out in two years by a student starting, more or less, from scratch; witness the trend to give the Computers and Thought Award to increasingly less recent graduates. The presence of a large, widely-accessible 'testbed' KB should enable a new round of important theses.

Many AI researchers search for an elegant solution in a desperate desire for scientific respectability. The name of our field – 'Artificial Intelligence' – invites everyone instantly to form an opinion. Too bad it was not called quantum cognodynamics. 'But perhaps, by interposing a layer of mathematical formalism, we can come to be accepted as hard scientists.' Hence the physics-envy!

Formalizing has never driven any early science along. In designing new drug molecules, the biochemist knows it is too inefficient to apply Schroedinger's wave equation to compute the energy minimizations, hence from his or her point of view the fact that such a deep understanding even exists *is irrelevant* to the task at hand. He or she relies on crude design heuristics, and the drug companies, using this methodology, occasionally are enriched. As Minsky remarked about the A* algorithm in 1970: 'Just because it's mathematical doesn't mean it deserves to be taught.'

Eventually, we *will* want layers of increasing 'neatness'. For example, in physics, students learn each year that last year's equations were a special case. We always try to reason at the highest, most superficial, most efficient level at which we can, and delve down one level deeper when we are forced to. But devoting so much effort to the attempt at 'neatness' today just drains time and intellectual energy away from the prime enterprise of the field.

One popular type of aestheticism that deserves mention is the trend to highly parallel (for example, connectionistic) and ever faster devices. The trouble is that most difficult tasks in knowledge-rich areas cannot be highly parallelized. If we were to set one million people to work trying to find a cure for cancer, we would not find one in 0.2 s. Each cancer experiment takes months or years to perform, and there are only a moderate number of promising experiments to do at any one time; their *results* will determine what the next round of promising experiments should be.

Parallelism is useful at one extreme for implementing very carefully engineered algorithms (for example, systolic algorithms), and at the other extreme for allowing a community of meaningfully-individuated agents to act independently, asynchronously. For most technical tasks, until we understand the task very well, the size of such an actor community that we can design is typically only about 100.

The time to perform a task often increases exponentially with its size (for example, looking ahead n moves in chess). Taking a microcoding approach or a parallelizing approach cuts off a constant factor; taking a knowledge-based approach may add a constant overhead but, more importantly, for the long run, it may chip at the *exponent*. Look at Table 3.1 again. On the other hand, it is worth remarking that there are some special tasks where the desired level of performance (x-coordinate) is fixed: beating all humans at chess, understanding spoken words in real time, tracking the space shuttle in real time, etc. In such a case, getting a large enough constant factor speedup really could solve the problem, with no need to apply the KP, BH, or EH. As our ambition to attack ever more difficult problems grows, though, the exponential nature of the search hurts worse.

8.2   Our position regarding expert systems

The KP underlies the current explosion of work on expert systems. Still, there are additional things our position argues for, that are not yet realized in today's ES.

One major power source for ES, the reason they can be so readily constructed, is the synergistic additivity of many rules. Using a blackboard (Erman *et al.*, 1980) or partitioned rule sets, it is possible to combine small packets of rules into mega-rules: knowledge sources for one large expert system.

The analogue at the next higher level would be to hook hundreds of large ES together, and achieve even greater synergy. That dream fails to materialize. As we increase the domain of each 'element' we are trying to couple together, the 'glue' we need gets to be larger and more sophisticated. It seems to us that it will require the large system mandated by the Breadth Hypothesis, before the true potential of ES technology will be realized.

> **Plateau-hopping requires breadth**   To couple together a large number of disparate expert systems will require something approaching full consensus reality – the million abstractions, models, facts, rules of thumb, representations, etc., that we all possess and that we assume everyone else does.

The INTERNIST program is carefully engineered to do a good job of diagnosing diseases from symptoms. But consider coupling it to a machine learning program, which tries to speculate on new disease mechanisms for epidemiology. The knowledge in INTERNIST is not stored in 'the right way', and much of the needed mechanism knowledge has *already* been compiled away, condensed into numeric correlations. Clancey encountered similar difficulties when he tried to adapt MYCIN's diagnostic KB to *teach* medical students.

As we try to combine ES from various tasks, even somewhat related tasks, their particular simplifications and idiosyncrasies prevent synergy. The simplifying was done in the interests of highly efficient and competent problem solving; breadth was not one of the engineering goals.

This naturally results in each ES being a separate, simplified, knowledge universe. When you sit down to build an ES for a task – say scheduling machines on a factory floor – you talk to the experts and find out the compiled knowledge they use, the ways they finesse things. For instance, how do they avoid general reasoning about time and belief? Probably they have a very simple, very specialized data structure that captures just the bits of information about time and belief that they need to solve their task. How do they deal with the fact that this milling machine M has a precise location, relative to all the others; that its base plate is a solid slab of metal of such and such a size and orientation; that its operator is a human; that only one operator at a time can use it, etc.?

If someone accidentally drills a hole through the base plate, most human beings would realize that the machine can still be used for certain jobs but not for others; for example, it is OK if you want to mill a very large part, but not a very small one that might fall through the hole! People can shift fluidly to the next more detailed grain size, to reason out the impact of the hole in the base plate, even if they have never thought of it happening before; but the typical ES would have had just one particular level built in to it, so it could not adapt to using the crippled milling machine.

Sometimes the ES's precipitous fall into incompetent behaviour is obvious, but sometimes its explanations remain dangerously plausible. Meta-rules about the system's area of competence can guard against this accidental misuse, but that is just a patch. A true solution would be to provide a broad KB so that the plateau sloped off gently on all sides, and so that we could hop from one ES's plateau to another. Knowledge space *in toto* is not a homogeneous solid surface, but more like a set of self-supporting buttes, and one ought to be able to hop from one to its neighbours.

This raises a point which is appropriate both to ES and to the aesthetes (Section 8.1) as well. Both positions tacitly assume a kind of global consistency in the knowledge base. Inconsistencies may exist for a short period, but they are errors and must be tracked down and corrected. We expect, however, that this is just an idealized, simplified view of what will be required for intelligent systems. Namely, we advocate:

The Local Consistency Hypothesis There is no need – and probably not even any possibility – of achieving a *global* consistent unification of several ES' KBs (or, equivalently, for one very large KB). Large systems need *local consistency*.

The Coherence Hypothesis Moreover, whenever two large internally-consistent chunks $C1$, $C2$ are similar, their heuristics and analogies should *cohere*; if the 'going up' metaphor usually means 'getting better' for $C1$, then it should again mean 'getting better' for $C2$, or else it should not apply at all there.

As regards local consistency, Stefik points out how physics advanced for many decades with inconsistent particle and wave models for light. Local consistency is what permits each knowledge-space butte to be independent of the others; as with large office buildings, independent supports should make it easier for the whole structure to weather tremors, such as local anomalies. In a locally consistent system, inferring an inconsistency is only slightly more serious than the usual sort of 'dead-end' a searcher runs into; the system should be able to back up a bit and continue on. Intelligent behaviour derives not from the razor's edge of absolute true versus absolute false – from perfect matching – but rather is suggested by plausibility heuristics and supported by empirical evidence.

Coherence is what keeps one from getting disoriented in stepping from one KB butte to its neighbour. Having the metaphors line up coherently can make the hops so small that one is unaware they have hopped at all: 'Her academic career, her mood, and her prospects were all going up' – see Lakoff and Johnson (1980). Coherence applies at the conceptual level, not just at the word level. It is not so much the *words* 'going up' as the concept, the *script* of moving upwards, that applies coherently in so many situations.

9 Problems and solutions

Problem 1 Possible 'in-principle' limitations

There are several extremes that one can point to where the Knowledge Principle and Breadth Hypothesis would be inapplicable or even harmful: perceptual and motor tasks; certain tasks which must be performed in small pieces of real time; tasks that involve things we do not yet know how to represent well (time, space, belief, mass nouns, counter-factuals, . . .); tasks for which an adequate algorithm exists; tasks so poorly understood that no one can yet do them well; and tasks involving large amounts of common sense.

Our response – in principle and in CYC – is to describe perception, emotion, motion, etc., down to some level of detail that enables the system to understand humans doing those things, and/or to be able to reason simply about them. As discussed in Problem 2, we let a large body of examples dictate what sorts of knowledge, and to what depth, are required.

A similar answer applies to all the items which we do not yet know how to represent very clearly. In building CYC, for example, a large amount of effort is being spent on capturing an adequate body of knowledge (including representations) for time, space, and belief. We did not set out to do this, the effort is driven completely by need, empirically: looking at encyclopaedia and newspaper articles, and developing machinery that can handle those cases encountered.

Tasks which can be done without knowledge, or which require some knowledge that no one yet possesses, should be avoided. One does not use a hammer type with.

The huge KB mandated by the Breadth Hypothesis is AI's 'mattress in the road'. Knowing that we can go around it one more time, AI researchers build a system in six months that will perform adequately on a narrow version of task X; they do not pause for a decade to pull the mattress away. This research opportunity is finally being pursued; but until CYC or a similar project succeeds, the knowledge based approach must shy away from tasks that involve a great deal of wide-ranging common sense or analogy.

The remainder of the problems in this section are primarily pragmatic, engineering problems, dealing with the mechanics of constructing systems and making them more usable. As can be seen from our response to the in-principle limitations, we personally view Problem 1 in that very same category! That is a view based on the EH, of course.

Problem 2   How exactly do we get the knowledge?

Knowledge must be extracted from people, from data bases, from the intelligent systems' KBs themselves (for example, thinking up new analogies), and from nature directly. Each source of knowledge requires its own special extraction methods.

In the case of the CYC project, the goal is to capture the full breadth of human knowledge. To drive that acquisition task, Lenat and his team are going through an encyclopaedia, sentence by sentence. They are not just entering the facts stated, but – much more importantly – are encoding what the writer of that sentence assumed the reader already knew about the world. They are the facts and heuristics which one would need in order to understand the sentence, things which would be insulting or confusing for the writer to have actually stated explicitly (for example, if coke is consumed to turn ore into metal, then coke and ore must both be worth less than metal). They also generalize each of these as much as possible (for example, the products of commercial processes are more valuable than their inputs). Another useful place they focus is the intersentential gap: in a historical article, what actions should the reader infer have happened between each sentence and the next? Yet another focus: what questions should anyone be able to answer having just read that article? These foci drive the extraction process. Eventually, CYC itself should help add knowledge, for example, by proposed analogues, extending existing analogies, and noticing gaps in nearly-symmetric structures.

This methodology will collect, for example, all the facts and heuristics about water that every article in the encyclopaedia assumed its reader already knew; we expect this will be close to what everyone does know and needs to know about water. This is in contrast to, for instance, naïve physics and other approaches that aim to somehow capture a deeper theory of water in all its various forms.

Problem 3   How do we adequately represent it?

Human experts choose or devise representations that enable the significant features of the problem to remain distinguished, for the relevant connections to be quickly found, etc. Thus, one can reduce this to a special case of Problem 2, and try to elicit appropriate representations from human experts. CYC takes a pragmatic approach: when something proves awkward to represent, add new kinds of slots to make it compactly representable.

Problem 4   How will it be used?

The representation chosen will, of course, impact on what inference methods are easy or difficult to implement. Our inclination is again to apply EH: when you find out that some kind of operation needs to be performed often, but it is very inefficient, then you need to adjust the representation, or the inference methods available, or both. As with Problem 3, there is a temptation to early specialization: it is a local optimum, like swerving around a mattress in the road. Pulling this mattress aside means assembling a large repertoire of reasoning methods, and heuristics for choosing, monitoring, and switching among them. Earlier, we sketched an opportunistic (non-monolithic) control structure which utilizes items in the control-strategy region of the KB.

To take a more specific version of this question: how do we expect to 'index' efficiently – find relevant partial matches? Our answer is to finesse it for now. Wait until our programs *are* finding many, far-flung analogies, for example, but only through large searches. Then investigate what additional knowledge *people* bring to bear, to eliminate large parts of the search space in those cases. Codify the knowledge so extracted, and add it to the system. This is a combined application of the Difficult Problems Hypothesis and the EH. It is a claim that the true nature of the indexing problem will only become apparent in the context of a large problem running in an already very large KB.

Problem 5   How can someone interact 'naturally' with KB systems?

Knowledge-based systems built so far share with their knowledge-free predecessors an intolerant rigidity of stylistic expression, vocabulary, and concepts. They rarely accept synonyms and pronouns, never metaphors, and only acknowledge users willing to wear a rigid grammatical straitjacket. The coming few years should witness the emergence of systems which begin to overcome this problem. As is only fitting, they will overcome it with knowledge: knowledge of the user, of the system's domain, of discourse, of metaphor. They will employ pictures and sound, as well as text, as means of input and output. Many individual projects (ONCOCIN, CYC) and expert system tools (ART, KEE) are already moving in this direction.

Problem 6   How can you combine several enterers'/systems' knowledge?

One solution is to sequentialize the entry, but it is not a good solution. Many EMYCIN-based programs designated someone to be the knowledge base czar, with whom all the other experts would discuss the knowledge to be entered. EURISKO, built on RLL, tried *explicitly* enforced semantics. Each slot would have a description of its intended use, constraints that could be checked statically or dynamically (for example, each rule's if-maybe-relevant slot should take less CPU time to execute than its if-truly-relevant slot). When someone enters rules that violate that constraint, the system can complain to them, to get everyone back on track using the same semantics again. CYC extends this to *implicitly* enforced semantics: having such a large existing KB that copy&edit is the clear favourite way of entering new knowledge. When one copies&edits an existing frame, virtually all of its slots' semantics (and even most of their values!) carry right over. There is a much more fundamental long-range solution to the problem of inconsistent KBs: live with them! Problem 7 describes this position:

Problem 7   How should the system cope with inconsistency?

View the knowledge space, and hence the KB, not as one rigid body, but rather as a set of independently-supported buttes. Each butte should be locally consistent, and neighbouring buttes should be maximally coherent. These terms are described in Section 8.2. The power of such systems should derive, then, not from perfect matching, but rather from partial matching, heuristic guidance, and (ultimately) confirming empirical evidence. Systems such as we are describing must encompass several points of view; they are 'open' in the sense of Hewitt (1982). It should be possible for new knowledge to flow compatibly and safely among them. At a much more exotic level, one can imagine mental immune systems providing (in the background) constant cross-checking, healthy skepticism, advice, and criticism.

Problem 8   How can the system builder, and the system user, not get lost?

'Getting lost' is probably the right metaphor to extend here, because what they need to do is to navigate their way successfully through knowledge space, to find and/or extend the relevant parts. Many systems, including CYC, are experimenting with various exploration metaphors and orientation tools: helicoptering through semantic nets; exploring a museum with 'Alician' entry into display cases and posters, etc. Both of these are physical spatial metaphors, which allow us to use kinesthetic memory to some extent, as the enterer or user gets more and more familiar with the layout of the KB. Several people at once can log into CYC's knowledge server, to add to its KB simultaneously; thus one's world sometimes changes a bit from under one, adding to the relevance of the (dis)orientation metaphor. For more elaborately scripted interface metaphors, see *True Names* (Vinge, 1984), *Riding the Torch* (Spinrad, 1984), or KNOESPHERE (Lenat *et al.*, 1984). The latter suggests clip-on filters to shade or highlight certain aspects of what was seen; models of groups and each individual user; and simulated tour-guides with distinct personalities.

Problem 9   How big a fraction of the million pieces of 'consensus reality' do you need to represent?

We believe the answer is around 20–50%. Why? When communicating with an intelligent entity, having chosen some concept X, we would expect the 'listener' to be familiar with X; if it fails several times in a row

– often! – then it is missing too much of consensus reality. A similar argument applies to analogizing, and to generalizing. Now to have a 30% chance for the chosen analogue to be already known by the listener, he, she or it might have to know 30% of the concepts that are analogized to. But how *uniformly* are good analogues distributed in concept-space? Lacking more data, we assume that they are uniformly distributed, which means the system should embody 30% of the full corpus of consensus reality. The distribution is, quite possibly, *not* uniform, which is why (the EH again) we need to build the KB and see.

10   Conclusion: beyond local maxima

Our position includes the statements that:

- One must include *domain-specific* knowledge to solve difficult problems effectively.

- One must also include both *very general* knowledge (to fall back on) and very *wide-ranging* knowledge (to analogize to), to cope with novel situations.

- We already have plenty of theories about mechanisms of intelligence; we need to proceed empirically: go off and build large testbeds for performing, analogizing, ML, NL . . . .

- Despite the progress in learning, language understanding, and other areas of AI, *hand-crafting* is still the fastest way to get the knowledge into the program in the 1980s.

- With a large KB of facts, heuristics, and methods, the fastest way would tip toward NL, and then ML.

- The hand-crafting and language-based learning phases may each take about one decade, culminating in a system with human-level breadth and depth of knowledge.

Each of those statements is more strongly believed than the one following it. There is overwhelming evidence for the KP and EH. There is strong evidence in favour of the BH. There is a moderate basis for our three-stage programme. And there is suggestive evidence that it may be possible to carry out the programme this century.

As a partial application of the Breadth Hypothesis, consider the task of building a knowledge-based system covering most of engineering design. Interestingly, this task was chosen independently by the Japanese EDR project and by Bob Kahn's National Research Institute. Both groups see this task as a moderate-term goal (around 1994). It is certainly much broader than any single expert system, yet much narrower than the universal knowledge base mandated by the BH.

Slightly narrower 'lawyers' workstations' or 'botanists' workstations', etc., are similar sorts of compromises (partial applications of BH) worth working on. They would possess a crown of very general knowledge, plus their specific field's next level of generalities, useful representations, etc., and some detailed knowledge including, for example, methods for extracting and using entries in that field's online databases. These have the nice side-effect of enticing the experts to use them, and then modify them and expand them.

The impact of systems mandated by the KP and BH cannot be overestimated. Public education, for example, is predicated on the *un*availability of an intelligent, competent tutor for each individual for each hour of their life. AI will change that. Our present entertainment industry is built largely on passive viewing. AI will turn 'viewers' into 'doers'. What will happen to society as the cost of wisdom declines, and society routinely applies the best of what it knows? Will a *knowledge utility* arise, like the electric utility, and how might it (and other AI infrastructures) effect what will be economically affordable for personal use?

When we give talks on expert systems, on common sense reasoning, or on AI in general, we are often asked about the ethical issues involved, the *mental environmental impact* it will have, so to speak, as well as the direct ways it will alter everyday life. We believe that this technology is the analogue of language. We cannot hold AI back any more than primitive man could have suppressed the spread of speaking. It is too powerful a technology for that. Language marks the start of what we think of as civilization; we look back on prelinguistic cultures as uncivilized, as almost belonging to a different species. In just such a fashion our distant descendants may look back on the synergistic man–machine systems that emerge from AI. To them, that may be the dividing line between civilized folk and savages. Can we even imagine what it was like when people could not talk with each other? Minsky recently quipped that a century from now people might look back on us and wonder 'can you imagine when they used to have libraries where the books didn't talk to each other?' We stand today, in 1987, at the interstice between the first era of intelligent systems (competent, thanks to the KP, but quite brittle and incombinable) and the second era, the era in which the Breadth Hypothesis will finally come into play.

Man–machine synergy prediction   In that 'second era' of knowledge systems, the 'system' will be reconceptualized as a kind of colleagular relationship between intelligent computer agents and intelligent people. Each will perform the tasks that he, she or it does best, and the intelligence of the system will be an *emergent* of the collaboration.

The interaction may be sufficiently seamless and natural that it will hardly matter to anyone which skills, which knowledge and which ideas resided where (in the head of the person or the knowledge structures of the computer.) It would be inaccurate to identify intelligence, then, as being 'in the program'. From such man–machine systems will emerge intelligence and competence surpassing those of the unaided human. Beyond that threshold, in turn, lie wonders which we (as unaided humans) literally cannot imagine today.

Acknowledgements

Many of the ideas in this paper emerged during a series of meetings with Mark Stefik, Marvin Minsky, Alan Kay, Bob Kahn, Bob Wilensky, Ron Brachman, and several others. The careful reader will also detect the welcome influence of many of our colleagues on our way of thinking: Woody Bledsoe, John Brown, John McDermott, Allen Newell, George Polya, Roger Schank, and Herbert Simon. Chuck Dement, Carl Hewitt, David Kirsch, and Bruce Porter provided very useful examples and critiques. References below prefaced by an asterisk (*) lie outside AI, yet have had a great impact upon our AI research strategy and upon our world view.

References

Abrett G. and Burstein M.H. (1986). The KREME knowledge editing environment. In *Proc. Workshop on Knowledge Acquisition for Knowledge Based Systems*, Banff

*Adams J.L. (1974). *Conceptual Blockbusting*. San Francisco: W.H. Freeman

Borning A. and Weyer S. (1985). A prototype electronic encyclopedia. *ACM Transactions on Office Information Systems*, 3(1), 63–88

Buchanan B.G., Sutherland G. and Feigenbaum E. (1969). Heuristic DENDRAL: a program for generating explanatory hypotheses in organic chemistry. In *Machine Intelligence 4* (Meltzer B. and Michie D., eds.), pp. 209–254. New York: American Elsevier

EDR. (1987). Personal communication. Japan Electronic Dictionary Research Institute Ltd

Erman L., Hayes-Roth F., Lesser V. and Raj Reddy D. (1980). HEARSAY-II speech understanding system. *Computing Surv.*, 12(2), 224–225

Feigenbaum E. (1977). The art of artificial intelligence: themes and case studies in knowledge engineering. In *IJCAI-5*

Genesereth M.R. (1984). The use of design descriptions in automated diagnosis. *J. AI*, 24, 411–436

Hewitt C. (1982). *Open Systems*. MIT AI Memo 691

*Hume K. (1984). *Fantasy and Mimesis*. New York: Methuen & Co. Ltd
*Kuhn T. (1970). *The Structure of Scientific Revolutions* 2nd edn. Chicago: University of Chicago Press
*Lakatos I. (1976). *Proofs and Refutations*. Cambridge: Cambridge University Press.
*Lakoff G. and Johnson M. (1980). *Metaphors We Live By*. Chicago: University of Chicago Press
Lenat D. (1984). Computer software for intelligent systems. *Scientific American*, **251**, 204–213
Lenat D. and Brown J.S. (1983) Why AM and EURISKO appear to work. *J. AI*, **23**, 269–294
Lenat D., Borning A., McDonald D., Taylor C. and Weyer S. (1984). KNOESPHERE: expert systems with encyclopedic knowledge. In *IJCAI-8*
Lenat D., Shepherd M. and Prakash M. (1986). CYC: using common sense knowledge to overcome brittleness and knowledge acquisition bottlenecks. *AI Magazine*
Minsky M. (1985). *Society of Mind*. New York: Simon & Schuster
Newell A. and Simon H.A. (1972). *Human Problem Solving*. Englewood Cliffs NJ: Prentice-Hall
Newell A. (1980). The knowledge level. *AI Magazine*
*Polya G. (1957). *How to Solve It*. Princeton NJ: Princeton University Press
Rich E. (1983). *Artificial Intelligence*. New York: McGraw-Hill
Spinrad N. (1984). *Riding the Torch*. New York: Bluejay Books
Stefik M. (1986). The knowledge medium. *AI Magazine*, 34–46
Strunk W. and White E.B. (1979). *The Elements of Style* 3rd edn. New York: Macmillan
Sussman G.J. (1975). *A Computer Model of Skill Acquisition*. New York: American Elsevier
*Tversky A., Slovic P. and Kahneman D., eds. (1982). *Judgment under Uncertainty: Heuristics and Biases*. Cambridge: Cambridge University Press
Vinge V. (1984). *True Names*. New York: Bluejay Books
Wall St. Journal (1987). What's news. **LXXIX**(65).

Appendix I: Goals and strategies for AI research

In Section 6, we briefly touched on the common confusion between AI goals and AI strategies. The next two sections list nine of each. As we mentioned in the body of the paper, much confusion in our field stems from several entries appearing on both lists. If one researcher chooses, say, the ultimate goal of language understanding, then he or she could approach that strategically in several ways. For example, humans first learn language by discovery, by imitating others' sounds, noting correlations and inducing simple vocabulary and grammar rules. Later, as we enter school, we improve our language abilities further by taking English classes, that is, by discussing, in natural language, the fine points of English vocabulary, grammar and composition.

Scientific disciplines not only *adopt* a paradigm, in the early stages they are *partitioned into subfields* by paradigms. If more than one paradigm remains viable for any length of time, it will soon come to see itself as a different discipline altogether and split off; AI faced this around 1970 with cognitive psychology, and is facing this again now with robotics and vision. People cannot mentally focus on too much at once; paradigms provide the needed cognitive simplifying.

All 9×9 pairs of the form $\langle$goal, strategy$\rangle$ could, in principle, be separate paradigms. Today there are only a small fraction of that number, and the groupings that have developed are, in many cases, poorly matched. For example, all pairs of the form $\langle$x, learning$\rangle$ unioned with $\langle$learning, x$\rangle$, come together for machine learning workshops every year. What is an instance of that ML confusion?

When one says that one is working on analogy, it might mean

1.   that one is using analogy as a strategy to pursue some other AI goal G. For instance, one might be building a program that parses or disambiguates English sentences by analogy; or it might mean

2.   that one is using some other strategy S, such as knowledge engineering, to investigate the phenomenon of analogy as the ultimate goal.

In the latter case, the program's final output would be a data structure that humans somehow recognize as symbolizing an analogy; but that data structure might be built by a set of if-then rules, or a neural net, or by talking with a human being, etc. The trouble is that, today, it is equally likely to mean that analogy is being pursued as a strategy or as a goal.

A1.1   Nine ultimate goals of AI

We share, or are sympathetic to, almost all of these:

1.   *Understand human cognition*   The goal is to understand how people think, not to have machine artifacts to put to work. Try for a deeper knowledge of human memory, problem solving abilities, learning, decision-making in general, etc.

2.   *Cost-effective automation*   The goal is to replace humans at various tasks requiring intelligence. This goal is met by programs that perform as well as the humans currently on the job; it does not

matter whether the programs think like people. The harder the problems it can solve, and the faster it solves them, the smarter it is.

3. *Cost-effective intelligence amplification* The goal is to build mental prostheses that help us think better, faster, deeper, more clearly. . . Science's goal – and measure of success – is how much it augments human beings' leg muscles, immune system, vocal cords, and (in this case) brain. This goal further divides depending on whose performance is being so amplified: do we want to amplify the average person's ability to diagnose disease, or the average GP's ability, or the world's best diagnosticians'?

4. *Superhuman intelligence* The goal is to build programs which exceed human performance. Crossing that particular threshhold could lead to an explosion of progress: technological innovation in manufacturing, theoretical breakthroughs, superhuman teachers and researchers (including AI researchers), and so on.

5. *General problem solving* Be able to solve – or at least plausibly attack – a broad range of problems, including some from fields you've never even heard of before. It does not matter if the programs fit human performance data perfectly, nor does it matter if they are at an expert's level. The point is that intelligent creatures can get somewhere on almost any problem; intelligence is flexibility and breadth of mind, not depth in some narrow area.

6. *Coherent discourse* This is similar to the Turing Test. The goal is to communicate competently with people, using complete sentences, in some natural human language. A system is intelligent iff it can carry on a coherent dialogue.

7. *Autonomy* This goal holds that a system is intelligent iff it can, on its own initiative, do things in the real world. This is to be contrasted with, say, merely planning in some abstract space, or 'performing' in a simulated world, or advising a human who then goes off and does things. The idea is that the real world is always so much more complex than our models of it, that it is the only fair test of the programs we claim to be intelligent.

8. *Learning (induction)* This goal is to have a program that chooses what data to gather and how; gathers it; generalizes (or otherwise converts) its experiences into useful new beliefs, methods, heuristics and representations; and reasons analogically.

9. *Information* Storing lots of facts about a wide range of topics. This is more of a 'straw man' view than the others, as it could be satisfied by an online textual encyclopedia, or even by a hard copy one! The other views all require the intelligent entity not merely to possess information but also to use it appropriately.

A1.2   Broad strategies for achieving those goals

Most of these are not *our* strategies:

1.   *Duplicate low-level cognitive performance*   Get your program to duplicate even micro-level measurements that psychologists have gathered from human subjects, such as memory storage and recall times, STM size, forgetting rate, errors, etc. Hopefully, if you do that, then your program's internal mechanisms will be similar to humans', and your program will be able to scale up the same way that human low-level mechanisms scale up (even though we do not know how that is, we will not have to know if we get the lowest level built the same way). One variation is:

2.   *Duplicate low-level structure*   Mimicking the human brain's architecture will lead to mimicking its functionality. This strategy traditionally makes the further assumption that McCulloch–Pitts threshold logic is the right level at which to abstract brain cell structure (rather than, for example, at the chemical and enzymatic levels). It gained attention as Perceptrons, and now enjoys a renaissance due to the promise that VLSI technology holds for producing parallel neural nets of immense size soon.

3.   *Simulate a society of mind*   This is yet another variant on the 'duplicate and hope' strategy, but this one is not so low-level as either of the previous two strategies. Build a program that consists of hundreds of specialized mental beings or actors – think of them as kludged knowledge sources – and marshall them to solve problems by cooperating and communicating among themselves. This is how nature managed to evolve us, and it may be the easiest way for us, in turn, to evolve AI.

4.   *Knowledge engineering*   Talk with human experts who perform the task, and extract from them the facts, representations, methods, and rules of thumb that they employ in doing the task. Encode these in a running prototype system, and then extract more and more knowledge, as the program runs and makes mistakes which the expert can easily translate – in context – into additional pieces of knowledge that should have been in the system all along. Have faith that this incremental knowledge acquisition will attain an adequate level of competence.

5.   *Natural language understanding*   Have a program talk with people, read articles, etc. People achieve intelligence that way – so can machines!

6.   *Learning (induction)*   Build a program that can learn. Then let it. People get to be smart by learning, starting from a *tabula rasa*; so can machines.

7. *Formalizing and advanced reasoning*   Marshall a toolkit of sophis-
    ticated deductive procedures for maintaining consistency and
    inferring new assertions. Having such a set of snazzy mechanisms
    will be necessary and sufficient. The strong version of this view says
    'It worked for physics; we must strive to find the "Maxwell's
    Equations" of thought.' The mild version is more conservative: 'as
    you formalize, you find the gaps in your understanding'.

8. *Intelligence amplification*   Build some intelligent interfaces that
    allow us to write programs more easily, or synthesize ideas more
    rapidly, etc. Then let these improved man–machine systems loose
    on the problem of achieving AI, whichever goal we choose to
    define it. In other words, instead of tackling the AI task right
    away, let us spend time getting prostheses that let us be smarter,
    then we will come back to working on 'real' AI.

9. *Superhuman intelligence*   An extreme form of the previous
    strategy. Build a program that does AI research just slightly better
    than people do, and then go sit on a beach while it investigates
    low-level cognition, or language understanding, or whatever your
    chosen AI goal.

Part Two
Applications

4
Expert Systems in the State Bank of NSW

Sue Zawa

State Bank of New South Wales

The State Bank's approach to expert systems has been to implement practical, commercial systems, rather than to fill a research role. This strategy has resulted in the creation of two useful prototype systems in the space of a year. The first, the Personal Loan Assistant, has already met with success. This paper discusses the methods used by the Bank to identify, develop and test expert systems. The Personal Loan Assistant, an expert system to assess applications for personal loans, is used as a case study.

Introduction

The State Bank of NSW is the third largest trading bank in New South Wales and the fifth largest in Australia. The Bank has assets of almost A\$ 12 billion, with 6500 employees and over 270 branches throughout New South Wales and the Australian Capital Territory. There are also branches in New York and London, and offices in Melbourne, Los Angeles and Tokyo.

As in most retail banks, the Retail Banking Division (called the Community Banking Group in the State Bank) is, by far, the largest section of the Bank. This Division contains two-thirds of the Bank's staff, consisting of the Branch network and a Head Office section. Other major sections of the Bank include the Wholesale Banking Group, which deals with large corporations; the Treasury Division, which deals with foreign exchange and money market transactions; the Electronic Data Processing (EDP) Division (with a staff of 550); Corporate Services; Human Resources and other support groups.

The State Bank has a reputation for innovation in the Australian banking sector. It was the first Australian bank to have user-modifiable passwords instead of PIN numbers on automatic teller machines (ATMs), and to use talking ATMs. The Bank has pioneered the use of advanced banking concepts in Australia through the State Future Banks. These branches incorporate the latest technology, with Personal Computers on most desks and a functional open plan architecture that looks both modern and pleasing to the eye.

As part of its high-tech image, the Bank was eager to investigate the full potential of expert systems technology. Management decided to hire someone with expert systems experience, rather than train a member of the Bank's existing staff.

Initial research

The first step towards introducing expert systems in the Bank was to carry out a study of the potential areas in which they could be used.

Initially, most EDP managers and other key EDP personnel (approximately 30 in all) were interviewed, both to inform them about expert systems and to obtain their ideas about potential applications.

Approximately 25 users outside EDP were interviewed. In addition, selected key division heads were sent memos informing them about expert systems and possible applications that would fall under their control. Presentations were given to various groups and the Bank's Operational Plan was carefully reviewed to identify the major projects planned for the next year.

Aside from potential users of expert systems, a number of areas were identified that could be affected by the installation of any expert systems. People from these areas were visited and given information about expert systems. The areas were:

- internal audit,
- training and
- marketing.

It was important to tell these people about potential systems early, as they would, almost definitely, be exposed to them later on. This way, they could provide input about their needs in systems before any serious development started.

A list of potential applications was assembled. Later, the applications were prioritized and a detailed evaluation of each one performed. In total, 42 applications were identified, although some of these were given a low priority, meaning that they were not very suitable for an expert system solution.

Generation of a report

After six weeks, a report detailing the potential for expert systems in the Bank was distributed. The major sections of this report were:

- *introduction to expert systems* (explaining what expert systems are, how they are built, their advantages and their potential risks);
- *applications within the Bank* (discussing the areas surveyed within the Bank, criteria used to prioritize applications, and an outline of each application identified, giving its priority, the source of experts, the targeted users, a description of the application, and advantages and disadvantages of an expert system solution);
- *recommended approach for the Bank* (discussing the recommended application, its intended scope, the hardware and software to be used, and the estimated resources required to develop it);
- *expert system hardware* (a thorough review of LISP machines and other workstations); and
- *expert system shells* (a thorough review of expert system shells, categorized into products for PCs, for workstations/minicomputers, and for mainframes).

Categories used to classify hardware were:

- producer,
- Australian distributor,
- comments,
- models,
- price,
- underlying language,
- languages supported,
- shells supported,
- operating systems supported,
- screens available,
- main memory size,
- virtual memory,
- disk storage,
- word length,
- underlying processor,
- machine cycle,
- communications protocols, and
- maximum number of users.

When researching software, it was decided that only shells would be evaluated, as development time is typically much longer using an AI language such as LISP or PROLOG. Categories used to classify software included:

- producer,
- Australian distributor,
- comments,
- hardware product runs on,
- price,
- main memory requirements,
- type of disk storage (hard disk, diskettes),
- underlying language,
- external interfaces,
- knowledge representation,
- inference mechanism,
- certainty factors,
- explanation facility,
- graphics,
- user interface rating,
- ease of development rating,
- flexibility rating, and
- speed rating.

Although much of this information was gathered from brochures and advertising material, the ratings and comments could not be determined without actually working with the products. Advertising material usually stresses the *features* of the product without giving an indication of the *usability* of these features.

Often the products with the most AI-type features were found to be of no use to business applications, as they were missing vitally important business features, such as a good user interface, the ability to communicate with outside programs/data, and reasonable debugging facilities.

Selection of the first application

The criteria used to prioritize applications were:

- must be an acknowledged problem area, possibly due to lack of training, high staff turnover, shortage of skills/personnel, or the impending retirement of an expert;

- an expert system solution would provide significant benefits (that is, monetary or improvement of working conditions);
- management must be committed to the system;
- users in the affected department have positive attitudes to technology;
- the problem has an identifiable solution;
- the solution of the problem does not rely on intuition, gut feelings, a large general knowledge, or the knowledge of current world situations (except where the system can be directly told these attributes);
- the problem's scope can be defined exactly;
- the problem is not trivial;
- the problem is not suitable for easy implementation using conventional DP techniques;
- the problem is not one-off, that is, it occurs regularly;
- the system will not be made redundant in the foreseeable future; and
- at least one expert in the area exists, who is available and willing to spend time developing the system, and is able to communicate expert knowledge.

The following additional criteria were used for the first system to be developed:

- the system must involve low risk;
- the system must have high exposure in the Bank;
- the system must not influence large amounts of money (as this is typically risky);
- the problem must be able to lend itself to prototyping; and
- speed must not be a critical factor.

Applications were classified as high, medium, low or deferred priority. Those with a priority of deferred were largely influenced by some future development, such as the design of a major new database, and were to be reviewed at a later date.

Of the applications identified, four were selected as satisfying these criteria well (that is, high priority). The best of these four was a system to assess applications for personal loans. Personal loans account for a high proportion of the Bank's customer borrowings. They are usually used for finance for cars, holidays and other personal expenses. Some of the reasons why this application was chosen were:

- it is an acknowledged problem area, due to fairly high staff turnover and, in some cases, a lack of adequate training;

- the system could significantly reduce the Bank's bad debts from defaulting personal loans;
- the system would lead to consistency in loan assessment;
- the system would be a useful training tool;
- the system would improve customer service;
- users were enthusiastic;
- the scope of the system is not too large, but is large enough to be non-trivial;
- the problem domain is not very complex, and is commonly taught to people without specialist degrees – therefore, there was a good chance that the knowledge engineer would be able to formulate accurate rules;
- lending is an area where expert systems have been successfully employed at other institutions (Lubich, 1986; Kupfer, 1987; Turner, 1987);
- although not a low-risk system, the risk could be effectively controlled through pilot testing before installation throughout the Bank;
- the system would receive very high exposure throughout the Bank; and
- the concept is something most Bank staff can relate to, whether they are junior branch staff or senior management – thus, it would make a good demonstration of the potential of expert systems.

A rule-based approach was chosen as the most appropriate paradigm for the system.

Hardware/software selection

It was decided that the system should run on personal computers, for the following reasons:

- the cost of development and software on PCs is generally lower than on other machines;
- the problem was not sufficiently complex to warrant a more expensive machine; and
- PCs are readily available as development and delivery machines.

The expert systems software available on PCs was reviewed. The criteria used for selection were:

- must have a good user interface (users will often have no prior experience with PCs, and very little experience with any computers);

- must run on an XT-compatible, preferably needing a maximum of 512 K main memory (this was the minimum PC configuration in branches);
- a separate run-time version must be available, so that users cannot look at or modify the knowledge in the system;
- must support rules and backward chaining;
- must allow saving of responses given to questions during a consultation (this turned out to be unnecessary);
- must have the 'how' facility so that users can ask how the system concluded its result (this turned out to be unnecessary);
- preferably gives the programmer a lot of flexibility;
- preferably allows interfacing to other programs and/or databases;
- preferably allows for forms to be defined, that is, a screenful of questions can be answered at once;
- preferably allows saving of intermediate results; and
- preferably has an uncertainty feature.

Keeping these criteria in mind, the PC product list was reviewed. The product that best matched the criteria was Aion Development System, an expert system shell running on PCs and IBM mainframes. Its features include:

- satisfies all required criteria, except that the 'how' facility is only available in the development version, not the run-time version (this turned out not to be a problem, for reasons discussed later in this paper);
- satisfies all the optional criteria;
- has inbuilt links to dBase, R:Base and Lotus, and the shell can call any executable program from DOS;
- has an excellent end user interface;
- has excellent debugging facilities;
- has excellent knowledge base editing facilities;
- written in Pascal, avoiding memory management problem of LISP-based products;
- knowledge is structured in a format that is very easy to develop and maintain;
- has a migration path upwards from PCs;
- contains very few bugs;
- has been purchased by a number of major organizations in the USA (although it was not directly sold in Australia at the time of evaluation);

- the product runs reasonably quickly, compared to other expert system products, on an Olivetti M24 SP (the Bank's standard PC XT-compatible), although knowledge bases are not compiled; and
- the product costs US$ 7000.

Scope of the system

The initial scope of the personal loan system was defined in the report. Although small changes were made during system development, the scope remained essentially the same in the final system. The definition of the initial scope was:

- the system determines approval of personal loans only, but the design should allow for possible future extensions to approve other types of loans;
- the system asks for customer details, mimicking the existing application form (although it can additionally check for accuracy of data);
- help is provided wherever possible;
- the system applies rules to the information given to it, and gives the user a recommendation about whether or not to approve the loan;
- the user may ask the system how it derived its result;
- loan information is stored on diskette or hard disk, for later transfer to Head Office; and
- development time was estimated at 3 months.

Creation of the user interface

Development of the system was commenced in February 1987.

The first and most difficult task was to find a name for the system. Any name indicating 'Expert Systems', 'Artificial Intelligence' or similar terms could be threatening to users, and informing them of what lay behind the user interface would not help them. The name had to be descriptive and non-threatening. 'Personal Loan Assistant' seemed like a good choice, especially as it indicated that the system was not intended to replace officers, but to assist them.

The expert was to be an interviewing officer from a branch. Interviewing officers normally carry out personal loan interviews with customers and make initial decisions about approval of applications.

The selection of the expert was fairly random, as there were literally hundreds to choose from. The manager of a nearby branch was approached and asked to select his best interviewing officer to work on the system. The officer chosen was an experienced interviewing officer, who is well-respected throughout the Bank.

The expert was given a half-hour crash course on expert systems, then asked how he would go about assessing a personal loan application. A series of general and detailed questions, along with the examination of many examples, determined the basic set of rules. Sessions with the expert lasted from 1–4 h. There were also a number of quick telephone calls.

Early in the project it became clear that the bulk of the work in creating the system would be the development of the user interface. Up to 130 pieces of information had to be gathered just to fill in the application form. There were an additional 20 pieces of information needed for back-office work, necessary before the application could be evaluated properly. A number of reports (such as the application form, which must be signed by the applicant) were also identified.

The user interface was intially created in Aion. This took 4 weeks, and produced around 15 screens and 120 rules. However a few deficiencies which were fairly minor, but indicated potential problems with ease of use and future maintenance, became evident:

- Aion could only read files sequentially. Therefore, reading through a database of information about all customers could take a long time if the required information was near the end.

- Although it allowed multiple fields on a screen ('form-filling'), Aion insisted on putting a box around each field, thus using at least three lines for each field. This restriction meant that, in some places, information belonging on one screen had to be split between two screens due to a lack of space. The title of each box had to appear on a single line above the input field, meaning that questions more than one line long could not be asked.

- Error checking for interrelationships between fields on the same screen could not be done; for example, validations such as: 'If field1 = A, field2 must be B or C' were impossible. Thus, some errors could not be trapped.

- It was impossible to specify default values for input fields where the value was to be selected from a menu (for example, 'What is the purpose of the loan? Car Boat Travel etc.' with a default of Boat.)

- Input fields of type 'string' could not be specified as 'mandatory'; for example, it was impossible to specify that the applicant's name *must* be filled in by the user.

- It was impossible to define new functions for function keys: for example, to create a function key that accepts all information on a screen as is, without the user having to press the Enter key on each field on the screen.

- A lot of processing and programming effort was wasted trying to make a non-procedural tool behave procedurally.

While these limitations seemed small, it was vital that users found the system as friendly and easy to use as possible. Therefore, a decision was made to rewrite the user interface in a more conventional product. (The user interface did not involve any 'expert' decisions.) The product chosen was dBase III Plus, the Bank's standard PC database management system.

The user interface was rewritten in dBase and later compiled with Clipper, a dBase compiler (as dBase response times were up to 30 s!). Of the 3 months development time, the user interface took over 2 months.

Completion of the system

When the first pass at the user interface in dBase was completed, Aion was used to develop a knowledge base containing expert information about the assessment of personal loans.

During development, the system was shown to the expert and to a large number of interested people throughout the Bank. It was important to get management involved as early as possible, so that their comments could be incorporated into the system. The user interface and the knowledge base were thus developed iteratively.

A slight hitch occurred 6 weeks into the project: the expert went on holiday for a month, giving one week's notice. As the project was to last for 3 months, with management expecting results at the end of this time, this was serious. Another expert from Head Office filled in.

When refinements to rules had stabilized, the system was tested against 60 actual cases from the files of one of the branches. It was found that three personal loans that were approved, but later defaulted, would have been refused by the system. This could have saved the Bank thousands of dollars in write-offs and legal costs. There was one case where the system refused a loan that should have been approved. However, it can cost 10 times the profit from a good loan to try to recover a bad debt, so this failure rate is more than acceptable.

All of the rules were typed up in plain English and distributed to appropriate managers. The managers found this very useful, as they could understand the reasoning well enough to know whether they agreed or disagreed with it.

At the end of the project a report was produced, outlining the scope and functional and technical design of the system. This was distributed widely throughout the Bank.

In total, the system took 3 months to develop, using one knowledge engineer full-time, 3 days of the experts' time, and 3 days of other managers' time. It should be noted that the prototype Personal Loan Assistant is a *complete* stand-alone system. The only work needed to turn it into a production system is to add tracking modules and links to mainframe databases.

System features

The size of a rule-based expert system is normally measured by the number of rules it contains. The Personal Loan Assistant originally contained around 40 rules. This figure has now been reduced to 26, as rules were later reviewed and consolidated, and a new release of Aion allowed for more efficient use of rules.

Although this sounds like a trivially small system by usual standards, Aion supports 'if-then-else' and 'nested if' rules. Also, a lot of processing that would require rules in another shell can be done with other structures in Aion. Therefore, the 26 Aion rules would translate to 100–120 rules in an EMYCIN-like shell, making the Personal Loan Assistant a small- to medium-sized expert system.

The maximum depth of rules (that is, the number of rules that can be pending at any one time) is five, with an average of three to four. Had the system been written in an EMYCIN-like shell, the maximum depth would have been around seven. Therefore, the reasoning is not very deep, but is deep enough to make the system difficult to write and maintain in a procedural language.

Communication between dBase and Aion is achieved by extracting the relevant information from dBase databases and reading it into Aion data structures. Aion outputs the results of its assessment to a file that is merged into a dBase database. The process takes around 30 s in each direction on a 10 MHz PC XT-compatible computer. Otherwise, response times are generally between 1 and 3 s.

At the end of processing an application the system's final recommendation is displayed on the screen. The user may print an Aion-generated report, which gives the final conclusion and a summary of intermediate results leading to this decision.

The explanations are generated by rules in the knowledge base, not by an automatic explanation generator. Therefore, information given to the user is totally controlled. The lack of a 'how' facility in Aion actually turned out to be a benefit, as it is impossible for users to see any of the rules in the system. ('How' explanations are typically generated by quoting rules to users.) Users would be confused if shown actual rules. Also, if rules were made public, the system could be abused by officers trying to force loans to be approved. Confidential rules could easily be leaked to competitors.

During system development, special effort was made to ensure that the system was easy to maintain. Attention was paid to grouping of rules and other structures for clarity, to consistent naming of rules and parameters, and to the use of comments and external technical documentation.

The system was designed so that it degrades gracefully: that is, if a problem is beyond its scope, it can still give reasonable answers. The sensitivity of the system was also considered. If one question is answered incorrectly by the user, the system should not give a completely incorrect answer. This problem was addressed by performing validation of all user responses, where possible, and by giving explanations of how results were attained so the user could easily spot the error.

The Personal Loan Assistant performs at the level of an experienced interviewing officer. However, it does not perform at an 'expert' level. When true experts assess loans, they look not only for normal evaluation criteria, but also for any unusual circumstances. An example of an unusual circumstance is that the officer has heard that the applicant's employer is about to go out of business, meaning the applicant's source of income may disappear. Factors such as these could be identified and incorporated in the system, but the user of the system would have to be asked many questions that would only rarely provide significant answers. A compromise had to be reached between the level of expertise in the system and the level of annoyance users would have when they are asked too many questions.

The pilot test

The next logical step was to try out the system in a real branch situation. User management was asked to approve a pilot test of the system for 3 months.

At this time, the Bank was closely considering the purchase of a credit scoring system. Credit scoring systems are statistically-based analysis systems, often used for the assessment of credit cards and/or personal loans. However, as credit scoring systems are very expensive, and the Bank would have to rely on an outside bureau for the development of the system, users decided to pilot the Personal Loan Assistant before making a decision. One distinct advantage of an expert system approach is that users can understand the information in the system well enough to know whether they agree or disagree with it. Credit scoring produces a list of scores, which the client must accept as correct.

The pilot was initially run in the expert's branch, commencing in August 1987. In October, seven more branches were added. The pilot was scheduled to finish in January 1988 but, due to changes made to the system during pilot, it was extended to April 1988.

Participants in the pilot attended a formal training course, where it was stressed that they could override the system's decision at any time.

Participants were also given short questionnaires to fill in each time they used the system. These were used to pinpoint any problems early in the pilot. Questionnaires covered both the ease of use of the system and the quality of the decision-making.

As a result of the questionnaire responses, two new releases of the system were introduced during the pilot test. Most changes related to the user interface. Wording on data entry and help screens was altered for increased clarity and extra error checking was added where necessary. Alterations were also made to reduce response times and memory usage. Some rules were altered during the pilot test when it was discovered that certain fairly rare cases had not been anticipated.

Customers were sent short questionnaires when their loans were approved, asking whether they felt the use of the system made a positive or a negative difference to the quality of service. However, very few responded, even though reply paid envelopes were provided.

The major problem encountered during the pilot was that there are wide variations in the ways different branches assess personal loan applications. This can depend on the location of the branch, the attitude of the branch manager, and a number of other factors.

Overall, the officers who benefited most from the system were the trainees. Many trainees stated that the system helped them remember all the steps they needed to carry out, and helped explain any difficulties along the way. It also helped develop their judgement in assessing applications. The more experienced officers were generally less enthusiastic, with some seeing the system as a threat.

Surprisingly, most customers who responded thought the system was excellent, and that the level of service they received from officers using it was high. It was expected that customers would see the use of the computer system as impersonal.

Conclusions

Before the Personal Loan Assistant can go into production, user management must decide if the system will be beneficial to the Bank, based on the pilot test results. Also, some technical issues, such as uploading and downloading of data to and from mainframes, must be resolved.

The State Bank has been investigating many other areas for expert systems, with an emphasis on expert systems that integrate seamlessly with conventional computer systems and databases.

Due to the high exposure of the Personal Loan Assistant in the Bank, managers throughout the Bank have been able to identify additional expert systems applications that they would not otherwise have realized were possible to automate.

By starting with a small system with low risk of failure and high visibility, the way was paved for more ambitious expert systems work in the future.

References

Kupfer A. (1987). Now, live experts on a floppy disk. *Fortune*, Oct 12, 47–52

Lubich N. (1986). Large financial institutions lead the way for AI. *Applied Artificial Intelligence Reporter*, Aug, 7–8

Turner G.J. (1987). How an outside expert views expert systems. *J. Commercial Bank Lending*, Jan, 8–11

5

Bridging the Gap Between Prototype and Commercial Expert Systems – A Case Study

Amanda E. Crofts
McMullan Kilvington Pty Ltd

Victor B. Ciesielski
Wayne Jenkins
Royal Melbourne Institute of Technology

Michael Molesworth
Federation Life Ltd

Timothy J. Smith
Richard Y. Lee
McMullan Kilvington Pty Ltd

Developing an expert system prototype in many domains can be done in a matter of weeks. However building a commercial expert system from a promising prototype can take many man-years of effort. This paper describes the development of a commercially funded expert system for life insurance underwriting and analyses the process of extending the prototype into a commercial system. It was found that limiting the scope of the system to 85–90% of cases for the delivered system was commercially attractive. Furthermore, only about half of the effort of building the system using a PC shell product was expended in knowledge engineering tasks. The remainder of the effort involved conventional programming to extend and modify the behaviour of the shell to generate a product of acceptable commercial quality.

1   Introduction

There appears to be considerable consensus that expert system technlogy has commercial potential in domains such as finance, law, insurance and medicine (Waterman, 1986; Harmon and King, 1985; Michaelson and Michie, 1983). This is evident in such indices as the number of expert system shells being sold to companies within these industries, the increasing number of job advertisements for knowledge engineers, and private and government surveys.

Despite this level of interest, as Donald Michie pointed out in 1986, 'the number of systems which are out in the marketplace actually earning money could, [I think], be counted on the fingers of two hands' (Michie, 1987). Thus, apart from the traditional difficulties associated with the implementation of an expert system for any purpose, there appear to be additional difficulties associated with commercial delivery and use of such systems. This paper outlines the commercial potential of expert or knowledge-based systems in one particular domain, the life insurance industry. It alleges that the lack of completed systems reflects a failure to exploit the expert system potential. The difficulties associated with the implementation of a life proposal underwriting system are discussed as an example of the tasks necessary in delivering an expert system as a commercially viable product.

2   Potential of expert systems in the insurance domain

Computers and application programs already play an integral role in the insurance domain. For expert system technology to play a similarly important role, it will be necessary for research project managers and third party software developers to convince insurance company managements that expert systems have capabilities and potential beyond those of conventional programs.

2.1   Class of tasks and problems

Within the insurance industry, there are a large number of tasks which depend on the knowledge and experience of specialized personnel. Such activities include the underwriting of insurance proposals, the assessment of insurance claims and the planning of investment strategies.

These tasks have the following features in common:

- There is no single 'right' answer that can be reached by way of simple – or even complex – formulae or algorithms.

- It is commonly held that those people who have more knowledge, or more experience, in these fields will make more informed, 'better' decisions than novices.

- People making decisions in these domains will be able to explain and justify their decisions and reasoning.

Harmon and King (1985) state that if 'task performance depends on knowledge that is subjective, changing, symbolic or partly judge-mental, the domain may very well be a good candidate for an expert system'. The insurance tasks mentioned, therefore, would appear to be suitable as potential domains for expert system development.

2.2   Cost advantages

In choosing whether or not to explore and exploit new technologies, commercial ventures have the primary aim of determining the effect on their bottom line. For expert systems to be of interest in the insurance domain, their use must be capable of reducing existing costs or, alternatively, of providing competitive advantage in the marketplace.

The potential cost advantages include:

- much faster prototyping and development time when using expert system technology for appropriate tasks;

- release of staff from duties and decision-making which can be accomplished by the expert system;

- the possibility of having clerical staff do some of the work previously done by highly paid experts; and

- more efficient staff training, using expert systems knowledge as training source, instead of the senior expert.

2.3   Marketing advantages

The insurance industry, in particular life insurance, depends on the sales of policies by agents for its survival and growth. A very strong impetus in our development of an underwriting system for life insurance proposals was the substantial time reduction in 'turn around' from proposal to policy issue. It was felt by our client, a life insurance company, that this advantage would make it far more likely for agents to market their products in preference to their competitors, as agents would respond to the improvements in the quality of service and support from the Life Office. In addition, as the insurance industry is a service industry, the facility to issue policies to clients at the time of proposal places the Life Office in a unique position servicing their clients.

2.4   Consistency advantages

By removing 'human factors', such as unreliability and inexperience, from a decision-making process, far more consistency is achievable. From a management point of view, company experience and policy can be embedded in a knowledge base. For example, if a company finds it has an inordinate number of claims arising from a particular occupation group, it can bias the loading in its underwriting system.

2.5   System development and maintenance advantages

There is one very tangible maintenance advantage with expert systems, as opposed to traditional applications programming. If the knowledge within an expert system for a specified domain were static, it would be feasible to 'hard code' its knowledge into a decision tree. However, as knowledge about diseases, their prognosis and their treatment as they relate to underwriting is not static, the knowledge base must be readily expandable and able to be edited. Expert systems offer this facility since the knowledge (rules or frames) is separate from the control mechanism (inference engine). This is not possible in applications software where changes in the embedded knowledge require changes in the control code.

Expert systems, and expert system shells, are particularly suitable for prototyping. In our implementation, our domain expert became very proficient at editing the knowledge base because he could concentrate on the knowledge and not be concerned with control structures.

3   Commercial reality in the insurance domain

3.1   Level of interest

In a survey of the North American insurance market Coopers and Lybrand (1986) found an extremely high level of expressed interest in expert systems technology. Only 32.6% of companies indicated that there was no activity taking place, and only 13% of companies surveyed indicated that they would never begin development, or that they were not sure when development would begin.

In terms of a breakdown in interest in specific applications, over 80% of the insurance companies surveyed indicated an interest in underwriting tasks, with other potential applications in the areas of claims and investments being secondary areas of interest.

3.2   Level of achievements

Despite the expressed level of interest in expert system technology, Coopers and Lybrand (1986) indicated that only 2% of the insurance companies they surveyed had applications in use. In part this could be accounted for by the relative infancy of the field; however, there were strong indications from our development activities with Computed Life Underwriting Expert (CLU_E) that other factors are contributing to this failure to produce finished products.

4   Design criteria for the CLU_E system

4.1   Choice of application

Our initial prototype sought to emulate the decision-making of the senior underwriter from a Life Company. After initial discussions with the expert it soon became clear that what seemed to be a homogeneous task was one that could quite easily be partitioned into 'easy' and 'hard' cases. A very large proportion (estimated at 85–90%) of policies could be issued with no information from the proposer, except a personal statement. In some cases, for example, where the proposer suffered from epilepsy or asthma, further information was traditionally required from the proposer. This was obtained via an additional questionnaire relevant to the disorder. In the remaining proportion of proposals, medical examinations or reports were required either as a result of very large sums insured, or as a result of evidence about pre-existing medical conditions outlined in the personal statement. Tackling the 'hard' cases usually requires multiple sources of information as diverse as medical examination reports, doctors' comments and analysis of blood pressure readings. In addition, to underwrite the hard cases, the information that must be accessed is confidential between the insurance company and the medical attendant. The underwriting process traditionally, therefore, takes the following form:

1.   the agent sends the personal statement to head office via branch offices;

2.   an underwriter at Head Office decides whether additional information in the form of questionnaires or medical evidence is required;

3.   the agent is advised by Head Office of the additional information required and the client is contacted and advised; and

4.   the additional information is sent to Head Office, the proposal is underwritten and the policy finally issued.

Obviously, any system which would make this time-consuming and clumsy process more effective would, we felt, be seen as highly desirable by the management of insurance companies. With this experience in mind we took into account the natural partitioning of the process and work began on a prototype system. CLU_E addressed the 'easy' part of the problem. It was our opinion that developing a system that could underwrite and issue immediate policies for 85–90% of cases was an excellent starting point for maximum commercial gain. By not attempting to prototype a system that could do the 'whole' underwriting task, we considered that we would get a maximum commercial payoff whilst still producing a very valuable tool within a realistic development time.

4.2   Design and implementation of the system

The prototype was developed using the EXSYS shell, and a very simple production rule structure. Knowledge sources for the prototype were a very experienced senior life underwriter and a number of underwriting reference books and manuals used by underwriters.

The prototype took a couple of months to develop and enabled the developers to investigate possible structures for the rule base, and to examine how we should handle tasks which it appeared could not be handled within a shell. These tasks included accessing tables, handling date intervals and string searches within files.

The prototype became a commercial development when Federation Life Ltd commissioned McMullan Kilvington Pty Ltd to implement the complete system.

The actual system development took place over 7 months. There were two people involved almost full-time for 4 months, the knowledge engineer and the underwriting expert. The knowledge engineer and the programmers were already familiar with both expert system technology in general, and the EXSYS shell in particular. In addition, the services of three programmers, each of whom is expert system 'literate', were used as necessary, adding, in effect, another man-year to the project. The high level of commitment of the expert underwriter, who had, in fact, commissioned the commercial system, was an essential ingredient in the success of the project.

When completed, the rule base was composed of approximately 1200 rules of varying complexities. It is estimated that the main purpose of 5% of the rules was to control the firing of other rules. Examples of the rules are shown in Figure 5.1. These are indicative both of the typical level of information used by the system, and of how more generalized conditions were used to 'block' more specialized questions being asked of the user.

The EXSYS shell was chosen in preference to other PC shells for a number of reasons. The main reason was that a fairly extensive rule base

RULE NUMBER:421

IF: [TMR] < = 130
and   [TMR] > = 125
and   [AGE] < = 39
and   [AGE] > = 30
THEN: [TMR] IS GIVEN THE VALUE 100
         Mortality Classification is 100 − Probability = 10/10

RULE NUMBER:270

IF: Have you ever had or do you now have symptoms of or been diagnosed having
         any disorder, disease or discomfort of the respiratory system (lungs, bronchi,
         trachea, etc.) including TB, asthma, emphysema, bronchitis, pleurisy etc.? yes
THEN: Respiratory system disorders are indicated
ELSE: Respiratory system disorders are not indicated

RULE NUMBER:361

IF: Respiratory system disorders are indicated
and   The respiratory system disorder is bronchitis
and   Between bronchitis episodes you suffer from 'morning cough', persistent
         cough or shortness of breath on exercise or exertion
THEN: The type of bronchitis is severe

RULE NUMBER: 370

IF: Respiratory system disorders are indicated
and   The respiratory system disorder is bronchitis
and   The type of bronchitis is severe
and   [AGE] > 40
THEN: HEAD OFFICE WILL REQUEST FURTHER INFORMATION FROM YOUR
         ATTENDING DOCTOR.
and   [TMR] IS GIVEN THE VALUE [TMR] + 150

Figure 5.1

had to be delivered on the lap-top personal computers used by life insurance agents. From the documentation with the shell, it appeared that we should experience no difficulty doing this. The shell also had some development features which we felt would be useful. EXSYS has external hooks to the C programming language. In the insurance environment, it would be necessary to access tables without reference to a database and a table utility – although primitive – was available.

At the point of writing, the expert system is fully developed and case tested. It is anticipated that field use of the system will commence in June 1988, when Federation Life begins underwriting superannuation and term policies. The percentage of cases which will be fully underwritten by the system is initially expected to be between 70–80%, depending on the financial underwriting limits which are yet to be set.

5   The CLU_E system

5.1   The underwriter's perspective

CLU_E assesses a proposal form for a life insurance policy using personal, medical and occupational criteria. It determines an underwriting rating which will be used by the Life Office in determining premiums, loadings, and exclusions in term cover and policy options. Collection and storage of data from proposals is a prime consideration. Reports are generated which are the hard copy proposal signed by the client.

The following features are encompassed:

- collection of personal data;
- collection of contract data;
- collection of essential screening medical information,
- facility to tailor the questioning process according to the option required by each client for each policy,
- facility to determine a rating for each proposer based on the deviation from standard life,
- facility to determine relevant exclusions to the policy,
- facility to advise the end-user of what additional medical information will be required before the proposal may be under-written, and
- user defined criteria – the Life Office has full control over the level of substandard lives and the size of coverage accepted without referral to a human underwriter at Branch or Head Office level.

5.2   Management's perspective

Fundamental to our implementation as a commercially funded project was meeting the needs of our clients and their end-users. Whilst the management of the Life Company was aware that expert system technology was being used for their application, at the bottom line their concerns were very much practical ones:

- Was it doing the task correctly?
- Would it streamline the underwriting process?
- Would the interface quality be of an acceptable level?
- Would the system be acceptable to their agents?

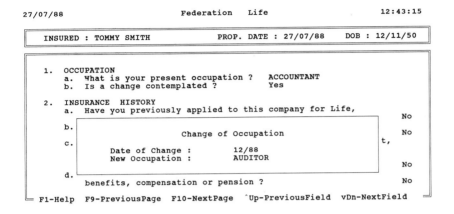

Figure 5.2

Some of the features normally considered to be integral parts of an expert system were of no interest to our clients in the delivered system. Not only was the management uninterested in the explanation facility of the system, they requested the facility be made inaccessible to the end-user. The rule set of the delivered system was fairly broad but quite shallow in its reasoning process, and handling of uncertainty was not required.

5.3   The agent's perspective

Whilst it has not yet been feasible to field test the system, the agent's major concerns will be similar to those expressed when processing conventional proposals. Fundamental concerns include minimizing the turn around time in the proposal to commission cycle. A further concern is that using the computer system should not be more difficult to use than a 'paper' system. Some sample screens from a consultation are shown in Figures 5.2–5.4.

6   Bridging the gap

A large gap was found to exist between the prototype we could develop in an expert system shell and a deliverable commercial system. Whilst acknowledging that available shells are becoming more and more

```
27/07/88                    Federation   Life                    13:13:44
 ╓───────────────────────────────────────────────────────────────────────╖
 ║  INSURED : TOMMY SMITH          PROP. DATE : 27/07/88    DOB : 12/11/50  ║
 ╙───────────────────────────────────────────────────────────────────────╜
 ┌─────────────────────────────────────────────────────────────────────────┐
 │                                                                           │
 │    5.  BUILD / HABITS                                                     │
 │                                                                           │
 │        a.  What is your height ?          180 cms    70  ins              │
 │                and  weight ?               67 kgs   147 lbs               │
 │                                                                           │
 │        b.  Have you ever smoked tobacco or any other substance ?     Yes  │
 │        c.  Have you ever taken alcohol ?                             No    │
 │        d.  Have you, in the last 5 years, either occassionally or         │
 │            regularly taken medications, drugs, stimulants or sedatives ? No│
 │                                                                           │
 │                                                                           │
 └─────────────────────────────────────────────────────────────────────────┘
   F1-Help  F9-PreviousPage  F10-NextPage  ^Up-PreviousField  vDn-NextField
```

Figure 5.3

```
27/07/88                    Federation   Life                    13:14:03
 ╓───────────────────────────────────────────────────────────────────────╖
 ║  INSURED : TOMMY SMITH          PROP. DATE : 27/07/88    DOB : 12/11/50  ║
 ╙───────────────────────────────────────────────────────────────────────╜
 ┌─────────────────────────────────────────────────────────────────────────┐
 │    7.  MEDICAL  HISTORY                                                   │
 │                                                                           │
 │        i.  Have you ever had, or now have, symptoms of or been            │
 │            diagnosed as having any disorder, disease or persistent        │
 │            discomfort of the following systems :                          │
 │                                                                           │
 │            a.  Respiratory  (lungs, bronchi, trachea, etc) including TB,   │
 │                asthma, emphysema, bronchitis, pleurisy, etc ?         No   │
 │            b.  Circulatory  (heart, blood, arteries, veins, etc)           │
 │                including high blood pressure, heart trouble,               │
 │                chest pain, stroke, murmur, etc ?                     No    │
 │            c.  Digestive  (throat, stomach, intestine, liver, bowel,       │
 │                gall bladder, etc)  including ulcers, haemorrhoids,         │
 │                hernis, etc ?                                         No    │
 └─────────────────────────────────────────────────────────────────────────┘
   F1-Help  F9-PreviousPage  F10-NextPage  ^Up-PreviousField  vDn-NextField
```

Figure 5.4

sophisticated in terms of facilities offered to the user, many facilities of conventional packages are not provided to developers.

In our application, for the system to be useful, it had to be deliverable on a personal computer. Although much development activity in academia takes place on mainframes or workstations, it is at the place where the expert is not available that the expert system becomes valuable. For our clients' purposes, the expertise was needed in the proposer's home, or agent's office. Access to a mainframe was not available, access to a PC was.

Our evaluations of PC shells before implementation of the prototype showed that most of the PC tools were deficient in the data handling facilities we needed to solve a real problem.

6.1   Data handling

This application required that the system be able to make decisions and impose premium loadings on the basis of information such as how long ago the proposer suffered the last attack of some disorder. Whilst it would have been possible to gather this information from a multiple choice response, such as:

The last asthma attack was
1.   less than 1 year ago
2.   more than 1 year but less than 2 years ago
3.   more than 2 years ago

the level of detail required made this option very cumbersome. It was necessary to attach to the variable collecting this information an external program call to calculate the difference between two dates.

6.2   Tables

The application required substantial table access to gain information about premiums relevant to age and policy code. Whilst a table utility is available within EXSYS, the storage and retrieval of values are very inefficient.

6.3   Arrays

The availability of arrays would have been a very useful feature. We needed a facility to store and access the same type of information about an indeterminate number of diseases. For example, a proposer suffering from asthma, chest pain and shingles would need to indicate when each of these started. We had to create individual variables for each disease and relevant piece of information.

6.4 Selection

Whilst a fairly common scenario in an expert system consultation is the selection of an appropriate value from a predetermined list, our application required selection from a number of very large lists. For example, to provide the level of detail necessary about occupation, the user has to choose from a list of several hundred possibilities. In addition, the underwriter wanted the user to access this selection process by entering the initial letters of a choice. This specific type of requirement also had to be handled external to the shell environment.

To implement this, a program FSELECT was written, which searched a sequential file in response to the first three letters entered by the user at the prompt, 'What is your occupation?' (see Figure 5.2).

If the occupation selected by the program was not acceptable to the user, the user could cursor up and down until the most appropriate response was found.

6.5 Interface

To meet the interface requirements of the management, CLU_E had to be fairly similar in appearance and usage to their other application programs. It was necessary, therefore, to hide as much as possible of the expert system shell behind a windows package.

6.6 Explanation and justification

Whilst a major feature of an expert system is the ability to explain decisions and justify reasoning, our clients felt that this would enable confidential and sensitive information to be freely available. Although some PC shells offered the facility to provide 'canned text' explanations, or different levels of information, our clients wanted this feature removed altogether.

Conclusion

In order to exploit the commercial potential of expert or knowledge-based systems, developers should take into account several factors. They should closely examine what tasks are suitable for expert system development within their domain of interest and which parts of the whole problem can be cost-effectively solved by expert systems. They should determine what features will be necessary for their system to be usable in the marketplace.

A vast source of potential applications is, at present, largely untapped. Kaplan (1984) contends that commercial developers should be exploring 'the automation of routine advice and standardization of service'. In our choice of scope for CLU_E we purposely partitioned the underwriting task, filtering off the hardest 10–15% to be examined by the human underwriter. This left us with an application with a high commercial payoff with a relatively modest development cost, as we could do a substantial portion of the whole task.

Unfortunately, the present PC shells, although sophisticated enough to handle different representations and inferencing strategies, do not supply sufficient facilities to enable production of commercially viable systems. One of the main priorities in a commercial development is that someone will use the system – it has, at least, to meet with interface standards that end-users are expecting from traditional application programs. In order to meet this expectation we found that about 50% of development time for CLU_E was spent in tasks not related to knowledge engineering.

Bridging the gap between prototype and commercial expert systems will require recognition by the system developers that they must do much more than code knowledge within some representation formalism; this will only ever be part of the commercial solution.

References

Brakenridge R.D.C. (1977). *Medical Selection of Life Risks*. London: Undershaft Press

Coopers and Lybrand. (1986). *Expert Systems in the Insurance Industry: A Survey Report*. Coopers and Lybrand Management Consulting Services

Harmon P. and King D. (1985). *Artificial Intelligence in Business – Expert Systems*. John Wiley & Sons

Hayes-Roth F., Waterman D.A. and Lenat D.B. (1986). *Building Expert Systems*. Reading MA: Addison-Wesley

Kaplan S.J. (1984). The industrialisation of artificial intelligence. *AI Magazine*, **5**(2)

Michaelson R. and Michie D. (1983). Expert systems in business. *Datamation*, 240–246

Michie D. (1987). Current developments in expert systems. In *Applications of Expert Systems* (Quinlan J.R., ed.). Wokingham: Addison-Wesley

Waterman D.A. (1986). *A Guide to Expert Systems*. Reading MA: Addison-Wesley

6

The Application of Artificial Intelligence in the Financial Services Industries

Nancy Irene Lubich

BankAmerica Corporation

In the face of declining profits, firms in the financial services industries are developing strategies to increase revenues, decrease costs and become more competitive. Among these strategies is a move into the area of Artificial Intelligence. This paper discusses problems faced by these firms and the ways in which they are attempting to apply advanced technologies to solve them. It also investigates specific systems developed by some of the leading financial and technological companies. Finally, the paper discusses some of the issues that a firm should consider before investing the large sums which can accompany the use of this technology. This is especially important in the financial industries where so much of the expertise is based on judgemental decision-making.

Introduction

In the face of deregulation, increased competition, and adverse market conditions, the financial services industries have recently experienced an unhealthy contraction of profits. Many of the historically strongest companies have suffered to the extent that they are posting unprecedented losses. In an attempt to reverse this trend, companies are implementing strategies to increase revenues, reduce costs, and gain competitive advantage. One area to which firms have looked in doing this, is the increasingly complicated world of advanced technology. Specifically, commercial and investment banking institutions, and insurance firms are looking to Artificial Intelligence technologies.

This paper will discuss some of the problems faced in each of these industries, and will explain why Artificial Intelligence, especially expert systems, will be useful in combatting them. It will also address areas where this technology may be inappropriate or of limited benefit. Finally, actual projects and systems undertaken by financial services and technological firms will be discussed to the extent disclosed in the current literature.

Commercial banking applications

Recent deregulation in the commercial banking industry has caused banking institutions to change drastically the way in which they do business. Whereas the government used to regulate costs and revenues, companies are now having to implement product pricing and cost-cutting strategies. Banks have typically been slow to take advantage of new technologies, preferring to wait until all of the bugs have been corrected before purchasing new hardware or software. Today, however, they are cautiously investigating advanced technology as a means of increasing revenue, decreasing costs, increasing productivity, and attaining a competitive advantage. It is estimated that a bank which implements Artificial Intelligence applications now will be about two years ahead of most of its competitors.

Of the various divisions of Artificial Intelligence research, those which have applications in banking are natural language processing, expert systems and, to a limited extent, vision and voice.

Banks typically maintain enormous databases of market, competitor, personnel and customer information. Natural language interfaces are being developed to assist the current users of the data, and to encourage use by others within the corporation. For example, in the past, managers have had only indirect access to employee files, necessitating numerous special requests through the personnel department. With natural language front-ends and special access codes, managers can now access information directly to be used in employee reviews and staffing searches.

Markets which commercial banks have previously been unable to enter because of legal restrictions pose a new threat. The expertise required to conduct business in these markets is not readily available within the firm and, because of the need to control costs, it may not be possible to go outside of the company and hire trained professionals. Yet, banks may be in the position to retrain employees or hire entry level personnel at an affordable level. Expert systems are being used to leverage scarce financial and technical expertise in these new markets and in existing lines of business. Examples of applications are commercial and personal loan application processing, investment planning, economic forecasting, optimization of corporate investment portfolios, strategic planning, personnel development, cash management, cross-product sales, insurance claims processing, securities analysis, money transfer processing, loan monitoring and teller training.

Expert systems may also have applications in what is referred to as the 'back room' (the operations side of the bank). Among these are letters of credit processing, pre-audit of electronic funds transfer and paying and receiving account reconciliation. It is more likely, however, that the major contribution of Artificial Intelligence in this area will be in machine vision and voice. The ability of a machine to read forms, especially cheques, will have a major impact on item processing, the operation of clearing cheques and reconciling accounts. Voice technology will also impact this area directly by assisting the personnel who must key in all of the information pertaining to each of the millions of banking transactions carried out each business day.

All of these technologies will not only assist bank employees with their work but will also have an impact on consumers. Over the years, technology has completely changed the relationship between banks and their customers. Most recently we have witnessed this in the proliferation of home banking pilot programs by most of the major commercial banks in the USA. Automated teller networks are another example of the impact of technology on traditional banking. In order to maintain these changing relationships, the companies must make the interface between customers and machines as easy as possible. Expert systems, natural language processing, vision and voice recognition and response should all be incorporated to facilitate this interface.

Investment banking and financial planning applications

Investment banking and financial planning are appropriate areas of application for expert systems technology. First of all, the expertise involved is complex enough so that the decisions are far from trivial, yet the required knowledge is sufficiently static so that the implementation of the system is meaningful. Secondly, the technology is ideal for the required synthesis of numerous financial inputs, investment alternatives and market conditions. In other words, the combination of quantitative and qualitative information can be accommodated. While many financial planning professionals do exist, few have actually mastered all of the interrelated areas of investment advising, tax shelters, retirement planning, cash flow management, insurance planning, taxation, trust and inheritance law. Through the use of expert systems, knowledge of all of these areas can, indeed, be combined. Finally, because the systems can be used for training purposes they augment the corporations' human resources group and decrease personnel expense. In an area which can command high salaries this can represent large savings.

Historically, complete financial planning services have cost consumers approximately US$ 2000 per individual, precluding all but the very wealthy from obtaining professional direction in this area. With the advent of Artificial Intelligence technology, however, financial advice can be offered to families with incomes of between US$ 20 000 and US$ 70 000 for about US$ 200. Not only is this attracting many new clients to investment banking firms, but it is also benefiting commercial banks who, through deregulation, can now offer financial planning services. Previously, it has only been cost-effective to offer such advice to the wealthiest of customers, but financial planning services can now be included in account packages at a cost which the banks can afford.

From the point of view of the consumer, computer-assisted financial planning has two important psychological effects. Many individuals feel intimidated by the human professionals. Through the experience they have with the machine surrogate, they learn how to define their questions and problems. They then gain self-confidence before going to a financial counsellor. In addition, dealing with a computer instead of a person overcomes a certain amount of resistance which is encountered when people are asked to disclose personal financial information.

As technological applications in the area of financial planning become more sophisticated, commercial and investment banking institutions will be able to offer more diverse and more affordable services to their customers. Individuals will be able to access these services in branch lobbies, customer service areas and at home, and be fully prepared for follow-up visits to planning professionals.

Insurance applications

In recent years the insurance industry has experienced a steady decline in its profit margins. This decline has resulted not only from costs, which are rising faster than revenues, but also from a change in the underlying structure of the industry. Standard insurance companies are facing substantial threats in the form of substitute products and services, increased competition from non-insurance institutions and self-insurance, and from the increased bargaining power of consumers. The latter derives both from commercial clients' new found expertise in risk determination and from consumers' increased knowledge of the market.

In an attempt to solve the cost/revenue portion of the profit problem, most companies' rates have been moving up while operating expenses have been decreased. This, however, has not restored the desired levels of net profit and return on equity. In addition, marketing departments have segmented their customers and begun selectively targeting them, while financial departments have realigned the risk and exposure of investment portfolios. From the standpoint of competitive threat, companies have realized that competitive advantage is derived from having better and more easily available information. Expert systems reduce the cost of knowledge reproduction and exploitation and are thus being used as a means of disseminating information and attaining the competitive edge.

The majority of Artificial Intelligence research in the insurance industry has concerned the field of underwriting. The squeeze on profits necessitates a change in organizational structure. The structure is changing toward entrepreneurial units which emphasize front-line production in the field with proactive marketing support from the home office. This implies the need for highly efficient underwriters in the lower ranks of the corporation. Ideally, the decisions should be made by those who are dealing directly with the customers. The insurance industry, though, is plagued by an inconsistent level of quality of decision-making in the field. Expert systems, however, can provide decision support comparable to a consultation with one of the company's most experienced underwriters. Thus, normally widely decentralized and judgemental decision-making processes are coordinated.

Examples of underwriting decision processes which have been successfully represented by expert systems are product design, customer interaction models, information gathering, information analysis, risk evaluation, premium rating, risk transfer analysis, and premium administration.

Better decision-making capabilities not only allow authority to reside in the lower ranks of the company, but also imply three additional benefits:

1.   It is more likely that those policies that are actually written will be more attractive, that is, they are more likely to be written at profitable premiums.

2.   Risks will be more completely and accurately classified. This assures that the rate quoted is better matched to the actual exposure and that the risk is properly interpreted when loss experience is reviewed.

3.   The best alternatives for structuring the risk, including deductibles, credits, conditions and reinsurance, will be identified.

Another benefit of applying expert systems technology in this industry is that underwriting policies may differ within a company according to geographic location. The practice of underwriting is based on the underlying assumption that risks in various groups are relatively homogeneous, and geographic fluctuations can seriously undermine this homogeneity. The result is that the effects of local changes in risk cannot be separated out from the underlying loss experience. Thus, the rate structure does not correctly represent the risks. An expert system, however, can recognize local conditions while maintaining corporate underwriting consistency. The system can then be used to adjust the rate structure accordingly.

The features of an underwriting expert system include:

- judgemental inputs,
- advice tailor-made to the specific risk under consideration,
- the ability to assess the case at any time during the evaluation,
- the ability to make connections between seemingly unrelated facts,
- the immediate presentation of warnings and suggestions during the evaluation, and
- the explanation of the reasoning behind each recommendation.

An application with these features is superior to any previously provided 'rating modules' which have been based on standard actuarial techniques.

Among the other techniques used in the industry are computational models, decision trees and checklists. Expert systems exceed the capabilities of computational models in that they can account for qualitative and incomplete information. Standard statistical models can only include quantifiable data which must be completely specified. Decision trees suffer from the inability to jump to a different 'branch' of the decision-making process when faced with an unanticipated combination of new evidence. Finally, checklists are too inflexible for complex decisions with interrelated variables which typically differ in importance.

Underwriting expert systems proves to be more prevalent and beneficial in the commercial lines rather than the personal lines segment of the industry. The age of data processing has not increased the productivity of the industry as it was first hoped. This is due to the fact that most of the time and effort involved is spent not in transaction processing but in decision-making processes which have eluded computerization. Personal lines, however, have gained from advances in data processing because of a higher volume of similar transactions. On the other hand, commercial lines typically include a small number of diverse and complex transactions, and also deal with widely varying types of risk. In contrast, personal lines deal with risks that are homogeneous enough to fomulate ratings structures for every aspect of the risk. In other words, simple statistical scoring models can be estimated to represent the risks fully. Two final reasons for the inappropriateness of applying this technology to personal lines are:

1.   there are relatively few alternatives for structuring the coverage so that the decisions themselves are much simpler, and

2.   the small average premiums do not justify the development costs.

The systems which have been put into production are designed in two parts. An applications processor compiles the application data and judges the importance of any missing information. This utility minimizes the return of applications to clients, maximizes information quality and reduces the costs of external data aquisition. Once the application is complete, the data is analysed by an underwriting assistant. This system accounts for company standards while incorporating geographic and market differences. Most companies have found that a rule-based system with 250–400 rules is sufficient for the initial screeing of a policy. Only the largest and most complex policies are then passed on to specialists.

From the human resources standpoint, expert systems have several benefits. Rather than attempting to automate the process, it has been humanized as more attention can be spent with those clients with specialized needs. Junior staff members have the flexibility to work on a wider range of cases earlier in their careers, making the industry more attractive as a career choice. With the average tenure in the field being 2–3 years, training costs have historically been very high but can now be decreased through the use of these applications. Finally, the systems which have been implemented are being taken back into the research areas. There they are being studied to identify the impacts of hypothetical changes in underwriting policies.

Perhaps the most stunning implications of underwriting expert systems occur in the areas of product design and distribution channels. Due to the ability of expert systems to test hypothetical situations efficiently, they are being used in the design of specialized products for the high income markets. They are also being considered for the support of alternative distribution channels. Companies are thinking forward to a time when underwriting 'vending machines' may appear in bank branches, credit unions, car dealerships, real estate brokerages, stock brokerages and the offices of financial planning professionals.

While underwriting systems have predominated in insurance applications, research has been done in three other areas. Claim reserve estimation requires a very high level of expertise. Artificial Intelligence systems have increased the accuracy of reserve predictions and have reduced the seniority of the personnel required in this task. Currently, aggregate loss reserve estimation models require users with actuarial experience. Expert systems now act as front-ends to these applications, leaving the actuaries to work on refining the underlying statistical models. Finally, companies like Metropolitan Life are experimenting with general risk assessment projects. However, to date, they have not been able to incorporate enough expertise into the knowledge base to make the system financially feasible to run.

Who is doing what

Commercial banking applications

- *Bank of America (BofA)* has been very cautious about its involvement with Artificial Intelligence. Thus far, BofA has developed several prototype expert systems but has not put any of them into production. Perhaps the most interesting of these systems is one which evaluates pieces of real estate for potential branch placement. The decision is made after the user is prompted for information pertaining to 16 individual expert systems which are linked together. The advantage of linking smaller systems is that much of the decision-making process can be avoided if the site can be ruled out on the basis of a decision derived from one of the subsystems. Other systems being considered throughout the bank involve loan application scoring, credit card fraud detection, credit training, automated teller network problem detection and diagnosis, cross product sales training, loan classification, credit limit analysis, account reconciliation diagnosis, product pricing analysis and financial planning. Bank of America has also purchased Intellect from Artificial Intelligence Corporation and has begun the development of natural language query systems for many of its internal databases.

- *Chase Manhattan*'s efforts have resulted in three prototype systems. The first deals with credit analysis and is being used as a guidance tool for junior relationship managers when they are analysing loan applications. Telex routing will soon be carried out by a combination natural language processor and expert system that will read the message, analyse its content, and route it to the appropriate department. In the case of funds transfer, it will instruct the bank's account production system accordingly. Finally, Chase is planning on using Artificial Intelligence technology to replace many of its current forms of internal communication. These include bulletin boards, supply catalogues, training listings, and the corporate telephone directory. In developing these capabilities, Chase has been very reluctant to use outside consultants. Using outside consultants prompts the question of who owns which part of the resulting system, whereas the Bank wants to maintain any competitive advantage which it gains through its use of this technology.

- *Cognitive Systems, Inc.* of New Haven, Connecticut has developed a prototype system which, like Chase's system, reads and understands unstructured telex funds transfer messages. This capability was developed for a European bank.

- *First National Bank of Chicago* has purchased M1 by Teknowledge, Inc. and has used it to develop expert systems in the areas of auditing, credit analysis, financial products development and training.

- *Security Pacific National Bank* is the commercial bank which is most involved in the application of Artificial Intelligence. The first project which the Bank attempted was the cloning of its top two foreign exchange traders. This project was chosen for two reasons:

  1.   there is, indeed, a scarcity of experts in this area and the ability to replicate their expertise would be invaluable, and

  2.   foreign exchange is a field where large profits can be made on each transaction and, as such, the stakes are very high.

Security Pacific soon found out that this task is impossible for two very important reasons. In reality, even the experts are wrong approximately half of the time. They make money because they lose less when they are wrong than they earn when they are correct. In fact, ordinary traders using the expert system were right only one-third of the time. In addition, foreign exchange decisions involve variables which cannot be specified in advance and which may be highly subjective. It was thought that this problem could be overcome by including data on the market's responses to historical events. However, there is still no way to account for the infinite number of happenings which can affect market behaviour. Human decision-makers can incorporate such events into their thought processes because they can make huge leaps in their thinking which machines cannot.

After realizing that the foreign exchange project would not succeed, Security Pacific turned to something more manageable. An expert system was designed which is based on the knowledge of its top two computer troubleshooters. The system is used by junior technicians and general users to diagnose hardware and operating system problems. As yet it does not have a natural language interface so the user has to have some computer skills to operate it. Plans are under way to apply this to Security Pacific's Automation Network which will incorporate point of sale and credit verification terminals.

Like Bank of America, Security Pacific has purchased Intellect and has used it to develop a front-end for its personnel records. Managers at all levels of the bank can use it to access personnel data directly which is used for employee evaluations, personnel searches, and staff and succession planning.

Finally, Security Pacific has developed an expert system which supports foreign exchange arbitrage decision-making and is selling it in the Bank's package of cash management services. As technology advances the Bank will be investigating possible applications in leasing, commercial lending, securities analysis, financial planning and interest rate swap analysis.

- *Syntelligence, Inc.* has realized that a bank's poor lending record may have nothing to do with the judgements of the credit experts but may be due to the inconsistent application of these judgements throughout the organization. As such, they have developed the Commercial Lending Analyst (CLA) which was made available in 1986. The system analyses, structures and prices the loan. It is based on standard loan application data and the expertise of seasoned credit analysts and officers. While the initial version was written in conjunction with a major bank, Syntelligence feels that 80% of the knowledge base is transferable to other institutions. This 80% is the portion which deals with standard firm and industry analysis and can be gleaned from any credit analysis textbook. The remaining 20% concerns the institution's specific lending policies. This portion can be customized for future clients. The bank working with Syntelligence on CLA feels that the system will be most useful in middle market lending where the risks tend to be greater. They also plan to use it in the training of junior loan officers.

Investment banking and financial planning applications

- *Applied Expert Systems (APEX)* of Cambridge, Massachusetts, has had a securities industry expert system on the market since June 1983. The specifications and users of this system have not been disclosed, but APEX says that its three major benefits are that it helps brokers to understand customer needs, it leverages the field sales force, and it supports the sale of new products.

- *Astec Consulting Group* of New York has developed a system which assists corporate trust departments in the evaluation of multiple tender offers.

- *Cognitive Systems* of New Haven, Connecticut has worked with a Belgian bank to write a stock market advice system called 'Le Courtier'. In Belgium, commercial banks are allowed, by law, to offer investment advice. Until recently, however, there has not been a great demand for this advice because tax laws precluded all but the very wealthy from participating in the stock market. Changes in the tax laws have now made it attractive for individuals in all income brackets to invest. As such, the banks have become overwhelmed with requests for advice, leaving little time for the officers to attend to their other duties. 'Le Courtier' not only offloads work from the officers to the computer system, but it also ensures the consistent quality of advice across the branch system. 'Le Courtier' offers advice based on the customer's answers to questions regarding age, income, desire for liquidity, current debts, future intentions, and the desired degree of risk.

- *Salomon Brothers, Inc.* has incorporated Artificial Intelligence technology with its ongoing research projects to produce sophisticated scenario analysis capabilities for its clients. An example of this is an expert system which compares possible combinations of face value, maturity and return, to optimize a bond portfolio.

Insurance applications

- *Metropolitan Life Insurance Co.* has developed expert systems which fall into three categories:
  1. underwriting screening,
  2. medical preadmission review (this system allows hospital admitting offices to determine whether a particular illness or hospital service is covered by a patient's insurance policy), and
  3. dividend calculation for group insurance and risk assessment.

  In addition to the actual development of these systems, Metropolitan has invested a large amount of research time studying knowledge representation and the intricacies of the PROLOG language.

- *Syntelligence, Inc.* has produced the Inland Marine Underwriting System which determines premiums and evaluates risks for several property and casualty insurance companies, including American Insurance Group, Inc.

Other financial services areas

- *Dow Jones Information Systems* has used natural language programming to create front-ends for many of its financial databases, including those which report news, stock quotes and financial disclosure information.   ˙
- *IDS/American Express, Inc.* uses an expert system which advises customer service representatives in the proper way to handle customer requests and complaints. The Corporation feels that by making this knowledge available to its representatives, it can guarantee a uniform service of high quality.

Conclusions

The application of Artificial Intelligence technologies in the financial services industries will be key in the reversal of the decline in profits which has been experienced in the recent past. However, because these are areas of expertise in which vast amounts of knowledge are manipulated with an enormous amount of judgement, firms will have to be sure that chosen applications are, indeed, appropriate. In deciding this, several things should be kept in mind. If a conventional solution to a problem already exists, the costs involved in developing an Artificial Intelligence capability will probably not be justified. On the other hand, the problem must be one for which an expert does, indeed, exist. Furthermore, this expert must be willing to participate in the project. The expertise must be of realizable benefit to the unaided user. The conditions surrounding the problem, that is, the knowledge and expertise, should be sufficiently static so that the implementation of the system is still valuable. Finally, the political climate must be favourable for the project to proceed. This implies the attention and commitment of top management, the minimization of interdepartmental conflict, and a clear understanding of what Artificial Intelligence actually is.

In summary, financial services companies, like any others, should ask themselves the following questions when they are considering investments in this technology:

- Do we have an immediate demand for this technology?
- What would happen to the company if the competition established a 2-year lead in Artificial Intelligence techniques?
- Do we want to understand the Artificial Intelligence technology instead of having faith that it works?
- How big is the project?
- How difficult will the system be to code, modify and debug?

The answers to these questions will determine whether or not the firm is ready to become involved with Artificial Intelligence technology.

Bibliography

Arndt S. (1984). Information key to success in changing market. *National Underwriter*, 16 Nov, 52–53

Bennett R.A. (1985). Copy cat computers that couldn't copy. *American Banker*, 3 June, 26, 28–29

Cook S. (1984). Financial expert systems. In *Proc. 1984 Annual Conf. of the ACM*

Friis W. (1985). Artificial intelligence systems: some banks have them, others will. *ABA Banking J.*, June, 203–204, 206, 208

Garsson R.M. (1985). The gut feeling goes electric. *Am. Banker*, 3 June 20–22

Iovacchini A. (1984). Computers simulate human reasoning, utilize problem solving methods. *Bank Systems and Equipment*, Nov, 99–107

Kutler J. (1985). It's 1985: does the computer know where your money is? *Am. Banker*, 3 June, 24–26

Raimondi D. (1985a). Insurer supporting commercialy viable AI programming. *Computerworld*, 27 May, 12–13

Raimondi D. (1985b). Maximizing benefits of AI a slow process, firm cautions. *Computerworld*, 27 May, 13

Schreiber N. (1984). Artificial intelligence in finance: a challenge to put mind into matter. *Wall Street Computer Review*, October 75–77

Shpilberg D. (1985). A promising new frontier. *Best's Review*, May, 36, 38, 40, 42

White D.G. (1985). Expert systems to the rescue. *Best's Review*, May, 52–54, 56, 109

(1985). The Banker's Magazine interview – John Diebold. *The Banker's Magazine*, March–April, 15–19

7

ADVISER: A Manufacturing Diagnostic Expert System

K. Horn
M. Brown
L. Lo

Telectronics Pty Ltd

This paper describes an expert system for the electronic fault-finding of a cardiac pacemaker circuit. The system is currently in use in the manufacturing line for assisting technicians to interpret the output of an automated test device providing a diagnosis of the circuit's faults and advice for its repair. The system employs shallow reasoning and, as a result, cannot address novel circuit faults. A deep model is proposed based on the functional structure of the pacemaker using cause–effect relationships between modular elements of the circuit.

Introduction

The manufacturing of complex electronic goods is not perfect; typically a percentage of production will fail to work or not meet quality standards. The product then has to be repaired or reworked and passed again through electronic test systems and/or quality checks. The reasons for products failing are many: components can be incorrectly placed on circuit boards, soldering joints can be dry or bridge onto other parts of the circuit, components can be faulty or out of tolerance and faults can exist in the design of the product.

In order to improve the speed and quality of the rework process, AI techniques have been employed by many companies. Today a large number of AI-based electronic troubleshooting programs have been implemented and have demonstrated considerable success (Bennett and Hollander, 1981; Cantone *et al.*, 1984; Hofmann *et al.*, 1986). These programs aid the technician by interpreting the results of automated test equipment and/or guiding the technician through the fault-finding exercise. To date, many electronic troubleshooting systems have been based on programs, such as MYCIN (Shortliffe, 1976) that accept a set of symptoms and find a match with an if-then rule that contains a diagnosis (fault) and a treatment (rework/repair). Unfortunately, such a strategy is far from that used by the electronic troubleshooter, who is armed with schematic diagrams and a knowledge of electronic principles and laws (that is, Kirchhoff's and Ohm's laws). Using this type of knowledge, the competent troubleshooter can build a model of the structure and function of the system under test. This is not to say that the troubleshooter does not compile his or her knowledge into simple symptom–diagnosis patterns with enough experience but, given a difficult or novel problem or when required to explain his or her reasoning, deeper structural-based knowledge is employed (Davis, 1984).

A simple symptom–diagnosis-based electronic fault finding system will be bound to fail given problems such as multiple faults, open circuit links or wires and short circuits. Furthermore, novel problems, such as a new brand of component used in manufacturing producing new faults, cannot be addressed by a simple expert system formalism. To overcome these limitations the AI-based electronic troubleshooter has to employ deep structural knowledge, as does its human counterpart.

A structure-based expert system to be used in the electronic manufacturing industry has another advantage in that it can capture product knowledge from the earliest phase of product design. In many electronic manufacturing companies the development phase for a product model involves the development of the product plus the production electronic test system. During this phase the capability of the product is defined and the potential for problems is evaluated and expressed as a specification for tests that need to be performed plus the conditions surrounding the tests. What tends not to be recorded are the reasons behind the test specification. This knowledge, accordingly, fades away and important product knowledge is lost.

Problems encountered during the remaining life cycle of the product model and resolved through failure analysis and further research may add to this body of knowledge but, in practice, it is mostly a rediscovery of prior knowledge. The effect is an excessive delay in the resolution of difficult problems and a potential for further occurrences before they can be checked. In order to correct this situation, the expert system should be capable of capturing knowledge acquired during the development and test phase of a product.

This paper examines a prototype electronic troubleshooting system developed at Telectronics Pty Ltd. The application involved the fault-finding and rework of an MPT cardiac pacemaker circuit that has failed manufacture tests. An MPT pacemaker is a particular model pacemaker with Magnetic and Telemetric Programming features. The system interprets the results from an automated test jig, attempts to diagnose any faults present and offers advice to help the repair of the circuit. Presently, only one technician is experienced in the rework of this model pacemaker and the loss of this technician by the company would slow down production significantly. The personnel hired for the rework process are not electronic engineers and gain competence mainly through experience rather than by modelling the faulty device in the manner of an experienced engineer. A faulty pacemaker often is repaired by trial and error, not by fault isolation, and thus time and components are wasted as the product stays in the test rework loop until its quality is assured. It may take new rework personnel a long time to recognize the correct symptom–diagnosis correlations apparent when a novel fault occurs in production.

Aims of the project

In order to assess the applicability of expert systems technology to the rework process it was decided to build a simple prototype expert system to capture the shallow knowledge used by the rework personnel. If this system was as good as the human counterparts, research would progress into a model-based system that could fulfil the benefits mentioned above. This paper will discuss the simple system and then outline the current state of the model-based system.

Information available to the system

The information available to the system consists of the output report from the MPT automated test equipment. This report (see Table 7.1) lists the results of 116 individual test results. Each test result is in the form: a fault ID number, a fault name, the lower limit for the test value, the value of the tested pacemaker and the upper limit for the test value. The tests that fall outside their upper or lower limits are flagged in the report with asterisks. The use of the electronic testing system assumes that any fault in a component of a pacemaker will be reflected by failure in one or more of the automated tests. The automated tests exercise the functionality of the pacemaker and do not test the actual components. The aim of the rework personnel is to bridge the gap between a behavioural malfunction of the pacemaker, as reported by the test system, and the faulty components.

The system utilizes information distilled from design specifications, knowledge acquired from an engineer experienced in fault-finding and interviews with rework staff. A database recording the past actions of the rework personnel and the fault report was examined. The data was discussed with the experts and their fault strategies observed. It is intended to use inductive learning techniques (Quinlan et al., 1987) to mine this database in the future and see if knowledge can be artificially generated. This was not possible for the present system as the actions performed by the rework personnel were not recorded in any standard format.

Table 7.1 Output report from MPT automated test equipment.

	SERIAL: 238600 MODEL: 5281B PAGE 1 DATE: Thu JAN 14:01:18 1988				
NUM	TEST NAME	LOWLIM	RESULT	UPLIM	FAIL
1	RESET MODE REGISTERS	1	1	1	
2	CHANNEL SHUTDOWN TEST	1	0	1	***
3	CHANNEL OPEN TEST	1	0	1	***
4	PACER PROGRAM ACKNOWLEDGE	1	1	1	
5	PROGRAM ACKNOWLEDGE 2.0V	1	1	1	
6	DATE REGISTER CHECK	1	1	1	
.					
.					
40	INTERVAL (746/757 MS)	744	746	760	
41	CELL R (BASK INT = 1070 MS)	34.00	37.79	42.00	
42	INTERVAL (1070 MS)	1068	1070	1072	
.					
.					
100	SENS. 2.5mV,EOL,10V	2.42	2.64	2.82	
101	SPREAD 2.5mV,EOL,10V	0.00	0.05	1.00	
102	10V AMPLITUDE AT EOL	5.55	4.02	6.75	***
103	PROGRAMMABILITY @ 10V & EOL	4.02	3.71	6.00	***
104	MAX. RATE TEST AT 130PPM	920	921	924	
105	MAX. RATE TEST AT 100PPM	596	597	600	
.					
.					
111	PACE COUNTER CHECK	18	18	18	
112	TELEMETRY SENSITIVITY	3.00	0.00	3.00	***
113	CURRENT, STD,PACE,LINK	25.00	62.40	40.00	***
114	CURRENT, STD+10V,PACE,LINK	85.00	94.10	150.00	
115	CURRENT, STD+10V,PACE,AD,LINK	105.00	300.10	175.00	***
116	CURRENT, STD,PACE,A/D,LINK	35.00	80.30	53.00	***

A four-fold knowledge base

The knowledge base was divided into four independent sections reflecting the diagnostic strategy of the expert engineers themselves. The first section of the knowledge base was concerned with the grouping of individual failed tests into an embracing qualitative description. For example:

IF   one of Tests 31,32 failed
THEN   Group is power

IF   one of Tests 16,17,18,19,20,21,22 failed
THEN   Group is A/D

This grouping enables test failures to be addressed as a group, i.e. the later rule suggests an analog to digital converter (A/D) problem rather than a number of individual failed tests.

The second section of the knowledge base examines the actual test results and assigns a qualitative description to the values. The numeric results of each test are compared against their upper and lower limits and a collective description is applied to the group of tests. A number of 'English-like' qualitative descriptions were employed to describe the set of test results, as shown in Figure 7.1. For example, a result that was less than 1.3 times its upper limit was described as 'slightly high', if it was more than 1.5 times its upper limit it would be 'excessively high' and a 'catastrophic' result was one greater than 2.0 times its limit. For some of the qualitative descriptions the results are compared to other test results: for example, test values not repeated across tests and one test less than another. Two qualification rules are shown below:

The qualification for the sensitivity tests:

IF   one or more out of spec: 62
          and less than: 62, 60
THEN   1.4 mV test value is just out of spec but does not exceed the value
          measured for the 1.8 mV test

The qualification for the power tests:

IF   one or more slightly high:
          31,32,49,113,114,115,116
THEN   current just in excess of specification

Some of the qualitative descriptions mentioned in Figure 7.1 refer to normal values, that is, ones within their respective test limits. For example, the description 'have space to drop' is used to test if a result's value can be moved up or down and not fall outside its limit. Some failures can be fixed by changing a component's value to shift its measured effect. If this shift results in the tests staying within their limits, the fault is rectified. Another description, 'all more than 4% drop of previous value', describes a series of results, each value being normally within 4% below the previous test result. Again, a fault can be rectified if a component value can be altered and the effect does not shift any of the results from 4% of the previous test.

The third section of the rule base is made up of hierarchy rules. These rules contain knowledge relating primary faults to secondary faults. A failure in one part of the pacemaker circuit will cause modules down-

---

. under spec: T1
over spec: T1
less than: T1, T2
in spec: T1, T2, T3 ...
have space to drop: T1, T2, T3 ...
all more than 4% drop of previous value: T1, T2, T3 ...
no repeats: T1, T2, T3 ...
no catastrophic: T1, T2, T3 ...
some similar: T1, T2, T3, ...
all the same: T1, T2, T3 ...
all catastrophic: T1, T2, T3 ...
one or more out of spec: T1, T2, T3 ...
one or more slightly high: T1, T2, T3 ...
one or more just slightly high: T1, T2, T3 ...
one or more excessively high: T1, T2, T3 ...
one or more catastrophic: T1, T2, T3 ...
shifted in the same direction: T1, T2, T3 ...

Figure 7.1   The qualification operators employed in ADVISER. Most of the operators act on test lists (T1, T2, T3 ...); however, some act on a single test (T1) or a pair of tests (T1, T2).

line of this module to malfunction also, producing secondary faults. Secondary faults may also be produced by the adjacency of components as a result of effects such as heat, magnetic inductance and radio frequency interference. The hierarchy rules thus encode the structure of causally affected circuit modules. The system reports repair advice only for primary failures but mentions those test failures that are secondarily related. A hierarchy rule for the coil test is shown below:

    IF   the results of coil test(s) is fail
    THEN   the secondary test(s) are 2, 3

The result of this rule is that the fault group list is changed from containing coil (failure of test 112) and channel open/shutdown (failure of tests 2 and 3) to just a coil failure. The channel open/shutdown fault is moved to the secondary fault list. This rule encodes the causative knowledge that a failure of the coil used for telemetry communication with the pacemaker results in the failure of tests trying to open and shutdown communications.

The final section of the knowledge base contains rules that link the primary failures discovered by the system with both a description of the fault and advice as to how to repair the fault. The following rule illustrates the advice generated with a particular conjunction of descriptions of 'vario' group failures:

Advice rule 1
IF   Vario failure described as:
          One or more of the vario amplitude tests were out of spec
          and the test did not fail catastrophically
          and no amplitude values were repeated
THEN   Advice is:
          Attempt to move the vario ladder by altering C4. This
          could rectify a few step failures due to the fact that
          the step amplitude differences are not all identical.
          Failing this, replace the 668 IC.

The system first attempts to find an advice rule in the knowledge base which matches the list of groups and qualitative descriptions exactly. If it is successful in this search the advice is output by the system. Otherwise the system tries to find an advice rule which best matches the failure list. If (for example) three of the four failures are described in a rule then the advice is output and the search continues with the remaining failures. When as many of the failures as possible have been accounted for, the system terminates its search.

The prototype expert system shell

The expert system has been developed in UNSW PROLOG (Sammut and Sammut, 1983) as this language allows for rapid prototyping of rule-based expert systems. Furthermore, no commercial tools were available that could run in the test system's computing environment. UNSW PROLOG also offered the advantage of being a local product with the source code available. The availability of source code offers the knowledge engineer the flexibility to modify the system and tailor it to the minor quirks of the domain. In developing this system, essential modifications to the PROLOG source had to be made. Two PROLOG systems were employed, both written in UNSW PROLOG. A run-time batch system was developed to run under UNIX on an NCR Tower. A rule editor and consultation environment was developed on an IBM AT microcomputer. The flexibility offered by separating knowledge from control in the expert system shell will allow for different model pacemakers to be considered using the same expert system shell.

Batch operation

The ADVISER batch system is now an integral part of the production process. The electronic testing system produces a log file of devices tested and a pointer to their test report. The expert system is run from a UNIX shell program that passes the expert system the appropriate report file and then appends the expert system output onto the report. The reports are then printed and collected by the rework personnel. The failure data from Table 7.1 produces the following ADVISER output:

Summary of input information:

Failed test line numbers:
2,3,102,103,112,113,115,116.

Description of failure of power test was:
Excessively high current drain.
Description of failure of coil test was:
Fail.

Advice related to this module:

The result of the power test being:
Excessively high current drain will result in the failure of test(s) 102,103.

Advice relating to the failure of the power test(s):
Visual check for short circuits, reversed diodes, reversed capacitors, leaking filter capacitor on the supply rail.
Failing this, separate PCBs to isolate the board drawing high current.

The result of the coil test being:
Fail will result in the failure of test(s) 2,3.

Advice relating to the failure of the coil test(s):
Check the telemetry coil. If OK replace the telemetry IC.

The rules used to diagnose this case are shown below divided into their appropriate sections:

1. The group rules are consulted and fault groups are assigned:

    IF   one of Tests 31,32,49,113,114,115,116 failed
    THEN   Group is power

    IF   one of Tests 2,3 failed
    THEN   Group is channel open/shutdown

    IF   one of Test 112 failed
    THEN   Group is coil

2. The fault groups are each checked against the appropriate qualification rules. By default, test groups such as 'coil' and 'channel open/shutdown' that have no qualification rules are described as fail.

    The qualification for the power tests:

    IF   one or more excessively high:
                3,32,49,113,114,115,116
    THEN   excessively high current drain

3. The hierarchy rules are now considered, resulting in faults 2, 3, 102 and 103 becoming secondary faults. Since all the 'channel open/shutdown' tests (that is, 2 and 3) are included in the rule

below, it is removed as a primary fault. The tests 102 and 103 relate to 'amplitude' and 'EOL' group failures, respectively; as no other tests in these groups have failed they are also removed as primary faults. It is important to note that, if test 48 (another 'amplitude' test) had failed, for example, this hypothesis would remain a primary fault despite the following rule:

> IF   the results of coil test(s) is fail
> THEN   the secondary test(s) are 2, 3
>
> IF   the results of power test(s) is fail
> THEN   the secondary test(s) are 102, 103

4.   The advice rules are finally considered:

> Advice rule 5
>
> IF   Coil failure described as:
>   Fail
> THEN   Advice is:
>   Check telemetry coil. If OK replace the telemetry IC.
>
> Advice rule 16
>
> IF   Power failure described as:
>   Excessively high current drain
> THEN   Advice is:
>   Visual check for short circuits ... etc.

Consultation operation

In consultation mode, the user may choose to select a particular knowledge base as different pacemaker models use different knowledge bases. This mode differs from the batch mode in operation as the actual test results are not considered; the user is prompted instead to describe the fault in terms of group failure descriptions. A multiple choice format is used to prompt the user for these qualitative descriptions. A session with the consultation system is shown below:

> Input of information:
> Enter the list of failed line numbers.
> Separate each entry by a space or a comma.
>
> For a group of failed tests it is only necessary to enter
> one line number from the group? 18, 19, 20
>
> Choose from the following to best describe
> the failure of these test(s):
>   1. Failure of A/D count and/or A/D spread.
>   2. All or some A/D slew rates and times shifted out of spec.
>   3. None of the above.
> Description number? 1

Summary of input information:

Failed test line numbers: 18,19,20.

Description of failure of A/D test was:
Failure of A/D count and/or A/D spread.

Advice related to this module:

Replace telemetry IC. (Noisy delta modulator.) This advice takes priority over any other advice statements.

Success rate

The initial expert system knowledge base contained 80 rules: 27 group rules, 19 qualification rules, 8 hierarchy rules and 26 advice rules. On selecting 45 test results for failed MPT pacemakers, at random, from the company's failure database, accurate and relevant advice was given for about 80% of the modules. The cases that did not pass were examined by an expert engineer and none of them posed problems when the new or changed knowledge was added to the system. Since this initial test run, 31 new rules have been added; the system now has 33 qualification rules and 43 advice rules, bringing the total to 111 rules. The success rate of the system is now estimated to be over 90%.

The major problem with this system is that it relies entirely on previous experience. This creates the situation where novel problems become fatal to the system. To resolve this problem, a more sophisticated approach requires the construction of a causal model of the pacemaker. This approach will thus enable the system to reason from first principles when a new problem is being presented. It could also suggest possible design errors.

The qualitative pacemaker model

A prototype causal model of the MPT pacemaker has been written in the language Smalltalk. The model is based on a modular conception of the pacemaker. Figures 7.2 and 7.3 illustrate the modular units and the causal links between these modules. The top level of the model defines the qualitative behaviour of the pacemaker. The bottom level of the pacemaker model defines modules that are not affected by other modules. Each module has a number of properties that describe its normal and possible abnormal behaviour. Rules are then used to link the behaviour of one module (a cause node) with other modules (effect nodes) that are causally related.

The model is expressed in a simulation language which is executed by a Smalltalk interpreter. The language allows nodes and links to be

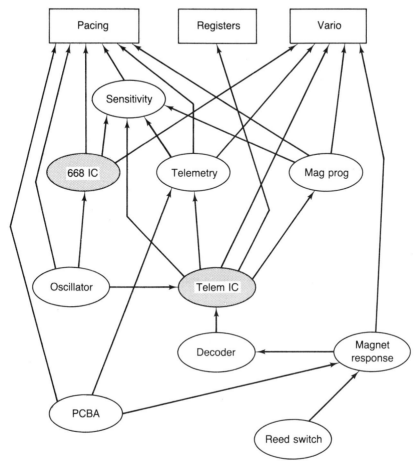

Figure 7.2   The MPT pacemaker model showing the model nodes and links. The square nodes represent the top level behaviour nodes. The shaded nodes are complex modules described in Figure 7.3.

defined independently of one another. When the model builder describes enough nodes and links, the model itself can be defined by specifying which nodes and which links make up the model. Many different models can be created using the same nodes and links already defined. This property allows many pacemaker models to reuse modules of other pacemakers without having to recreate the shared modules. Figure 7.3 illustrates the use of two submodules, component ICs used in a range of pacemakers, that are parts of the MPT pacemaker illustrated in Figure 7.2. A further property of the language is that a number of different models can be spliced together with links to form a more comprehensive simulation.

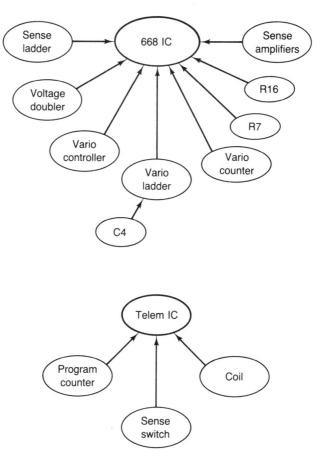

Figure 7.3   The two IC submodules of the MPT pacemaker model.

Structure of the model

The structure of the model can be graphically output from the Smalltalk program, producing graphs similar to those of Figures 7.2 and 7.3. These diagrams are only a summary representation of the model, as each line representing a link may involve different properties and, in some cases, may represent many properties. Unfortunately space does not allow each individual link to be labelled in these figures. Figure 7.4 illustrates those nodes and links only involved with magnetic programmability. The properties associated with individual links and nodes are defined with link description rules. The following link descriptions show that the pacing and sensitivity nodes are only linked with one property, whereas the sensitivity and 668 IC nodes are linked with two different properties:

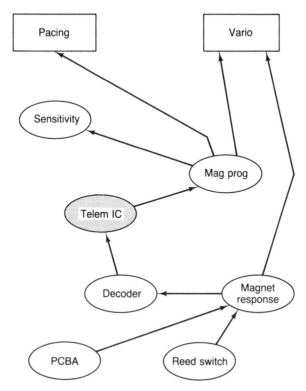

Figure 7.4   The MPT pacemaker model showing relevant nodes and links, with the pacing node set to 'pacing settings not magnetically alterable'.

Link 27:

  causels Sensitivity with 'operation' as 'over sensing'
  effectls Pacing with 'operation' as 'inhibited'

Link 39:

  causels 668IC with 'sensitivity' as 'over sensing'
  effectls Sensitivity with 'operation' as 'over sensing'

Link 21:

  causels 668IC with 'sensitivity values' as
    '0.7 under spec, 4.4 over spec'
  effectls Sensitivity with 'values' as
    '0.7 under spec, 4.4 over spec'

Fault finding with the causal model

The operation of the model is illustrated with an example. The example shows how the pacing and vario nodes behaviour can be influenced by changing the reed switch 'response' from 'normal' to 'under spec'. The default value for a property of a node is 'normal'.

The user enters:

Reed switch response is under spec.
Propagate.

The model runs and the effects of the changed node propagate through the model. The nodes affected by the change in the reed switch function are illustrated below:

Reed Switch node:
   response is under spec.
Magnet response node:
   value is under spec.
Decoder node:
   reed switch function is fail.
Telem IC node:
   vario entry is normal.
   program counter is normal.
   magnet operation is fail.
   telemetry operation is normal.
   sensitivity control is normal.
Mag Prog node:
   operation is fail.
Sensitivity node:
   operation is normal.
   value is not magnetically alterable.
Pacing node:
   presence is normal.
   rate is normal.
   setting is not magnetically alterable.
   output amplitude is normal.
   width is normal.
Vario node:
   operation is normal.
   entry is normal.
   state is not magnetically alterable.
   amplitude is normal.

The effect of the reed switch change can be seen to influence the overt behaviour of the pacemaker in two ways: the state of the vario settings cannot be magnetically altered and the pacing settings cannot be magnetically altered. The path through the model can be seen if Figures 7.2 and 7.4 are examined with the above output. It is important to note that, although the sensitivity node is affected, it does not affect the pacing node; rather, the pacing node was affected by the mag prog node. This effect occurs as the sensitivity and pacing nodes are not linked with a property 'magnetically alterable': only the mag prog and pacing nodes are linked with this property.

The operation of the model for the fault-finding task requires it to be run in reverse. If the behaviour of the pacemaker is specified from a top-level node this can be propagated down the model to the lower-level nodes, providing a chain of possible places where a fault could have occurred. For example, if we enter into the model 'pacing settings not magnetically alterable', then propagate this down the model, the result is similar to the output above except that the vario node would be 'normal' and its state would be 'magnetically alterable'. The lowest level node affected is the reed switch node, suggesting a possible fault at this node. Other low level faults that could cause this overt behaviour would also be output, suggesting the possibility of multiple faults. In this case the PCBA (printed circuit board assembly) node is also output, as a short circuit across the reed switch would affect the magnet response node in the same manner as a faulty reed switch. Any of the following nodes could also be faulty: pacing, mag prog, telem IC, decoder, magnet response.

The fault-finding exercise is now a matter of finding at what level in the tree or chain of faults the module behaviour becomes faulty. If the model was now run forward, the lowest level reed switch and PCBA behaviours just discovered would again produce the output above, demonstrating that both pacing and vario node changes should be observed in this situation. However, the vario behaviour is not observed, only the pacing problem, suggesting the problem may not be at the reed switch or the PCBA. Examining Figure 7.4 reveals that the mag prog node is one point where the pacing and vario nodes are mutually affected. The fault could therefore lie at, or between, the pacing and mag prog nodes. The mag prog node could not be faulty as it would effect the vario node. The pacing node or the connection to the mag prog node must be faulty. Again, it is necessary to note that the sensitivity node could not be the culprit as it is not linked to the pacing node with the necessary property. This hypothesis is further supported by the observation that a fault at the reed switch, PCBA or magnet response nodes would also result in a fault at the vario node, which is also not observed.

The model-based approach described above has the main advantage that a product can be modelled at any stage in development and its behaviour examined. This is an extremely important quality for fault-finding tools in high technology manufacturing industry, as knowledge can be captured before the faults are experienced in manufacturing and before the knowledge is lost getting from the research and design staff to manufacturing staff. The model can help designers at all stages of product development, not just the rework staff in manufacturing.

This model-based system is a distinct improvement over the previous shallow implementation of ADVISER; however, it is not yet in a

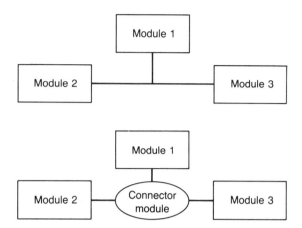

Figure 7.5   The top diagram illustrates the conventional model and wires connecting the three modules. The bottom diagram shows the wires represented as a connection module (adapted from Pipitone, 1986).

usable form. One may ask, how does the information get into the model? It is proposed to use qualification rules of the form described above, in the ADVISER system, to relate the automated test equipment failures to behavioural malfunctions of the pacemaker. At each node in the model, rules can be attached relating the node's qualitative behaviour to measurable behaviours exhibited by the test system. For example, a failure of test numbers 106 or 107 would suggest the reed switch is 'under spec'.

Extensions to the model

Three important extensions to the model are proposed. The first is to link with each node heuristics, as in the form of ADVISER's 'advice' rules, that capture experience-based knowledge. This knowledge would allow well recognized symptom–diagnosis patterns to be expressed, allowing the faulty module to be found without the need to run the entire model. The second extension relates to the problem of short and open circuits. The present model includes short circuits as a property of the PCBA node. Figure 7.2 suggests that common short and/or open circuits on the PCBA affect the pacing, telemetry and magnet response nodes. The model is to be extended so that wires themselves are modules and not expressed by the model links, as illustrated in Figure 7.5 (Davis, 1984; Pipitone, 1986). Wires and circuit board tracks that are close together could be linked by relations expressing possible short circuits. Open circuits are modelled when propagation through the network via connection modules is not concomitantly observed in the circuit under test.

The final extension relates to the use of fault probabilities. The output from the ADVISER system, as shown in the consultation example, suggests that some faults are more important than others, revealed by the statement 'This advice takes priority over any other advice'. The system has to be enhanced to include a conflict resolution strategy that allows only the most probable failures to be output. Pipitone (1986) has proposed that Bayesian probability-based methods, as opposed to other methods of representing uncertainty, such as certainty factors in MYCIN (Shortliffe, 1976) or odds in PROSPECTOR (Duda *et al.*, 1977), are best suited to electronic fault-finding. The main assumption behind this view is that electronic devices can be broken up into modules (see Figure 7.5) which exhibit faults that are independent of each other, as opposed to natural systems where faults are often interdependent. Furthermore, reliable probabilities can be gleaned from the past records of device failures stored in manufacturing databases and continually updated as more devices are manufactured. Telectronics is presently changing the format of its fault record databases so that information of this type can be gained in the future.

Conclusion

The deep model-based system proposed offers many advantages over shallow expert systems used for electronic fault-finding. The model can predict failures not yet experienced by human counterparts and copes with multiple faults, shorts and open circuits. The system allows knowledge of both causal and experiential form to be mixed. The design of the model makes the knowledge acquisition process more organized as it is based on structure rather than an unrelated recollection of experience. Furthermore, the organization of knowledge linking rules to model nodes makes the knowledge updating process extremely organized. Many large expert systems built using shallow knowledge only are currently being reported as being extremely difficult to manage (Compton *et al.*, 1988). The final advantage relates to the ability of the system to exist and grow with the development of the product from conception.

References

Bennett J.S. and Hollander C.R. (1981). DART: an expert system for fault diagnosis. In *7th IJCAI*, Vancouver, pp. 843–845

Cantone R., Lander W.B., Marrone M.P. and Gaynor M.W. (1984). INATE 2: interpreting high-level fault modes. In *Proc. 1st Conf. on Artificial Intelligence Applications*. Denver CO. pp. 470–473

Compton P., Horn K.A.R., Quinlan J.R. and Lazarus L. (1988). Maintaining an expert system. (In this volume)

Davis R. (1984). Diagnostic reasoning based on structure and behaviour. *Artificial Intelligence*, **24**(1–3), 347–410

Duda R.O., Hart P.E., Nilsson N.J., Reboh R., Slocum J. and Sutherland G.L. (1977). *A Computer-Based Consultant for Mineral Exploration.* Artificial Intelligence Center, SRI International, Menlo Park CA

Hofmann M., Caviedes J., Bourne J., Geale G. and Brodersen A. (1986). Building expert systems for repair domains. *Expert Systems*, **3**(1)

Pipitone F. (1986). The FIS electronic troubleshooting system. *IEEE Computer*, July, 68–76

Quinlan R., Compton P., Horn K. and Lazarus L. (1987). Inductive knowledge acquisition: a case study. In *Applications of Expert Systems*, (Quinlan J.R., ed.). Reading MA: Addison-Wesley

Sammut C.A. and Sammut R.A. (1983). The implementation of UNSW-PROLOG. *Aust. Computer J.*, **15**(2), 8–64

Shortliffe E.H. (1976). *Computer-Based Medical Consultations: MYCIN.* New York: Elsevier-North Holland

8

An Expert Operator Guidance System for an Iron Ore Sinter Plant

L.G. Lock Lee
K. Teh
R. Campanini
BHP Central Research Laboratories

The development of a commercial knowledge-based expert system requires more than a good understanding of the technology. To be successful, the expert system must be closely integrated into the information systems environment of the application. The user interface must also provide a level of comfort that ensures natural interaction between the user and the knowledge/information that he or she is being provided with. Clearly, the implementation of a successful expert system application requires a combination of skills from knowledge engineering, data processing and user interface design. This paper describes the development of an expert system to provide control advice to operators of a complex iron ore sintering process. The issues encountered in building this system to the on-line test stage are discussed and some advice offered to new expert system developers.

1 Introduction

The operation of complex processing plants is potentially a very profitable area for the application of expert systems technology (Nida *et al.*, 1986; Barrett, 1984; Moore *et al.*, 1984). Much has been written and several prototypes built to assist with interpretation of the numerous alarm conditions that can occur in nuclear power plants (Embrey and Humphreys, 1986; Yufik and Sheridan, 1984). While BHP may not operate processes that are as potentially dangerous as a nuclear reactor

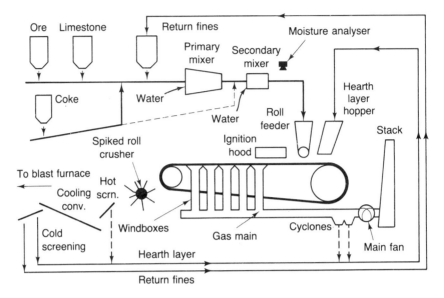

Figure 8.1   Iron ore sinter plant.

plant, many of the processes are equally as complex and, as yet, not well understood. Given the complexity of these processes, reliance on experienced and expert operators is commonplace. The iron ore sinter plant at the Company's Newcastle Steelworks was selected as an appropriate application area for the Company's first serious effort in applying expert systems technology. The sinter plant offered an appropriately sized problem and an enthusastic expert. A prototype system is now in the field for continuous on-line testing. This paper reports on the development of the prototype, to date, and relates some of our experiences during the course of the project.

2   Application description

2.1   Sinter plant description

An iron ore sinter plant prepares ore for feeding to the blast furnace. The plant takes a mixture consisting primarily of fine iron ore, a flux material (limestone), fuel (coke) and returned sinter fines (reject material), dampened with water, to form a loose granular mixture, which is placed on a moving steel strand. Figure 8.1 provides a schematic description of the process. The mixture is ignited as the bed passes under the ignition hood. The coke particles in the upper layer start to burn as air is drawn through the bed by a series of windboxes. The flame front moves down the bed as the material moves towards the end of the strand. The combustion of coke generates the heat to cause the partial melting of the mixture to form a strong agglomerate, that is, sinter. The operational objective is to produce material of sufficient average size and chemical composition to optimize blast furnace operations. Many of the major parameters that the operators must monitor are not directly measurable: for example, the permeability on the bed. The operator must use his or her judgement to infer the process status from the instrumentation that is available.

The control problem for iron ore sinter plants is an extensively studied topic. The process is complicated by the complex interrelationships between multiple variables and long time constants. There are very few, if any, examples of sinter plants under full automatic control. Perhaps the most successful practitioners have been the Japanese, who have heuristically based 'operator guidance systems' operating quite successfully (Watanabe *et al.*, 1985). These systems make use of fuzzy logic technology (Larsen, 1980; Umbers and King, 1980; Zadeh, 1973), in cooperation with sophisticated process sensing and data analysis systems to maintain control.

The difference between the expert system approach and the fuzzy logic approach is purely one of scope. Fuzzy logic relies on a small number of heuristically derived rules about key parameters, whereas an expert system attempts to take into consideration all factors which may impinge on the control problem. For example, equipment malfunction, prewarning of material contamination, long-term quality and production aims, alarm conditions etc., are not taken into account by closed loop controllers, such as fuzzy logic controllers or statistically-based adaptive controllers. These factors will often cause large process upsets that adversely affect the operation of the controller. In this sense, the expert system would be responsible for managing the operation of the closed loop controller, ensuring maximum control of the process.

Figure 8.2 represents how a short-term closed loop controller could be incorporated under the management of a supervisory expert system.

2.2   Potential application areas within the sinter plant

Figure 8.3 summarizes the major application areas identified within the sinter plant. The major application area identified was to provide guidance on the application of control strategies. As the time cycles for response to operator actions taken can span well over an 8 h shift, it is important to maintain consistent operating practice over shift changes. By offering consistent advice 24 h/day, the expert system could help maintain the required consistency. The sinter plant management saw the educational value of an expert system as important. Our 'expert' had 25 years experience as General Foreman on this plant and has now retired. A number of the current operators will retire in the next few years. The

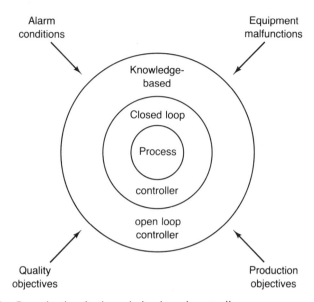

Figure 8.2   Organization for knowledge-based controller.

Figure 8.3   Application areas within the sinter plant.

management was keen that no de-skilling of the workforce should occur. In response, much of the advice offered by the system is accompanied by concepts and theoretical explanations as to why a certain action should be taken.

A module was included to simulate the starting up and shutting down of unit processes to be used as a training aid. The simulation would be knowledge-based. The module for alarm interpretation was included, though this particular plant's alarm system is not overly complex. The final two areas, plant maintenance (diagnosing faulty equipment) and resource management were identified as other potential areas of application.

2.3   Positive features of sinter plant application

The development of expert systems for commercial profit, rather than purely technical interest, ensures that the selection of a suitable application is critically important. There is still a considerable element of risk when undertaking an expert system project – and not all the obstacles are technical. Some features of the sinter plant application that have a positive impact on the likely success of this project are summarized as follows:

- *An enthusiastic expert and champion*   During his career, our expert had earned the respect of all levels of staff at the sinter plant. His enthusiasm and 'salesmanship' to the eventual users has helped smooth the introduction of the system.

- *Supportive management*   Supportive management at the sinter plant has ensured that the project would not suffer from 'organizational' obstacles.

- *An aging operator workforce*   It was the announcement of our expert's intention to retire early and the age of the existing operator workforce which prompted the sinter plant management to undertake this project.

- *An old plant*   Old plants rely more on operator heuristics than modern plants. The situation for many old plants is that modernization costs may not justify the additional productivity gained. An expert system could be a very cost-effective means of improving productivity without huge expenditure on new instrumentation.

- *Sufficiently complex to be a serious demonstration of the technology*   As a first application of expert systems technology, it was important to select an application that clearly could not be done using other technologies. The sinter plant was selected as being 'about the right size'. We had the option of concentrating only on the control strategies if the project started to look too large.

- *Relatively high value*   If the project is taken right through to full implementation, the level of savings would have a significant impact on the profitability of the plant.

- *Abundant case data* Regardless of how well a system is developed, unless there is sufficient case data, the system cannot be evaluated as successful or not. With the sinter plant the case data is abundant. The plant operates 24 h/day and data is collected either on a computer data logger or by manual means on a routine basis.

3   Objectives

3.1   Technical objectives

The technical objectives could be summarized as follows:

- demonstrate that 'process knowledge' could be captured and applied using currently available technology;
- demonstrate a variety of applications, for example, control advice, fault diagnosis, simulation as being amenable to expert systems technology; and
- demonstrate the value of advanced user interfaces in the control room environment.

3.2   Business objectives

The business objective was to prove the viability of expert systems technology. The management of any business centre is faced with a variety of technologies suitable for investment. The objective is to demonstrate to the Company that expert systems technology can prove to be a highly profitable and strategically important investment opportunity.

The specific objectives for the sinter plant are:

- a reduction in fuel usage resulting from stable process operation;
- increased production through improved tuning of the process and reduction in non-scheduled stops; and
- increase in operator skills, available through using the knowledge base as a training aid for new operators.

4   System design

4.1   Software design

Figure 8.4 summarizes the software design for the system.

4.1.1   Knowledge base

The knowledge base development was divided into three separate tasks: the 'control strategies' knowledge base, an 'alarm interpretation' knowledge base and a 'startup/shutdown simulation' knowledge base.

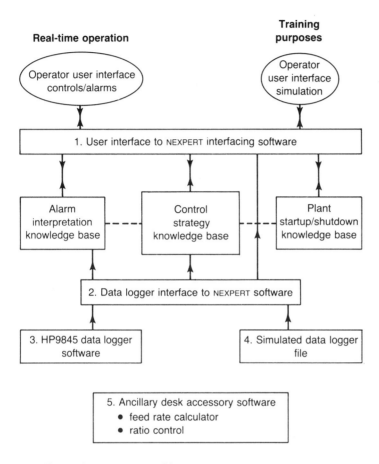

Figure 8.4   Sinter plant operator guidance system – software design.

Each knowledge base was built as a stand alone off-line prototype and then implemented for on-line testing. The control strategies and alarm interpretation knowledge bases will ultimately be incorporated into a single knowledge base. The startup/shutdown simulation knowledge base has been implemented as a stand-alone knowledge base for training purposes. The knowledge bases all use production if-then type rules and are described below.

Control strategies knowledge base   The task of the control strategies knowledge base is to capture all the major factors which may impinge on the successful control of the process. These factors can be divided into short-term and long-term factors. The short-term factors cover parameters which might vary in time cycles of up to 2 h. These parameters are monitored directly by the operator or, if available, some form of closed loop controller. The longer term factors are normally measured over days or even weeks. Factors such as quality and production requirements are monitored by management staff in cooperation with operations staff.

The first task in building the control strategies knowledge base was to structure the knowledge into the major control parameters and their relative interrelationships and importance. This task was performed using a combination of rule induction techniques (Thompson and Thompson, 1986) and reference to the literature on sinter plant control (Watanabe *et al.*, 1985; Miyagi, 1980). The initial prototype was built over a period of 2 months. Off-line testing was performed over a period of 2 months. Conversion to on-line testing required the implementation of a data logging computer to feed plant information to the knowledge-based system. The control strategies knowledge base consists of approximately 120 rules.

Alarm interpretation knowledge base The alarm interpretation knowledge base provides an explanation and interpretation of alarm conditions. There are approximately 70 rules covering different alarm conditions. The interrelationship between alarms is not complex and the interpretation is often straightforward. The value of the knowledge base is, therefore, more in the availability of on-line documentation of procedures for servicing alarms, especially those that only rarely occur. There is, however, an important relationship between alarm conditions and the control strategies knowledge base. Disruptions to the physical process caused by equipment malfunctions will often result in process upsets. The control strategies knowledge base must be aware of such disruptions in managing the control of the process.

Startup/shutdown knowledge base The building of the startup/shutdown knowledge base was prompted by examples from the literature on the use of knowledge-based simulations (Faught *et al.*, 1980) and the use of knowledge bases to build complex logic based systems, for example, control of materials handling equipment in a steel billet mill (Baba *et al.*, 1985). The billet mill example involved the use of expert system building tools to codify the complex logic required to control the automation equipment.

The authors claimed that the engineer designing the system was able to build the system in one-third the time it would normally take using conventional methods. The startup/shutdown knowledge base contains approximately 60 rules and simulates the complex logic involved with starting up and shutting down the sinter plant. The system was built over a period of about 6 months. Though no direct comparison with conventional development is available, it was felt that the testing of the system in cooperation with the expert was made much easier by the transparency of the logic or rules afforded by expert system building tools. tools.

4.1.2   Software tools

The use of a commercial expert system shell was necessary to enable us to meet our project objectives within the time frame available (12–18 months). The tool selected was a package called NEXPERT, developed by Neuron Data. NEXPERT, initially available only on the Apple Macintosh, provides a user interface approaching that of the more advanced hybrid tools, such as KEE and ART. The processing speed was of little concern as sintering is a slowly changing process, so the processing speed of the Macintosh was adequate. NEXPERT provides an excellent interface to the user and knowledge engineer. The package also possesses some sophisticated inferencing techniques to control the forward chaining requirements of the application. Perhaps the feature of NEXPERT which distinguishes it from other commercial 'shells' is the ability to embed the package within user written code. The package is supplied with a library of routines which enable user written programs to examine the status of the knowledge and initiate inferencing sessions. This ability is essential if the system is to be comfortably integrated into the 'information system environment' of the application.

4.1.3   Real-time software interface

As the system is required to operate in real-time, there is a requirement to embed the knowledge-based system within a shell, which can provide plant information to the knowledge base and provide a suitable user interface to the operator. This software was coded in Pascal and effectively 'manages' the operation of the NEXPERT knowledge base.

For testing purposes, the interfacing software is able to read status information from a disk file for simulated testing of various plant conditions.

4.1.4   Data logging software

Conventional data logging software is normally required simply to collect plant data and report either the raw or averaged data as on-screen plots or daily reports. The data logging software for the operator guidance system was given the additional task of interpreting the data collected into judgements that an expert operator would agree with. For example, when a rule in the knowledge base says:

'If the suction pressure is HIGH then. . . .'

what it may really mean is:

'If the average of the 6 suction pressure sensors (excluding any that are not working) is over 10.5 kPa and has been at that level for the last 5 min, then . . .'.

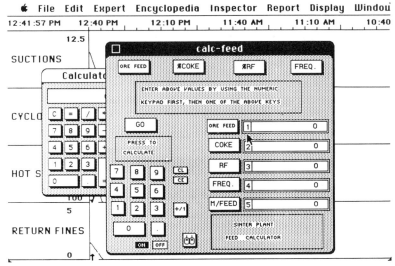

Figure 8.5   Ancillary software.

In other words, to implement the rule as it is written in the knowledge base may require substantial pretreatment of the raw data values. And if there is some debate as to what values constitute 'HIGH', a fuzzy logic approach may be required.

While the rules in the knowledge base could be tested off-line to ensure their validity, it is the tuning of the judgement determinations which will ensure that the advice arrives at the right time. The data logging software has been implemented on a Hewlett Packard HP9845 data logging computer in BASIC.

4.1.5   Ancillary software

An advantage of the Apple Macintosh is the 'desk accessory' feature, which provides tools such as calculators, notepads, scrapbooks, etc. In keeping with the objective to provide an advanced user interface, extra software was designed to perform some of the ancillary tasks for the operator, to enhance further the environment offered by the Macintosh. One of these is a customized calculator to assist with determining feed rates. Another is a system for controlling the chemical composition of the sinter mix.

Figure 8.5 shows an example of the ancillary software in operation.

4.2   Hardware configuration

Figure 8.6 describes the hardware configuration. The configuration describes the planned, rather than current, implementation. The knowledge-based system will exist on a separate processor, communicat-

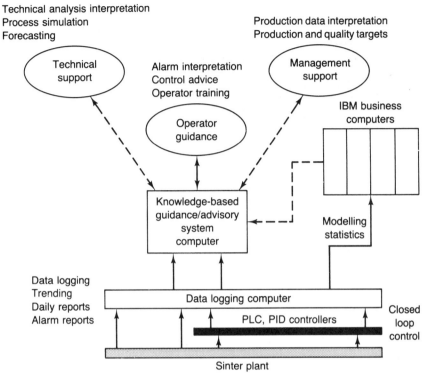

Technical analysis interpretation
Process simulation
Forecasting

Production data interpretation
Production and quality targets

Figure 8.6   Hardware configuration.

ing directly with the process data logging computer and the business mainframe. The plan is to have the knowledge-based system integrate all of the knowledge acquired from process models, statistical models and management targets with expert operator knowledge to assist with advising the operator. The present configuration has no links to the business mainframe computers or links to PID and PLC controllers.

4.3   System operation

4.3.1   Control adviser

The control adviser polls the data logging computer for all plant parameter judgements every 60 s. If the status has changed, the knowledge base is updated with the new status and an inferencing session commenced. The rules are forward chaining, so that the system attempts to infer from plant data whether a control action is necessary. The main operator screen will be updated if any single parameter has changed. The operator is alerted to the change by both a message on the screen and computer-generated voice. The change is also logged to a disk file and the printer. If a recommendation results from the last inference, a message

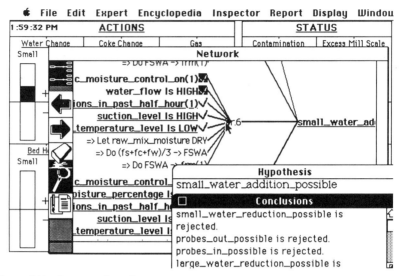

Figure 8.7   Operator interface.

stating the current plant status, the recommended action and the reason for the action is presented in a Macintosh window. At the end of each inference session the operator is able to view and print each message received, as well as use some of the NEXPERT menu options to explore the current status of the knowledge base. If, during an inference session, a piece of information is required that is not provided by the data logging computer, the operator will be asked for it. The operator then has the opportunity to ask why, to see the current rule being examined. Figure 8.7 shows an example of a typical screen that the operator may be faced with.

The top line displays the menu options available through NEXPERT. Other windows are used to ask questions, output recommendation windows or monitor rules as they are being evaluated during an inferencing session. These windows overlay a plant mimic display whenever an inferencing session is initiated by a change in plant status.

The knowledge contained within the control adviser knowledge base is of both a short-term and a long-term nature. Short-term control knowledge caters for the fine adjustments an operator may need to make to stabilize the process in the short-term. Long-term control knowledge refers to more fundamental changes to standard operating practice due to longer term drifts in quality or changed production requirements.

4.3.2   Alarm interpretation and troubleshooting

The alarm interpretation knowledge base provides mostly text and graphical explanations of what an alarm means, why it has occurred and a procedure for recovering from it. The use of this knowledge base is

Alarm:
Fresh Water Head Tank Low Level.

Low levels in the head tank suggest insufficient pumping pressure to the tank.

Action:
Put another pump on.

If no pump is available call millwright and foreman. This fault must be rectified quickly.

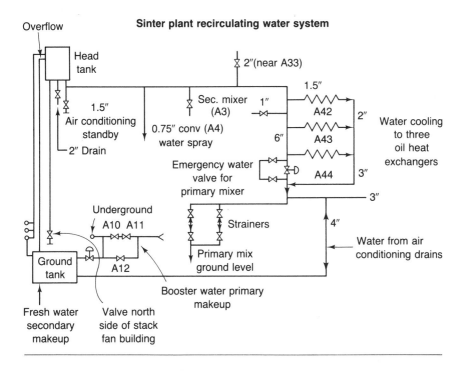

Figure 8.8   Alarm messages.

mainly to provide the operators with an accepted procedure for servicing the alarm. Some of the rarer alarms are associated with schematics which may assist maintenance personnel correct a fault. Figure 8.8 shows a typical message from the alarm system.

4.3.3   Startup and shutdown simulation

The startup/shutdown simulation has been developed as a separate knowledge base. NEXPERT was used initially to extract the knowledge about electrical interlocks, switch positions and accepted procedures. While there is no real call for transparency of rules in this application, it was thought that the use of an expert system building tool like NEXPERT

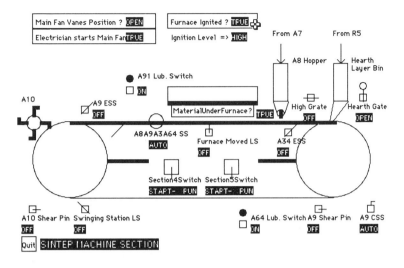

Figure 8.9   Startup/shutdown simulation.

could speed the development of the logic required of the system. After validation, using NEXPERT, the rules were then recoded in Pascal for speed. The simulation allows new operators to experiment with different ways of starting or shutting down the plant from different situations. Though the task is one of pure logic, it is still very complex. While there are standard procedures available, the experienced operators are able to perform the task much more quickly than if the standard procedures are followed. The other major benefit gained from this knowledge base is that it contains knowledge about how the equipment is designed to operate and it forms the basis for troubleshooting equipment failures. The system offers a graphical interface to the operator. A sample screen is shown in Figure 8.9.

5   Current status

The present status of the system is that the control strategy knowledge base has been installed on the plant and is now under field trial 24 h/day. The data logging software has been tuned to the extent that the judgement and timing of judgement values for plant parameters appears to be satisfactory. The operators are in general agreement with the rules in the knowledge base. However, initial evaluation of the system has shown the operator to be making more changes and earlier changes than the system is recommending. A supposition from these early results is that one cannot necessarily conclude that how an operator views the interaction of a number of parameters is merely the sum of how he or she views each parameter individually. For example, if we have a rule, such as:

IF A is High AND B is Low AND C is High
THEN condition true

being able to judge the size of A, B and C individually may not ensure that the rule will become true at the correct time. The knowledge in the rule may be perfectly correct. However, the mechanisms for judging the size of a parameter may change depending on the situation. For example, suppose an operator normally judges conditions A, B and C by the parameter moving outside a predefined limit and he or she sees that conditions A and B have become true. Rather than wait for C to reach its limit, in practice, the operator may be just looking for a hint of C moving upwards before acting. That is, the operator may be increasing the sophistication with which he or she judges a given parameter, depending on the status of other related parameters. The situation suggests the incorporation of fuzzy logic techniques to provide the operator with a quantitative 'strength' of recommendation above some predefined threshold. The incorporation of fuzzy logic techniques to manage the short-term control problem is now being undertaken.

When incorrect recommendations have been made, it has usually been due to insufficient conditions within a rule, rather than errors or conflicting rules in the knowledge base. Additions to the knowledge base are now mostly to cater for special situations that may only occur periodically and were overlooked in the initial building of the knowledge base.

The conclusion drawn from early evaluations is that the knowledge of control strategies can be extracted and represented adequately using production rules. But to make the knowledge base functional in real-time, the problem is one of careful tuning of knowledge covering the control of short-term factors and then integrating this within the knowledge required for longer term control.

Systems are now installed to collect plant data over an extended period of time, to build up sufficient case data on each type of operator change. The system could then be tuned using both statistical evidence of when past changes were made and comments by the more experienced operators on past cases.

6 Summary of experiences gained to date

Most of the literature on practical applications of expert systems have concentrated on technical issues, such as knowledge representations, inferencing mechanisms and languages. Our experiences, to date, in building a system for commercial use show that the challenge is far from purely a technical one. The following advice is offered for those contemplating a commercial expert system development.

- *Application selection is critical* Selecting the right application will be critical to the eventual success of the project. The aim should be to select applications that:
  - require only relatively small and manageable knowledge bases,
  - have an enthusiastic expert who can promote the project,
  - are easily commercially justifiable, and
  - have abundant case data available for testing purposes.

  It is important that the first serious application require a relatively short development time (say less than 2 years) yet be a convincing demonstration of the technology.

- *Integration of an expert system is critical* It would be rare to find an expert system application that did not require integration with a database, plant instrumentation or other EDP systems. Developers should be aware that the expert system development may constitute less than 50% of the total project. In fact, we see a major benefit of an expert system is the ability to integrate a variety of diverse information sources, such as statistical models, mathematical models, database information, plant instrumentation etc., into a single source of advice.

- *Expert system building tools can build serious systems* Current expert system building tools do not suffer from the many restrictions imposed by their predecessors. Our experiences mimic those of a growing number of companies who have built serious expert systems using tools on personal computers. While an expert system shell must place some restrictions on how a system is developed, one must consider the maintenance cost of supporting systems written in LISP or PROLOG, not to mention the extended development time required.

- *Live testing of expert systems is essential* Every effort should be made to have the system tested 'live' at the earliest opportunity. Our experiences have shown that an expert will typically offer 'general' rules by which to operate and a few special cases. When live testing commenced, many more special cases were thought of. Having a system in the field may help the expert and other experienced operators recall special cases for early inclusion in the knowledge base.

- *Be responsive to the user* User acceptance of any expert system is going to be difficult, especially with experienced operators. A significant hurdle to overcome is the time it can take to lift the performance of the system to a sufficiently high level.

After the novelty of the new equipment has worn off, it is easy for scepticism to set in. Our response to this situation has been to try and be as responsive to operator criticisms as possible. One of the major features of an expert system is its transparency. This can be a big selling feature with users, as they can see and understand the logic that the system is using and, therefore, be constructively critical of the system. By responding quickly to requests for rule changes or additions, the experienced operators can start to feel a part of the system. Schlumberger have reported (Smith, 1984) benefits gained from the use of an advanced user interface, providing the user with easy access to all relevant information from a single source. Their experience with the DIPMETER ADVISOR expert system was that users found the system useful well before the system was complete. Our experience using a Macintosh-style user interface and providing plant information from a single source has proved an important aid in maintaining operator interest while 'evolving' the knowledge base to a usable level. All of the operators are now comfortable with the operation of the system after only very minimal training.

Despite all of the above endeavours, ultimate acceptance will only come when the system consistently provides faster and better advice than an experienced operator could offer.

7   Future work

Our immediate aim is to monitor closely the performance of the system by comparing its recommendations with case data of previous operator actions taken. In this way the system could then be tuned, at least to match the performance of the present operating staff.

Our overall direction is to understand better the 'mental model' by which the experienced operator controls a process (Yufik and Sheridan, 1984; Edwards and Lees, 1974) and implement knowledge-based systems which represent and mimic operations based on such a model. We view the current system as a part implementation of this mental model.

In conjunction, some experimentation with statistical techniques for early detection of trends in plant data will be conducted on the plant database with a view to their use by the knowledge base. The early detection of a change in plant status should enable the system to outperform the operator in the early recommendation for control actions.

Some research work is planned to investigate further the use of inductive techniques for synthesizing 'general' operating procedures from historical plant data. While it is difficult to foresee these techniques detecting many of the special case situations that can periodically occur, they could assist with confirming what the general operating procedures are and provide some preliminary information on how to tune the system, at least to match past performance.

Incorporation of knowledge from the startup and shutdown simulation with the control strategy knowledge base is planned. The rationale for this is that, on occasions, the cause for some instability in the process may be due to equipment malfunction, rather than some inherent problem with the process itself. Not all equipment malfunctions result in alarm conditions, but monitoring of different bin levels and feed rates can assist with the diagnosis of this type of malfunction. This task, however, will require significant expansion of the existing data logging facilities.

8   Conclusions

In building an expert operator guidance system for an iron ore sinter plant, many facets of expert systems development that are not commonly reported in the literature have been experienced. While there is still considerable work to be done before the project could be deemed a success, one of the overriding thoughts coming from our experiences to date is that it is not purely technical considerations, such as knowledge representation or inferencing techniques, that will ultimately determine the success of an expert systems project. Ultimately, it will be the ability of the developers to integrate the expert system within the existing information processing environment and their ability to gain user enthusiasm for the system that will determine its success or failure.

Acknowledgements

The assistance of Maurie Saunders, General Foreman BHP Rod and Bar Products Sinter Plant (now retired) and the Sinter Plant operations and management staff are gratefully acknowledged. Programming assistance from Mr. K. Lloyd of Computer Cellar, Mayfield is also acknowledged.

References

Baba K., Yamasaki J., Nakanishi T., Kikugawa H., Takahashi T. and Fujimoto T. (1985). *Development of Process Computer Control System for a New Billet Mill*. Kawasaki Steel Corporation, Mizushima Works, Japan
Barrett M.L. (1984). *Expert Systems in Process Development Knowledge-*

Based Systems and New Generation Computing – Trends and Implications for Management. Technical Report, Dept. Management, University of Queensland

Edwards E. and Lees F. (1974). *The Human Operator in Process Control*. London: Taylor and Francis

Embrey D. and Humphreys P. (1986). Support for decision-making and problem-solving in abnormal conditions in nuclear power plants. In *Knowledge Representation for Decision Support Systems* (Methlie L.B. and Sprague R.H. eds.). North-Holland: Elsevier Science Publishers

Faught W., Klahr P. and Martins G. (1980). An artificial intelligence approach to large-scale simulation. In *Proc. 1980 Summer Computer Simulation Conf.*, Seattle WA, pp. 231–235

Larsen P.M. (1980). Industrial applications of fuzzy logic control. *Int. J. Man–Machine Studies*, **12**

Miyagi T. (1980). Process Control System of Sintering Plant. *The Sumitomo Search* No. 24, 45–55

Moore R.L., Hawkinson L.B., Knickerbocker C.G. and Churchman L.M. (1984). A real-time expert system for process control. In *IEEE Proceedings of the First Conference on Artificial Intelligence Applications*, Denver

Nida K., Itoh J., Umeda T., Kobayashi S. and Ichikawa A. (1986). Some expert system experiments in process engineering. *Chem. Eng. Res. Des.*, **64**, Sept.

Smith R.G. (1984). On the development of commercial expert systems. AI Magazine, **5**(3)

Thompson B. and Thompson W. (1986). Finding rules in data. *Byte*, 11 Nov., 149–160

Umbers I. and King P. (1980). An analysis of human decision-making in cement kiln control – the implications for automation. *Int. J. Man–Machine Studies*, **12**(1), 11–23

Watanabe M., Sasaki Y., Sogawara M., Takahashi H. and Saino M. (1985). Development of operation guide system and its application to Chiba no. 4 sintering plant. In *Proc. 4th Int. Symp. on Agglomeration*, Toronto, Canada, June 1985

Yufik Y. and Sheridan T. (1984). A Framework for Design of Operator Planning/Decision Aids: Expert System Approach, SPIE Vol. 485 Applications of Artificial Intelligence

Zadeh L.A. (1973). Outline of a new approach to the analysis of complex systems and decision processes. *IEEE Trans. Sys. Man and Cybern.* SMC-**3**(1), 28–44

9

DESPLATE: A Diagnostic Expert System for Faulty Plan View Shapes of Steel Plates

L.D. Cung
T.S. Ng
The University of Wollongong

This paper describes an expert system, DESPLATE, developed in conjunction with BHP Steel International Group, Slab & Plate Products Division, Port Kembla, to diagnose faulty plan view shapes of steel plates. In particular, a methodology for knowledge acquisition from multiple experts with different disciplinary backgrounds will be presented and discussed.

1 Introduction

The paper describes an application of an expert system technology in the diagnosis of faulty plan view shapes of the steel products in the Plate Mill, BHP Steel International Group, Slab & Plate Products Division, Port Kembla, Australia.

The project is aimed at applying the technology to an industrial environment where heavy machinery is largely controlled by digital computers. The Plate Mill can be considered as a typical site for such an application. It is an old mill which requires professional experience or so-called 'heuristics' to operate, and has been undergoing significant upgrades through application of modern state-of-the-art technology. The number of real experts is small, while the need for their expertise is great. Thus, there is strong incentive to develop an expert system to make such valuable expertise available to less experienced operators and to assist them in fault diagnosis of the mill.

Knowledge acquisition has usually been viewed as the 'bottle neck' in the process of building expert systems. The process becomes much more complicated and time-consuming when multiple experts from different backgrounds are involved. This project requires the inputs of domain experts from several disciplines, namely electrical engineering, mechanical engineering and operations. To achieve the goals set out for the project, it is important to have an appropriate methodology for knowledge acquisition. The paper presents such a methodology and discusses its application to the project.

The paper is organized as follows. In Section 2, a brief overview of the production process at the Plate Mill is given. In Section 3, problems that motivate the development of a diagnostic expert system for faulty plates, DESPLATE, are mentioned. In Section 4 we discuss a number of issues that arose in the course of developing DESPLATE. In particular, the use of both forward and backward chaining techniques and the classification of knowledge are described with reference to DESPLATE. The present status of the project is also given. Finally, in Section 5, a methdology used in the project to acquire knowledge from multiple experts from different disciplinary backgrounds is discussed.

2   The Plate Mill

To understand the extent of the fault diagnosis problem in the Plate Mill, it is necessary to have a brief overview of the setting and the production process in the mill.

The Plate Mill first started production in 1964. It is one of several rolling mills at the BHP Steel International Group, Slab & Plate Products Division, Port Kembla, Australia. Originally it was an old, traditional rolling mill where heavy machinery and men worked together around the clock to catch up with schedules. However, within the last decade, the mill has been upgraded massively with installations of new equipment, computer control systems, new control pulpits and the introduction of new rolling practices. The function of the mill is to roll reheated slabs into plates of scheduled thickness and dimensions (Kelly, 1984). The final products are of rectangular plan view shapes, up to 3300 mm wide and 180 mm thick. Each year, about 700 000 tonnes of steel plates are produced by this mill.

A schematic layout of the mill is shown in Figure 9.1. The mill has two major rolling stands, namely No. 1 and No. 2, equipped with large rolls (up to 508 mm in diameter) driven by high power electric motors (up to 4470 kW). Roll gaps and forces are maintained by large hydraulic cylinders.

Slabs coming from the reheating furnace initially go through the No. 1 stand for thickness reduction to desired width. The slabs proceed

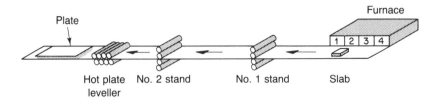

Figure 9.1   Schematic layout of the mill.

through the No. 2 stand where finishing passes are carried out and finally through the hot plate leveller which provides each slab with a smooth finishing surface.

The mill is controlled by complex and sophisticated computer systems with provision for manual override. A top-down picture of the control system is outlined as shown in Figure 9.2, where the mill control computer (MCC) receives schedules of products and performs all necessary calculations, such as mill gap settings, number of passes, etc. This information is then down-loaded to automatic gauge control (AGC) computers which directly control the hydraulic system in both stands. The equipment (motors, decoders etc.) communicates with the MCC and AGC computers through programmable logic controllers (PLC). Another auxiliary computer is used to control the final part of the mill which consists of the hot plate leveller and the cooling bed.

The mill is designed for automatic operation. However, manual override is provided to allow operators to attend to situations in which computers cannot operate effectively due to unexpected conditions, such as temperature deviations in the furnace, incoming faulty slabs, etc.

While the implementation of a sophisticated computer control system has greatly improved the productivity of the mill, as well as the quality of products, operation has also become more complex and thus faults are harder to identify. The impact of new technology is yet to be comprehended fully as only a limited number of senior staff are fully knowledgeable of the changes in the system. With their invaluable experience and knowledge acquired over years of practice, these people have quickly absorbed the new concepts, adapted themselves to changes and are considered to be experts in their fields.

Despite large budget allocations and enormous effort spent in preparing documentation for the mill, the information could not be presented in a manner that was readily suitable for fault diagnosis. In practice, there is little or no time to refer to these hard copies once alarms come on or the mill is down. In such situations, experts have to be called in regardless of time. This may become very inconvenient and time-consuming if, for example, the mill is stopped at midnight.

A remedy to the above situation is to have an expert system to assist in fault diagnosis. An expert system is a program that captures the

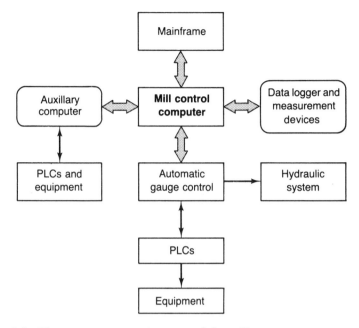

Figure 9.2   The computer control system of the mill.

knowledge of experts in a certain field and makes this knowledge available to less experienced people within that field. An important property of such a system is the ability to provide an explanation for any given advice. Therefore, if equipped with diagnostic knowledge of recognized domain experts, the expert system can become a very valuable tool in helping to reduce down-time and to improve productivity.

3   The specific problem

After reheated slabs are rolled into plates, they are transferred to the plate finishing area where they are cut to customized dimensions. The ideal plan view shape is a perfect rectangle which minimizes the waste. However, that perfect shape rarely occurs. There are unwanted operating conditions that cause the products to fall into one of the following faulty categories: camber, off-square, taper, concave or convex end, etc. Figure 9.3 illustrates an exaggerated plan view picture of the plates. Among them, camber is the most difficult shape to diagnose and it occurs quite frequently. On some occasions, as faulty plates fail to meet certain requirements, they have to be cut into smaller dimensions. This is a costly exercise and is of great concern to the Company. The goal of DESPLATE is to locate the possible causes for a particular shape and to suggest appropriate remedies.

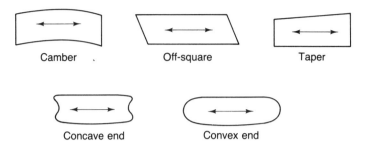

Figure 9.3 Examples of faulty shapes.

Due to complex mill settings, problems can arrive from various sources, such as:

- electrical failures;
- mechanical breakdowns or wear;
- operational errors; or
- prerolling conditions, such as incorrect temperature, faulty shapes or variable slab thickness before rolling, etc.

The diversity of domain expertise involved led to one of the great difficulties in developing DESPLATE, that is, knowledge acquisition from multiple experts with multiple disciplinary backgrounds. The approach taken to tackle this problem will be discussed in Section 5 of this paper. In Section 4 we will look at how DESPLATE works.

4   DESPLATE

In a typical consultation session, DESPLATE first prompts its user with a set of possibly observable facts that may have been noticed by the user prior to, or during, the session. Step by step, responses from the user will lead DESPLATE to come up with a set of most likely causes, as well as appropriate corrective actions. The user may be asked to carry out certain tests or measurements and to provide results to DESPLATE, which will then carry out analysis and provide interpretation of the results. Graphic routines written in Turbo-Pascal are also used to convey information to the user whenever description is either lengthy or confusing.

To understand how the system works, it may be desirable to look at the principle underlying its control strategy and knowledge representation.

Control strategy

There are two basic control strategies for expert systems, known as 'forward chaining' and 'backward chaining'. In forward chaining, the reasoning proceeds from data to conclusion. Given data or symptoms, the system makes appropriate deductions until a certain conclusion is reached. In backward chaining, the process is reversed. A certain goal is initially assumed and the inference engine would seek relevant data to prove it. If the goal turns out to be false, the system can undo a previous assumption and start with another.

According to our experience in this project, neither of these strategies alone seems to simulate adequately the way human fault finders appear to exercise their expertise (Merry, 1983). For diagnosis in an environment like the Plate Mill where sources of faults are widespread, experts would first rely on observable symptoms to distinguish between areas of fault by rejecting negative possibilities. When a particular domain is identified, relevant tests may be used to identify the fault. However, it is not always possible to prove explicitly that a particular fault exists. In such cases, experts have to make some educated guesses to reach appropriate conclusions.

To simulate this type of activity, a combination of both strategies is used. The mixed strategy works like this:

- start with forward chaining to narrow down the search;
- when the search domain is reasonably narrow, a certain fault can be assumed and if all symptoms required to prove that fault are known, backward chain to prove it; and
- if it is not possible to carry out backward chaining (perhaps due to missing subsets of knowledge), continue forward chaining.

The concepts are implemented using an expert system shell, LEVEL 5, which supports both forward and backward chaining. The changes in strategy are controlled by careful arrangement of production rules within the knowledge base (LEVEL 5 Users' Manual, 1987).

An example of the type of rule that generates forward chaining is as follows:

RULE 2.0.2 For speed mismatch between slew rolls

IF Slab twists while running over a set of slew rolls
AND Observe more closely and select \ Bar slews when broadsiding
THEN Check for faults when start and stop
AND NOT Check for speed mismatch

Now, if the conditions of this rule are satisfied then the inference engine would continue with the subdomain where the simple fact 'Check for faults when start and stop' is true. For example, there are 7 rules in that family, and each is similar to rule 2.2.1 shown below.

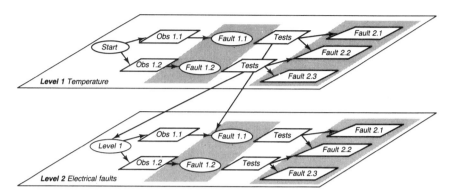

Figure 9.4   An example of the classification of knowledge.

RULE 2.2.1 For faults when start and stop

IF Check for faults when start and stop
AND Run the roll in short bursts, you find \ A slow starting roll
AND Check sideguards \ Roll is not rubbing on sideguards
THEN Problem with bearings

In rule 2.2.1, backward chaining is applied. The goal 'Problem with bearings' is assumed and all conditions are exhausted before the next rule is considered.

Meanwhile, all the rules belonging to the family of 'Check for speed mismatch' are inhibited as the result of rule 2.0.2.

Classification of the knowledge

The knowledge is classified into a number of hierarchical levels. There are two main principles which govern the arrangement of the entire knowledge base: time and frequency of occurrence of fault. The mill is rolling continuously 24 h/day to meet its schedules. Thus, observations or tests that can readily be carried out would have higher priority. On the other hand, faults that rarely occur should only be tested when everything else has failed.

The priorities determine the order in which information is presented to the user. By doing so, the most common faults should be detected after a short consultation session.

The structure of the knowledge base is illustrated in Figure 9.4, where:

- *Obs* Observations. These are carefully chosen facts or symptoms that help the user to identify certain 'families' of faults.

- *Tests* Special tests or actions normally carried out by experts to generate further information necessary to identify a particular fault.

- *Faults* These are causes of the problem we are trying to solve. They are divided into several hierarchical levels due to their nature. Normally, first level faults are not shown to the user, they only help to narrow down the search. However, the final faults are very specific and are usually followed by a set of corrective actions.

If all tests at level 1 fail, DESPLATE will continue to search for faults at level 2. However, it is also possible for the system to infer directly from a positive test result at level 1, some conclusion in another level (see Figure 9.4).

Current status

The project of developing DESPLATE started in January 1987. It is presently deployed at three locations within the Plate Mill. The knowledge bases consist of a total of about 200 production rules, while the source files occupy approximately 200 Kb of memory. The system runs either on IBM PC or compatibles, preferably with enhanced graphic adapter card. It can assist less experienced operators in the diagnosis of three common faulty shapes: camber, off-square and taper.

In a recent demonstration to experienced operators, the system was found to be satisfactory; solutions and recommendations it provided matched nicely with the operators' anticipations. The only complaint that one operator had was, 'How come it doesn't know what I don't know?'

5 A methodology for knowledge acquistion from multiple experts from different disciplinary backgrounds

There are many different approaches to the problem of knowledge acquisition (KA) from multiple experts (Mittal and Dym, 1985; Hart, 1986; McGraw and Seale, 1987a). The main emphasis of these techniques is on group interactions and group dynamics. Nevertheless, little concern is given to the problem of multiple disciplinary backgrounds, where each member of the group possesses a different subdomain of expertise. Moreover, these methodologies do not readily lend themselves for KA, in general, as the experience acquired from each expert system is quite unique. A knowledge engineer should always carry out preliminary analysis of each case before applying a suitable methodology.

The following section describes a four-stage methodology for knowledge acquisition that has been applied to this project. The concept of modelling experts will be discussed in relation to the methodology and shown to improve the effectiveness of the KA process (Cung and Ng, 1987).

The methodology consists of four stages. First, we discuss factors concerning identification of a model for multiple experts. Next, we consider important attributes in forming the multiple expert team (MET). The most important part of the methodology will follow with detailed description of the KA techniques and finally the process of verifying the acquired knowledge will be discussed.

5.1   Identification of a model for the multiple experts

The first step in building an expert system (ES) is to select competent domain experts. Various techniques have been proposed for selecting domain experts (McGraw and Seale, 1987a). These range from interviewing each expert individually to giving a sample problem to a group of nominated experts and using their performance in this problem to select the most suitable persons. In this project, the later method is applied. The sample problem is to construct a diagnostic ES for the off-square pattern which the domain experts agreed unanimously to be the most straightforward case. Our knowledge engineer also visited the Plate Mill frequently to gain a better view of the problem domain as well as more accurate evaluation of the domain experts.

In dealing with experts from different disciplinary backgrounds the important factors are:

1. *Domain expertise*   The person must possess a level of knowledge commensurate with other colleagues in the same field.

2. *Communication ability*   The person must be willing to cooperate and be able to communicate relatively well with the knowledge engineer and other experts.

Consequently, a group of multiple experts was chosen with one member from each discipline. The remaining domain experts were invited to be consultants whose contributions are valuable at a later stage.

During this initial stage the knowledge engineer and the selected domain experts worked together to identify the problem under consideration and to set an overall goal for the project (Buchanan *et al.*, 1983). Camber was then chosen to be the next target.

An essential task for the knowledge engineer at this stage is to construct a model for each expert (Cung and Ng, 1987). Multiple experts from multiple disciplines usually possess two types of expertise:

1. *Isolated expertise*   The area of expertise known and practised by one of the experts of which the others have no significant knowledge.

2.   *Related expertise*   The area of expertise that involves the knowledge and experience of at least two experts; each has relatively important contributions to the solution.

The amount of 'related expertise' required to solve a set problem would give a good indication of whether to treat the experts as a group or, alternatively, to acquire information from each expert individually.

The ability to express oneself systematically or to solve problems analytically should also be noticed. It is well known among the knowledge engineering community that it is far easier to retrieve information from those with an analytical mind than from those without one. This information would help the knowledge engineer in choosing a more appropriate way to communicate with the experts.

5.2   Formation of a multiple expert team (MET)

With careful analysis of results of the sample problem (off-square), we decided to form a multiple expert team (MET) and to prepare the team for information retrieval (Cung and Ng, 1987; McGraw and Seale, 1987a).

In a typical knowledge acquisition process, the sequence of questions asked by the knowledge engineer would fall into the 'WHAT-HOW-WHY' pattern, that is:

1.   The questions should be designed to identify the specific problem(s) to be solved, for example:

   '*What* do you want to diagnose?' or
   '*What* do you want to design?' etc.

2.   Extract the problem-solving techniques of the experts, for example:

   '*How* do you diagnose "this"?'

3.   And, finally, the explanations of why certain conclusions are arrived at, for example:

   '*Why* do you use this test to detect that fault?'

Similarly, to maximize the chance of retrieving the most relevant information, the domain experts must be prepared to know *what* information they are expected to provide, *how* the information would be acquired, and preferably *why* the acquisition process should be carried out using the proposed method.

If domain experts are well aware of what they are expected to contribute they may be more active, not only in answering specific questions, but also in extending answers to relevant issues.

We clearly explained to the MET all techniques to be used in the next stage and encouraged them to ask questions such as, why such techniques should be used. The purposes are to gain consensus from the experts and to create a relaxed atmosphere necessary for the next stage.

To reduce the representation mismatch between the way experts state their knowledge and the way it must be represented in a program, we briefly introduce to the MET the proposed structure for the knowledge base.

At the end of this stage, the multiple experts are ready for information retrieval. There is a direct tradeoff between efforts spent in this stage and the time required for the subsequent stages. The more clearly the domain experts know what they have to supply, the fewer iterative steps will be needed to refine the knowledge base.

5.3   Information retrieval from the multiple expert team

During this stage, the multiple expert team members are brought together to provide specific problem-solving expertise. The process is divided into two phases.

Phase 1: brainstorming (Osborn, 1953)

Initially, this is designed to stimulate ideas and to encourage experts to provide as much information as possible on the subject under consideration. Information acquired in this phase is to be evaluated in phase 2.

Phase 2: group evaluation techniques (Cung and Ng, 1987)

The underlying principle in this stage is to concentrate only on problems that require elaborations from more than one expert. The major activities involved in this phase are:

1.   The knowledge engineer presents to the multiple expert team members all the available information. This information includes techniques or strategies used by the multiple expert team members to solve the problem under consideration.

2.   The multiple expert team members classify the information into two major groups:

   (a)   *Isolated expertise*   To save the experts' time, information in this category will be dealt with outside the meeting. The concerned experts will be approached individually using conventional methods (Buchanan *et al.*, 1983; McGraw and Seale, 1987b).

   (b)   *Related expertise*   The involved experts are invited to join an evaluation process.

The rules for this process are presented in Cung and Ng (1987). The main idea is to take advantage of the meetings to make the experts resolve their solutions together and this combined effort should be carefully recorded. The model is continuously updated to keep record of areas of related expertise identified during this process. Knowing the ability of each expert, the knowledge engineer could carefully conduct the KA process at the most appropriate level to suit those involved.

5.4   Verification of the acquired knowledge

In this stage the information acquired is exposed to experts, both participants and non-participants, for thorough verification. The aims are two-fold: first, to enhance the validity of the information, and second, to allow the domain experts to familiarize themselves with the way their knowledge is represented explicitly, thereby reducing representation mismatch.

The information acquired will be transcribed into a readable form, for example, a 'knowledge tree', and then given back to each multiple expert team member for assessment. Collaboration between the knowledge engineer and each individual at this stage would be useful to achieve the following goals:

1.   correction of incorrect terminologies or misinterpretation of certain ideas and concepts,

2.   acquisition of more detailed explanations, and

3.   identification of missing or incomplete subsets of information.

Feedbacks from experts are evaluated using the group evaluation techniques (GET) mentioned in Section 5.3. This interactive process is carried out until the information is satisfactory. The acquired information can now be exposed to 'consultants' (refer to Section 5.2) for further assessments. The feedback from these, including criticisms and contributions, will then be subject to discussion using GET. At the end of this stage the knowledge base should be ready for encoding into an expert system.

Conclusion

This paper has reported the development of DESPLATE, an application of expert system technology at the Plate Mill, BHP Steel International Group, Slab & Plate Products Division, Port Kembla. The project involved contributions from multiple domain experts from multiple disciplines. An appropriate methodology for knowledge acquisition has also been presented with reference to the project. The system also incorporates graphics routines written in Turbo-Pascal to provide users with useful colour graphics interfaces.

DESPLATE can assist operators to diagnose the off-square, camber and taper shapes. At the present time, further development of the system is being carried out. The completion date of the project is expected to be mid-1988.

Acknowledgements

We acknowledge the valuable contributions from the multiple expert team members: M. Bogovac, G. Hall, D. Mather, P. Tolhurst and G. Venables. We also thank the consultants: J. Wood, W. Taylor, D. Goard and B. Baker for their valuable comments on the acquired information. We deeply appreciate the ongoing support from Mr. R. Evans, Mr. D. Riley, Mr. G. Rozmus of CEED and the Plate Mill managerial staff.

References

Buchanan, B.G., Barstow D., Bechtel R., Bennett J., Clancey W., Kulikowski C., Mitchell T.M. and Waterman D.A. (1983). Constructing an expert system. In *Building Expert Systems* (Hayes-Roth F., Waterman D. and Lenat D.). Reading MA: Addison-Wesley

Buchanan B.G. (1986). Expert systems: working systems and the research literature. *Expert Systems*, 3(1)

Cung L.D. and Ng T.S. (1987). *Modelling Multiple Experts For Knowledge Acquisition*, submitted for publication.

Hakami B. and Newborn J. (1983). Expert system in heavy industry: an application of ICLX in British Steel Corporation works. *ICL Technical J.*, 3 November, 347–359

Harmon P. and King P. (1985). *Expert Systems, AI in Business*. John Wiley and Sons

Hart A. (1986). *Knowledge Acquisition For Expert Systems*. St. Louis, MO: McGraw-Hill

Hayes-Roth F., Waterman D. and Lenat D. (1983). *Building Expert Systems*. Reading MA: Addison-Wesley

Kelly P. (1984). 3500 mm plate mill and plate finishing equipment summary. *Australian Irons and Steels*, April

LEVEL 5 User's Manual, PC Version. (1987). Information Builders, Inc.

McGraw K. and Seale M. (1987a). Multiple expert knowledge acquisition methodology. In *Proc. 3rd Third Australian Conf. Applications of Expert Systems*, May

McGraw K. and Seale M. (1987b). Structured knowledge acquisition for combat aviation. In *Proc. NAECON 1987*, May

Merry M. (1983). APEX3: An expert system shell for fault diagnosis. *GEC J. Research*, **1**(1), 39–47

Mittal S. and Dym C.L. (1985). Knowledge acquisition from multiple experts. *AI Magazine*, **6**(2), Summer

Osborn A. (1953). *Applied Imagination: Principles and Procedures of Creative Thinking*. New York: Scribner's

Pau L.F. (1986). Survey of expert systems for fault detection, test generation and maintenance. *Expert Systems*, **3**(2)

Simon H.A. (1969). *The Science Of The Artificial*. Cambridge, MA: MIT Press

10
Expert System Techniques in Spatial Planning Problems

R.B. Stanton

Australian National University

H.G. Mackenzie

Commonwealth Scientific and Industrial Research Organization

The paper describes the use of deductive rule-based techniques in spatial planning problems. These problems are characterized by having spatial predicates in rule antecedents, and by the need to generate objects with spatial properties within the deductive process. One such problem, that of 'region management' planning, is discussed in some detail, whilst another in the command and control area is described briefly. In 'region management' planning, the goal is to classify a set of geographic regions into a number of region zone types according to rules which represent knowledge of managing the regions. A consistent and complete set of management policy rules is developed by interactively modifying the rules in response to the detection of conflicts in classifying regions. The deductive consequences of the rules are made available to the planner in each cycle of the planning process. In the command and control problem, regions where incompatible activities might occur are inferred from an operations plan. To provide appropriate forms for representing planning policies, extensions to the standard backward chaining rule forms are described.

1 Introduction

There is now a very wide literature on expert systems and their distinguishing characteristics (for example, see Waterman, 1986). Central to the distinction between expert and other kinds of systems are the issues of acquiring problem domain knowledge and representing it in a form suitable for use in finding reasoned solutions to problems. This paper discusses a class of spatial planning problems in which domain knowledge is about deriving plans for the management of regions according to their spatial and aspatial attributes. We will be interested in the representation, acquisition, consistency and completeness of such knowledge. Much of the discussion will revolve around case studies.

Planning problems have long been of interest in AI partly because they can be described as search problems in which goal predicates, initial states and formation rules have clear problem domain interpretations (as world states, actions, and so on). In their general form such problems explore an extremely large search space since they involve reasoning about plans as sequences of conditional actions. However, in their particularized form, they can often be construed as classification problems. The 'region management' planning problem can be put into this form.

A region management plan divides an area (often geographic) into zoned regions, each region having a single zone and each zone standing for a set of permissions allowing or denying particular activities in any region so zoned. Regions can overlap and may or may not cover their associated area. Region boundaries might be synthesized in the planning process.

Zones are described by the set of activity permissions and prohibitions they license. Activities may be singular with persistent effects (such as the construction of a road in a land-use plan) or generic with multiple transitory effects (such as defining a flight corridor in an air-space plan).

An area to be planned is described by a group of objects having a number of aspatial attributes (some fixed, some under the control of the planner) and having spatial attributes which interrelate them to the area in which they are embedded.

The planning task takes place in the context of overall policy criteria which must be satisfied by any resultant plan. Typically, overall policy consists of general guidelines rather than prescriptions for the generation of plans. It is the planners' responsibility to integrate their knowledge of planning issues with policy directives and thereby to develop the basis for determining a particular plan. From this point of view, the planning task can be regarded as one of extending policy until it becomes strong enough to determine a plan for a specific situation (that is, until a plan can be seen as a preferred inference from the extended policy). Such extensions must form complete and consistent knowledge bases.

The classification planning problem then has two main require-ments. The first is for a plan generation system which assigns zones to regions in ways that satisfy management policies for the region. The second is for an acquisition system which allows planners to develop policy by adding their expertise to the knowledge base used in plan generation.

The remainder of the paper describes a system, SPECS, which meets these requirements. SPECS has three subsystems: one for inferencing, one for spatial database support and one for interactive graphics support. The operational theme running through the operation of SPECS is that, as planners develop and refine policy rules, they are given ready access to the deductive consequences of the rules viewed as constructors of, or constraints on, possible zone maps. In common with the use of expert systems technology in other areas, SPECS provides explanations for all inferences made from its knowledge base.

The SPECS system has been applied to problems in National Park planning and to command and control operations planning. These applications are used below to illustrate the operation of SPECS.

2   Illustrative example: two approaches to spatial classification planning

This section describes a spatial classification planning task associated with the management of a National Park. The approach promoted by the SPECS system is compared briefly to a constraints satisfaction approach to the same task.

The Great Barrier Marine National Park consists of five sections, one of which is called the Cairns Sections. The Cairns Section is covered by approximately 500 regions which have been designated 'atomic' regions for the purpose of assigning zones. Typically, each region either contains a geographic feature, such as a reef or shoal, or is an expanse of water either closely associated with such features or identified for its existing uses (such as shipping, fishing, etc.).

The problem of planning the Cairns Section has been studied by Cocks et al. (1982), using an approach based on LUPLAN (ibid), a 'land use' planning system developed at the CSIRO. The base data used in the LUPLAN study was made available for the SPECS experiment. Region boundaries were obtained by digitizing a large scale map of the Section. Figure 10.1 shows regions in the Cairns Section classified by two properties: those containing commercial shipping lanes and those containing reefs or shoals.

Activities to be controlled by zoning include fishing, swimming, collecting, trolling, sight-seeing, recreational boating, and so on. The relationship between zones and activity permissions can be found in Cocks et al. (1982). More or less in order of increasing permissibility, the zones are named Preservation (P), Scientific Research (SR), Seasonal Closure (S), Marine National Park Type A and B (MNPA and MNPB),

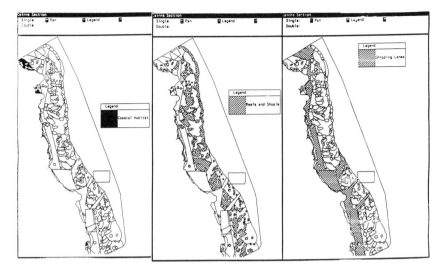

Figure 10.1

General Use Type A and B (GUA and GUB). (These abbreviations are used freely below.)

Policy rules given in Cocks *et al.* (1982) are illustrated by the following examples.

- A.1   All mapping units (regions) classified as SC (coastal shipping lane) or ST (transverse shipping lane) will be zoned GUA.

- B.7   As far as possible, ensure that areas associated with existing offshore national parks or within 5 km of existing coastal national parks and nature reserves are zoned as MNPA, MNPB or S.

- B.11   As far as possible, ensure that inter-reef areas are not zoned GUA.

- B.12   As far as possible, ensure that fringing reefs and near-shore areas are zoned MNPA or MNPB.

Before looking at the representation problems for the expert systems approach to plan generation associated with policies of this kind, we will briefly review the way LUPLAN solves the generation problem.

In the LUPLAN scheme, policy rules are translated into components of an objective function used in a hill climbing search for a zone map of 'maximum goodness'. 'Goodness' here is a measure of the extent to which regions which are suitable for certain activities are zoned so as to permit those activities to take place, and vice versa for activities which are not suited to particular regions.

The planner provides an 'initial zone map' as the point in the search space where the climb begins. Different start maps may lead to different 'final zone maps' as, of course, do variations in the coefficients provided for the objective function. By providing different initial zone maps, local 'best' solutions can be obtained. By changing coeffients in the objective function, different weights can be given to competing policies.

As mentioned above, the SPECS solution to the zoning problem is based on an approach very different from the one used in LUPLAN. Both systems accept that region data taken together with given policy statements result in a highly under-determined system (initially at least). Whereas the LUPLAN approach accepts this low level of determinism and proceeds to find local maxima on a surface defined by coefficients relating rules and region attributes, the SPECS approach is to assist the planner to remove the non-determinism (as far as possible) by refinement and development of policy (that is, by strengthening rules in one way or another).

The extent to which most of the non-determinism can be removed from typical region use planning tasks by this method is an experimental matter. However, for some classes of problems, it is clear that planning decisions do, indeed, remove all non-determinism. Further, by seeing the planner's task as one of decision-making through rule strengthening, the SPECS approach provides a base both for justification of reasoning and for generating explanations about particular zone maps.

3   Representation and inferencing: plan generation

System design issues fall into the following areas:

- descriptive adequacy of the usual antecedent/consequent rule schemas;
- the need for interactive graphics to be integrated into the deduction/answering process;
- the use of external databases as persistent stores for rules and spatial and aspatial data;
- the need for efficient recovery of spatial relations from a large spatial database; and
- the detection of consistency and completeness among sets of policy rules involved in planning experiments.

Knowledge representation and associated inferencing issues are discussed below. The other matters, mostly concerned with software engineering problems, are outside the scope of the paper.

The design of SPECS proceeds from standard ideas about building rule-based systems. For example, a zoning plan can be seen as a binary relation over the set of regions and the set of zone classifications, each member of the relation being deduced from base region attributes by policy seen as deduction rules. However, the policy rules illustrated earlier challenge knowledge representation and inferencing techniques in a number of ways. Specifically, difficulties are caused by:

1.   disjunctive consequences,

2.   negated consequences,

3.   spatial predicates over regions, and

4.   the qualifier 'as far as possible'.

Rules in SPECS allow disjunctive and negated consequences to be expressed directly. The associated inferencing processes are described below.

The need to compute a range of spatial relationships over relatively large amounts of coordinate data are handled with a deductive spatial database system using techniques described in Abel and Smith (1984).

The 'as far as possible' qualifier is used to finesse the problem of consistency since it can always be appealed to in rejecting any rule that would otherwise generate conflicting classifications. For this reason, the qualifier is not supported in SPECS. Instead, unqualified versions of the rules are used. The conflicts generated by the unqualified rules are detected in the plan generation process and resolved by refining the conflict supporting rules accordingly.

Difficulties 1–4 aside, the standard antecedent/consequent rule representation techniques are used to capture planning policy. The resultant rule set is used to answer queries in a backward chaining inferencing procedure. Procedural attachment is used in rules for spatial database access.

Plan generation consists of inferring the zone(_region,_zone-class) relation from the policy rule set, and the subsequent display of that relation as a map. Figure 10.2 shows a map of regions in the northern part of the Cairns Section. The map illustrates several points.

The policy rules unambiguously classify some regions as members of a particular zone class (for example, Preservation zone). A complete, consistent rule set will classify all regions in this way.

Regions labelled 'Possibly ...' are those which have the embedded classification in a possible world. Possible worlds are generated by disjunctive consequents as described below.

Regions labelled 'unassigned' indicate rule set incompleteness. Those labelled 'conflict' indicate rule set inconsistency.

The systems provide expert system-styled explanations for each of these categories. In particular, explanations of inconsistency give the supports for conflict and thereby assist the planner in finding a resolution. The planning cycle is based on this kind of explanation.

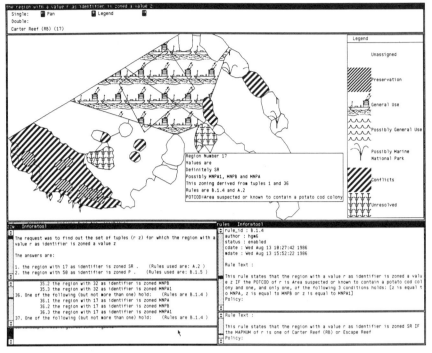

Figure 10.2

4   Inconsistency detection and resolution: the planning cycle

Policy rules vary from guidelines for assigning a zone to a particular region to strict criteria for acceptance of a final zone map. The construction of zoning maps involves planners in mixing the directives of policy rules with a range of unformalized practical considerations. When represented in rule form, the result of the combined policy and planning knowledge can inadvertently give rise to inconsistencies.

It is apparent that a zone relation inferred from a consistent set of rules is a total function. During the development of a plan, however, for reasons just mentioned, rules may not be consistent and accordingly the relation will not be functional. In turn, this will cause multiple assignment of zones to some regions and no assignments at all to others (see Davis, 1985). Incremental removal of inconsistencies of this kind form the basis of the planning cycle.

The derivation of the zone relation can be examined both textually and graphically (see Figure 10.2). For any region, the rules involved in the zoning for that region, the zone values derived, and the base data held for the region are made available through a graphical browser.

The derivation tree for any tuple generator may also be examined by means of the explanation subsystem. The explanation system also explains why tuples were not derived.

Conflicts are resolved by modifying the rule set, typically by strengthening the antecedents of rules (so that they are less general). Strengthening rules in this way can cause incompleteness in an otherwise complete set. In this case, the rule set has to be broadened to make the relationship bigger (usually by adding rules).

If the 'zone' relation were a function from _r to _z, we could display it by assigning colours or textures to values of _z and colouring each region _r with the appropriate colour or texture. However, when it is not a function, 'conflicts', or regions occur where the functionality condition is violated and must be displayed differently. A full discussion of this is given in Stanton and Mackenzie (1987b).

5   Rule extensions

This section contains an overview of the mechanism used in SPECS for deriving relations. Stanton and Mackenzie (1987b) contains a more detailed account.

A relation computed by SPECS is a set of 'tuple' objects, each of which has the following form, where the θ and φ are substitutions:

- θ, a simple tuple generator derived from the standard type of rules which do not contain constructive negations or disjunctive consequents;

- $\langle \theta$ except $\varphi 1, \varphi 2, ...\rangle$, an exception tuple generator derived when a constructive negation operator appears in the antecedent of a rule; and

- $\langle$choose $\theta 1, \theta 2 ...\rangle$, a disjunction tuple generator, from rules with disjunctive consequents.

Given a set of variables $\{x1, x2 ...\}$ a simple tuple generator represents the set of ground instances of the term 'tuple(x1, x2, ...)' under the substitution θ. SPECS is explicitly designed for grounded answer relations so questions of intepretations of variables will not be discussed here.

The usefulness of constructive negation arises where it is not convenient or efficient to fix the domain of interpretation for an expression. For example in:

not P(x) $^\wedge$ Q(x) ...

we wish to restrict the tuples satisfying Q(x) to those not satisfying P(x) without enumerating the domain of P.

Rules B.7 and B.12 in Section 2 have disjunctive consequents.

Such rules are not represented in that way but as standard rules which have a consequent which is the 'most specific' generalization of the set of disjunctions, and with an 'exclusive or' expression in the antecedent. This syntactic constraint was imposed for efficiency in searching the database. The XOR operator constructs 'multiple worlds', one for each of the disjuncts. Subsequent unifications take place independently within each of the worlds. Thus rule B.12, represented by:

fringereef(_r) ^ (_z = "MNPA" XOR _z = "MNPB") => zone(_r,_z)

can produce a disjunction tuple generator in which two new worlds are established, the associated substitution for one containing "MNPA" for _z and the other, "MNPB". Disjunction tuple generators also carry identification of the choice points which produced them, allowing split worlds to be reunited by an answer processing operation which carries out case analysis. In this way SPECS can deduce 'zone(r1,"P")' from the three rules.

dugong_habitat(_r, high) => zone(_r, "P") dugong_habitat(_r, medium)
=> zone(_r, "p")
=> dugong_habitat(_r, medium) or dugong_habitat(_r, high)

since both worlds generated by the choice point in the third rule eventually contain 'zone(r1,"P")'.

Rule B.11 in Section 2 has a negated consequent. Rules of this form are supported in SPECS by constraint rules of an 'if deduced' kind, where demons prohibit the existence of certain answer tuples.

Thus we could represent rule B.11, (naïvely 'inter-reef(_r) => not zone(_r,GUA)') as a demon which checks for the generation of an assertion unifying with 'zone(_r,GUA)' and allows it if it is not the case that 'inter-reef(_r)' for that unification.

6   Another example

This section describes an application of the SPECS system to a command and control problem. In contrast to the park planning application where the extent of regions to be zoned is given as part of the fixed attributes of regions, in the problem described here, such boundaries are inferred by the management rules.

The map shown in Figure 10.3 contains two patrol paths and two artillery bombardment areas. Part of the command and control problem sketched here is to take collections of such objects and to check them for compatibility from an operational viewpoint; that is, for the presence of mutual interactions which should be brought to the attention of the planner.

Knowledge about potential incompatibilities between objects in the

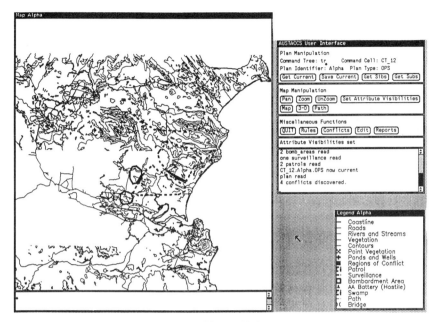

Figure 10.3

controlled area is encoded as rules of the kind described earlier. For example, one source of incompatibility is captured by:

> friendly patrols should not be placed in close temporal and spatial proximity lest misidentification difficulties occur

This planning rule rests on definitions about 'closeness' in time and space. In practice, the latter can be a complicated relation on the terrain over which patrols are scheduled. These definitions are encoded in additional rules which currently compute temporally overlapping patrols for closeness in time and intersecting, fixed width corridors around patrol paths for closeness in space.

Another incompatibility is:

> patrols must not be routed such that they are likely to pass through a bombardment area

that is, for a patrol and a bombardment area which overlap temporally, the patrol corridors cannot intersect the bombardment region. There are a large number of similar rules which are used to guide operations planning.

The results of applying such rules to the objects shown in Figure 10.3 are displayed in Figure 10.4. In this case, regions of incompatibility found by SPECS are shaded on a scaled map of the terrain.

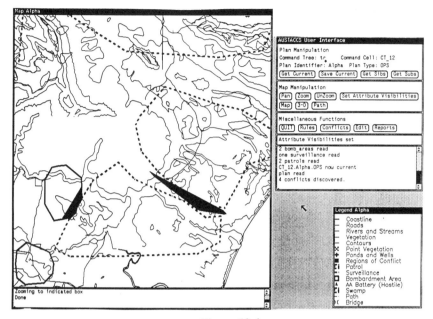

Figure 10.4

Spatial predicates in rule antecedents are recovered by procedural attachment to the spatial database component, a deductive database containing a computational geometry engine.

7   Summary

The central thesis of the work reported in this paper is that expert systems technology can be used to construct effective solutions to spatial classification planning problems.

The method involves seeing the planning task as one of devising complete and consistent policy by iteratively strengthening the set of rules and making their deductive consequences readily available to the planner. Solutions for an interesting range of problems are being constructed using this method. Ongoing developments are expected to produce improvements in the following areas:

- rule forms for expressing policy and associated reasoning strategies;

- detection of rule set completeness;

- efficient spatial inferencing techniques over large databases; and

- interactive graphics services tightly coupled to the deduction processes.

Acknowledgements

Some passages in this paper are edited versions of work previously reported in Stanton and Mackenzie (1987a). They are included with permission of the Australian Computer Society. The work is part of a joint project on 'spatial inferencing systems' between the Computer Science Department, ANU and the Division of Information Technology, CSIRO, and is supported, in part, by an Information Technology Grant. John Smith, CSIRO, a co-researcher in the program, directed the construction of the spatial database interface and contributed to the analysis of the reefplan application. The authors would like to thank the Division of Water Resources, CSIRO and the Great Barrier Reef Marine National Park Authority for making available the data involved in the LUPLAN study.

References

Abel D.J. and Smith J.L. (1984). A data structure and query algorithm for a database of areal entities. *Aust. Comput. J.*, **16**(4), 147

Anderson J.R., Wood N. and Baird I.A. (1982). *Mapping Units and Data for the Cairns Section Planning Exercise*. Technical Memorandum 82/9, CSIRO Division of Water and Land Resources

Cocks K.D., Baird I.A. and Anderson J.R. (1982). *Application of the SIRO-PLAN Planning Method to the Cairns Section of the Great Barrier Reef Marine Park, Australia*. Technical Memorandum 82/1, CSIRO Division of Water and Land Resources

Davis J.R. (1985). ADAPT: an aid for devising zoning schemes. In *Microcomputers for Local Government Planning and Management* (Newton P. and Taylor A., eds.). Melbourne: Hargreen

De Kleer J. (1986). An assumption based TMS. *Artificial Intelligence*, **28**, 127–162

Doyle J. (1979). A truth maintenance system. *Artificial Intelligence*, **12**, 231–272

Stanton R.B. and Mackenzie H.G. (1987a). A graphical oriented deductive planning system. *Aust. Comput. J.*, **19**(2), 76–83

Stanton R.B. and Mackenzie H.G. (1987b). Deduction based region use planning. In *Proc. IJCAI 10*, 584–587, Los Altos: Morgan Kaufmann

Waterman D.A. (1986). *A Guide to Expert Systems*. Reading MA: Addison-Wesley

11

The Development of Victorian Business Assistance Referral System – VBARS

Stephen Nethercote

ANZ Bank

This case study stems from the development of the VBARS expert system. The development was undertaken as a research and development exercise to test the TODAY-ES shell we had incorporated into the TODAY 4GL.

This paper chronicles our experiences while designing and developing the VBARS application. The reader should acquire an understanding of how this expert system works and how we approached the development. Our major points of interest – knowledge acquisition and integration – have received extra attention.

---

1 Introduction

This report covers aspects of the use of TODAY-ES to build the VBARS expert system. VBARS was written for the Department of Industry, Technology and Resources (DITR) in Victoria, Australia.

Section 2 refers to the background of the project and the reasons for its existence. The project was undertaken as an R&D exercise. The cost–benefit will be in terms of knowledge gained and publicity.

Section 3 discusses the project itself. The reader should gain an understanding of what the expert system is trying to achieve. VBARS is more than an expert system: it is written as an application. It has file maintenance, logging and reporting aspects which support the expert system but are not actually part of it. The central feature of the application is the expert system.

Sections 4–6 discuss some of the project management and technical issues encountered in building VBARS. The two technical issues considered are, firstly, knowledge acquisition with multiple experts and, secondly, the performance of TODAY-ES as an expert systems tool.

On the project management side we concluded that managing an expert system is not significantly more difficult than most other projects. The exception is that a working knowledge of expert systems and access to good technical knowledge is essential for quality results.

In the matter of expert systems tools TODAY-ES proved to be a good tool for the task. Throughout most of this paper decision trees are emphasized. This is because rules only became available after the completion of development. TODAY-ES's integration with the TODAY 4GL and its development capabilities were significant factors in building this application.

2 Background

The expert systems tool – TODAY-ES

BBJ Computers International Ltd is one of the larger software houses in Australia. The Head Office is in Melbourne. Their main products are accounting and supply packages. In 1983 BBJ commenced development of the successful 4GL, TODAY, in order to free itself from the constraints of the HP3000 marketplace. In 1987 BBJ developed an expert systems environment, called TODAY-ES, as a companion product to TODAY.

TODAY-ES and TODAY were used to write the VBARS application.

TODAY-ES uses a variant of the C4 algorithm, a successor to ID3, to build decision trees and rules. Knowledge induction is only part of the ES development environment which includes substantial reporting and example file maintenance facilities.

At the time of VBARS development, TODAY-ES's inference mechanism used decision trees to establish decisions. Following the completion of VBARS, rules were added to TODAY-ES. With both rules and decision trees TODAY-ES uses backward chaining. TODAY-ES is best suited to classification and diagnostic tasks.

Project objectives

DITR's objectives as paraphrased from the brief for the expert system were:

1. to develop an expert system to provide accurate advice on enquiries for business assistance,

2. to develop an expert system which can be used to demonstrate a practical expert system in use,

3. to provide the developer with experience in expert systems development,

4.   to provide software developers with information about the process of developing a real and useful expert system, and

5.   to provide research workers with experience and information about the process of developing a real and useful expert system.

The last two points involve giving papers at conferences and involving external research institutions in the project. This is one of several papers on various aspects of the project. This project also provides some of the subject material for a master's degree which is now in progress.

BBJ's objectives in undertaking the project were:

1.   To test TODAY-ES. TODAY-ES is not just an expert systems tool but, rather, a new kind of tool. The incorporation of expert systems technology into 4GL application development environments is new. We had heard reports that our competitors were headed down the same track but we had not seen any of their results.

2.   To research expert systems development. Expert systems appeared to be different in their project management. In fact, this difference may be largely illusory.

3.   To research knowledge engineering. We have considerable theoretical knowledge about the management and manipulation of knowledge which we wished to consolidate.

4.   To promote TODAY-ES. This is a high profile project which will demonstrate the capabilities of TODAY-ES.

Profit was not a major incentive for either BBJ or DITR: the project was costed to break even. In fact, it cost BBJ money. The main objective was to learn about expert systems tools and development because these are seen as future directions for BBJ.

3   The project

The problem

Many individuals or small businesses seek business advice and assistance. There are a number of agencies which can assist them. The expert system is required to refer an enquiry to the most appropriate agency or agencies. The appropriateness of an agency is determined by estimating the enquirer's current need and finding an agency which can fulfil that need. For instance, an inventor may be assisted by several of the agencies known to the system. The best assistance may be technical, marketing or financial. Further, the degree of agency involvement varies from brief counselling sessions to embarking on projects lasting months or years. VBARS works out what kind of assistance is required and which agencies are suitable.

While at first glance this may appear straightforward there were a number of issues which complicated the picture. Firstly, although each of the eight agencies initially included in VBARS has a major focus for its services, there is frequently considerable overlap of services provided by agencies. There is also considerable competition for the right to provide these services. Secondly, the enquirers often do not know what assistance they require. They may think they know but, for a variety of reasons, they may not be correct. Thirdly, it was a criterion in the specification of the system that provision be made for expanding the number of agencies covered.

VBARS is not intended to offer business counselling. It is restricted to advice on sources of assistance.

The agencies

The agencies represented in VBARS are listed below, together with the major focus of their activities. The first four agencies were employed in developing the prototype. The rest were included after the prototyping stage.

1. Australian Productivity Council (manufacturing efficiency);
2. Centre for the Development of Entrepreneurs (training entrepreneurs);
3. Small Business Development Corporation (small business counselling);
4. Victorian Innovation Centre (developing new products);
5. Australian Microcomputer Industry Clearinghouse (business computing);
6. Department of Industry, Technology and Resources Industry Assistance Group (general business advice, export);
7. Industrial Design Council of Australia (product design); and
8. Victorian Economic Development Corporation (development finance).

Scale of the VBARS expert system

This is a substantial expert system. In both size and sophistication it rates as a real expert system. Its major limitation is that it covers only eight agencies. These agencies give a reasonable coverage of the services and skills available. However, the coverage is not complete.

Increasing the coverage to 25 agencies should be a relatively minor task, except where new services are to be added. We do not expect that many new services would be added.

There are 107 referrals for 41 services. Each referral consists of an agency/service pair. In some consultations more than one referral is made. To achieve this, VBARS has 38 decision trees, each using 10–15 attributes. These decision trees are arranged to make use of structured induction and context limiting strategies.

VBARS is a huge system when compared with other decision tree-based systems. Those systems discussed and demonstrated at recent expert systems conferences commonly consist of only one tree (for example, Carter and Catlett, 1987).

Comparison with rule-based systems is harder. The common means of comparing rule-based systems is to count the number of rules. This is unreliable because each rule is of different importance. Sizes of rule-based systems tend to vary from 50 rules to over 5000 rules.

Decision trees are a kind of composite rule. Each path from root to leaf of a decision tree roughly corresponds to a rule. This is further complicated by the effects of combining decision trees to build the system. In decision tree form VBARS equated to 1022 rules. When these decision trees were converted to rules this was reduced to 750 rules as a consequence of removal of duplicated and subsumed rules.

In addition TODAY's procedural logic is used where appropriate to validate, test and set values. This further obscures the scale of the system by increasing its capabilities and reducing the code complexity.

The users

There are three classes of users catered for in VBARS. At the outset of the project it was thought that most users would be 'New Users'. As the project progressed it has become apparent that most users would be 'Experienced Users'.

The 'Administrative User' has access to the system administration menu and controls the maintenance of the 'agency' and 'service' files and setting of system parameters for configurable features.

An 'Experienced User' is normally a staff member of an agency and is conversant with the system. The system appears to be more terse. Help messages and text-defining terminology are not displayed unless requested. Some extra reporting and enquiry facilities may be available.

A 'New User' is an occasional or first-time user. The system is more friendly and provides a degree of guidance to the user. Reporting facilities are limited to reports of referrals. Help messages are displayed to define terminology. Access to the system is through the enquiry introduction screen.

4   Building the expert system

Stages of development

The brief for the expert system was issued in late 1986 with proposals for the system due in November. We were told that there were 11 proposals received. On Christmas Eve we officially heard that we had the job.

The first project management meeting was in late February and meetings continued once a fortnight. We decided to start with a prototype, the development stages of which are summarized below:

Prototype development: (first four agencies)

Late February	1.	First project meeting.
	2.	Introductory meeting with each agency.
March	3.	Exploratory meetings at each agency.
	4.	First design of prototype.
	5.	Attempt to use questionnaires to gather data fails.
April	6.	Meetings with experts at agencies.
Early May	7.	Demonstration of prototype.

Application development:

Late May	8.	Design of VBARS proper.
June	9.	Introductory meetings with the second four agencies.
June/July	10.	Exploratory meeting with each new agency.
June/July	11.	Building of VBARS (initially with agencies used in the prototype).
July/Aug/Sept	12.	Meetings with experts (held at BBJ). Separate meetings for each agency with 3–10 meetings with each agency.
October	13.	Installation.
November	14.	Acceptance.

Prototyping

The initial development was done as a prototype. TODAY proved to be a good prototyping language. The prototype was developed as one large amorphous system. For the prototype this was reasonable but it would never have worked in the finished system. It would not have had the flexibility or capabilities required.

When the prototype was completed it was demonstrated and discussed with each of the agencies. This encouraged further participation from the agencies because they felt that they understod the project better and could see their contributions. We did not present the prototype any earlier for fear of losing their interest and support.

The prototype gave us a chance to orient ourselves to the problem at hand, which included time to get a basic understanding of the agencies and their interrelationships, and time to learn what the knowledge consisted of. It also gave us time to learn how the knowledge could be structured and confidence for both DITR and ourselves that the system could be built.

By the time the prototype had been developed we knew what we could achieve, what was possible, and what was required. It was, in effect, a feasibility study.

We took what we had learned and the comments we had received when demonstrating the prototype and designed the real system. The prototype had served its purpose and was discarded. The new design proved much easier than the prototype to develop and was not substantially altered in the course of development.

Both the quality and the structure of the VBARS application were enhanced through the understanding gained in the prototype.

Expert system architecture

This describes the expert system enquiry component of the application. Maintenance and reporting facilities are in other parts of the system.

The system may be viewed as a series of stages, each dependent on prior stages. The enquirer begins with an introductory message displayed on the screen. The enquiry is initiated by selecting the REFERRAL option shown in Figure 11.1. In most stages the enquirer is questioned regarding his or her experience and requirements. The enquirer selects an answer from a menu of possible answers.

Stages in processing an enquiry

Figure 11.2 describes the processing stages that a consultation goes through in order to decide on a referral. These stages closely parallel those of our experts in the early stages of their interviews when they are trying to work out whether they can do anything useful for a client.

1. *Initial enquirer screen*   The screen shown in Figure 11.1 introduces the enquirer to the system. From here the enquirer can either run VBARS or can request more information regarding use of the system.

2. *Get enquirer's request*   This finds out, in general terms, what the enquirer wants and focuses it into one of eight topics, and gives a sense of direction and relevance to the enquirer.

    Figures 11.3 and 11.4 show typical consultation screens. In Figure 11.3, the portion of the screen above the dividing line displays previous questions and answers. This area may also be

```
┌─────────────────────────────────────────────────────────────────┐
│                                                                   │
│           VICTORIAN BUSINESS ASSISTANCE REFERRAL SYSTEM           │
│           ════════════════════════════════════════════           │
│                                                                   │
│     This computerized referral system helps people seeking business │
│     advice and assistance.                                        │
│                                                                   │
│     It knows about the services supplied by a selected number of  │
│     business assistance agencies and can match these to the business │
│     needs of the enquirer. In some cases it may find needs and    │
│     opportunities of which the enquirer was not aware.            │
│                                                                   │
│     A series of questions will be asked. Most of them are multiple-choice. │
│     If your answer is not one of those listed please choose the nearest │
│     available answer.                                             │
│                                                                   │
│        For a REFERRAL, type 1 and then RETURN.                    │
│                                                                   │
│        For further HELP, type 2 and then RETURN.                  │
│                                                                   │
│  Control : _____                                        │
└─────────────────────────────────────────────────────────────────┘
```

Figure 11.1   This is the initial screen seen by all users of VBARS except for the system administrator.

used to display information for the guidance of the user. The area between the dividing line and the Control line, labelled Control:, displays the current question and the possible answers. Selection is made by entering the number of the user's choice in the space provided. Where the user is required to provide a value rather than a selection then a data field is provided in this area and the answer validated appropriately. The function keys provided on the Control line allow the user to terminate the consultation, start another consultation and to access the explanation facility. In this application 'why' is more relevant than 'how'.

It should be noted that TODAY has been designed to be used with character mode terminals. This was a design decision made in respect to the marketplace in which TODAY is sold.

The question being asked in Figure 11.3 is the first question in this section. The answers listed for the question approximate the topics into which the next stage is divided. Further questions are asked to verify the choice of topic. The topic area actually chosen depends on all answers given in this stage.

These topics are not mutually exclusive, in fact, there is considerable overlap between them. The training topic overlaps with all other topics. Each topic has a number of subtopics to qualify further the enquirer's area of interest. If an enquirer gives as

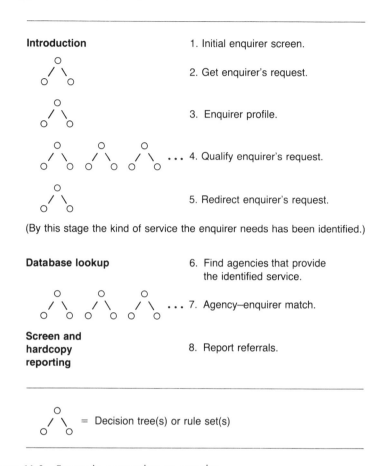

Figure 11.2 Stages in processing an enquiry.

his or her main area of enquiry export and then indicates that he or she wants finance for export then this would be processed under the finance topic.

The effect of this stage is to allow the enquirer a degree of flexibility in nominating his or her area of interest and to focus this into the topics covered by the expert system.

3. *Enquirer profile* This gathers basic information on business and industry experience and on the enquirer's business. It is also intended to give the user a feeling that the expert system is responsive to the particular background and needs of the enquirer.

4. *Qualify enquirer's request* The topic selected for the enquirer is examined for suitability. Each topic is subdivided into various aspects relevant to the subject. The system tries to match the enquirer to one of these subtopics.

```
┌─────────────────────────────────────────────────────────────────────────┐
│              VICTORIAN BUSINESS ASSISTANCE REFERRAL SYSTEM                │
│         ═══════════════════════════════════════════════════════          │
│                                                                          │
│                                                                          │
│  ─── 1) A Profile of Yourself and Your Business ───                      │
│  How many full years' experience do you have in managing a               │
│  business?                                                     5          │
│  How many full years have you worked in this industry or                 │
│  a related industry?                                           5          │
│                                                                          │
│  Does this enquiry concern a business you:                               │
│  1) are employed by   2) own   3) wish to buy                            │
│  4) wish to start   OR   5) licensing a product to a manufacturer   already own │
│  How old is the business? (Give the answer in completed years)   5       │
│  Which industry sector is the business in?                  manufacturing │
│                                                                          │
│  ─── 2) Subject of Enquiry and Associated Questions ───                  │
│ ─────────────────────────────────────────────────────────────────────── │
│  What is the main area of your enquiry?                                  │
│  1) new_business   2) training      3) products   4) computing           │
│  5) efficiency      6) marketing   7) finance     8) export              │
│  9) other                                                                │
│                                                                          │
│  Input the number of the choice selected : [   ]                         │
│                                                                          │
│  Control :_____ Start   pf1   End   pf2   Why   pf3          │
└─────────────────────────────────────────────────────────────────────────┘
```

Figure 11.3   A consultation screen.

It is this stage and the next that are the most crucial to the expert system. These stages have a broad knowledge of the services available and the prerequisites which make those services appropriate. The myriad of combinations and the general lack of clarity in this area mean that approaching this task by conventional programming is impractical. Attempts to do this tend to fall short because of the complexity of the problem.

Not all possible topics are covered. For instance, industrial relations are not completely covered in the present system. The topics represented cover the agencies that we have. Further subjects will have to wait until agencies which have those topics are added to VBARS. Even so, the representation of services at present is pretty good considering the number of agencies involved. We do not expect many new topics to be added. When the time comes they will be relatively easy to incorporate.

The system seeks to classify the enquirer's needs within the topic area. Each topic area is divided into a number of subclasses.

```
┌─────────────────────────────────────────────────────────────────────┐
│              VICTORIAN BUSINESS ASSISTANCE REFERRAL SYSTEM            │
│              ══════════════════════════════════════════             │
│                                                                      │
│   Does this enquiry concern a business you:                          │
│   1) are employed by   2) own   3) wish to buy                       │
│   4) wish to start   OR   5) licensing a product to a manufacturer   already own │
│   How old is the business? (Give the answer in completed years)    5 │
│   Which industry sector is the business in?      manufacturing       │
│                                                                      │
│   —— 2) Subject of Enquiry and Associated Questions ——              │
│   What is the main area of your enquiry?      finance                │
│   In what area of finance do you require assistance?    obtain funds │
│   Do you have a business plan?     have                              │
│                                                                      │
│   —— 3) Finding Suitable Agencies ——                                │
│   For what purpose do you need the finance?      expand business     │
│                                                                      │
│  ─────────────────────────────────────────────────────────────────  │
│   Do you have any plans to export?                                   │
│   1) have   2) have not                                              │
│                                                                      │
│   Input the number of the choice selected:                          │
│   Control :———————————  Start  pf1   End  pf2   Why  pf3            │
└─────────────────────────────────────────────────────────────────────┘
```

Figure 11.4 Matching the enquirer with agencies which provide the appropriate service. In this case an interest in export would bias the agency towards this enquirer. The services of the agency being considered are far broader than simply export assistance but the agency has a special interest in export oriented companies.

The subclass classification is either a service within the topic or an indication that no service is appropriate under that topic.

If the result of the classification is a service within the topic area then the system proceeds to finding appropriate agencies (step 6 in this list). If the classification is not a service then the enquirer failed to be qualified under that topic area and the request is redirected.

5. *Redirect enquirer's request* If the enquirer fails to be qualified in the previous stage then the system takes a diagnostic approach to determine the enquirer's needs.

There are two main reasons for reaching this section.

(a) The enquirer may lack sufficient business experience. This indicates that the enquirer does not really know what he or she wants or needs, and would not benefit sufficiently from services under the topic area chosen. These people are mostly new starters in business and would benefit from a variety of the available training courses.

Note that many of the services in step 4 are available to enquirers lacking business experience.

(b)   The business may be an existing business which has been identified as being at risk. One of the aims of this system is to detect businesses which are in trouble and refer them to agencies which can help solve their problems. There are a number of indicators which show that a business has problems and that the request for assistance may be a misguided attempt to solve those problems. In this case, a diagnostic approach is taken to the enquirer's business and the referral is made on the basis of the best agency to tackle the problem.

The knowledge in this stage reflects common business failings. This knowledge is used to examine the status of the business, identify possible problems, and select appropriate services to handle the problem.

By the end of this stage we have determined the service for which the enquirer will be referred.

6.   *Find agencies that provide the selected service*   This is a search of the 'agency/services' database to find agencies which provide the service.

Each of the agencies provided us with details of the services they provide. These details are stored on a file which is read when we need to find the agencies providing the required service.

The database allows the various agencies' services to be added and deleted independently of the expert system knowledge. The type of service must already be known to the knowledge base (in stage 4). It also allows the many-to-many relationship between agencies and services to be represented and thus provides better referrals.

The database lookup finds a list of agencies which provide the service. Since the different agencies have different customer criteria, some of these agencies may be inappropriate.

7.   *Agency–enquirer match*   For each of the agencies found in the previous step the enquirer is matched with the kind of clients the agency will service. The knowledge in this section reflects both statutory requirements and agency preferences.

Each agency has some TODAY and expert system logic to determine whether the enquirer is an appropriate client for that agency. For most agencies a single criterion is sufficient to cover all services. Only one agency requires a separate set of criteria for

```
┌─────────────────────────────────────────────────────────────────────┐
│                                                                     │
│              VICTORIAN BUSINESS ASSISTANCE REFERRAL SYSTEM          │
│              ══════════════════════════════════════════════        │
│                                                                     │
│  REFERRAL to :–                                                     │
│  The VEDC has loan and leasing facilities available to support the  │
│       development                                                   │
│       and/or expansion of any business entity within Victoria. In   │
│       particular, the VEDC                                          │
│       supports export oriented or import replacement manufacturing  │
│       and                                                           │
│       processing concerns, rural exporters and tourism. Loans which │
│       are free of                                                   │
│       establishment costs, service and valuation charges are        │
│       available from as low                                         │
│       as $20,000 with no stated maximum                             │
│  (Leasing – $10,000 minimum).                                       │
│  Interest rates are commercially structured. The VEDC can usually   │
│       provide greater                                               │
│       flexibility with regard to repayment and security requirement │
│       than most other                                               │
│       lenders.                                                      │
│  Equity funds are also available in certain areas.                  │
│                                                                     │
│     Contact :    Victorian Economic Development Corporation         │
│                  23rd Floor ANZ Tower                               │
│                  55 Collins Street                                  │
│                  Melbourne 3000                                     │
│                  Telephone (03) 655 3200                            │
│                                                                     │
│  Control :─────────────── Start  pf1  end  pf2  Why  pf3            │
└─────────────────────────────────────────────────────────────────────┘
```

Figure 11.5   This referral recommends the Victorian Economic Development Corporation for business loans.

each of its programs. It appears to me that this agency has inherited the programs which it runs and lacks a cohesive ethos.

The knowledge of the agencies is separated from the knowledge about services. This makes the system easier to build and expand. In this system there is only one body of knowledge about services. Being independent of the agency knowledge, the services knowledge is easier to maintain. Maintaining the agency knowledge separately makes it possible for the developer to add and remove agencies with a minimum of fuss.

The differences of policy and belief between the agencies on matters of business theory and practice tended to be solved by arbitration and negotiation. Most of these differences were not major. If substantial unresolvable issues arose they would have been handled in the agency-specific knowledge. The very existence of the agency-specific knowledge in VBARS indicates that differing beliefs are already being handled. The depth of knowledge required for this system is not very deep. Had VBARS been a counselling system then greater difficulties would have been encountered.

8.   *Report referrals*   For each agency found to be suitable the referral details are displayed to the enquirer. Figure 11.5 shows a referral to one of the agencies. A hard copy report is also available.

Where several agencies are found to be suitable, a ranking scheme has been introduced. It consists of a combination of agency preferences and a bias towards the major functions of each agency. Only the highest ranking are reported as referrals.

The enquirer may make further requests of the system. Information regarding the enquirer's profile and business status may be retained and used in further requests so that on subsequent enquiries the enquirer would not be asked about his or her business experience.

Other components of the application

There are several other aspects to this application which are relevant to understanding its scope.

The System Administrator has control over the administration and maintenance components of the application. This includes maintenance of the 'agency' and 'service' files. The 'agency' file has the details of how to contact the agency. Normally this is name, address and phone. The 'service' file is used for matching agencies with services. The data in both of these files is subject to change and needs to be kept separate from the rest of the system. The administrator's menu is shown in Figure 11.6.

At the administrator's discretion all enquiries are logged with comments from the user. The log includes all answers to questions and significant decisions, and will be used to improve the quality of the referrals and report the distribution of referrals.

The log enquiry screen in Figure 11.7 shows significant details of the enquirer's profile, request and referral(s). The hard copy log report shows all the details of the enquiry.

How and why explanations of the system's reasoning are available. They show how decisions were reached and why questions were asked. Why explanations have been arranged to provide clarification of the current question.

System complexity

The first major complexity was the scope of the knowledge domain. The knowledge required by this system covers most aspects of assistance to small to medium sized business. This is a fairly large body of knowledge by any standards. It is a complex body of knowledge containing a variety of seemingly unrelated subjects including finance, computing and export.

```
* TODAY-ES *
            VICTORIAN BUSINESS ASSISTANCE REFERRAL SYSTEM


        1 User Menu

        2 System Control

        3 Agency Details

        4 Log Files

        5 Training Files


  MAIN MENU

  Control : _____
```

Figure 11.6   The Administrator's menu. Selecting 'User Menu' gives access to VBARS. The other selections give access to menus of maintenance and enquiry screens. Training files are the example files used in the inductive rule learning.

Fortunately, the expert system was not required to go into great depth on any subject. However, VBARS was required to cope with a large body of knowledge on diverse and disjoint subject matters.

None of the experts used in building the system knows everything that the system knows. Some experts think they know all there is to know, but most are aware that there are aspects with which they are not fully conversant. This limitation was particularly true of the experts' understanding of the services of other agencies or even other parts of their own agency.

The most time consuming aspect was the 'multiple experts' dimension. It was originally envisaged that there would be one expert who would guide and instruct the development of the system. In the end, each agency was separately represented. We needed to use multiple experts firstly because each agency has to be fairly represented by VBARS and, secondly, because no one expert understands the whole problem domain.

Multiple experts added to complexity and slowed development due to:

1.   the logistics of arranging meetings with so many experts,

```
* TODAY-ES *                                                    2/9/87
           VICTORIAN BUSINESS ASSISTANCE REFERRAL SYSTEM
           ═══════════════════════════════════════════════


Enquiry Number         1 [    1047]        Topic     2 [finance
Date of Enquiry        3 [ 1/ 9/87]        Subtopic  4 [obtain funds

Business Exp           5 [1           ]  Industry Exp      6 [8        ]
Business trained       7 [none        ]  Industry trained  8 [–        ]
Business Status        9 [already own ]  Industry Sector  10 [service  ]

Service   1 [finance           ]    Subclass    12 [planning        ]

Referrals:    Agency 13 [SBDC   ]      Rank 14 [ 1]
              Agency 15 [       ]      Rank 16 [  ]
              Agency 17 [       ]      Rank 18 [  ]
              Agency 19 [       ]      Rank 20 [  ]
Comment:      21 [                                               ]
              22 [                                               ]
              23 [                                               ]
              24 [                                               ]
              25 [                                               ]
              26 [                                               ]
Control: _____ Delete f1  Print  f2  Next  f3  Prev  f4
```

Figure 11.7 Enquiry log browse screen.

2.   contradictory and/or competing beliefs of experts, and

3.   conflict between experts/agencies.

The tactics and logistics of using so many experts added a considerable amount of time taken for the project. Most agencies provided two or three experts on a regular basis. From the entire eight agencies we had 21 experts at various times.

The knowledge in VBARS benefited from the use of multiple experts. In the end we sought more experts to cover areas incompletely covered by our existing experts.

5   Knowledge acquisition

This section describes the various means used to acquire knowledge for VBARS. As the project progressed we tried a variety of methods, each with some degree of success. The main factors influencing knowledge acquisition were:

1.   the breadth of the knowledge domain to be covered,
2.   the depth of knowledge required for the system,
3.   the number of experts we were required to use, and
4.   the interrelationships of the experts/agencies.

Questionnaires

One recommended way to gather examples for inductive learning systems is to use questionnaires. They were used in an expert system for troubleshooting a smelter for what appeared to be a similar inductive learning process (Brew and Catlett, 1987). Each completed questionnaire represents an example. When sufficient examples have been collected they are recorded on file for use as a training set. Using questionnaires has been said to be an easy way of gathering the data. In the cases we are aware of, there was a single expert and the scope of the problem was considerably smaller than in the current case.

The chief benefit of using questionnaires is that they provide a close relationship between the experts' knowledge and the knowledge base that is built. In effect, the knowledge engineer builds the training set directly from expert supplied data and, therefore, has less opportunity to distort it.

A questionnaire is not a stable item. It is continually modified to suit the requirements of the expert and the problem domain. Questions and their answers may be added, changed or deleted to try to capture the knowledge domain more thoroughly.

We tried several forms of questionnaire. There were questionnaires which covered the entire problem domain and questionnaires for particular topics and subproblems. All were deemed to be obscure by our experts.

There were a number of reasons for this obscurity. Firstly, the number of questions on the larger questionnaires was too big to be manageable. Some questionnaires we produced had more than 50 questions, each with up to 15 answers. For each case somewhere between 5 and 15 questions were relevant and the rest served to confuse the issue. If we had stuck with this approach then later questionnaires could have exceeded 150 questions.

Dividing the larger questionnaires into smaller ones solved very little. Deciding which questions were relevant depended on the point of view of the expert and his or her agency. Smaller questionnaires would probably have worked with a single expert. With multiple experts there was a problem of trying to create questionnaires which suited everybody.

Different experts saw relevance in different questions. Questions which were not clearly related to their portion of the knowledge domain were hard to answer. Although they had the option of marking questions as irrelevant to the case, they were reluctant to do this.

Terminology was a problem in interpreting questionnaires. Different experts used different terminology. Even common everyday terms such as 'product' have a variety of meanings. It was by no means clear that users would understand the terms to have the meanings assigned by the experts. We thought of developing a glossary for the questionnaire but this would only make the questionnaires more cumbersome.

In the end questionnaires were inappropriate to this problem. Multiple independent experts have too many different views of the problem domain. These differences need to be resolved in the questionnaire for it to be effective. The logistics of trying to develop such a questionnaire were daunting. We found that designing questionnaires and getting them completed was going to be too hard a task and so we tried other means of acquiring the knowledge.

Meetings

We decided that our knowledge acquisition would need to be done by interviewing our experts and applying the knowledge to the expert system. For the most part, this knowledge acquisition process was characterized by meetings. There were several kinds of meetings.

Fortnightly project meetings with DITR reviewed progress and tried to keep the project on track. They also served to review some of the progress of our meetings with the agencies, particularly the political aspects.

With each new agency and each new group of experts we held an introductory meeting in which we discussed the objectives of the project and the reasons why they should be involved. Murray Frazer, as instigator of the project and as DITR's representative, explained the goals of the project. BBJ's representative explained how they saw the project and what assistance was desired from the agency. Normally we asked for 5 days of their time spread over the period of development. In the event, this turned out to be reasonably accurate.

Following the introductory meeting we had several meetings with each agency. These were held at the agency, usually in the expert's office. Originally these were to investigate the problem domain and to ascertain questions for the questionnaires. From these meetings we gained a basic understanding of the problem domain. When the questionnaires failed, these meetings were conducted as interviews and became the primary source of knowledge for building the prototype.

Our demonstrations of the prototype were the first occasions on which the agencies' representatives saw the system. These marked a change in approach. Instead of us going to the agencies, we now had them coming to our premises. We had made as few demands as possible on our experts' time while building the prototypes. The prototype gave us some credibility in their eyes. Following the acceptance of the prototype there was a lull in our contacts with the experts while we applied what we had learnt to building the real expert system.

An extensive series of development meetings followed the substantial completion of the real expert system structure. In these meetings we asked our experts to try cases through VBARS and recommend improvements. This formed the major part of the teaching and tuning of VBARS. These meetings continued until our experts were comfortable with the operation of the system.

6   Integration and TODAY-ES

This may appear to be a very straightforward application of expert systems. In fact building this system using most other expert systems tools may not have produced as good a result for the effort. BBJ have integrated the expert systems environment into the 4GL environment. Without access to TODAY's screen handling, reporting, procedural logic and file handling, the system would be considerably weaker. We would not have been able to structure the system as we did or achieve the success we have.

Support function – system interfaces

4GLs provide an environment which interacts with users, data bases and conventional applications. 4GLs provide a powerful vehicle for delivering expert systems.

TODAY-ES uses files of examples to learn inductively the rules for building the expert system. TODAY was used to maintain and report these examples files.

TODAY's screen handling, reporting, procedural logic and file management were used to write the application to support the expert system. The TODAY HELP subsystem provides substantial assistance to the users of the expert system.

Enhancement function – integration

The integration of expert systems with 4GL features enhances the power of the expert system tool. In particular, conventional procedural logic can combine with traditional expert systems techniques to achieve better systems.

This is particularly true in managing attributes. Attributes are the data items used to hold the values used by the decision tree and are fundamental to decision tree processing.

Using TODAY's procedural logic we gained the following benefits:

1. *Context limiting* – limiting the scope of the knowledge being addressed at any one time. The system becomes simpler to develop because smaller amounts of knowledge are easier to handle. Questions do not become unfocused. The user gets a sense of the relevance of the questions and fewer questions are asked because the problem is more focused. The division of the knowledge into topics is an example of this.

   The disadvantages are that there are more decision trees/rule sets to maintain and some issues may not be considered because they were not part of the context. These can be minimized by careful subdivision of the knowledge domain.

2. *Structured induction* – dividing a decision tree into smaller decision trees. Just as dividing the knowledge domain into topics simplified developing the system, dividing the trees into smaller trees with explicit relations between them made the system more manageable. It also made it possible to share knowledge between contexts. The decision tree may be used in several contexts.

3. *Forward chaining* – driving the expert system with data orientation at appropriate points. This provides the expert system with considerably greater flexibility than is available with only backward chaining. At present, TODAY-ES does not support forward chaining but conventional TODAY logic can mimic it.

4. *Simplifying decision trees.* TODAY procedural logic was used to supplement or replace decision trees with logic where appropriate. TODAY logic was also used to create different views of attributes which, in turn, simplified the decision trees.

5. *Evaluation/calculation of attributes.* TODAY logic provides alternative means of acquiring attribute values. Any means of accessing or computing data that TODAY has may be used.

6. *Assume attribute values.* TODAY logic can be used to assume the values of attributes where other data suggests the correct value.

7. *Validation.* TODAY logic can be used to test that an attribute has a valid value and that the value is reasonable in the situation.

Decision trees and rules sets

Throughout this paper I have referred to decision trees and rule sets. TODAY-ES's structure allows these to be used interchangeably. The emphasis on decision trees is purely because this was the original representation available in TODAY.

The decision trees were converted to rules when they became available. There are slight variations in the questioning but, in general, the appearance is the same. Occasionally an extra question is asked when a rule is tried that would not have been used by the decision trees and sometimes a question is not asked because the attribute was redundant in that rule. The processing of the rules requires more CPU time but, in the cases I have seen, this does not visibly slow down TODAY-ES. Rules are more flexible but can be more cumbersome to work with.

Given the time over again I would use inductive learning to build the system even though we had to create the data. The inductive learning process tests the trees/rule sets for completeness and conflicts resulting in a more thorough system and one in which I have more confidence. The examples files used for the induction were not too difficult to maintain. I would use decision trees while developing the system and convert these to rule sets towards the end of development. This conversion took less than a day because the rule sets are created directly from the decision trees.

7   The current state of VBARS

BBJ's development of VBARS has been successfully completed. In October 1987 VBARS was delivered and in November it was accepted. VBARS has since received some internal use at DITR. Our comments that eight agencies were not enough have been accepted and, prior to general release, VBARS is being expanded to around 20 agencies. In the interests of technology transfer this is being done by another software house, Intrinsic Software Pty Ltd. As I understand it there has been a delay in implementation due to the time required for Intrinsic to take over responsibility for VBARS.

8   Conclusions

The technology employed in building this system is not difficult to use. The project followed a pattern fairly common to applications development. It went through phases of prototyping and development. There were regular project meetings to control the course of the project, meetings with experts to solicit knowledge for the system, and meetings and demonstrations at which the strengths and failings of the system were discussed.

The project was late but both BBJ and DITR expected that this might happen as neither had experience in this kind of project. The main reason for lost time was that, after the project commenced, we discovered that there was no single expert and we therefore had a problem of dealing with multiple experts.

To attempt to build an expert system the project leader must have a knowledge of expert systems, and members of the team should have an understanding of knowledge engineering. You should also choose a tool appropriate to the task; in our case this was TODAY-ES.

TODAY-ES did the job. It was our estimate that the combination of 4GL development techniques (for example, prototyping) and the integration of the product saved considerable time and effort and resulted in a more powerful and complete expert system application.

Traditionally, decision tree-based expert systems have been very limited in their scope and abilities. TODAY-ES appears to have overcome most of these limitations. Now that rules have been incorporated, its major limitations are the lack of a formal forward chaining capability and the fact that it is not a graphics-based system and so does not present as well as the competition.

Acknowledgements

I have been responsible for developing TODAY and TODAY-ES and for project leading the VBARS project. The original design of TODAY was done by Stuart Evans. David Harper has been of great assistance with TODAY-ES and VBARS.

References

Brew P.J. and Catlett J. (1987). SA: an expert system for troubleshooting a smelter. In *Applications of Expert Systems* (Quinlan J.R., ed.). Wokingham: Addison-Wesley
Carter C. and Catlett J. (1987). Credit assessment using machine learning. In *Proc. 3rd Australian Conf. on Applications of Expert Systems*, Sydney, Australia
Frazer M.V. (1987). Victorian Business Assistance Referral System: Development and early use. In *Proc. AI 1987 Conference*, Sydney, Australia

12

Assisting Seasonal Adjustment Analysts: A Joint ABS/Fujitsu Prototype Expert System

Peter Cox
Terry White
Andrew Sutcliffe

Australian Bureau of Statistics

Chris Liles
Fujitsu Australia Ltd

The Australian Bureau of Statistics (ABS) and Fujitsu recently completed a joint development of a prototype expert system. The prototype solves a real-world, practical problem that requires true expertise, and by its very size, complexity and purpose the prototype is a non-trivial expert system. The prototype was designed as an expert's aid to assist the expert seasonal adjustment analysts judge whether a seasonal adjustment is acceptable and, after further validation, could be used as such. The experts believe that the prototype could be developed into a full production expert system, usable by both experts and non-experts, thus spreading valuable expertise. The joint project has been a successful one and demonstrates the applicability of using expert systems technology to solve practical problems.

1 Background to Expert System Development

1.1 A joint project is born

In October 1986 the ABS made a commitment to redeploy staff to work on areas of new technology. Part of this effort was to be directed towards evaluating the applicability of expert systems technology to the ABS, and to determine what approach is needed for the future. This activity was to cover initial investigations into, and possible developments of prototypes for, the use of expert systems in various areas of ABS activity.

As part of this work, a joint project was established between the ABS, Fujitsu Australia Ltd (FAL), and Fujitsu Ltd in January 1987 to build a prototype expert system, using Fujitsu's mainframe-based expert system shell, ESHELL, and evaluate the results by November 1987. A team was formed consisting of two ABS officers and a FAL Systems Engineer together with project management support from ABS and FAL.

The major goals of the joint project were agreed as:

1.   to develop a relevant prototype system that can be demonstrated,

2.   to examine the effects of expert systems on ABS applications systems,

3.   to assess expert systems as an alternative to traditional DP tools, and

4.   for ABS and FAL* to obtain practical experience with an expert system.

1.2   Assistance from Fujitsu Japan

The team received training in Fujitsu's expert systems development shell, ESHELL, and the Expert Systems Development Methodology (ES/SDEM) from Fujitsu Japan.

The components of ESHELL most pertinent to this paper are the knowledge representation facilities and the blackboard. The knowledge representation facilities available in ESHELL are production rules and frames. **Production rules**, or rules, establish a relationship between two facts and are typically expressed in the form if-then. Production rules grouped together as a module are called a **knowledge source**. **Frames** are knowledge representation structures which hold information about an object and will typically be arranged hierarchically. The **blackboard** is addressable dynamic working memory which contains intermediate results generated during the processing of the expert system, typically by the then part of rules.

The ES/SDEM is a Fujitsu developed methodology for developing expert systems, which facilitates a rapid prototyping approach and allows the expert's knowledge to be acquired in a systematic way, based on a predetermined model. Section 3 describes how the methodology was used for this application and how the acquired knowledge was expressed in ESHELL.

The team was assisted by an on-site visit by a knowledge engineer (KE) from Fujitsu Japan during the initial design of the expert system in June 1987, and a review of the system by Fujitsu KE's in Tokyo in August 1987.

1.3 Selection of application

As a starting point, applications that could benefit from expert systems technology had to be identified. Several applications covering a broad spectrum of the ABS's activity were chosen and examined on the basis of a fairly standard expert systems selection criteria checklist. From these examinations the team drew up a list of applications and, on the basis of criteria to help select an application for the initial prototype, established a short-list. With the assistance of Fujitsu Japan an application was chosen as being the most suitable for the prototyping exercise. The application chosen was seasonal adjustment reanalysis and, at this point, a senior expert from the Seasonal Analysis Section joined the team on a part-time basis.

2 The application

2.1 Nature of the application

Much of the data held by the Bureau is in the form of time series, which are statistical records of particular social or economic activities measured at regular intervals over time for a long period.

ABS clients who use time series data are usually interested in the current figures – they want to know what the recent movements have been and whether there have been any turning points – for example, whether retail sales are declining or increasing. This information is typically used to make projections about future activity. It is difficult for clients to make accurate projections using raw series data because of the presence of variations in the data, some of which can be attributed to more or less regular seasonal factors – for example, Australian retail sales are usually much higher at Christmas time. Seasonal adjustment consists of identifying and making allowance for these variations, in the form of adjustment factors, producing seasonally adjusted time series, which represent any underlying trends and any irregular variations. The irregular variations are then 'dampened' down to show more clearly the underlying trends, facilitating more accurate projections. Seasonal adjustment reanalysis is the process of analysing the most recent adjustment of series which have previously been adjusted for, over a number of years.

At the ABS, adjustment factors are produced each year by expert seasonal adjustment analysts within the Seasonal Analysis Section, an area which provides a service to the other sections within the ABS which are responsible for the collection, classification, and publication of the data. One of the tasks of the seasonal analysis experts is based on the use of the X11-ARIMA computer program, which is used worldwide by major statistical agencies and which has been adopted by the ABS as its standard method of seasonal adjustment. The program reads adjustment factors set up by the analysts, adjusts raw time series data using several statistical techniques, and produces a lengthy report consisting of tables of data, results of statistical tests, graphs and diagnostic messages. All of these must be examined by expert seasonal adjustment analysts to ascertain whether X11-ARIMA has produced a technically acceptable and reliable adjustment.

The ABS has recognized that the highly specialized and skilled personnel available for this work are in short supply. Currently, up to eight staff do the work of providing seasonally adjusted figures for publication of about 1000 series each year, which entails submitting up to 10 000 X11-ARIMA jobs. As a general rule, because of staff constraints, only time series that have a significant user demand are considered for analysis.

2.2 Domain of the expert system

The expert system has been designed to examine the X11-ARIMA output resulting from the reanalysis of a series to ascertain if the program has produced an acceptable adjustment and, if not, to identify problems and recommend changes to allow an expert to correct them.

3 Expert system development

3.1 The conceptualization stage

The first and most crucial step in the ES/SDEM is the modelling of the experts' decision-making process. The ES/SDEM assumes that an expert working to solve particular problems will have a set of objects about which decisions are to be made. Additionally, these objects will typically contain information about the decision-making process. It also assumes that the expert uses rules of thumb according to a problem solving strategy to establish one hypothesis after another, and then, using expert knowledge, selects the most appropriate solution or picks an optimum solution by comparing hypotheses against possible solutions.

The aim of this stage is to generate a draft expert model showing the relationships between these components. By focusing on WHAT-type questions (that is, WHAT sort of knowledge the expert uses to do WHAT in the process of solving the problem) the team was able to formulate the following model after several initial interviews with the expert.

1.   *The object model* The experts' knowledge about the particular series, its relationship to other series and the current and previous years' X11-ARIMA outputs for the series.

ES/SDEM	Project Name	SEASONAL ANALYSIS	Date	
EXPERT MODEL	Version – Concept Oriented Design Chart		Name	P.Cox

(Problem solving process)

TABLE CHECK → GENERAL CHECK → DIAGNOSE → CHARTS → RECOMMEND

(Strategy)
- SCAN AND COMPARE X11 OUTPUT FOR BOTH YEARS AND NOTE SIGNIFICANT RESULTS
- CHECK X11 PARAMS
- GENERAL EVIDENCE FOR HYPOTHESES
- GATHER VISUAL EVIDENCE FROM CHARTS
- MAKE RECOMMENDATIONS

(Method)

C1-CHECK-KS
B1-CHECK-KS
A1-CHECK-KS
- CHECK TABLE VALUES
- CREATE RESULT

SEASONAL-BREAK-KS
TRADING-DAY-KS
TREND-BREAK-KS
- GENERATE EVIDENCE FOR HYPOTHESES

CROSS-CHECK-RECOMMEND-KS

RECOMMEND-KS
- WEIGH EVIDENCE
- GENERATE RECOMMENDATION

ASK-KS

GENERAL-CHECK-KS
- CHECK X11 PARAMETERS

CHART-KS
- DISPLAY CHARTS
- GENERATE EVIDENCE

OBJECT

SA-GROUP   X11   TABLE

HIRM (RETAIL GROUP)

X11002
UCNB918 (SERIES)   X 11001 (NEW×11)   TABLE-001 (TABLE A1)

X11 OUTPUTS   LOAD TABLES   Original data (MATRIX)

(Object model)

SEASONAL-BREAK LEVEL
TRADING-DAY LEVEL
TREND-BREAK LEVEL

(Hypothesis set)

INSERT-SEASON
CHANGE-TRADING
INSERT-TREND-BREAK

TEXT → DISPLAY RECOMMENDATIONS EXPLANATION

(Known solution set)

- RECOMMENDATIONS
  - ACCEPTABLE ANALYSIS
  - UNACCEPTABLE ANALYSIS
- NOTES
- EXPLANATION
  - EVIDENCE
  - TESTS

Solution

| Notes | -Expert Model- |

Figure 12.1

2. *Solution set*   Initially established possible solutions, in this case, the recommendations of the experts, for example, 'Change the Seasonal Moving Average used in the X11-ARIMA run' and the explanations of those recommendations, that is, the evidence that caused the recommendations.

3. *Hypothesis set*   Hypotheses were identified as being possible problems with the series. Examples are 'Seasonal break indicated', 'Seasonal moving average change indicated'.

4. *The problem-solving method*   The experts' strategy for solving the reanalysis problem involves the study of X11-ARIMA reports for

both years, gathering evidence for hypotheses, testing hypotheses and making recommendations based on those hypotheses that held.

5. *The rule sets* Several different types of rule sets were discovered:

(i) Control rules, for example, 'If the X11-ARIMA Sigma Limits parameter is not 1.5 to 2.5 discontinue the check'.

(ii) Table checking rules, for example, 'If the f-test value is within 2% of the threshold for this series then it is a significant result'.

(iii) Evidence generating rules, for example, 'If the I/S ratios are significantly above 6.5 and are higher than last year's then the seasonal moving average may need changing'.

(iv) Recommendation rules, for example, 'If there is enough evidence to suggest a trading day effect in the series and there are no trading day factors then recommend the insertion of a trading day block'.

The relationship between these components was drawn on a worksheet and became the draft expert model, which was then used to design the structure of the system.

3.2   The structuring stage

The purpose of this stage is to formalize the expert model and to define the structure of the expert system. During this stage the KE focuses on HOW-type questions, that is, HOW the expert represents and uses the objects to solve the problem. The seasonal analysis expert system (ES) was structured such that the object model is represented as frames, the hypotheses and solution sets as blackboard elements and the rule sets as knowledge sources.

The final expert model (Figure 12.1) is described below.

A   The object model

The frames in the object model and their contents are:

- OBJECT   A generic frame containing the methods of instantiation and reference to be inherited by other frames.

- SA-GROUP   A generic frame for groups of series. SA-GROUP contains values which are shared (inherited) by all groups but which could be overridden by specific values in a particular group or series. For example, weights of evidence, table check values, standard X11-ARIMA parameters, and so on.

- HIRM   A generic frame representing the 'monthly retail sales' group of series. All series belonging to this group are instances of this frame. There will be a generic frame for each group of series introduced to the system.

- **UCNB918** An example of a series frame, an instance of HIRM. This frame contains general documentary information, such as contact name, specific testing values for this series, exception conditions (for example, a series may be part of a higher level aggregate and must always be adjusted) and input parameter values from last year's X11-ARIMA run. Values in this frame will be updated at the end of a successful check of an X11-ARIMA run, that is when the analysis is acceptable.

- **X11-ARIMA** Instances of this frame are created dynamically at system initialization, one for the previous X11-ARIMA run, one for the current run. Each of these instance frames contains links to the table instance frames for an X11-ARIMA report.

- **TABLE** Instances of this frame are created dynamically at system initialization. One frame is created for each table in each of the previous and current X11-ARIMA runs. Each table frame contains data values and pointers to vectors (created by a LISP function) for table data. An example of a slot in this frame may be 'F-TEST-VALUE'; the slot can have a VALUE facet (for example, 8.6539) and a RESULT facet (for example, 'significant-change').

B   The hypothesis set

There is a blackboard (BB) level for each hypothesis and evidence is written as nodes of that level. The BB attributes vary for each level but two of the important common ones are:

- **WHAT** The text description of the evidence.

- **WEIGHT** The weight to be given to that evidence (a measure of how much this evidence contributes to the hypothesis). In some cases, the same evidence will contribute to more than one hypothesis, with a different weight for each.

C   The solution set

The solution set is represented by the BB level RECOMMEND, the attributes of which are:

- **WHAT** The text description of the recommendation, for example, 'Remove the Easter correction factors'.

- **WHY** The BB level name for the hypothesis which held and caused the recommendation. This attribute will be used for the explanation facility.

D   The problem solving method

The basic inference process of the system has been designed to imitate generally the way the expert approaches the problem. The major processes built into the system are grouped into rule sets (knowledge source – KS) as follows:

- INITIALIZATION   The instance frames of X11-ARIMA and TABLE are created from files generated by a PL/1 program (which translates the X11-ARIMA output into a suitable form). A blackboard node containing data that will remain static for the run is created. Finally, the initial KS schedules the appropriate TABLE CHECK KSs and the GENERAL CHECK KS.

- TABLE CHECK   There is one KS for each possible table in the X11-ARIMA report; however, not all tables appear in every report. These KSs systematically check the relevant data values and messages in a table – this includes comparisons between previous and current reports. The KSs do not attempt to diagnose problems – they only record significant results in the RESULT facet of the TABLE frame slots. This parallels the expert examining tables and making mental notes of significant results. An example of a rule in this type of KS is:

  > IF   (CURRENT-F-TEST GREATER THAN F-TEST-THRESHOLD)
  >   AND   (CURRENT-F-TEST GREATER THAN PREVIOUS-F-TEST)
  > THEN
  >   (! D9NEW RESULT 'F-VALUE 'SIGNIFICANT-INCREASE)
  >   (that is, a LISP function to set the $RESULT slot
  >   of the F-VALUE facet of frame TABLE D9)

- GENERAL CHECK   The GENERAL CHECK and ASK KSs are used to decide whether an analysis of the X11-ARIMA run should continue. Reasons for discontinuing may be X11-ARIMA parameter changes since the last run, data values which would have too great an effect on the adjustment, or illegal parameters. In some cases, the system will notify the user and stop the run, in others it will ask the user if it should continue. If the analysis is to continue, GENERAL CHECK schedules the necessary DIAGNOSE, CHART and RECOMMEND KSs.

- DIAGNOSE   There is one KS for each hypothetical problem in an analysis; examples are SEASONAL BREAK, TREND BREAK, TRADING DAY ADJUSTMENT. Each DIAGNOSE KS tests the RESULT facets of the TABLE frames of tables relevant to a particular hypothesis and generates evidence for that hypothesis, by adding a node to the relevant BB level. An example of a rule in these KSs is:

  > IF   (TRADING-DAY-WEIGHTS-IN)
  >   AND   (RESULT-TR-FTEST IS 'EXTREME-INCREASE)
  >   AND   (SERIES-LENGTH IS EITHER 'SHORT or 'VERY-SHORT)
  > THEN CHANGE TYPE: ADD
  >   LEVEL   : TRADING-DAY-ADJUSTMENT
  >   ATTRIBUTES   : WHAT = "Short series and F value
  >   increase > 1.0"
  >   WEIGHT= (MODERATE-WEIGHT)
  >   WHERE = 'C15

where (MODERATE-WEIGHT) is retrieved from frames
and 'C15 is a table indicator.

- **CHART** This corresponds to the expert's visual scan of the graphs produced by X11-ARIMA to check for evidence for some hypotheses. One graph is displayed for each month of the series and the user is asked to check for visual evidence. If the system has already identified potential problems this is noted on the graph. The reply from the user (confirming or denying a problem) is used to generate further BB evidence nodes for a hypothesis. If the system has any indications of potential problems with Easter or Australia Day holiday corrections, special charts are displayed for the relevant periods.

- **RECOMMEND** The CROSS CHECK and RECOMMEND KSs correspond to the expert's weighing up of evidence and making recommendations. CROSS CHECK KS ensures that evidence for one hypothesis does not cause another hypothesis to be incorrectly held true (for example, evidence for a large extreme data value in March of an Easter-March year may falsely indicate a need to include Easter correction factors). RECOMMEND KS weighs up evidence for each hypothesis and generates nodes to the RECOMMEND BB level if any hypothesis holds. In some cases, a hypothesis holds if the sum of the weights of the items of evidence exceeds a specified value (retrieved from frames). In other cases, extra evidence will be generated if certain combinations of evidence are present. Recommendations for each hypothesis can differ depending on the total weight, for instance, a recommendation indicating a seasonal break may range from 'definite' to 'strong' to 'some'. Also, in some cases, one recommendation will override another, for example, a recommendation of a seasonal break will override a recommendation to change trading day weights.

- **POST** The post processing function initially displays either a list of recommendations or the message 'analysis is acceptable' since the indication of an acceptable analysis is the lack of sufficient evidence to cause a recommendation. Other functions allow the user to:
  - display the hypotheses which caused the recommendations to be made (or the major hypotheses if the analysis was acceptable),
  - display all the hypotheses examined by the system,
  - display all the items of evidence which support (or deny) a particular hypothesis, and
  - display all tests done by the system for a particular hypothesis.

These functions provide an explanation facility to allow the user to find out why certain recommendations were or were not made. This is required both to convince the expert of the accuracy of the recommendations and to assist the trainee expert to learn about seasonal adjustment analysis techniques.

The demonstration system, constructed by the end of June 1987, had only one hypothesis and a single rule in each knowledge source but it demonstrated that the design was sound and that hypotheses could be added on a stand-alone basis.

3.3   The detailing stage

Successive prototypes were developed via the ES/SDEM detailing stage during which more detailed knowledge was acquired from the expert and added to the system. The strategy used was to interview the expert to formulate rules for another hypothesis, enter these rules into the system and test the hypothesis using the project teams' own test data.

Entering rules into the system required the construction, especially in the TABLE CHECK KSs, of LISP functions to carry out the mathematical checks of data. These functions were written to facilitate the readability of rules, for instance:

```
IF    (ANY-SEASONAL-FACTOR-REVISIONS-SIGNIFICANT)
      where   (ANY-SEASONAL-FACTOR-REVISIONS-SIGNIFICANT)
              causes the execution of a LISP function which
              compares the vector of this year's factors
              against the vector of last year's forward
              factors and checks that the difference is within the average
              percent change of the irregular.
```

During the detailing stage extra rule sets were discovered but this was to be expected since, at this stage, the team was becoming more aware of the techniques of knowledge acquisition.

3.4   The validation stage

By mid-October 1987 the team was of the opinion that the system was ready for testing by the experts. The experts in the seasonal analysis area ran several series through the system over the next month and any problems they encountered were reported to the project team. Due to the system design these problems were easily and quickly resolved.

The experts' comments on the testing of the system are discussed in Section 4.

3.5   Size and cost

The current prototype system has 239 rules in 39 knowledge sources, 203 user-defined functions (written in UTILISP), 19 frames (plus one for each series introduced to the system – currently 18) and a medium sized PL/1 program to convert the X11-ARIMA output to a form suitable to be read by the expert system.

The total staff cost has been 39 staff-weeks consisting of 31 weeks input by KEs, 4 weeks input by experts and 4 weeks input by a PL/1 programmer. Machine costs for development are not known since the bulk of the system was developed on FAL's Canberra Test Centre. However, running costs of the expert system are less than 1 CPU second per series.

4   Experts' comments

4.1   Testing of the ES

Initially, the system was tested on some artificial cases and gave the correct recommendations. Next, a set of 10 live series were chosen to commence more substantial testing. The series are all published in seasonally adjusted form and were chosen because they covered a wide spectrum of the types of monthly series handled by the section.

Three experienced analysts were involved in the testing. The series were run through the system, both unmodified and with artificial problems introduced. The strategy used for testing involved the expert analysing a series and then consulting the ES to:

1.   check that the ES's recommendation was correct, and
2.   to check that the evidence supporting the recommendation agreed with their own thoughts.

The impression of the analysts (who had no initial input into the development of the system) was that the system was performing well with no major problems. A summary of the testing so far is given below:

1.   the system can identify problems occurring in the seasonal adjustment of a time series,
2.   most of the time (95%) the experts agreed with the system's recommendations, and
3.   certain interactions between hypotheses can, in some cases, cause the system to be unable to identify the exact nature of the problem.

4.2 Evaluation of the system

The prototype expert system for seasonal adjustment has the capacity to provide a reliable indication of problems with the seasonal adjustment of reanalysed series.

Further testing is required to 'fine tune' the system. To do this and establish that the system is of a sufficient standard to 'trust', requires a period of actual use. This would involve the analysts doing their normal reanalysis work but, at the same time, running the series through the system and comparing their recommendations and the system's recommendations. Given the current demand for seasonally adjusted data and the shortage of 'experts', it is believed that the system should be further developed to enable 'non-experts' to use the system.

4.3 Potential benefits of the system to the ABS

Should the seasonal analysis readjustment prototype be developed into an expert system usable by non-experts, statisticians will be able to adjust their own data without recourse to the experts. This means that the ABS will be able to produce many more seasonally adjusted series. The seasonal analysis experts, freed of the job of analysing all but the most complex adjustments, will be able to spend more time developing their expertise.

The retention of valuable expertise is another benefit. If the seasonal analysis experts' knowledge is held in the ES, the impact to the organization of losing that expertise is lessened. It should be noted, however, that this expertise will need to be continually updated so that it does not become dated.

4.4 Summary

After further development and testing the system's batch mode could be used to alert the experts to only those series for which the adjustment is judged to be unacceptable. The expert could then work through these series in the system's interactive mode. It is estimated that approximately 50% of the current series would not need to be investigated by the experts.

Further development should make the system usable initially by statisticians within the ABS and then by general users outside the ABS.

5   Benefits of a joint approach

5.1   In the beginning

To implement an expert system from scratch is a very difficult task. There is a variety of expert system software tools available and choosing one is a large task in its own right.

The most immediate advantage to the ABS of the joint development was access to:

- an expert systems development shell which has been used to implement expert systems,
- the experience and support of the knowledge engineers who have already implemented many systems,
- extensive training in the use of the shell, and very importantly
- a rigorous methodology.

All of these factors gave ABS and FAL a springboard to the development of a prototype expert system, from which both organizations could gain an appreciation of the technology. At the end of the prototyping exercise several conclusions were reached about the applicability of expert systems.

5.2   At the end

All three organizations agreed that all of the goals had been met and that the joint development had been very successful.

From the ABS's perspective, the training of staff, the knowledge of what is involved in developing expert systems and the ability to identify potential applications has given the ABS staff confidence in further expert systems developments. A representative from Fujitsu Japan believed that the technology transfer had been a success. A benefit to Fujitsu Japan was the successful Western use of the methodology which had previously only had Japanese exposure. FAL's perspective was in accord with the ABS, in that FAL now had experienced knowledge engineers who could help their organization solve new and difficult problems and had created new career paths for staff. The joint development had also given all three organizations further common interests, and regular meetings on expert systems will continue between FAL and the ABS.

6   Conclusion

The ABS and Fujitsu have successfully developed a prototype expert system. The prototype has user acceptance and could well be used as the basis for a large production system.

The success of the project is largely attributable to its joint nature. Fujitsu's development methodology (ES/SDEM) and development shell (ESHELL) and the support of Fujitsu Japan were all vital to the project. Another vital factor was the team structure and the contributions of both the ABS staff and FAL staff. The contributions of Fujitsu facilitated the transfer of expert systems technology to the ABS.

On a broader spectrum the joint development has proven the practical aspect of the technology.

References

Fujitsu Ltd (1987). *Development Methodology of an Expert System*.

Harmon P. and King D. (1985). *Expert Systems: Artificial Intelligence in Business*. New York: John Wiley and Sons

Hayes-Roth F., Waterman D. and Lenat D. (1983). *Building Expert Systems*. Reading MA: Addison-Wesley

Matsumoto S. (1987). ES/SDEM – Software development engineering methodology for expert systems. In *Proc. Int. Conf. and Exhibition on Artificial Intelligence*, Osaka, Japan

Matsumoto S. and Ota T. (1988). *Software Development Engineering Methodology for Expert Systems*. Fujitsu Ltd

13

AI in Analytical Chemistry: An Expert System for the Diagnosis of Problems in Hydroponic Agriculture

R. Finlayson
D.B. Hibbert

University of New South Wales

Water, nutrient solution and plant tissue of hydroponically-grown strawberries have been analysed for trace elements by inductively coupled plasma atomic emission spectroscopy (ICPAES). The data is collected by a microcomputer and is assessed by an expert system (HYDROPONICS) for elemental imbalances. HYDROPONICS also interrogates the farmer for observations of the crop which leads to a second set of identified problems. Rules are provided to resolve conflicting diagnoses and reports are issued detailing possible causes and suggesting remedies. A typical analysis and session with HYDROPONICS is given.

Introduction

In this paper we report the use of an expert system (HYDROPONICS) to aid the diagnosis of excesses and deficiencies in plants grown in a soil-less medium. The expert system is implemented on a microcomputer that is interfaced to the analytical instrumentation. This allows information to be transferred directly into the expert system which runs in real-time during the analysis.

AI in analytical chemistry

The first task of analytical chemistry is to determine what? and how much? This mainly requires the techniques of conventional analysis, although the DENDRAL project (Lindsay *et al.*, 1984) is an example of the use of AI to understand complex patterns that arise in mass spectra. Methods of analysis that provide an excess of complex information (for example, most spectroscopic techniques) are amenable to statistical treatments (factor analysis, pattern recognition) and, where human judgement is required in the interpretation of the data, AI. Recent examples of this approach are from mass spectrometry (Gregg *et al.*, 1984), infra-red analysis (Tomellini *et al.*, 1985) and nuclear magnetic resonance (Dumoulin and Levy, 1984). Another use of expert systems in analytical chemistry is in the optimization of methodology. Thus, it is possible to be advised on the best conditions for high performance liquid chromatography given a mixture of organic or biological molecules (Dessy, 1984), or in the use of an ultracentrifuge (Pierce and Hohne, 1986). Much of this work stems from the USA and has recently been reveiewed in an ACS symposium (Pierce and Hohne, 1986).

AI will make further inroads into analytical chemistry when it helps to answer the questions behind the questions given above. In the example of this paper, the hydroponic farmer wants to know why his or her strawberries taste bitter and why the plants are yellowing, and what to do to correct and prevent this situation, rather than be given pages of chemical analysis data.

Hydroponic agriculture

In hydroponic agriculture (Darley, 1987) plants are grown in a soil-less medium where all the nutritional requirements (except for carbon ex atmospheric carbon dioxide) are supplied by a nutrient solution to the plant roots, which may be supported in an inert mineral material (rock wool, vermiculite) or simply suspended in the solution. Plastic tubes (100 mm diameter, 6–20 m long), suspended at a convenient height are often used to contain the crop.

Hydroponic culture, though more capital intensive than traditional soil culture, and requiring more technical expertise, is perceived as a cost-effective alternative if:

1.   soils are absent or hostile, or farm land costly (Middle East, Pacific atolls);
2.   soil diseases persist or transfer as in monoculture cropping (for example, carnations in Australia);

Table 13.1 Limits of concentration of elements and ions needed for proper growth of strawberries.

Species	Raw water (ppm)	Nutrient solution (ppm)	Leaf tissue (ppm)	Fruit[†] (ppm)
Determined from ICPAES				
Al[‡]	<5	<5	<300	2
Ca	<100	110–210	10 000–20 000	1300
Fe	<2	1–4	70–250	33
Mg	<45	27–43	1000–4000	1300
Na[‡]	<30	<150	<3000	100–250
P	–	18–44	3000–5500	3200
S	<80	70–120	18 000–30 000	1000
B	<0.2	0.1–0.7	30–150	20
Cu	<0.1	0.1–0.4	5–40	5
K	–	90–220	15 000–25 000	22 000
Mn	<0.4	0.05–0.6	40–400	35
Zn	<0.1	0.05–0.4	20–90	10
From other methods of analysis				
NO_3^-	–	90–150	–	–
NH_3	<10	<20	–	–
Total N	–	–	25 000–35 000	–
pH	–	5.5–6.5	–	–
Cl^-[‡]	<50	<200	1000–5000	–
Mo	–	0.001–0.04	<0.5	–

[†] Fruit values from limited analyses, ranges taken as ± 30%.
[‡] Toxic elements, minimum value 0 ppm.

3.   top quality produce, commanding a premium price, is to be produced (lettuce, strawberries in NSW);

4.   the bench top height of the crop reduces the labour requirements, weeds and soil-borne pests;

5.   water supply is limited or costly (there are no evaporation losses).

Unlike natural soil that is capable, to some extent, of buffering nutrients and poisons, in hydroponic agriculture the operator must maintain all the nutrients in the optimum concentration range in the nutrient solution and be ever vigilant so that any deficiency in the system may be quickly corrected. Most elements are needed in a given range of concentration: too little and they are ineffective, too much and they are toxic. Some (for example, aluminium) are not necessary at all and are toxic above a certain lower limit. Chemical analysis can determine the levels of a range of elements and also important anions (for example, Cl^-, NO_3^-). Table 13.1 shows the limits of elements and ions that are important in the growth of strawberries. It is to be noted that there are different limits to the concentrations of the elements in the growing solution, the water that is used to make up this solution, the leaves and the fruit of the plant. Indeed, when considering the analysis of leaf tissue attention should be paid to the type of leaf and its age. In practice, the nutrient solution and the leaf tissue are analysed when diagnosing problems in a crop. In our studies of strawberries, we have observed that the fruit does not show such great diversity in concentration of elements.

Aspects of the requirements of an expert system

The information that is required to diagnose an excess or deficiency of species in a hydroponic system is a mixture of concrete facts (the chemical analysis), human observation (the farmer's view of the crop) and the rules of the diagnosis (see Figure 13.2). The rules that a human expert would use comprise a set of about 200 ranging from simple rules relating to the analysis ('the sodium content is adequate if it is less than 150 ppm') to more complex juxtapositions of facts ('if each chemical analysis shows no fault but the leaves have purple spots then either the analysis is wrong and there is a deficiency of phosphorus or there is an infection'). This latter example shows the need to check one set of information against another with a good knowledge of the system. For example, a deficiency of iron is accompanied in the tissue by an excess of potassium, so an apparent discrepancy between the analysis of nutrient and leaf may not be caused by an error. The chemical analysis should not be wrong, but rogue values can occur and it is important to identify which observations need to be queried in the case of conflict. Finally, there may be help to be given as to the source of the problem ('a galvanized metal article – roof, pipe etc. – has yielded a toxic zinc concentration') and counselling as to the correct procedure ('remove offending galvanized hardware, dilute with low zinc dam water, remove zinc from solid nutrient').

Choice of programming environment

Of the fifth generation languages, the authors were most familiar with PROLOG and the nature of the problem suggested that this language would be a reasonable choice for the expert system. Although there is access to networked DEC VAX 11/780 and 11/750 machines, we decided to implement the system on an IBM AT-compatible micro-computer. The reasons were three-fold:

1.   the output from the main analytical instrument is directly transportable to an MS-DOS machine,
2.   part of the commercial exploitation of the system will be selling a diagnostic package for use with microcomputers, and
3.   the problem is of a tractable size for running on a microcomputer.

The need for an expert system here stems not from the level of complexity (there are a limited number of rules) but from the different types of expertise needed – that of the analytical chemist and the hydroponics expert.

The system is in two parts with data from the Inductively Coupled Plasma Atomic Emission Spectrometer (ICPAES) and other chemical instruments coming directly into LOTUS-123 which performs the initial manipulation and then exports the results into the expert system written in the shell Xi-PLUS (Expertech Ltd). Xi-PLUS is a shell written in Micro-PROLOG that provides a highly interactive environment for creating and consulting knowledge bases. Its principal elements are **identifiers** (atoms) that are manipulated in **facts**, **rules** (if-then), **demons** (when-then), **queries** and **defaults** by English-like language rules and menus. Extensive help and reporting facilities are available. For example, any conclusion reached on the way to the top level goal may be changed to see 'what if . . .' and its derivation may be charted. The knowledge base (in Xi-PLUS several 'knowledge bases' may exist in a single 'application') may be modified at will and new knowledge bases may be chained and run automatically or from a menu. Interfaces to LOTUS-123, C and different graphics programs are provided. Both backward and forward chaining can occur and may be controlled from the knowledge base. Questions, with suitable help and reporting screens, to ascertain the values of identifiers may be written, but Xi-PLUS can also generate its own questions automatically, including only those possible values that are relevant to the goals under investigation.

Against Xi-PLUS the manipulation of variables is awkward and restrictive. For example, variables cannot take numerical values (there are ways around this using identifiers that are then reset). The operation of even a modestly sized knowledge base is slow – the assessment of the ICP results of 14 elements takes about 1.5 min on a 10 MHz IBM AT clone.

However Xi-PLUS has allowed us to write a usable system in about one man-month.

Experimental

The majority of elements may be conveniently analysed by ICPAES (see Table 13.1). In this technique a high temperature radio frequency plasma in a carrier gas (argon) atomizes a sample introduced as an aerosol from an aqueous solution. Hot elements emit light of characteristic wavelength, the intensity of which is proportional to the concentration of the element in solution. A scanning monchromator allows each element in Table 13.1 to be determined from a single sample, the time taken being about 2 min. ICPAES analyses were performed on a Labtam Plasma Lab with Labtam 3000 computer and software. The raw water and nutrient solution were analysed directly. Two standards per element were run to provide calibration. The calculation of concentrations was performed by the Labtam software and the results transported to LOTUS-123 as parts per million (ppm) of the original solution. The error in the ICPAES analysis was typically ± 4%. Weighed samples of dried plant tissue were mineralized in nitric acid and the resulting solution was analysed by ICP as described above.

Chloride, nitrate, ammonia and hydrogen ions were determined potentiometrically by ion selective electrodes which follow the Nernst equation (emf is proportional to log (a_i) where a_i is the activity of the ion which may be taken as the concentration in dilute solution). This data may also be logged by the microcomputer and manipulated in LOTUS-123. Total N is determined in the plant tissue by Kjeldahl digestion and titration. Molybdenum deficiencies are rare and, because of the very low amounts of this element, the analysis is complex and costly, requiring concentration by liquid chromatography before analysis.

Results

Data is available for the suitable limits of elements and ions in raw water and nutrient solutions (Resh, 1978), but for many plants there is little comprehensive data on values in plant tissue, in particular fruit (Reuter and Robinson, 1986). We are compiling such information for, *inter alia*, strawberries, the results of which are given in Table 13.1. The range of concentrations represent values from a series of plants, both healthy, diseased and showing an elemental imbalance. The limits for elements are taken when the yield of fruit falls by 10%. We have a smaller data set for strawberry fruit and the ranges may be prone to a greater error.

The analysed concentration of each element is converted in LOTUS-123 into a value between ± 100 with 0 being the optimum value and the output is presented to the expert system and graphically (Figure 13.1) to the operator.

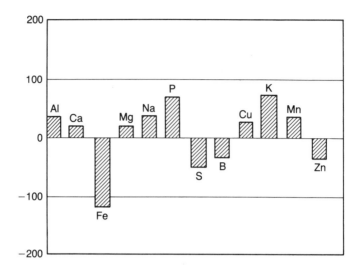

Figure 13.1   Elemental analysis by ICPAES of a nutrient solution scaled to a normal range of ± 100, showing a deficiency of iron.

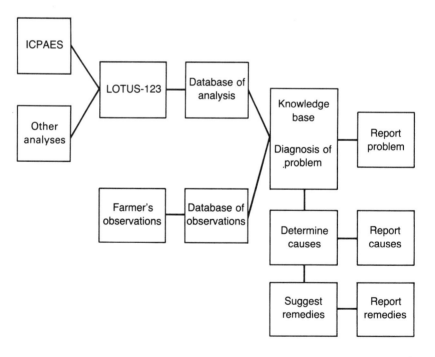

Figure 13.2   Schematic representation of the HYDROPONICS analysis and expert system.

HYDROPONICS – the expert system

The overall relationship between aspects of the expert system and the analysis procedure is shown schematically in Figure 13.2. A small knowledge base is initially loaded to establish if the analysis includes ICP or the farmer's observations or both. If both, a check for conflicts between their conclusions will be performed. HYDROPONICS answers the top level goal analysis? which takes the value normal only if both the farmer's observations and the ICP analysis are clear. It is important to alert the farmer to problems with the nutrient, water supply or crop, even if this has not become noticeable. Equally, the farmer may still have the guidance of an expert if the analysis is clear but there is a problem with the crop. This part of the expert system offers a limited guide to diseases, and also points to elemental imbalances that may help in the absence of a full chemical analysis. In answering the top level goal, questions may be asked by the program, and reports (including graphs) and help screens are generated at suitable junctures. General rules and decision trees are available (Resh, 1978) to diagnose elemental imbalances from observation of the crop and these are included in the solution of the goal problem includes? In discussions with local farmers we have discovered the importance of gaining individual expert knowledge for a particular crop, and in the exact expressions used to detail observed problems.

ICP analysis

The name of the species followed by the analysis in water, nutrient, leaf tissue and fruit tissue are read one species at a time from LOTUS-123 as species, conc of water, conc of nutrient, conc of leaf and conc of fruit. The rules for handling chemical data are of the form:

> if list of species includes Any_element
> and species is Any_element
> and conc of water > 100
> then list of excess elements in water includes Any_element.

In Xi-PLUS, floating variables begin with upper case letters while identifiers commence with lower case letters. In a future version two warning states, a bit high and a bit low, will be generated. Then the lists of species that are imbalanced are used in the rules that report the problems and suggest solutions. Amounts of chemicals to be added or removed by dilution with water are automatically generated in LOTUS-123 and may be read in to HYDROPONICS as necessary.

Table 13.2 Allowed values for the attributes of the observations made on a crop by the farmer.

Attribute	Values may include (and unknown)
affected leaves	older leaves, newer leaves
effects	generalized, localized
terminal buds	die, remain alive
leaves are	wilted, "not wilted"
leaves have	no dead spots, small dead spots, large dead spots
leaf colour	light green, dark green, yellow, red
stalks	slender, thick, bent, normal
roots	normal, stumpy
fruit taste	bitter, normal

Farmer's observations

The observations of the farmer are statements that give values to attributes. Allowable attributes and the values each may take are given in Table 13.2. In addition any attribute may be unknown. All excesses and deficiencies are possible at the start of the question and answer session with the grower because values for the attributes are unknown. Questions are asked, in turn, to establish the truth of each rule that adds particular problems to the list of problem. Thus the rule for deficiency of iron is:

```
if affected leaves are new leaves or unknown
and effects are localized or unknown
and terminal buds are alive or unknown
and leaves are "not wilted" or unknown
and leaves have no dead spots or unknown
and leaf colour is yellow or unknown
and stalks are slender or unknown
and fruit taste is bitter or unknown
then problem includes deficiency of iron
```

The grower is encouraged to answer unknown if he or she is not sure. In the above example, iron deficiency is ruled out if the fruit taste is normal. There are currently 22 rules for deficiencies and excesses of 11 elements; if each attribute has a definite value then a problem is uniquely identified or all are ruled out and the default that the problem includes no answer fires. As more attributes are unknown, more possible elemental imbalances are revealed. We have defined a certainty index for each imbalance identified and added to the list of problem, as the ratio of the number of attributes that are in each rule that are not unknown to the total number of attributes. If nothing is known then all imbalances are listed with certainty of 0; if all are known a single problem is found with certainty 1.

Dealing with conflicts

Having both ICP analysis and the farmer's observations is a luxury that may lead to conflicts. HYDROPONICS has a series of rules that deal with potential conflicts between the observations and chemical analysis. For example, if iron is deficient in the tissue of a plant, potassium, phosphorus and nitrogen may appear to be high in the tissue while being normal in the nutrient solution. Imbalances with similar observable attributes are flagged (for example, iron and sulphur deficiency), with the ICP analysis being the arbiter. The imbalances are also ranked as being common, uncommon and rare. So, if iron deficiency or molybdenum toxicity are indicated, the iron deficiency will be chosen as the major problem. All conclusions are available to the user so the grower has the possibility of finally overriding HYDROPONICS.

Reporting causes and remedies

Each problem has a series of causes that are reported if they have not already been ruled out. In the above example one cause of excess phosphorus in leaf tissue may be iron deficiency. If the iron is normal then this possibility is not offered to the user. Iron may be deficient if the pH > 6.3. If the pH < 6.3, high pH is not the cause of that case of iron deficiency.

Each cause has a remedy and these are reported to the user. In LOTUS, a calculation of the amount of nutrient to add, or water to dilute with (in the case of an excess) is done to bring each element to its median concentration.

An example consultation

Iron deficiency is a common problem and we show in Table 13.3 the analysis of a recent plant and nutrient submitted to us, together with the observations of the crop and the responses of HYDROPONICS.

Table 13.3

HYDROPONICS	User	Comments
		HYDROPONICS uses multicoloured screens and menus. Here, only the text of the consultation is given.

The **analysis** includes
    just **ICP**
    just **observations of crop**
    both **ICP** and **observations** ....
	<<	<< indicates the choice of the user

Report: Loading ICP knowledge base.		A LOTUS-123 file (ICP.WKS) is automatically consulted that contains: (i) the limits of normal analyses of the species considered, and (ii) concentrations of the current analysis. These are direct from the ICP spectrometer.
Report: ICP anlaysis indicates a deficiency of iron in the nutrient solution.		
Report: Loading farmer's observations.		A question and answer session now follows to establish the goal – **problem** includes?

affected leaves are
    older leaves
    newer leaves ....
    unknown
	<<	A common distinction is whether the older, established leaves are affected or the newer, bud leaves as they come out.

effects are
    generalized
    localized ....
    unknown
	<<	Over the whole plant or just on some leaves?

terminal buds
    die
    remain alive ....
    unknown
	<<	

leaves are
    wilted
    "not wilted" ....
    unknown
	<<	

leaves have
    no dead spots
    small dead spots
    large dead spots
    unknown ....
	<<	This is difficult to decide ... Big spots grow from little spots.

HYDROPONICS	User	Comments

leaf colour is
  yellow
  red
  dark green
  light green
  unknown ....
	<<	Colouring, and how it distributes over the leaf is important, and difficult to express (see "further work").

stalks are
  slender
  thickened
  bent
  normal
  unknown ....
	<<	

fruit taste is
  bitter ....
  normal
  unknown
	<<	This is, after all, the ultimate test.

Report:
Certainty of manganese deficiency = 0.60
Certainty of sulphur deficiency   = 0.60
Certainty of iron deficiency   = 0.625   = 5 known/8 total attributes

Report: There is a consistent deficiency of
iron between the crop and nutrient solution.

Report: Possible causes of iron deficiency are: Note: as pH is correct this is not
 (i) Iron omitted from nutrient solution.   included, nor is high phosphorus.
 (ii) Iron added as sulphate not EDTA.
 (iii) Low temperature.
 (iv) Poor aeration of solution.

Report: Possible solutions of iron deficiency are:
 (i) Add Fe EDTA (20 g/L) to nutrient solution.
 (ii) Spray leaves with 0.1% iron solution.
 (iii) If it is not summer try warming roots at night
 (10–15°C).
 (iv) Increase aeration by splashing of return
stream to holding tank, increasing ventilation of
tank, or bubble air.

Future developments

The package is functioning on a limited number of elements and it remains to be seen whether the total number of elements and ions with their attendant rules can be programmed into a microcomputer system.

The language of the interaction with the farmer is important and we are conducting research into the preferred descriptors, for example 'yellow' or 'chlorotic' to describe a leaf colour. The exact patina of a mottled leaf is also critical to the diagnosis and we hope to use the graphics interface to offer pictures of leaves that a farmer can choose from, rather than descriptions such as 'reticulated with interveinal chlorosis'.

Acknowledgement

This work was supported by Unisearch Ltd.

References

Darley E., ed. (1987). *Hydroponics Workshop*. Sydney: NSW Department of Agriculture

Dessy R.E. (1984). *Anal. Chem.*, **56**, 1312A

Dumoulin C.L. and Levy G.C. (1984). *J. Mol. Spec.*, **113**, 299

Gregg H.R., Hoffman P.A., Crawford R.W., Brand H.R. and Wong C.M. (1984). *Anal. Chem.*, **56**, 1121

Lindsay R., Buchanen B.G., Feigenbaum E.A. and Lederberg J. (1984). *Dendral*. New York: McGraw-Hill

Pierce T.H. and Hohne B.A. eds. (1986). *Artificial Intelligence Applications in Chemistry*. ACS Symposium Series 306, USA: American Chemical Society

Resh H.M. (1978). *Hydroponic Food Production*. Santa Barbara: Woodbridge Press

Reuter D.J. and Robinson J.B. (1986). *Plant Analysis*. Melbourne: Inkata Press

Tomellini S.A., Hartwick R.A. and Woodruff H.B. (1985). *Appl. Spect.*, **39**, 331

14

Explanations and the SIRATAC Cotton Management System

Matthew Clarke

Digital Equipment Corporation (Australia) Pty Ltd

There is a wide variety of understandings of what constitutes a reasonable explanation. This paper summarizes the basic issues of computer generated explanation and examines one practical approach to these issues. To transcend the inadequacies of 'rule dumping', an explanation facility must be closely tied to the whole structure of an expert system, rather than appended as an afterthought. The SIRATAC cotton management system shows that the endorsement paradigm is a good basis for generating explanations. It also illustrates that while OPS5 does not have a standard explanation facility, it is not difficult to generate explanations from OPS5.

1 Introduction

Explanations are often cited as a requirement of an expert system. They are also frequently mentioned as a difficult feature to achieve adequately. However, it is rare to find in AI books or papers anything more than glimpses of the issues involved in this area.

The first section of this paper gives an overview of the issues involved in generating explanations from an expert system. Then follows a discussion of the SIRATAC cotton management system, focusing on its explanation facility.

The history and purposes of SIRATAC have been well documented elsewhere. In summary:

Cotton cannot be grown with commercial success in Australia without chemical control of pests costing from A\$ 100 to A\$ 300 per hectare. Excessive spraying is costly, may cause outbreaks of secondary pests, increases the risk of pests becoming resistant to insecticides and causes public concern about pollution. The SIRATAC system has been developed to assist growers to reduce these risks by making good tactical decisions in the use of insecticides. (See Hearn *et al.* (1986), which includes other references.)

The existing system (written wholly in FORTRAN) has grown to be unmanageable and a reimplementation is currently under way. This reimplementation is a joint venture between several groups. The expert system portion of this reimplementation has been designed by the Digital Equipment Corporation. SIRATAC Ltd and CSIRO's Division of Plant Industry provide the cotton growing expertise; CSIRO's Division of Information Technology coordinates the project and provides the programming resources to implement the system.

In the rest of this paper 'SIRATAC' refers to this reimplementation.

SIRATAC will integrate the latest in fourth generation and relational database technologies with a suite of FORTRAN simulation models and an intelligent decision maker written in OPS5.

2   Explanations

2.1   What constitutes a good explanation?

A good explanation is one which provides the user with well structured information to allow him or her to understand the conclusion which the expert system has reached.

This definition has many ramifications:

- Accurate and relevant information (**content**) must be presented in a way which is readily comprehensible (**form**).
- Explanation generation is a user-oriented task: the needs of the user community should dictate what constitutes an acceptable explanation. Explanations need to be understandable to the end user, not necessarily to the knowledge engineers or the experts.
- A good explanation needs to be affected by the level of expertise of the user. Ideally, it should generate different text depending on the user.
- An explanation need not mirror how the expert system came to the conclusion. A significant understanding of a particular conclusion may be quite independent of the exact flow of inference used to reach that conclusion. This happens to humans as well – the way we explain our conclusions is normally not by describing how we reached that conclusion.

- A good explanation system has to know when to stop. It should not reveal everything it knows about the conclusion, only that which is necessary to bring clarity to the user's mind. An explanation should only appear when requested.

- The main aim is to give *understanding*, not to *convince*. It is possible to convince someone without them having any understanding, just as it is possible for them to understand without being convinced. We should aim (in human-to-human relations just as much as in computer-to-human relations) to assist people to make decisions, rather than to make decisions for them. This gives people the dignity they deserve and allows them to add any extra knowledge they may have before choosing to accept or reject the expert system's advice.

2.2   Are explanations always necessary?

Explanation facilities are not always used in the way described above. Explanations are useful as a debugging tool (helping to track errors in inferencing and errors on the knowledge base). Explanations in some systems may be used as a tutor: to teach humans about the domain. More importantly, some applications for expert systems have no requirement for explanations.

It has been pointed out that non-expert users of expert systems often find explanations superfluous. They need to know what to do without wanting to know why (Browston *et al.*, 1985).

Indeed, some expert systems will never need to interact with humans: they will run as one module among many in a larger system. It would make no sense at all for one program to demand an explanation of another program.

2.3   What sort of questions might the user want answered?

Here are some of the most common questions which need to be addressed by explanation facilities. Innumerable variations on these are likely to be asked. Yet even these basic questions are not universally applicable. In any particular expert system only some subset of questions will be both appropriate to the domain and required by the users.

- Questions of definition, like:
  - What does ⟨term⟩ mean?
- Questions of method, like:
  - How was the value of ⟨variable⟩ deduced?
  - What factors led to ⟨conclusion⟩?

- Questions of appropriateness, like:
    - Why was that method of evaluation used rather than some other method?
- Questions of motivation, like:
    - Why is it necessary to deduce ⟨variable⟩?
- Questions of hypothesis, like:
    - What would happen if ⟨variable⟩ was ⟨value⟩?

For a more detailed examination of types of questions and answering strategies, see Neches *et al.* (1984).

2.4   How can expert systems produce explanations?

There are four key techniques used in explanation generation – canned text, form sentences, execution trace and 'deep' reasoning. It is normal for an expert system to use some mixture of these.

2.4.1   Canned text

In the simplest case, where an expert system has a small set of possible conclusions, each conclusion may have associated with it some hard coded English text indicating the reasons why that conclusion is appropriate. Similarly, more complex systems may have hard coded text associated with individual inference steps or with subgoals achieved along the way to deducing the conclusion.

A major problem with any use of canned text is that maintenance is made more difficult. Whenever the knowledge base is changed, the canned text must be examined to see if it is still correct. Otherwise the knowledge in the explanations may no longer reflect or enhance the knowledge in the knowledge base. Clearly it would be better if the expert system could generate explanations from the knowledge base itself.

Using canned text is normally the best way to answer questions of definition.

2.4.2   Form sentences

The next step is to augment canned text with actual values. This makes the explanation more relevant to the specific task at hand. This is achieved by inserting variables into some predefined sentence structure.

This style of explanation may become quite complex, including values deduced at run-time and information extracted from the knowledge base. For instance, the explanation:

The car requires a visit to the garage since a terminal discharge level of
0.0 V indicates a faulty battery.

could be generated from the form sentence:

The ⟨singular form of object⟩ requires ⟨problem solution⟩ since a ⟨variable⟩
level of ⟨value⟩ ⟨variable units⟩ indicates ⟨problem⟩.

2.4.3   Execution trace

The vast majority of expert system explanation facilities use some form of
execution trace (often called 'rule dumping'). The purpose of an
execution trace is to show the user what inference steps were used to
reach a conclusion.

This may simply be a verbatim display of the current rule being
fired. There may also be the option of displaying rules which have
previously fired. In most cases, a literal rule dump is quite opaque. Hence
some massaging is normally necessary to make the rule more readable.

This form of explanation can describe *what* happened to reach the
conclusion, yet says little about *why* that path of inference was chosen
over another. This limitation can be somewhat lessened by including
sections of canned text which seek to clarify *why* a particular rule was
appropriate at that time.

Quite reasonable explanations can be produced in this way for
positive questions of method. But explanations for negative queries (for
example, 'why *didn't* you recommend so-and-so?') are somewhat more
difficult.

Questions of motivation can often be answered satisfactorily by,
first, examining the execution history to discover what goal triggered this
line of inferencing and, second, expressing the goal and its consequences
via a form sentence.

2.4.4   'Deep' reasoning

One can readily see that the role of canned text is to add knowledge to
the expert system which is either not coded in the knowledge base or not
extractable from the knowledge base. An alternative, therefore, would be
to include that knowledge somehow in the knowledge base in a
retrievable way. Trying to encode knowledge *about* the expert system's
knowledge is the essence of deep reasoning.

If an expert system understood itself, then it could more easily
explain itself. Some expert system technologies go so far as to say that an
expert system *must* be able to reason about its own processes since
explanations are a by-product of self-knowledge (Brachman *et al.*, 1983).
This seems to imply that for each expert system there needs to be a
separate explanation generation expert system whose domain is 'facts that
have been deduced and knowledge about the deduction process'.

Certainly the *best* explanations come from the ability to 'reason from first principles', but *reasonable* explanations can be achieved without this ability.

Questions of appropriateness and questions of motivation generally require more underlying knowledge than can be gained by examining the system's chain of inferencing. Hence, deep reasoning techniques would be of most use in answering those types of questions.

2.5   Comprehensiveness and generality

An important corollary to Section 2.4 is that an effective explanation system needs to be closely tied to the overall structure of the expert system. It is inadequate to append an explanation facility as an afterthought. If an expert system needs to have an explanation capability then it needs to be designed around that requirement.

Unfortunately, this close coupling of explanation generation with the rest of an expert system limits the generality of the explanation facility.

Any form of rule dumping aids generality but the explanations generated are normally less comprehensive than what the user really wants. On the other hand, making use of deep reasoning techniques can aid comprehensiveness, but binds the explanation facility to the domain being addressed.

Since most tasks have different explanation requirements and because of the dependence of an explanation facility on the structure of the rest of the expert system, it is generally very difficult to transport an explanation facility from one expert system to another. Hence, there are currently few explanation facilities which are comprehensive as well as being general-purpose.

3   SIRATAC

3.1   The OPS5 decision maker

The OPS5 module in SIRATAC has three main sources of information: the number of pests present in a field; predictions of pest and plant development; and characteristics of pesticides. The module deduces which chemicals (or combinations of chemicals) should be sprayed on the crop, based on criteria such as efficacy towards the current pest population, cost, government regulations and environmental impact. The most favourable application day (today, tomorrow or the next day) is also recommended.

As an indication of the complexity of the task, there are:

- about 20 chemicals to choose from, plus mixtures of any 2 or 3 chemicals; and

- between 20 and 30 factors by which chemicals are judged.

The decision-making process is based on a system of *endorsements*. This approach is a variation on the endorsements of Cohen (1984), and Sullivan and Cohen (1985).

Cohen uses endorsements to make explicit the reasons for believing or disbelieving uncertain propositions. In SIRATAC there are no levels of certainty: we assume all data and inferences are accurate. But it is necessary to keep track of the many reasons for choosing or not choosing particular spray recommendations. Each of these reasons has an associated **level of importance**.

The relationship between levels of certainty and levels of importance deserves more study. It could be that the two are isomorphic. In real life, we allow both of these factors to affect how we respond to new data. We are certainly concerned about the truth of an assertion ('how reliable is the source of this data?'). But we also filter new data based on relevance ('how important is this fact to the task at hand?'). Many expert systems deal with certainty but ignore importance. In SIRATAC, certainty is ignored while importance is dealt with in a similar way to standard certainty manipulation: there are mechanisms for assigning importance levels to assertions and mechanisms for combining those levels.

3.2   Endorsements: an example

Endorsements form the basis of the importance manipulation mechanisms. They also form the basis of the explanation facility.

As an example, let us consider the issue of **phytotoxity**. Some chemicals do not adversely affect the cotton plant, but others (those said to have high phytotoxicity) are, to some degree, detrimental. Phytotoxicity is quite an important issue when the plants are young. But later in the season, the plants are hardy enough to make phytotoxicity unimportant. These factors are drawn together by a small set (3 or 4) of OPS5 rules when a chemical is being evaluated. The product of these rules is an endorsement for that chemical. An endorsement is a working memory element (a piece of OPS5 data) which is represented like:

```
(endorsement   ˆ chemical-id   G:23
               ˆ type           PHYTOTOXICITY
               ˆ reasons        | has average phytotoxicity |
               ˆ level          60)
```

In creating this working memory element, the OPS5 knowledge base is asserting that 'on the issue of phytotoxicity, I endorse chemical G:23 with 60 votes'.

The chemical-id field is an internal identifier which points to another working memory element containing details of the pesticide (or mixture of pesticides) being evaluated.

The level is based on knowledge of the particular chemical's phytotoxicity and the current importance of phytotoxicity. The level represents a *vote count* which may be either positive or negative.

The values in both the level and reason fields are computed at run-time. Hence, the information represented in those values can be arbitrarily complex.

The contents of the reason field are used for explanation generation.

3.3   Explanations in SIRATAC

3.3.1   What do the users require?

Users of SIRATAC do not always accept the recommendations produced by the system. The knowledge encapsulated in the computer system can, at times, seem remote and irrelevant to the cotton grower. Sometimes they prefer to trust their own experience-based knowledge. The purpose of SIRATAC's explanations is to minimize this remoteness by explicitly stating all the factors which were taken into account by the decision maker.

Typically, the users may have a different opinion of the relative importance of these factors. Having seen the explanation, the users can augment the system's reasoning with their own judgement before making a decision.

If the users disagree with a recommendation then the explanation allows them to see clearly *where* they disagree with the system. If they agree with the system's recommendation, they may still request some explanations in order to enhance their knowledge of the decision-making process; to increase their confidence in their own judgement; and to increase their confidence in SIRATAC's advice.

3.3.2   What does SIRATAC provide?

At any time after SIRATAC has made a pest management decision (even several days later) the user may issue explanation commands like:

- Display SIRATAC responds with its recommendation: a list of chemicals considered to be most appropriate for controlling the current pest population. The recommended application day is also displayed.

Table 14.1

Endosulfan was not recommended because it –	
Reason	Level
Should definitely not be used in stage 3 of the Heliothis resistance strategy	−999
Is moderately toxic to fish	−0.1
Is moderately toxic to bees	−0.06
Poses a resistance hazard	−0.06
Will control the Heliothis population well	0.96
Will control the aphid population moderately well	0.56
Is moderately reliable	0.24
Is inexpensive	0.18
Has a low resurgence hazard	0.12
Has low toxicity to beneficial insects	0.09
Has moderate residual mortality	0.06
Has low phytotoxicity	0.04
Has low toxicity to birds	0.04
Has low toxicity to humans	0.02
Takes a moderate time to kill	0.01
Is registered for the current pest population	0.0

- List   A complete list of chemicals evaluated (in order of merit).
- Why chlordimeform   SIRATAC answers the question 'why was the chemical chlordimeform recommended?' in the following style:

  > Chlordimeform (spray tomorrow) was recommended because it is moderately inexpensive, is not phytotoxic, will control the Heliothis population (reducing the egg count to 0.11) and spraying tomorrow will give a 12% better result than spraying today. These considerations outweighed the fact that chlordimeform could cause Heliothis resistance.

- Why not acephate   SIRATAC answers the question 'why wasn't the chemical acephate recommended?' in the following style:

  > Although acephate will totally control the aphid population and is not phytotoxic, it was not recommended because it is expensive and will not control the Heliothis population.

- Explain endosulfan   SIRATAC produces an exhaustive list of the reasons for and against the endosulfan recommendation (Table 14.1), along with the relative importance of those reasons.

An enhancement to this system would be to add a compare command. This would provide the user with a comparison of two chemicals. To do this, the explanation system would need to examine the endorsements for both chemicals and note where they differ.

3.3.3 How are these explanations generated?

Generation of these explanations is quite straightforward, since all the necessary information is already in the endorsements.

The central part of the explanation facility is the why and why not questions. To answer these questions the reason field of the relevant endorsements is used to fill in the slots in form sentences. For example, the answer to a why question uses the form:

> ⟨conclusion⟩ was recommended because it ⟨positive reason 1⟩, ⟨positive reason 2⟩, . . . and ⟨positive reason *n*⟩. These considerations outweighed the fact that ⟨negative reason 1⟩, ⟨negative reason 2⟩, . . . and ⟨negative reason *m*⟩.

Although the *form* of the explanations is very simple, the *content* is quite varied and comprehensive. The endorsement reasons (which were generated during the decision-making stage) may include binding conditions (such as requirements of Law), heuristically-deduced assertions, and detailed numeric information gained from the FORTRAN simulations.

Why and why not explanations only contain the *major* factors contributing to the recommendation. This follows the principle that an explanation system should only present as much information as is necessary to bring clarity to the user's mind. If the users wish to examine a chemical in more detail, they can use the explain facility.

Generating an explain list is a simple matter of formatting all endorsements for the requested chemical into a sorted table. From this, the user can see exactly what factors affected the decision and exactly how much weight was given to each of those factors.

By storing all the endorsements after a recommendation has been made, SIRATAC allows the users to return at any time in the future to request an explanation. The explanation facility can act on the stored list of endorsements without needing to repeat the whole decision-making process.

4 Concluding comments

- OPS5 is a programming language: it is used for too many different tasks to allow one explanation facility to be generally useful. But the lack of inbuilt explanation facilities does not imply that explanations are impractical in an OPS5 system.

- The fact that explanations needed to be an integral part of SIRATAC was a large influence on the choice of the endorsement approach. Endorsements can be expressed and manipulated quite naturally in OPS5.

- The SIRATAC project shows that endorsements provide a good basis from which to generate explanations. Using endorsements, generating explanations from OPS5 is not a major task.

- SIRATAC's explanation facility has been designed to operate with any system which uses the same endorsement structure. All information regarding how a decision was made is stored in the endorsement data structures. The code which generates explanations can operate on any list of endorsements, without the need to know how, when or by whom they were created. Hence some domain independence has been achieved.

- Rather than storing information about what rules fired when, endorsements record key points in the inferencing. They record justifications for accepting or rejecting certain conclusions. Formatting these justifications into English sentences gives a much more meaningful explanation than a massaged rule dump.

  This endorsement approach does not automatically produce a deep reasoning system. But it does provide a framework with which to make explicit the reasons underlying a decision.

5   Acknowledgements

The cotton examples in this paper are, of course, only possible because of the many years of experience which have been brought together in the SIRATAC development team. I am glad to have been able to rely on Neil Ashburner's understanding of the old SIRATAC system; Brian Hearn's expert knowledge of cotton management and his ability to funnel the diverse views of other cotton managers; Bob Jansen's extensive database and design experience; Bob Colomb's encouragement and managerial support; and John Coghlan, who first recognized the applicability of the endorsement approach.

References

Brachman R.J., Amarel S., Engelman C., Engelmore R.S., Feigenbaum E.A. and Wilkins D.E. (1983). What are expert systems? In *Building Expert Systems*. (Hayes-Roth F., Waterman D.A. and Lenat D.B., eds.). Reading MA: Addison-Wesley

Browston L., Farrell R., Kant E. and Martin N. (1985). *Programming Expert Systems in OPS5*. Reading MA: Addison-Wesley

Cohen P.R. (1984). Progress report on the theory of endorsements: a heuristic approach to reasoning about uncertainty. In *Proc. IEEE Workshop on Principles of Knowledge-Based Systems*, Denver CO

Hearn B., Brook K., Ashburner N. and Colomb R. (1986). SIRATAC, a cotton crop management expert system. In *Proc. 1st Australian Artificial Intelligence Congress*, Melbourne

Neches R., Swartout W.R. and Moore J. (1984). Enhanced maintenance and explanation of expert systems through explicit models of their development. In *Proc. IEEE Workshop on Principles of Knowledge-Based Systems*, Denver CO

Sullivan M. and Cohen P.R. (1985). An endorsement-based plan recognition program. In *Proc. 9th Int. Joint Conf. on Artificial Intelligence*, Los Angeles CA

Part Three
Techniques

15
Robustness and Transparency in Intelligent Systems

Randall Davis
Massachusetts Institute of Technology

Given the widespread interest in and use of knowledge-based systems, it is important to understand under what circumstances they will be **robust** – able to handle problems they have not previously been tested on, and **transparent** – able to make their operation comprehensible to an observer. This paper explores robustness and transparency by considering the potential use of knowledge-based systems in an environment where such attributes are crucial: a manned space station. We use this as a motivating example to understand how robustness and transparency arise and what research will be necessary to produce systems with these attributes.

Building and operating a manned space station will confront problems of enormous complexity in an environment that is both hostile and unfamiliar. The complexity of the station and the novelty of the environment preclude the creation of an exhaustive list of contingency procedures. Unforeseen events will inevitably occur, requiring real-time interpretation, diagnosis and response. As an example of the kinds of difficulties that arise, we briefly review the failure of a fuel cell during the second mission of the US space shuttle. We take this as a starting point, using it as an example of the kind of unanticipated event that can occur and examining the varieties of knowledge and engineering reasoning required to deal with it. We then consider what it might take to have a computer assist in this task by giving it understanding of 'how something works', a key concept developed through the rest of the paper.

We discuss briefly several non-solutions to the problem, demonstrating why existing technology is insufficient. This leads to the exploration of several research themes. We consider the nature and character of engineering models and suggest that their creation, selection, and simplification are key issues in the sort of understanding we wish to create. Recalling the difficulties involved in the capture of the Solar Max satellite, we argue for the necessity of complete design capture and speculate about what it would take to create a design capture system so effective that it would be almost unthinkable to create or modify a design without it. We also consider what can be done at the design stage to make models considerably easier to use and more effective; that is, how can we design in such a fashion that interpretation, diagnosis, and response become that much easier?

1 Introduction

Developing and building a manned space station will confront problems of significant complexity in an extraordinarily demanding environment. The station's size and complexity will make necessary the extensive use of automation for monitoring and control of critical subsystems, such as life support. The station complexity, along with the novelty of space as an environment, means that all contingencies cannot be anticipated. Yet the hostility of the environment means that consequences of failure can be substantial. In such situations, robustness and transparency become essential properties of the systems we develop.

This paper is concerned with these two properties – robustness and transparency – from a number of perspectives. We claim that they are crucial to the space station application and, in fact, to any situation with similar levels of complexity and similar consequences of failure. We argue that they are fundamental properties of models and system designs based on those models. As a result, robustness and transparency cannot easily be grafted on afterwards; they must be considered at the outset and designed in. We explore how this might happen, that is, how these two properties translate into constraints on system design and describe a number of research efforts that may lead to better understanding of how such design might be accomplished.

It is useful, at this point, to establish some simple vocabulary. By **system** or **device** we mean the hardware whose behaviour we wish to understand and control. The power distribution system, for example, would include all the cables, batteries, fuel cells, solar arrays, switches, etc., that supply power to the station. By **model** we mean a description of that hardware that will allow us to analyse, interpret, diagnose, and guide its behaviour. When expressed explicitly, it is typically written in terms of schematics, performance curves, engineering drawings, etc. The model may also be implicit in a program designed to monitor the hardware or it may exist in the mind of the human doing the same job. In any case, it provides the basic framework used to understand the device.

While we speak broadly of systems and models, our concern here is, for the most part, with systems of physical devices and the associated engineering models of them; much of what we say is likely to carry over to software as well. Models of human behaviour and social systems are largely beyond what we attempt to do here.

1.1   Unanticipated events: motivation

Because much of what we discuss is motivated by the difficulties of dealing with unanticipated events, it is worth taking a moment to consider what they are and why they are important. By unanticipated events we mean any occurrence requiring a response that has not been previously planned for, analysed, and the appropriate response determined. One compelling example might occur if the life support system monitors present a collection of readings that indicate a malfunction but do not match any known pattern of misbehaviour. The readings need to be analysed and an appropriate response initiated, yet this cannot be done 'by the book'; it requires that we reason through what could have happened to produce such readings.

The importance of such events arises from their inevitability, due to both the complexity of the space station and the novelty of the environment. Unanticipated events and interactions are a fact of life for complex, large-scale systems because the number of different kinds of things that can go wrong is so vast, and our ability to do exhaustive formal analyses of fault events has rather modest limits. Space is a sufficiently novel environment that we have no comprehensive catalogue of standard fault models that can be checked ahead of time.

1.1.1   Unanticipated events: example

During STS-2, the second mission of the US space shuttle, an interesting sequence of events led, at one point, to the recognition that a fuel cell was failing and later to the realization that in its degraded state it could conceivably explode. This sequence of events helps to illustrate both the inevitability of unanticipated events and the kinds of knowledge and reasoning needed to deal with them.

Some brief background will help make the events comprehensible. The basic function of the three fuel cells (Figure 15.1) is to produce electricity by combining hydrogen and oxygen in a carefully controlled reaction that uses potassium hydroxide as a catalyst. The combustion product is water, removed from the cell by the water removal system (Figure 15.2): damp hydrogen enters the condenser at the right, pulled along by the flow produced by the motor and pump at left. The motor is also turning a separator that pushes condensed water droplets toward the walls of the chamber where they accumulate due to surface tension (recall this is a zero gravity environment). The now drier hydrogen returns to the fuel cell, while the annulus of water continually being formed at the

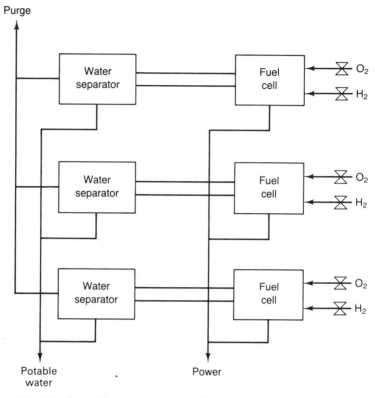

Figure 15.1 The fuel cell and water separation system.

separator is picked up and guided to the water storage area. A meter at the outlet monitors water pH, checking for contamination (for example, potassium hydroxide from the fuel cell), since the water is intended for consumption.

In a very much abbreviated form, the sequence of events leading to early mission termination of STS-2 proceeded as follows (adapted from Eichhoefer, 1985):

- Pre-launch   During pre-launch activities the fuel cell pH meters register high.
  Interpretation   Familiar, unexplained anomaly.

- Pre-launch   At various times, oxygen and hydrogen flow meters read high; at one point oxygen flow goes off-scale.
  Interpretation   Sensors malfunctioning.

- +3:00   Fuel cell 1 (FC1) begins to shed load; the other two assume more load.
  Interpretation   Cell may be failing.
  Controllers consider purging FC1. Degraded perform-

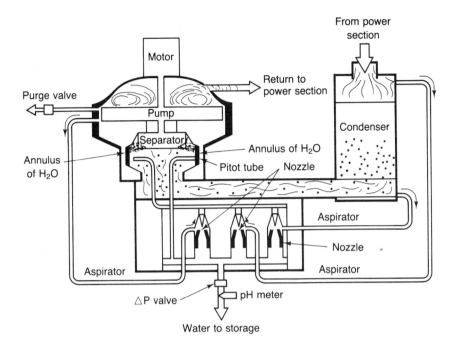

Figure 15.2 Details of the water separation unit. (Adapted from MITRE Corporation report of 16 July 1985 by Gerald Eichhoefer.)

ance suggests possible flooding; pH high also suggests flooding; purging will remove water. Purging FC1 rejected – purged KOH might solidify, blocking purge line that is common to all three cells.

- +3:25 Crew asked to test pH manually. If sensor is correct, potable water may be getting contaminated by KOH.

- +4:25 Crew too busy with other duties to perform test.

- +4:40 FC1 off-loads significantly.
          Interpretation Clear failure.

- +4:51 FC1 isolated from remainder of electrical system and shut down.

- +5:48 Mission evaluation room recognizes new failure mode for the cell in the current situation. Once it is shut down pressure slowly drops, but can drop at different rates on each side. If pressure differential becomes large enough, gas bubbles from one side can cross to the other, possibly combining explosively.

- +7.52 FC1 restarted with reactant valves closed; reactants consumed and voltage in cell drops to 0.

Post-mission analysis of the fuel cell and water separator revealed that the pH meter had been working correctly and that a small particle blocked the nozzle in the water separator of cell 1, preventing water removal to the storage area. The water backed up, first in the separator and later in the cell, flooding it (hence the high pH), leading to performance degradation, consequent load shedding, and eventual failure.

1.1.2   Lessons from the example

This example is useful for a number of reasons. It illustrates, first, robustness and transparency in the face of unanticipated events. The reasoning was robust in the sense that the blockage had not previously been anticipated, yet engineers were able to reason about how the device worked to recognize and predict a novel sequence of potentially serious consequences. The reasoning was transparent in the sense that the story above is comprehensible. Even given the very small amount of information in Figures 15.1 and 15.2 and the short description above, the description of the events 'makes sense'.

Second, it suggests the difficulty of *a priori* identification and analysis of all failure modes and all the ways those failures may combine. Even with all the careful design, testing, and previous experience with fuel cell technology, a new mode of cell failure was encountered.

Third, it illustrates the kind of knowledge and reasoning that was required to understand, diagnose, and repair the problem. The knowledge involved information about structure (interconnection of parts) and behaviour (the function of a component labelled 'motor' or 'pump'), supplied by Figures 15.1 and 15.2. Knowledge of basic chemistry and physics was also involved, used to understand the behaviour of potassium hydroxide in solution and the notion of surface tension. Importantly, the reasoning relies on **causal models**, descriptions of devices and processes that capture our ordinary notion of what it means for one event to cause another (for example, the motor causes the pump to turn which causes the hydrogen and water to move through the condenser, etc.).

The reasoning involved was of several varieties. The fourth event above, for instance, illustrates reasoning about behaviour to predict consequences: if the cell is flooded, potassium hydroxide can get in the water, meaning it can get to the water separator and then into the water storage. Another form of reasoning involved working from observed symptoms to diagnoses and then to repair actions: if FCI is shedding load, it is an indication of degraded performance, which suggests flooding. Flooding, in turn, suggests purging as a repair. Simple knowledge of connectivity and chemistry ruled out that action in the event at +3:00: it might have blocked the common purge line.

Finally, it offers a simple way of summarizing much of what this paper is about: while all of the reasoning above was done by people using their models of the devices in question, we suggest giving computers exactly the same sort of knowledge and reasoning abilities, The could, as a result, perform as far more effective assistants.

We believe this can be done by supplying them with something like Figures 15.1 and 15.2, with knowledge about structure, behaviour, an understanding of causality, chemistry, physics, electronics, and more. In short, we need to give them the same understanding of 'how things work' that we use in everyday engineering reasoning.

The aspiration, of course, is easy – execution is considerably more difficult; this is clearly no small undertaking. In the remainder of this paper we examine some of the research issues that arise in attempting to make this happen.

- How can we provide descriptions usable by a machine that are equally as rich as those in Figures 15.1 and 15.2? Consider, for example, how much knowledge is captured by the simple labels *motor*, *pump*, and *condenser*.

- How can we provide the kinds of reasoning abilities displayed above?

- How can we provide the ability to select judiciously the correct model for a given problem? Consider how our view shifted from one grounded in physics, to one oriented towards chemistry, to one grounded in electronics, as the need arose.

- How can we provide the ability to simplify a complex model, selecting out just the 'relevant' details? Consider what a drastic, yet useful, simplification of the actual devices Figures 15.1 and 15.2 are. (Consider, too, what a misleading statement it was, above, to say: 'Even given the very small amount of information in Figures 15.1 and 15.2 . . . , the description of the events makes sense.' It makes sense precisely because the right level of detail was chosen. How might we get a machine to do that?)

- For that matter, how do human engineers do all these things?

1.2   Agenda

Our discussion now proceeds in three basic steps. First, to help make clear the difficulties involved in robustness we explore briefly some non-solutions to the problem. Second, we identify two broad categories of attack that are likely to offer some leverage on the problem: developing models and reasoning methods powerful enough to handle unanticipated events, and developing techniques for coping with situations where only imperfect models are available. Finally, we describe a number of specific research topics that will help to develop the models, methods and techniques needed to produce robustness and transparency.

2   Some non-solutions to the problem

Before proposing a new attack on a problem, it is worth asking whether the problem can be tackled with known techniques. We consider three plausible approaches and explore why each of them fails to provide the degree of robustness we believe is necessary.

One traditional approach is the use of man–machine combinations, relying on the human to handle non-routine situations. This is, of course, useful and can be quite effective over a range of problems. In the fuel cell problem of STS-2, for instance, routine monitoring was handled automatically, while exceptions were analysed by human experts.

It is also clear, however, that systems currently being designed and used are so complex that this will no longer be sufficient, unless we can make our automated assistants smarter. Some nuclear power and chemical processing plants, for instance, are so complex that non-routine events lead to massive overload on human information handling abilities. So many alarms were triggered during the Three Mile Island accident, for instance, that not only was it effectively impossible to interpret them, even detection became problematic as multiple alarms masked one another. Somewhat more immediately relevant, during shuttle mission STS-9 an alarm was triggered more than 250 000 times over 3 days, due to an unanticipated thermal sensitivity in a Spacelab remote acquisition unit, along with an oversight in user software.

It is likely that similar, and perhaps higher, levels of complexity will be involved in the space station. As a result, we need to do more than rely on the human half of the team to handle all exceptions. We need to upgrade the ability of our machines to interpret, diagnose, and respond to unanticipated events, enabling man–machine combinations to remain effective in the face of complex systems and novel environments.

A second route of attack on the problem might appear to be the creation of more reliable software through improved software engineering, program verification, or automatic programming (Rich and Waters, 1986). Unfortunately all of these solve a problem different from the one at hand here. The issue is illustrated in Figure 15.3: techniques for production of reliable software all assist in ensuring that a program matches its specifications. Unanticipated events, however, will, by definition, not show up in the specifications. The problem in dealing with unanticipated events is not so much one of debugging code, it is the creation and debugging of the model and specifications.

Finally, given its wide popularity, we might ask what expert system technology (Davis *et al.*, 1977; Waterman, 1986) might be able to contribute to the difficulties we face. Here, too, the answer is that they have little to offer. The fundamental limitation in these systems arises from the character of the knowledge they use. Traditional expert systems

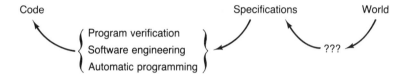

Figure 15.3

gain their power by collecting empirical associations, if-then rules that capture the inferences human experts have learned through experience. We refer to them as empirical associations to indicate the character of the knowledge they capture – associations, typically between symptoms and diseases, gathered as a result of human experience.

Importantly, those associations are typically **heuristic** rather than **causal**; that is, they capture what experts have observed to happen without necessarily being able to explain why it should be so. A medical diagnosis system, for example, might have a rule of the form 'a college student complaining of fatigue, fever, and sore throat is likely to have mononucleosis'. The rule offers useful guidance even if the experts cannot provide a detailed causal (that is, physiological) explanation for why the conclusion follows. Indeed, the power of the technology comes, in part, from the assistance it provides in accumulating large numbers of fragmentary rules of thumb for tasks for which no well-defined causal theory exists.

One important consequence of this kind of knowledge, however, is a kind of brittleness. Current generation expert systems are *idiots savants*, providing impressive performance on narrowly defined tasks and performing well when the problem is exactly suited to the program's expertise. But performance can degrade quite sharply with even small variations in problem character. In general, the difficulty arises from a lack of underlying theory: since the rules indicate only what conclusions follow and not why, the program has no means of dealing with cases that 'almost' match the rule, or cases that appear to be 'minor' exceptions. Indeed, they have no notion of what 'almost' or 'minor' could mean.

3 'Figuring it out'

Having reviewed some existing technology that does not appear capable of providing the degree of robustness needed, we turn now to considering what kinds of ideas and technologies would help solve the problem.

The basic thrust of our argument is quite simple. As the size and complexity of systems increase, we see a decrease in the opportunity to do an exhaustive *a priori* analysis and prespecify appropriate responses.

The space station will likely be complex enough to preclude such analysis; the novelty of the environment increases the chance of unanticipated challenges.

To deal with such situations we need a new approach to building intelligent systems, one based on a simple premise: when you cannot say in advance what will happen, the ability to 'figure out' how to respond becomes much more important. Where knowledge-based systems, for instance, 'know' what to do because they have been given a large body of task-specific heuristics, we require intelligent systems capable of figuring out what to do.

This ability should play a supporting role and is clearly not a replacement for existing approaches. Where we can anticipate and analyse, of course, we should, and where we can construct effective fault tolerant systems, we should. But as system complexity grows and the number and seriousness of unanticipated events increases, we need the flexibility and breadth of robust problem solving systems to deal with them.

The key question, of course, is how to construct systems with this property. In the remainder of this paper we suggest several ways of looking for answers to that question.

4   Models and engineering problem solving

Faced with an unanticipated event in a complex system, a powerful way to figure out what to do is by reasoning from an understanding of the system, a model of 'how it works'. A behavioural model, for instance, can be of considerable help in dealing with complex software, like an operating system. In dealing with a complex physical device, a model of structure and function (schematics and block diagrams), along with an understanding of causality can be essential in understanding, interpreting and debugging behaviour (Bobrow, 1984).

How might we proceed, for example, when faced with a set of sensor readings from the fuel cells that indicate malfunction but do not match any known pattern of misbehaviour? The most robust solution appears to be grounded in knowing how it works, that is, creating and using models that capture structure, behaviour, and causality at an appropriate level of detail. We need to know what the component pieces are, how they each work, how they are interconnected, etc.

We argue that, in the most general terms, the creation, selection, and use of appropriate models is the most powerful approach to the problem (Patil et al., 1981; Hobbs, 1985). It is in many ways the essence of engineering problem solving. Since, as we discuss in more detail below, models are abstractions, the process of model creation and selection is essentially one of deciding which abstraction to apply. Faced with a complex system to be analysed, an engineer can bring to bear a powerful collection of approximations and abstractions.

As a relatively simple example in electrical engineering, for instance, an engineer may decide to view a circuit as digital or analogue, linear or non-linear. But even to approach the problem as one of circuit theory means we have made the more basic assumption that we can model the circuit as if signals propagated instantaneously, and hence ignore electrodynamic effects. Models and their underlying abstractions are thus ubiquitous in this kind of problem solving.

We believe that an important source of power in the problem solving of a good engineer is the ability to create, select, use, and understand the limits of applicability of such models. Consequently, we believe that a powerful approach to building robust problem solving programs is to identify and capture the knowledge on which that modelling ability is based. Similarly, a powerful approach to building transparent problem solving programs is to make that knowledge explicit in our programs. One general thrust of the research we suggest is thus broadly concerned with advancing our understanding of model creation, selection, and use, and demonstrating that understanding by creating programs capable of doing such things.

A second general thrust is made feasible by the fact that the space station is an engineered artifact, a device intended to accomplish a specific purpose whose design is under our control. As a result we can also ask, how can we design in such a fashion that dealing with unanticipated events is easier? That is, given the inevitability of encountering such events and the difficulty of reasoning about them in complex systems, how should we design so that the reasoning and analysis task becomes easier? We speculate, for instance, about what 'design for comprehensibility' might mean.

Other approaches we discuss that share the same basic mindset include understanding (and hence capturing in programs) 'common sense' physical reasoning, and exploring the origins of robust problem solving in people, whose graceful degradation in performance is so markedly different from the behaviour of automated systems.

5 Research topics

In this section we discuss, in broad terms, a number of research topics relevant to the overall goal of building systems that are both robust and transparent problem solving programs is to make that knowledge explicit getting machines to assist in significant ways with reasoning about situations like the STS-2 fuel cell problem will require that they have appropriate models. We then ask how those models can be created and, indeed, how we can design the device from the outset in such a way that the model creation process is made simpler.

5.1 Model creation and selection

Selecting and creating models is perhaps the most fundamental issue in solving engineering problems and an important determinant of the robustness of the solution. It is a skill that is, in some ways, well known: it is what good engineers have learned to do through years of experience. The goal here is to understand that skill and experience well enough that it can be embodied in a program, allowing automated assistance in selecting and creating appropriate models.

In almost any design or analysis problem, the most basic question is how to 'think about' the object in question, that is, how to model it. Given the acknowledgement that all models are abstractions, it is futile (and, as we have suggested, inappropriate) to seek perfect completeness and robustness. That, in turn, means that the modelling decision concerns what to pay attention to, that is, which properties of the object are relevant to the task at hand and which can safely be ignored. The goal here is to find a model with two properties. First, it should be complete enough that it handles the important phenomena. Second, it should be abstract enough that it is computable and capable of producing a description at an appropriate level of detail. But naming the goal is easy; the research challenge is in finding a more precise understanding of what it means to 'consider the task' and to determine when a model is 'complete enough', 'abstract enough' and 'at an appropriate level of detail'.

One possible route to understanding the nature and character of models is to define the kinds of abstractions commonly used in creating them. This might be done by determining what kinds of abstractions are commonly (and often implicitly) employed by engineers. What are the rest of the terms like *digital, analogue, linear*, etc.? Is there just an unstructured collection of such terms or is there, as we would guess, some sort of organizing principle that can be used to establish an ordering on them? If so, we might be able to say more concretely what it means to proceed from a more abstract to a more precise model and might be able to develop programs capable of such behaviour. It is unlikely that there is a simple, strict hierarchy that will allow us to move in a single, unambiguous direction. Much more likely, we will find a tangled graph of models; part of the task is to sort out the different kinds of interconnections likely to be encountered.

A second possible route to understanding the nature of models arises from the simple observation that models ignore details. Perhaps, then, different kinds of models can be generated by selecting different combinations of details to ignore. The task here is to characterize different 'kinds' of details; the ideal set of these would not only generate known models but might suggest additional models as well.

By either of these routes – studying the kinds of abstractions used or the kinds of details ignored – we might be able to produce an array of different kinds of models. That brings us to the problem of model selection, determining which to use in a particular situation. Some assistance may be provided by knowing how the array of models is organized, that is, what it means to be a 'different kind of model'. Difficulties arise in determining what the important phenomena are in the problem at hand and selecting a variety of model capable of dealing with them. How is it that a human engineer knows which approximations are plausible and which are likely to lead to error?

It is unlikely that we will ever be able to guarantee that model selection is flawless or that the models themselves are flawless. We thus need to confront the problem of detecting and dealing with models that are inappropriately chosen for the task at hand or that are incomplete in some relevant detail. Human engineers, at times, make the wrong selection or use a faulty model, yet are capable of detecting this and dealing with it. How might we get machines to do the same?

Finally, note that progress on model selection will have an important impact on the somewhat loaded issue of system override. If, as we have argued, unanticipated events are inevitable, we may encounter some events that are outside the range of applicability of the model no matter how carefully it was chosen. This problem can be particularly difficult because selecting a model, in effect, determines 'how to think about' the current situation and can, as a result, produce subtle misinterpretations.

We argue that override is fundamentally a decision that a particular model is inappropriate. Consider the example of a program monitoring and controlling life support. We might be tempted to override its decisions if they seem sufficiently different from our own, but why should they differ? The most basic answer seems to be that the model the program is using to interpret sensor readings is inappropriate, that is, based on assumptions that are not valid in the current situation.

The only objective way to discover this is by determining why that model was chosen, what approximations it embodies, and what the limitations are on those approximations. Since much of this information was used to make the model selection to begin with, leverage on the override problem can come from understanding model selection and, importantly, from making explicit both the model itself and the assumptions underlying it. This would give us reasonably objective grounds for the override decision, since the model and its underlying assumptions will be available, and can be examined and compared to the current situation. It also reminds us how important it is that such information be made explicit, rather than left implicit in the program code or the mind of the program author.

5.1.1 Model specification needs to be less trouble than it is worth

We have repeatedly stressed the importance of models as a basis for robust reasoning about complex systems. But specifying those models is not an easy task, for several reasons. At the simplest level the issue is volume: there is an enormous amount of information to be captured. Existing design capture systems do not deal well with the problem because they do not make the information collection process easy enough, nor do they offer sufficient payoff once the information is entered to provide a motivation for doing it. They are, in general, more trouble than they are worth.

For design changes, in particular, it is today often easier simply to try out the change and then (maybe) go back and update the specification database. In the case of Solar Max, for instance, perhaps no one knew about the additional hardware because it had been added at the last minute and never documented. The problem of documenting code is similar: it is often easier to try it out, then document. Often the documentation never gets done because it simply is not viewed as critical to the undertaking.

The problem is both organizational and technical. Organizational issues arise because design documentation is typically of least use to the original designer, who is most familiar with the object. There should be a value structure within the organization that makes clear the importance of supplying complete design specifications and emphasizes that, as in Solar Max, the consequences of even minor omissions can be serious.

But there is a more radical position on this issue that is surely worth exploring. *It should be impossible to create or modify a design without doing it via a design capture system.* Put slightly differently, there should be a design capture system so useful that no one would think of proceeding without it. The thought is Utopian but not so far afield as it might seem; existing VLSI design tools, for example, provide sufficiently powerful functionality that no major design would be done without them. Even their basic functions – schematic capture and edit, design rule checking, simulation – provide sufficient payback to make them worth the trouble. (VLSI also has the non-trivial benefit of inaccessibility: once you have the chip in hand, you cannot change it manually, you have to go back through the design process – and hence the design tools.)

Existing tools also illustrate important limitations: they capture the final result, but not the rationales, not the design process. An effective system would be one that was useful from the earliest 'sketch on the back of an envelope' stage, and that captured (and aided) every step and decision along the way. The result would be a record that included not only the final design, but its intended functionality, all rationales for the design choices, etc.

The technical problems in creating such a system include standard concerns about a good interface, such as ease of use and portability; paper is still hard to beat. But the issues go considerably deeper than that. Engineers find communication with each other possible, in part, because of a large shared vocabulary and base of experience. Communication with a design capture system should be based on similar knowledge; the identification and representation of that knowledge is a sizeable research task.

The relevant vocabulary includes concepts about structure (shape, connectivity, etc.) and behaviour (what the device should do). Both present interesting challenges. While connectivity is relatively straightforward, a compact and appropriate vocabulary for shape is not obvious. Behaviour can sometimes be captured by equations or short segments of code, but descriptions in that form soon grow unwieldy and opaque. We need to develop a vocabulary for behaviour capable of dealing with considerably more complex devices.

There is also the problem of unspoken assumptions. If design capture systems simply transcribe what is expressed literally, forcing every fact to be made explicit, the description task will always be overwhelming. We need to understand and accumulate the knowledge and design conventions of engineers so that the system can make the relevant inferences about what was intended, even if not expressed.

5.1.2 Designing for testability, diagnosability, analysability, comprehensibility, transparency, etc.

We have argued that the complexity of the station and the novelty of the environment preclude an exhaustive *a priori* analysis of contingencies and require, instead, an ability to figure out what to do in the face of unanticipated events. We have suggested that this, in turn, is best facilitated by 'knowing how things work', that is, having a model of structure and behaviour.

The complexity of the systems we design clearly has an impact on both how easy it will be to create such models and how easy it will be to reason with them once they exist. Since we are, in fact, designing the station (rather than trying to model a naturally occurring system), it is worth asking what can be done at the design stage to facilitate model creation and model use.

Design for testability Design for testability is one relatively well known approach in this category (Breuer, 1985). It acknowledges that newly manufactured devices have to be exhaustively tested to verify their correct operation before they are placed in service and suggests that we design in ways that facilitate this task. Substantial effort has been devoted to this in circuit design, with some success. Given the likely need for equipment maintenance and the difficulty of a house (station?) call by service technicians, it will be useful to design the station in such a way that basic diagnostic tests can easily be run on devices that may be malfunctioning. Where well known concepts, like ensuring that signals are observable and controllable, are likely to carry over easily, part of the research task here lies in extending techniques developed for simple digital circuits to deal with much larger subsystems.

Design for diagnosability Design for diagnosability is a less well understood task. Where testing involves methodically trying out all the designed behaviours of the device, diagnosis is a process of reasoning from the observed symptoms of malfunction to identify the possibly faulty components. Diagnostic power is measured, in part, by discrimination ability: more powerful diagnostic reasoning techniques implicate fewer components. But some problems are inherently ambiguous – a device may be designed in such a way that the observed symptoms must implicate a large number of different components. Design for diagnosability would involve designing in a way that avoids this situation. Put more positively, it would mean designing in ways that seek to minimize the number of components implicated by a malfunction.

One very simple observation along this line can be made by considering the topology of the device: the only subcomponents that can be responsible for an observed symptom are those that are 'causally connected' to it. In an electronic circuit, for example, the most obvious causal connections are provided by wires. More generally, there must be some sequence of physical interactions by which the error propagates from its source to the point where it is observed. The fewer such interactions, the fewer candidate subcomponents. Simply put, this argues for 'sparse' designs, that is, those with relatively few interconnections.

Designs with unidirectional components (that is, those that operate in a single direction and have distinct inputs and outputs, like logic gates and unlike resistors), also have smaller candidate sets. In devices with unidirectional components there is a single direction of causality, giving us a notion of 'upstream' and 'downstream' of the symptom. Only components that are upstream can be responsible for the symptom.

Diagnosis also involves probing, taking additional measurements inside the device, as well as generating and running tests designed to distinguish among possible candidate subcomponents. We might also examine design styles that facilitate both of these tasks.

Designing for analysability, comprehensibility, transparency Given our emphasis on being able to figure out what to do, perhaps the most fundamental thing to do early on is what might be called design for analysability or comprehensibility. If we have to think about how the device works and reason through the possibly subtle effects of an unanticipated event, then let us, at least, make that easy to do. This may be little more than the traditional admonition to 'keep it simple', here given the additional motivation that we may need to do on-the-spot analysis and response.

Simplicity in design will aid in making that easy; it may present additional virtues as well. Simplicity often produces transparency, an important component in people's willingness to accept automated assistance with critical tasks. Simplicity will help achieve NASA's design goal of allowing crews to intervene at low levels in any station subsystem.

Finally, simplicity may also produce robustness by assisting in determining when a model is inappropriate. We argued above that the override decision can be viewed in terms of the model selection process and can be facilitated by making explicit the simplifying assumptions underlying each model. But those assumptions might not always be made completely explicit so, at times, it may be necessary to determine what they are. This is likely to be easier to determine if the model can be analysed easily.

5.1.3   Robustness requires common sense

Current expert systems are brittle, in part, because they lack common sense knowledge, that large collection of simple facts about the world that is shared across a culture. At the simplest, common sense may include facts such as: physical objects have mass and take up space; two things cannot occupy the same space at the same time; or objects that are unsupported will fall. In the absence of such an underpinning of world knowledge, the system must interpret its rules with complete literal mindedness and can do little in situations in which the rules 'almost' apply.

Consider, for example, a rule in a medical diagnosis expert system that is relevant if the patient is between 17 and 21 years old. Does the rule apply if the patient is 16 years 11 months old? How about 16 years 5.9 months? Our common sense knowledge of the world tells us that the human body does not change discontinuously, so the rule is probably still relevant. Compare this with a rule that says: 'If the postmark date is after April 15, then the tax return is late'. Here we know, again from common sense knowledge, that there is, in fact, a discontinuity. Each of these chunks of common sense is simple enough and easily added to a system; the problem is finding and representing the vast collection of them necessary to support the kind of reasoning people do with so little effort.

For engineering problem solving of the sort relevant to our concerns here, there is another layer of, what we might call, engineering common sense that includes facts such as: liquids are incompressible; all objects are affected by gravitational fields, but not all objects are affected by electromagnetic fields; electromagnetic fields can be shielded, etc. Engineers also know large numbers of simple facts about functionality, such as what a valve does, and why a door is like a valve.

The research task here is the identification, accumulation, organ-ization, and interconnection of the vast numbers of simple facts that make up common sense (Lenat *et al.*, 1986) and engineering common sense. Only with this body of knowledge will we be able to create systems that are more flexible and less literal minded.

5.1.4   What is the source of human robustness?

Since robustness in problem solving is a common trait of experienced engineers, we ought to take the obvious step of examining that behaviour and attempting to understand its origins. What is it that human experts do, what is it that they know, that allows them to recognize and deal with inadequate models? Why is it that human behaviour seems to degrade gracefully as problems become more difficult, rather than precipitously, as is the case with our current programs? Part of the answer may lie in the number and variety of models they can use, along with their body of common sense knowledge.

5.2   Multiple models

Thus far, our approach has focused on creating robustness by reasoning from detailed models. But how can we get robust behaviour in situations where no effective model yet exists? One quite plausible reason for this would be incomplete information: selection of an appropriate model might depend on a fact about the system or environment that we simply do not have as yet. In this section we speculate on one possible approach to such problems.

One idea explored to some degree in the HEARSAY system (Erman *et al.*, 1980) for speech understanding involves the use of multiple knowledge sources, each dealing with a slightly different body of knowledge. Our imperfect knowledge about the task – interpreting an utterance as a sentence – means that none of the knowledge sources can be guaranteed to be correct. The basic insight here is to employ a group of cooperating experts, each with a different expertise, in the hope that their individual weaknesses are distinct (and hence will, in some sense, be mutually compensated) but their strengths will be mutually reinforcing.

A similar technique might be useful in engineering problem solving: lacking any one model believed to be appropriate, we might try using a collection of them that appear to be plausible and that have somewhat different conditions of applicability. Even given such a collection, of course, there remains the interesting and difficult problem of deciding how to combine their results when the outcomes are (as expected) not identical.

6   Summary

We have argued that the complexity of the station and the novelty of space as an environment makes it impossible to predict and analyse all contingencies in advance. The hostility of the environment means the consequences of failure are substantial. In such situations, robustness and transparency become essential properties of the systems developed. Systems are robust to the extent that they can deal with events that have not been specifically anticipated and analysed. They are transparent to the extent that they can make their reasoning comprehensible to an observer.

Given the inevitability of unanticipated events, robustness is best accomplished by 'figuring out' what to do, rather than relying on a list of predetermined responses. But 'figuring out', the sort of analysis and reasoning routinely done by engineers, can only be done if you 'know how it works', that is, have a model of the device. We thus believe that a key source of power in engineering reasoning is the collection of models engineers use, along with the approximations and abstractions that underlie the models. One major thrust of research then should be directed toward understanding the processes of model creation, selection, and simplification.

Given the serious consequences of working from incomplete information, a second major thrust should be devoted towards model and design capture. Existing systems for VLSI design are effective enough to make them essential tools, and hence effective in some aspects of design capture. We need to provide similar levels of tools for all varieties of design and need to understand how to capture design rationales, as well as the final result of the design process.

We also noted that, even given complete design models, reasoning with them can be difficult, hence we suggest turning the question around and asking what we can do at design time to make the reasoning task easier. We have speculated about what design for testability, diagnos-ability, and comprehensibility might mean, and suggest further explora-tion there as well.

Finally, it appears that additional leverage on the problem is available from examining human performance to determine the source of robustness in our own problem solving behaviour, and from compiling the large body of common sense knowledge that seems to be a source of graceful degradation in human problem solving.

Acknowledgements

This paper is a shorter version of one prepared for the Symposium on Human Factor Needs in Space Station Design, National Academy of Sciences, Washington, DC, January 29–30, 1986.

Support for the preparation of this report came, in part, from a research grant from Digital Equipment Corporation, from the Defense Advanced Research Projects Agency of the Department of Defense, under Office of Naval Research contract N00014–84–K–0124, and from a research grant from the Wang Corporation. This paper benefitted significantly from comments on early drafts by Walter Hamscher, Brian Williams, Reid Simmons and Dan Weld. Dennis Webb of NASA's Mission Operations Directorate at Johnson Space Center was of considerable assistance in providing pointers and access to information about the STS-2, STS-9, and 41-C Missions.

References

Bobrow D., ed. (1984). *Qualitative Reasoning About Physical Systems*. Amsterdam: North-Holland. This is the book version of the December 1984 issue of *Artificial Intelligence*, a special issue on that topic. Nine articles illustrate the variety of models and tasks attacked, including diagnosis, design verification, behaviour prediction, etc.

Breuer M.A. (1985). *A Methodology for the Design of Testable Large-Scale Integrated Circuits*. Report SD-TR-85-33, Space Division, Air Force Systems Command. This provides a wide-ranging overview of different testability techniques.

Davis R., Buchanan B.G. and Shortliffe E.H. (1977). Production rules as a representation. *Artificial Intelligence*, Feb. 15–45. This provides an early overview of MYCIN, the first purely rule-based expert system.

Eichhoefer G. (1985). MITRE Corp report, 16 July. Los Angeles: MITRE Corporation

Erman L.D., Hayes-Roth F., Lesser V. and Reddy R. (1980). The HEARSAY-II speech understanding system: integrating knowledge to resolve uncertainty. *Computing Surveys*, June, 213–254

Hobbs I.R. (1985). Granularity. In *Proc. 9th Int. Joint Conf. on AI*, pp. 432–435. This speculates on ways of producing coarser grained models from fine grained ones.

Lenat D.B., Prakash M. and Shepherd M. (1986). Using common sense to overcome brittleness. *AI Magazine*, Winter, 65–85

Patil R.S., Szolovits P. and Schwartz W.B. (1981). Causal understanding of patient illness in medical diagnosis. In *Proc. 7th Int. Joint Conf. on AI*, pp. 893–899. This explores the combined use of three different kinds of models in diagnostic reasoning.

Rich C. and Waters R.C., eds. (1986). *Artificial Intelligence and Software Engineering*. Morgan Kaufmann. This is a recent survey of attempts to use AI approaches to this problem. It provides a historical overview and a wide-ranging view of the problem with extensive references. Also see the *IEEE Transactions on Software Engineering*

Waterman D.A. (1986). *A Guide to Expert Systems*. Reading MA: Addison-Wesley. This is a recent text oriented towards commercial applications of the technology and provides a large set of examples and references

16
Electronic Fault Diagnosis: Fault Trees and Expert Systems

Raymond Lister
University of Sydney

Test engineers used fault diagnosis trees long before the term 'expert system' was coined. This paper reviews the characteristics of expert systems and shows that fault trees are expert systems. However, they are an opaque, cumbersome method of knowledge representation. The construction and maintenance of a fault tree are labour intensive. Fault trees cope poorly with the complexity of contemporary electronic devices. In some circumstances, inductive learning techniques can automate the construction process. These circumstances are discussed. The paper then goes on to describe other forms of knowledge representation used in electronic fault diagnosis expert system applications – rules, frames, and constraints – and concludes that these techniques offer advantages over fault trees when the diagnosis system can only be constructed manually.

1 Introduction

Fault diagnosis consumes a considerable portion of the manpower in the electronics industry. It is performed under two circumstances: when a newly manufactured product fails to work ('reworking'), and when a product fails in the field. There is potential for considerable savings, both direct and indirect, through automating the process. The time to perform each diagnosis may be reduced, and thus fewer workers are required. Less skilled, and thus less expensive, workers may be able to perform the task. Deskilling can also alleviate the problem of staff turnover. Reworking is not a glamorous occupation, but manual fault diagnosis requires considerable skill. Many skilled people resent being pushed into this work. Even when workers are happy to perform diagnosis, there can arise a need to move them on to other projects. By having an automatic diagnosis system for the product on site, a customer may be able to repair simple problems without having to call in an expert or return the product for servicing. When the user cannot find the problem, the extra information supplied by the automatic system may help the service engineer to arrive better prepared, and possibly save a return visit. When transport costs are high, a diagnosis may be attempted 'over the phone', or via some other communication medium. However, it is often an inefficient and frustrating tactic, and the cost of long distance communication can also be high. In some circumstances, such as those involving on-line computer systems or process plants, it is extremely important to minimize down-time, and an automatic system can help, through speeding up the diagnosis phase (Kolcum, 1986; Grillmeyer and Wilkinson, 1985).

2   Characteristics of expert systems

The following subsections discuss the characteristics that differentiate expert systems from conventional programs (Quinlan, 1986; Waterman, 1986), placing emphasis on how these characteristics relate to fault diagnosis in electronic equipment.

2.1   Expert systems are knowledge-based systems

An expert system consists of two parts: a **knowledge base** and an **inference engine**. The power of an expert system comes from the knowledge encoded within the knowledge base, rather than the processing of that knowledge by a sophisticated inference engine. This idea has been called the **Knowledge Principle** (Feigenbaum, 1987). It is certainly possible to diagnose faults in electronic systems without specific knowledge of that system. Engineers do it often, by reasoning from 'first principles', that is, from electronic theory. However, there are many situations where fault diagnosis is carried out by technicians who do not not reason from fundamentals. Instead, they apply the knowledge they have built up through extensive experience with the faulty device. Such people use several types of knowledge:

- knowledge of the structure and correct behaviour of the system;
- knowledge of **fault models**, that is, how the system, or modules within the system, can fail, how likely each failure is, and how the fault manifests itself;
- knowledge of diagnostic tests; and
- knowledge of diagnostic strategies.

2.2   Expert systems perform a non-trivial task

Although the fault diagnosis task may have been transferred from an engineer to a technician, it usually remains a difficult task. The diagnostic process has merely been transformed from one requiring sophisticated reasoning to one requiring comprehensive knowledge.

2.3   Expert systems are transparent

Transparency means that an expert system must be understandable by human experts who may have little knowledge of computing, in general, and expert systems in particular. Transparency is necessary so that the human experts can satisfy themselves that the expert system has reached, or will always reach, correct conclusions. Also, the more transparent an expert system, the easier it is to maintain.

2.4   Expert systems can use redundant or inexact knowledge

There are three reasons why the ability to handle inexact data and knowledge is sometimes needed in the diagnosis of electronic equipment:

1.   The test result is not known with certainty. This is particularly the case with analogue measurements.

2.   A test exercises more than one component. Furthermore, the test may exercise each component to differing degrees, and thus the test casts a variable degree of suspicion on each component.

3.   Two or more components may be suspect, and no discriminating test has been applied, but each component has a different *a priori* likelihood of being faulty.

There are two reasons why the ability to handle redundant knowledge is useful:

1.   If a test has not or cannot be performed due to unpredictable and uncontrollable reasons, then an alternative test may be used.

2.   Two or more tests may give conflicting answers, and this inconsistency will need to be resolved.

In many testing environments, considerable effort has gone into eliminating these factors. Design techniques, such as design for testability (DFT) and built in self-test (BIST), are intended to increase the observability and controllability of modules within a system, making it easy to construct inexpensive tests that precisely and unambiguously identify faults (Bennetts, 1982). In these cases, an expert system may be superfluous. However, DFT and BIST add extra components, or may slow the system, so they cannot always be used.

2.5   Expert systems are capable of explaining their conclusions

In the simplest expert system applications, the explanation facility is merely a trace of the rules that have fired. In more ambitious systems, the explanation may enumerate assumptions, and describe the diagnosis strategy used. Explanation is very useful during system development, but it is often unnecessary for day-to-day use of an electronic fault diagnosis system. Whereas a doctor needs to satisfy him- or herself that a medical expert system's conclusions are reasonable before he or she acts, the user of an expert system for electronic fault diagnosis can often replace the component that seems faulty with little risk or cost. If the faulty behaviour is not fixed, then the user will report the problem with the expert system to the knowledge engineer.

3   Fault trees

The term 'fault tree' is actually used to describe two different structures used in fault diagnosis. One of these forms is very similar to the decision tree used in expert systems, and the other is similar to the inference net used in many expert systems (Reboh, 1981). Thus in order to distinguish the two forms, we will refer to the former structure as a **diagnosis decision tree** (DDT), and the latter as a **fault inference tree** (FIT).

3.1   Diagnosis decision trees

Diagnosis decision trees (DDT) are basically flow charts. They are a method for describing the sequences in which a given set of tests should be applied in order to find a set of faults. Each node in the tree represents a test. The diagnosis procedure starts at the test represented by the topmost root node. The result of the test at each node determines which path downward from that node will be followed. The diagnosis is complete when a leaf node (that is, a node with no children) is reached. Figure 16.2 shows a DDT, in which two tests diagnose faults in the circuit shown in Figure 16.1. In this example, each test has a binary result – pass or fail – and thus only two children but, in general, tests in fault trees may have an arbitrary number of results. If test1 fails but test2 is successful,

Input

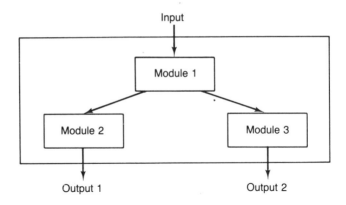

Figure 16.1   A simple example circuit.

then we suspect a fault in module2. If test2 fails but test1 is successful, then we suspect a fault in module3. If both tests fail, then we suspect a fault in module1, because it feeds into both module2 and module3. This last diagnosis is justified if a **single fault assumption** is reasonable. However, note that an alternative explanation for both tests failing would be that both module2 and module3 are faulty.

Test engineers used DDTs long before the term 'expert system' was coined, but they are very similar, and sometimes indistinguishable, from decision trees used in expert systems. The remainder of this section discusses the characteristics of expert systems identified in the previous section, with regard to DDTs.

DDTs pass the criteria set by Feigenbaum's Knowledge Principle. The method of inference is simply to move down through the tree, following the path indicated by the test result. Thus the power of the diagnostic system comes from the knowledge encoded in the tree, and not through a sophisticated inference technique.

DDTs have traditionally been constructed as the system is designed, by members of the design team. They consider each component in turn, enumerate its failure modes, and design a diagnostic procedure to identify each failure. These procedures are then combined, with some regard for overall diagnostic efficiency, to form the DDT. The engineer devises the DDT by applying his or her considerable knowledge of the system, but the DDT does not document that knowledge. Thus DDTs are an opaque method of knowledge representation (Kreiger, 1985). The different types of diagnostic knowledge identified in Section 2.1 are represented implicitly in the DDT. For example, knowledge of the relative likelihood of failure of components will affect the way the engineer orders the tests in the DDT, but it is very difficult to deduce the relative likelihood of failure by inspecting the tree.

DDTs are weak at representing inexact knowledge. First, in order

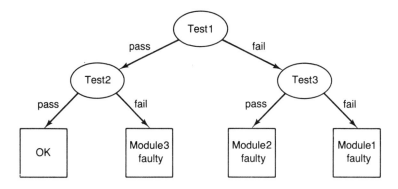

Figure 16.2   A diagnosis decision tree for the circuit in Figure 16.1.

to move down through the tree, the test at every node must be categorical. Secondly, a DDT assumes that the test at each node can be performed. (In principle, a DDT could have a cannot perform test subtree below each node, but this would add tremendously to the complexity of the tree.) Thirdly, the fact that a test result could be explained by a several fault hypothesis is only represented implicitly by the structure of the tree.

DDTs do not usually offer an explanation capability, but as noted above, electronic fault diagnosis applications often do not require it. In any event, a trace of the nodes traversed in the tree, together with the output of some set text, might prove to be a limited but useful explanation procedure, and as expressive as the rule tracing procedure used in many of the simple expert system shells.

3.2   Fault inference trees

The term **fault tree** is also used in engineering to describe a data structure used in studying the probability of failure in complex systems, such as nuclear power plants or spacecraft, by combining data about the likelihood of failure of individual components. Figure 16.3 shows a fault inference tree (FIT) for the circuit in Figure 16.1. Information flows from the bottom of a FIT towards the top. In this case, the FIT indicates that if any of the three modules fail, then the circuit fails. If probabilities of failure can be assigned to the three modules, then a probability of failure can be calculated for the whole circuit. If we replaced the OR node with an AND node, we would be describing the fault behaviour of a different circuit in which the three modules were redundant, thus providing some fault tolerance in the system. This simple example shows little of the expressive power of FITs. FITs have an arbitrary topology, and there are other node types for describing many other situations (Barlow and

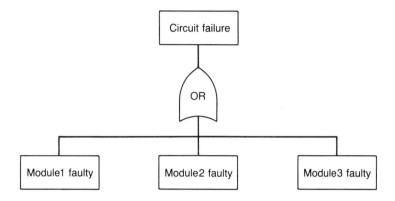

Figure 16.3   A fault inference tree for the circuit in Figure 16.1.

Fussell, 1975; Himmelblau, 1978). However, this simple example is sufficient illustration for the needs of this paper.

Although initially designed as a tool for analysing the likelihood of failure in systems, FITs have been adapted for fault diagnosis, such as in an oscilloscope (Cantone *et al.*, 1985), the electrical switch yard of a nuclear power plant (Rodriguez and Rivera, 1986), a nationwide communication network (Williams *et al.*, 1983), and the avionics of the F/A-18 aircraft (Hernandez, 1986). In these cases, diagnosis starts by locating the highest node in the FIT that describes the faulty observed behaviour, and proceeds by examining the nodes under it. In our simple example, the circuit failure would lead us to test each of the three modules. If we knew the internal structure of these modules, we could proceed further down the FIT to isolate the problem within the faulty module.

FITs, like DDTs, satisfy Feigenbaum's Knowledge Principle. Furthermore, the structure of a FIT reflects the structure of the device being tested. This aids transparency. However, fault diagnosis tests do not always map directly onto a device's structure, as described in Section 2.4; a test does not always identify a single faulty module. Usually a test indicates that a fault is present in one of a set of modules, perhaps with varying degrees of likelihood. FITs are not strong at representing this type of inexact knowledge. However, if the individual tests map well onto the system's structure, as will be the case for systems designed using DFT or BIST, FITs are an excellent knowledge representation mechanism. The great advantage of FITs as a diagnostic tool is that they often need to be constructed anyway. Large, costly or potentially hazardous systems are carefully analysed for failure modes, as part of the design process.

4   Diagnosis decision trees and inductive learning

Decision trees are commonly used in expert systems. They are generated by the widely used ID3 algorithm, and other inductive learning algorithms (Michie, 1986; Quinlan *et al.*, 1987). They are very similar to DDTs, but can differ in one respect; in cases where tests have not been run on the faulty device before diagnosis has begun, and where the cost of performing the individual tests varies and the overall cost needs to be minimized, the structure of a DDT indicates the order in which the tests should be performed. A decision tree, however, is constructed by assuming that all tests have already been performed, or the cost of the tests does not vary substantially. (The ID3 algorithm, which forms the basis of most commercially available inductive learning software products, does not account for test cost. However, appropriate extensions could be made to ID3, or other inductive learning algorithms could be used.)

The automatic construction of a decision tree is done by analysing a set of examples. If an electronic system is complex, the number of examples required may be high. A large set of examples is not always available, possibly because the system is not mass produced, it is a relatively new product, it has a low failure rate, or the data has simply not been collected.

In diagnostic cases where the ordering of tests to minimize cost is not relevant, and a sufficiently large set of example cases exists, inductive learning techniques have been applied to overcome the problems of manually constructing DDTs. Automatically generated decision trees have been applied to fault diagnosis systems for printed circuit boards in digital switching exchanges (Gunhold and Zettel, 1986), electronically controlled automobiles (Klausmeier and Allen, 1985), and the Texas Instruments (TI) 990 minicomputer system (Stuart *et al.*, 1985). We will examine, in greater detail, one part of the latter application, which diagnoses problems in the TI computer's WD500 disk drive subsystem. The subsystem contains two 130 mm Winchester drives and a floppy drive. Initial diagnosis procedures use the six lights on the front panel. Depending on the fault, these lights either are on, off or blink. Table 16.1 shows part of the troubleshooting chart for the drive, adapted from the system documentation (Stuart *et al.*, 1985). The decision tree shown in Figure 16.4 was produced from this documentation. This tree diagnoses most of the possible problems with the drive system. The manually generated diagnosis documentation that covered these and a few more faults was represented as a flow chart and was spread over 15 pages.

Table 16.1   Part of Texas Instruments 900 disk subsystem diagnostic documentation. (Adapted from Stuart *et al.*, 1985.)

LED indication	Probable cause
6 on, or 6 blinking, or all on, or 2–5 on with 6 blinking	Formatter failure .
2–6 blinking	P_BUX ID incorrectly set, or formatter faulty
2, 6 on, or 1, 2, 6 on	Winchester number 1 faulty, or Winchester number 1 cables bad, or formatter faulty
3, 6 on, or 1, 3, 6 on	Winchester number 2 faulty, or Winchester number 2 cables bad, or formatter faulty
2, 3, 6 on	Formatter faulty, and/or Winchester number 1 faulty, and/or Winchester number 2 faulty, and/or Winchester terminators faulty
4, 6 on, or 1, 4, 6 on	Flexible drive faulty, or flexible drive cables bad, or formatter faulty
5, 6 on, or 1, 5, 6 on, or 1, 5 on, or 5 on	PBIF connector faulty, or formatter faulty
No LEDs on	Blown fuse, or faulty internal power connections, or EMI filter faulty, or bad front panel cable, or faulty front panel PWB, or faulty power supply

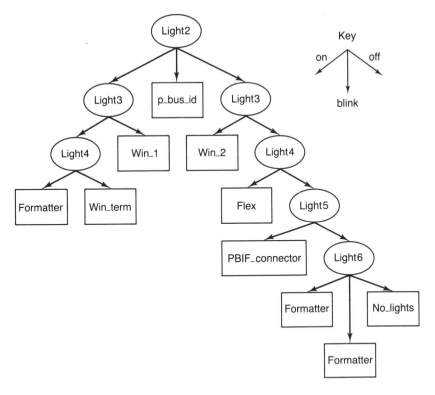

Figure 16.4 A diagnostic decision tree for the Texas Instruments 900 computer.

5 Knowledge representation for manual generation of diagnostic software

As mentioned above, it is not always possible to generate DDTs using inductive learning, because of the need to account for variable test costs, or lack of historic data. In these cases the automatic fault diagnostic system must be constructed manually. It is also highly likely that the system to be tested will change during its life, and thus maintenance changes will need to be made to the diagnostic software. Since DDTs are not a particularly transparent method of knowledge representation, they are expensive to build and particularly expensive to maintain. The remainder of the paper will discuss the advantages of more conventional knowledge representation techniques.

Electronic diagnostic expert systems are traditionally divided into two categories: 'shallow' and 'deep' systems. The reason for making this division may be more clear if one considers a scenario in which two people with appropriate, but different, backgrounds are set the task of repairing a television set. The first person has not repaired a television before, but he or she has a degree in electronic engineering. This person proceeds by tracing through the circuitry, reasoning with his or her knowledge of circuits, designing and carrying out tests that verify that each component is performing correctly. The second person is an experienced television repair technician. He or she notes the fault manifestation (for example, 'ghosting' of the image), and from his or her experience with televisions, settles quickly on a small set of likely faulty components, and applies a set of well chosen tests developed in the past to isolate the failed component. The engineer is reasoning deeply, which is sometimes called **causal reasoning**, **model based reasoning** or **reasoning from first principles** (Atwood *et al.*, 1986; Chandrasekaran and Mittal, 1983; Davis, 1987; Milne, 1987). The technician's approach is called **shallow reasoning** using **compiled knowledge** (Chandrasekaran and Mittal, 1983), or reasoning from **second principles** (Milne, 1985; 1986). There are two problems with this division. First, the Knowledge Principle tells us that the connotations associated with the word 'shallow' are misleading. Secondly, the 'deep' category itself contains a wide spectrum of knowledge representation and inference techniques. The author proposes to split the 'deep' category, and rename the 'shallow' category, to give three new divisions:

- black box systems,
- causal, or model-based systems, and
- introspective systems.

These three categories will be discussed in the remainder of this section.

5.1   Black box systems

These systems reason purely from the input/output behaviour of the device under test. The inference mechanism does not use knowledge of the internal construction of the system. Most of these systems use rules. Rules take the general form:

if ⟨antecedent⟩ then ⟨consequent⟩

In black box systems, the antecedent describes an input/output pattern for the device, and the consequent describes the component or components that are suspected of being faulty as a result of this test. The strength of these systems is their handling of inexact and redundant data, and their flexible, data driven control strategies (Reboh, 1981; Buchanan and Shortliffe, 1984; Kim and Pearl, 1983).

In many rule-based diagnostic systems, a variable with a value constrained to a prescribed range represents the degree of belief that a component is faulty. If the variable is at one end of the range, then the component is believed to be definitely faulty; if the variable is at the other end of the range, then the component is believed to be working properly; and if the variable is between these extreme values then both possibilities are entertained to some degree. This same technique is sometimes used to represent the confidence in a test result, where the user may be asked a question that could have a true/false answer, but he or she also has the option of entering a number in a prescribed range, reflecting his or her degree of confidence in the answer. This method of input is particularly useful for describing a user's degree of confidence that a given analogue parameter is within its correct range, or in assigning a degree of faith to data from a sensor whose performance may be degrading (Fox *et al.*, 1983).

Other numbers express the strength with which a test result implicates certain faults. An example of a rule from such a system is given below, from a system to diagnose faults in a part of the avionics of the B-1B bomber (Davis, 1986):

    if two consecutive bits fail in test 1 section 2, and
        the voltage at Pin 1A is greater than 5 volts
    then card3 is bad with 0.75 certainty

In some systems, an *a priori* measure of the likelihood of failure of each component is used (Merry, 1983; Cantone *et al.*, 1983).

Sometimes there exists more than one way of testing a component, and this redundant knowledge can be encoded in several rules. If one test cannot be performed, another rule that provides the same data may be able to fire. Conflicting answers from rules are usually handled in an *ad hoc* numeric fashion, such as producing some linear combination of the different numbers. Despite this lack of rigour, the expert system's performance often proves acceptable, probably because the human expert being imitated also uses a very coarse method of handling inexact data.

Diagnostic strategies are sometimes encoded as part of the inference engine, and thus independently of the application, or as part of the knowledge base. The former determines the next test to apply by using the degree of belief in each candidate fault and the cost of administering that test. The simplest systems apply classic backtracking and determine the next test by selecting the strongest test for the most likely fault, taking no account of the cost of that test (Merry, 1983). Systems which attempt to minimize test cost select the next test by constructing a game tree to some depth, where the moves of one of the 'players' are the test results (Cantone *et al.*, 1983; Pipitone, 1984). Ali and Scharnhorst (1985) describe a system for diagnosing faults in an aircraft in flight, and incorporate a measure of the danger of each fault in their selection strategy. Systems which encode the diagnosis strategy within the knowledge use a priority system where rules are assigned a numeric measure of their priority, which may be altered by other rules in the knowledge base (Laffey *et al.*, 1986; Prevost and Laffey, 1985).

In comparison to rules, fault trees are a cumbersome method of knowledge representation. For instance, consider the knowledge 'if one card in a set of N identical cards has failed, and one extra working card is available, then a good diagnosis procedure is to replace each of the suspect cards with the extra card until the faulty board is identified'. Many conventional expert system shells would allow this knowledge to be expressed concisely, possibly as a single rule, in which a variable representing the cards could be instantiated to N possible values. However, a fault tree would need to express this knowledge by enumerating all possible fault conditions with a tree of N nodes. In general, a fault tree and a rule-based system may be functionally equivalent, but the fault tree enumerates all possible diagnosis steps and conclusions, whereas the set of rules uses variables that may be instantiated to different values. All possible behaviour of the rule base has been 'hard coded' in the fault tree. Thus a fault tree and a rule-based expert system may be indistinguishable to the user, but the latter may offer advantages to the knowledge engineer who must construct or maintain the knowledge base.

There are many applications built on black box principles. Examples, other than the ones mentioned above, include diagnostic systems for computer systems (Bennett and Hollander, 1981), an oscilloscope (Cantone *et al.*, 1984), radar equipment (Chao *et al.*, 1986), and telecommunication networks (Vesonder *et al.*, 1983; Thandasseri, 1986). The market is full of development environments for this type of system. Black box approaches suit small, well understood systems and can be built by people with a minimal background in expert systems. However, the implementation effort increases very quickly as the complexity of the device increases, and the more sophisticated techniques described below are required.

5.2   Causal or model-based systems

An amorphous mass of rules can be as hard to understand as a fault tree. Expert systems require structure every bit as much as conventional programs. Sections 5.2.1 and 5.2.2 describe two ways of structuring a diagnostic knowledge base.

5.2.1   Constraint satisfaction networks

One obvious way to structure an electronic diagnostic expert system is to group the rules to reflect the modular structure of the artifact to be tested. Rules that describe the correct behaviour and possible faults of

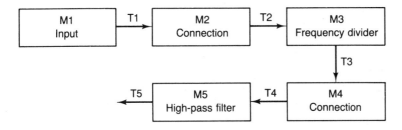

Figure 16.5   The example circuit for the FIS system.

each module are grouped together. Variables and their bindings are passed between groups of rules along channels that reflect the module interconnection structure of the device. Such a method of organization is called **programming by constraints** (Winston, 1984). Thus an engineer maintaining the diagnostic expert system will be able to find all rules affecting a module in the one place, and assess the effect of any changes to those rules by tracing along the module interconnection data structure.

The fault isolation system (FIS) is a system constructed in this way. It was designed to find faults in analogue systems, such as amplifiers, analogue multiplexers, voltage controlled oscillators, and power supplies (Pipitone, 1986). The knowledge required by FIS to test a device includes a list of modules, how the modules are connected, various tests and their costs, and a list of 'causal rules'. Figure 16.5 shows a portion of the circuit used by Pipitone (1986) to demonstrate the FIS system.

The following simplified subset of causal rules from that example describe how the frequency of the signal is affected by faults in the system:

- rule 1:   M1 causes T2 frequency high
- rule 2:   M3 causes T3 frequency high
- rule 3:   T4 frequency high causes T5 frequency high
- rule 4:   T3 frequency high causes T4 frequency high
- rule 5:   T2 frequency high causes T3 frequency high
- rule 6:   T1 frequency high causes T2 frequency high

The first two rules describe the faulty behaviour of two modules. Rules 3 to 6 describe how correctly functioning modules propagate faulty behaviour. These rules are either supplied directly by an expert or, in some circumstances, can be found in a library of rules for generic components.

If a failed test result is given, FIS chains through the rules, from the right-hand side of each causal rule to the left side, to identify all possible module failures that would explain the failed test. The candidate failed modules are referred to as an **ambiguity set**. Thus, in the above example, if we give 'T5 frequency high', FIS will generate the ambiguity set {M1, M3}. FIS can also use tests that are passed to deduce from the causal rules which modules must be working correctly.

Note how wires (called **connections** in the diagram) are modelled explicitly as modules in the above example. Though not illustrated by this example, wires have failure modes, such as open circuit and short circuit, and need to be represented.

The above example is smaller than the actual cases to which FIS has been applied, which have usually contained around 10 modules (Pipitone, 1986). It is merely an illustration. The example is too simple to make a causal system worthwhile. The number of modules is low, the number of possible faults is low, only one parameter (frequency) is being tested, and the linear interconnection topology is the most simple of the possible topologies.

FIS can cope with all three sources of uncertainty identified in Section 2.4. However, the first of these categories (the test result is not known with certainty) can only be represented in a clumsy fashion. Test results, which are usually analogue measurements, are converted into qualitative values, such as {low, ok, high}. Each conversion is categorical, that is, there is no mechanism for representing something like 'the test result is probably ok, but there is a small chance that it is high'. This limitation could be overcome in FIS by defining a more expressive set of qualitative values, such as {low, marginally low, ok, marginally high, high}. However, this approach would require rules to be altered or added to the knowledge base to cope with these new values, with the result that the transparency of the knowledge base would suffer. The second form of uncertainty (a test may cast a variable degree of suspicion on several components) is handled in several ways. First, by the ambiguity sets described above. Secondly, a probability is assigned to every fault hypothesis by an elaborate statistical approach. In addition, knowledge of the structure of the device reduces the need for this second form of inexact reasoning; if two tests fail, and the single fault assumption is appropriate, then the fault must be on the intersection of the paths exercised by the two tests. The final type of inexact knowledge – *a priori* knowledge – is implemented directly. FIS' inexact reasoning mechanism uses an *a priori* fault probability.

FIS can cope with redundant knowledge. It uses an elaborate technique based on information gain to advise the technician on the best test to perform next. However, it does not insist that the test be performed. FIS will attempt to find the data the user could not give by some other means, or proceed as best it can without the data. Expert systems based on constraint satisfaction networks are well suited to coping with conflicting test results. In fact, identifying constraints that lead to conflict, and relaxing those constraints, is a principal method of diagnostic reasoning within these systems (Davis, 1984). Constraint satisfaction techniques for diagnosis were also demonstrated by Chandrasekaran and Punch (1987), and an application in process control that uses structural knowledge to resolve problems with sensor data was described by Scarl *et al.* (1985, 1987). A system for reducing spurious error reports with in-circuit testing is described by Apfelbaum (1985). Constraints are not unique to diagnostic systems for analogue devices. In fact, digital systems are very well suited to constraint-based systems, as these examples for a logical 'OR' gate show (Davis and Shrobe, 1983):

if either input is 1, then the output is 1
if the output is 0, then both inputs are 0

Systems based on reasoning about the structure of a device reduce the need for the knowledge engineer to encode explicitly knowledge of diagnostic strategies. The structure implies much of the strategy. For instance, if a test result points to a fault in a particular set of components, then a good choice for the next test might be one that exercises some, but not all, components of that set.

As the experience of a human diagnosing faults in a product develops, they tend to move gradually from causal reasoning to black box reasoning. FIS cannot combine these two sorts of reasoning. However, other systems have attempted to do this (Downing, 1987; Fink, 1985; Fink and Lusth, 1987; Havlicsek, 1986; Kahn *et al.*, 1987; Pazzani, 1987; Peng and Reggia, 1987a, 1987b).

FIS is implemented in LISP, but a similar system has been implemented in PROLOG (Kriz and Sugaya, 1986).

5.2.2. Frames

Although the structural rules that describe the behaviour of the circuit in Figure 16.5 are an improvement on any 'flat', 'black box' description of the system, they treat each of the circuit modules as black boxes. On closer inspection of the circuit, we see that modules M2 and M4 are both wires, and rules 4 and 6 describe behaviour common to all wires. The following two facts and one rule demonstrate a more transparent method of representing this knowledge:

M2 is a wire
M4 is a wire

if a component is a wire
then a high frequency on the input will cause a high frequency on the output

In fact, all components in this example will propagate an incorrect high frequency input, so one rule could describe the same behaviour described in rules 3–6. However, the modules do not share all of their properties. For example, module M3, a frequency divider, can generate

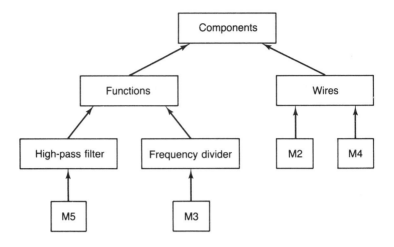

Figure 16.6   An example frame hierarchy.

an incorrect high frequency signal, but wires cannot. However, by organizing the rules in a frame hierarchy, we can capture properties that the modules share and properties that separate them. Figure 16.6 shows a simple frame hierarchy that might be used to structure knowledge of components in the example. Each node, or frame, contains knowledge which is inherited by nodes beneath it in the hierarchy. The knowledge may be data like that in a conventional database system, sometimes called 'facts'. However, frames may also store executable code, often represented as rules. Thus a rule is stored at a point in the hierarchy that reflects its generality; the rule describing the propagation of a high frequency signal is applicable to all components, so it would be stored in the highest, most general frame called components; rules specific to a particular component, such as the ability of M3 to generate an incorrect high frequency signal, would be stored in the lower frames. (FIS does use frames (Pipitone, 1986), but each frame is used in isolation; they are not organized hierarchically. The frame example described here was constructed by the author for the purpose of illustrating concepts described in this paper.)

Since electronic systems are often large, complex and man-made, they tend to have a natural structure well suited to description by frames. Other expert systems that use frames include diagnostic systems for a computer line printer (Young, 1987), a communications network (Mathonet *et al.*, 1987), a digital data logger (Laufmann and Crowder, 1987), a telephone switching system (Goyal *et al.*, 1985; Prerau *et al.*, 1985), a non-impact page printer (Strandberg *et al.*, 1985), avionics of the Boeing 737 (Ali and Scharnhorst, 1985), and a computer disk subsystem (Rolston, 1987).

5.2.3   Introspective systems

Of the types of diagnostic knowledge identified in Section 2.1, only knowledge of the structure and correct behaviour of the system is well developed when most systems are first manufactured. The other three forms of knowledge grow with experience. Also, if the production volume of a complex product is low, there may never be sufficient experience to build up shallow knowledge of how to diagnose faults in the unit. For instance, a survey of faults in British Royal Air Force aircraft found that 20% of all faults (not just faults in the avionics) were novel (Grant, 1986). Thus, there is a clear demand for automatic systems capable of reasoning from design data alone. Unfortunately, such systems remain in the research domain. Much of the research is aimed at producing very sophisticated methods of reasoning in which assumptions underlying the reasoning process are made explicit and are revised as more diagnostic data is collected. Hence the term **introspective systems**. Many of the research systems use a fundamental, completely general knowledge representation method, such as predicate calculus. The great strength of such methods is that the system is not limited to dealing with a restricted set of known fault models. Their weakness is their heavy computing requirements. These systems are moving away from the pure Knowledge Principle, and process their knowledge with a sophisticated inference engine. A more comprehensive treatment of the research issues is beyond the scope of this paper. The reader is referred to work by Davis (1984, 1987), De Kleer (1986), De Kleer and Williams (1987), Genesereth (1984), Reiter (1987), and Shapiro *et al.* (1986).

7   Conclusion

Fault trees have been the traditional method of representing knowledge about electronic fault diagnosis. However, the complexity of modern electronic systems makes constructing them a tedious process. Maintenance of them is particularly expensive, as they are a cumbersome and an opaque method of knowledge representation. Expert systems offer a solution to the problem. First, where appropriate, inductive learning techniques make it possible to automate the construction of fault trees. Secondly, expert systems technology provides more powerful methods of knowledge representation.

Electronic diagnostic expert systems can be divided into three categories: black box systems, causal or model-based systems, and introspective systems. There are many applications built on black box principles, and the market is full of development environments for this type of system. Black box approaches suit small, well understood systems, and can be built by people with a minimal background in expert systems. A diagnostic expert system for a more complex, but well understood, device requires a causal, or model-based approach. These systems require more sophisticated development tools and a stronger knowledge of Artificial Intelligence from the implementor, but applications have been built using this approach. If the faulty behaviour of a device is very poorly understood, reasoning from the design data is the only option. This sort of reasoning remains an open research topic.

The recent application of expert systems technology has been made possible by the dramatic increase in the power of computers. The very complexity and sophistication of electronics that is rendering fault trees impractical has made possible a technology better suited to coping with that complexity.

Acknowledgements

I am grateful for the help of Geoffrey Burn of GEC Research Laboratories, and Owen Mace of British Aerospace (Australia), in obtaining copies of several papers described herein, and also for the comments offered by the referees. This work was partially funded by a grant under the CSIRO Collaborative Programme in Information Technology.

References

Ali M. and Scharnhorst D.A. (1985). Sensor-based fault diagnosis in a flight expert system. In *Proc. 2nd Conf. on Artificial Intelligence Applications*, Miami Beach FL, pp. 41–54

Apfelbaum L. (1985). An expert system for in-circuit fault diagnosis. In *Proc. IEEE Test Conf.*, Philadelphia PA, pp. 868–874

Atwood M.E., Brooks R. and Radlinski E.R. (1986). Causal models: the next generation of expert systems. *Electrical Communication*, **60**(2), 180–184

Barlow R.E. and Fussell J.B., eds. (1975). *Reliability and Fault Tree Analysis*. USA: Society for Industrial and Applied Mathematics (SIAM)

Bennett J.S. and Hollander C.R. (1981). DART: an expert system for computer fault diagnosis. In *Proc. 7th Int. Joint Conf. on Artificial Intelligence*, Canada, pp. 843–845

Bennetts R.G. (1982). *Introduction to Digital Board Testing*. Edward Arnold

Buchanan B.G. and Shortliffe E.H., eds. (1984). *Rule-Based Expert Systems: The MYCIN Experiments of the Stanford Heuristic Programming Project*. Reading MA: Addison-Wesley

Cantone R.R., Pipitone F.J. and Lander W.B. (1983). Model-based probabilistic reasoning for electronics troubleshooting. In *Proc. 8th Int. Joint Conf. on Artificial Intelligence*, Germany, pp. 207–211

Cantone R.R., Lander W.B., Marrone M.P. and Gaynor M.W. (1984). IN-ATE/2: interpreting high-level fault modes. In *Proc. 1st Conf. on Artificial Intelligence Applications*, Denver CO, pp. 470–473

Cantone R.R., Lander W.B., Marrone M.P. and Gaynor M.W. (1985). Automating knowledge acquisition in IN-ATE using component information and connectivity. *SIGART Newsletter*, 93, July, 32–34

Chandrasekaran B. and Mittal S. (1983). Deep versus compiled knowledge approaches to diagnostic problem solving. *Int. J. Man–Machine Studies*, **19**, 425–436

Chandrasekaran B. and Punch W.F. (1987). Data validation during diagnosis: a step beyond traditional sensor validation. In *Proc. 6th National Conf. on Artificial Intelligence*, Seattle WA, pp. 778–782

Chao S.K., Caudell T.P., Ebeid N., Partridge D.R. and Sameshima S.T. (1986). An application of expert system techniques to radar fault diagnosis. In *Proc. IEEE Western Conf. on Knowledge-Based Engineering and Expert Systems (WESTEX-86)*, Anaheim CA, pp. 127–135

Davis K. (1986). DORIS (Diagnostic Oriented Rockwell Intelligent System). *IEEE Aerospace and Electronics Systems Magazine*, **1**(7), 18–21

Davis R. (1984). Diagnostic reasoning based on structure and behavior. *Artificial Intelligence*, **24**(1–3), 347–410

Davis R. (1987). Robustness and transparency in intelligent systems. (In this volume.)

Davis R. and Shrobe H. (1983). Representing structure and behavior of digital hardware. *Computer*, **16**(10), 75–82

De Kleer J. (1986). Reasoning about multiple faults. In *Proc. 5th Nat. Conf. on Artificial Intelligence*, Philadelphia PA, pp. 132–139

De Kleer J. and Williams B.C. (1987). Diagnosing multiple faults. *Artificial Intelligence*, **32**(1), 97–130

Downing K.L. (1987). Diagnostic improvement through qualitative sensitivity analysis and aggregation. In *Proc. 6th Nat. Conf. on Artificial Intelligence*, Seattle WA, pp. 789–793

Feigenbaum E. (1987). Knowledge processing: from file servers to knowledge servers. In this volume

Fink P.K. (1985). Control and integration of diverse knowledge in a diagnostic expert system. In *Proc. 9th Int. Joint Conf. on Artificial Intelligence*, Los Angeles, pp. 426–431

Fink P.K. and Lusth J.C. (1987). Expert systems and diagnostic expertise in the mechanical and electrical domains. *IEEE Transactions on Systems, Man and Cybernetics*, **17**(3), 340–349

Fox M.S., Lowenfold S. and Klienosky P. (1983). Techniques for sensor-based diagnosis. In *Proc. 8th Int. Joint Conf. on Artificial Intelligence*, Germany, pp. 158–163

Genesereth M. (1984). The use of design descriptions in automated diagnosis. *Artificial Intelligence*, **24**(1–3), 411–436

Goyal S.K., Prerau D.S., Lemmon A.V., Gunderson A.S. and Reinke R.E. (1985). COMPASS: an expert system for telephone switch maintenance. In *Proc. Expert Systems in Government Symposium*, Washington, pp. 112–122

Grant T.J. (1986). Maintenance engineering management applications of artificial intelligence. In *Proc. 1st Int. Conf. on Applications of Artificial Intelligence in Engineering Problems*. (Sriram D. and Adey R., eds.) Southampton, UK, pp. 1097–1121

Grillmeyer O. and Wilkinson A.J. (1985). The design and construction of a rule base and an inference engine for test system diagnosis. In *Proc. IEEE Int. Test Conf.*, Philadelphia PA, pp. 857–867

Gunhold R. and Zettel J. (1986). System 12 in-factory testing. *Electrical Communication*, **60**(2), 128–134

Havlicsek B.L. (1986). A knowledge based diagnostic system for automatic test equipment. In *Proc. IEEE Int. Test Conf.*, Washington, pp. 930–938

Hernandez J.L. (1986). AFTA – a platform to expert systems in ATE. In *Proc. AUTOTESTCON 1986: IEEE Int. Automatic Testing Conf.*, San Antonio TX, pp. 51–55

Himmelblau D.M. (1978). *Fault Detection and Diagnosis in Chemical and Petrochemical Processes*. USA: Elsevier

Kahn G.S., Kepner A. and Pepper J. (1987). TEST: A model-driven application shell. In *Proc. 6th Nat. Conf. on Artificial Intelligence*, Seattle WA, pp. 814–818

Kim J.H. and Pearl J. (1983). A computational model for causal and diagnostic reasoning in inference systems. In *Proc. 8th Int. Joint Conf. on Artificial Intelligence*, Germany, pp. 190–193

Klausmeier R. and Allen W. (1985). A prototype expert system for diagnosing electronically controlled automobiles. In *Proc. 1st Annual Workshop on Robotics and Expert Systems*, Houston TX, pp. 273–277

Kolcum E.H. (1986). NASA demonstrates use of AI with expert monitoring system. *Aviation Week and Space Technology*, March 17, 79–82

Kreiger D. (1985). *AUTOTESTCON 1985: IEEE Int. Automatic Testing Conf.*, New York, pp. 43–48

Kriz J. and Sugaya H. (1986). Knowledge-based testing and fault diagnosis of analog circuit boards. In *Proc. FTCS 16: 16th Annual Symp. on Fault Tolerant Computing*, Vienna, Austria, pp. 378–383

Laffey T.J., Perkins W.A., and Nguyen T.A. (1984). Reasoning about
fault diagnosis with LES. In *Proc. 1st Conf. on Artificial Intelligence
Applications*, Denver CO, pp. 267–273

Laffey T.J., Perkins W.A. and Nguyen T.A. (1986). Reasoning about
fault diagnosis with LES. *IEEE Expert*, **1**(1), 13–20

Laufmann S.C. and Crowder R.S., III. (1987). LVA: a knowledge-based
system for diagnosing faults in digital data loggers. In *Proc. 3rd Conf.
on Artificial Intelligence Applications*, Orlando, FL, pp. 144–149

Mathonet R., Van Cotthem H. and Vanryckeghem L. (1987). DANTES:
an expert system for real-time network troubleshooting. In *Proc.
10th Int. Joint Conf. on Artificial Intelligence*, Milan, 527–530

Merry M. (1983). APEX 3: an expert system shell for fault diagnosis. *GEC
J. Research*, **1**(1), 39–47

Michie D. (1986). Current developments in expert systems. In *Proc. 2nd
Australian Conf. on Applications of Expert Systems*, Sydney,
pp. 163–182

Milne R. (1985). Fault diagnosis using structure and function. In *Proc.
9th Int. Joint Conf. on Artificial Intelligence*, Los Angeles,
pp. 423–425

Milne R. (1986). Fault diagnosis using structure and function. In *Proc. 1st
Int. Conf. on Applications of Artificial Intelligence in Engineering
Problems*. (Sriram D. and Adey R., eds.), pp. 1043–1054.
Springer-Verlag

Milne R. (1987). Strategies for diagnosis. *IEEE Transactions on Systems,
Man and Cybernetics*, **17**(3), 333–339

Pazzani M.J. (1987). Failure-driven learning of fault diagnosis heuristics.
IEEE Transactions on Systems, Man and Cybernetics, **17**(3),
380–394

Peng Y. and Reggia J.A. (1987a). A probabilistic causal model for
diagnostic problem solving. Part I: integrating symbolic causal
inference with numeric probabilistic inference. *IEEE Transactions
on Systems, Man and Cybernetics*, **17**(2), 146–162

Peng Y. and Reggia J.A. (1987b). A probabilistic causal model for
diagnostic problem solving. Part II: diagnostic strategy. *IEEE
Transactions on Systems, Man and Cybernetics*, **17**(3), 395–406

Perkins W.A., Laffey T.J. and Firschein O. (1983). LES: A model-based
expert system for fault diagnosis of electronic systems. In *Proc.
17th Asimolar Conf. on Circuits, Systems and Computers*,
California, pp. 9–14

Pipitone F. (1984). An expert system for electronics troubleshooting
based on function and connectivity. In *Proc. 1st Conf. on Artificial
Intelligence Applications*, Denver CO, pp. 133–138

Pipitone F. (1986). The FIS electronics troubleshooting system. *IEEE
Computer*, July, pp. 68–76

Prerau D.S., Gunderson A.S., Reinke R.E. and Goyal S.K. (1985). The
    COMPASS expert system: verification, technology transfer and
    expansion. In *Proc. 2nd Conf. on Artificial Intelligence
    Applications*, Miami Beach FL, p. 597
Prevost M.P. and Laffey T.J. (1985). Knowledge-based diagnosis of
    electronic instrumentation. In *Proc. 2nd Conf. on Artificial
    Intelligence Applications*, Miami Beach FL, pp. 42–48
Quinlan J.R. (1986). What is an expert system? In *Proc. Nat. Workshop
    on Expert Systems*, Sydney, pp. 5–12
Quinlan J.R., Compton P., Horn K. and Lazarus L. (1987). Inductive
    knowledge acquisition: a case study. In *Applications of Expert
    Systems*. (Quinlan J.R., ed.). Wokingham: Addison-Wesley
Reboh R. (1981). Knowledge engineering techniques and tools in the
    PROSPECTOR environment. *SRI Int. Technical Note*, No. 243
Reiter R. (1987). A theory of diagnosis from first principles. *Artificial
    Intelligence* **32**, 57–95
Rodriguez G. and Rivera P. (1986). A practical approach to expert
    systems for safety and diagnnostics. *InTech*, **33**(7), 53–57
Rolston D.W. (1987). A multiparadigm knowledge-based system for
    diagnosis of large mainframe peripherals. In *Proc. 3rd Conf. on
    Artificial Intelligence Applications*, Orlando, FL, pp. 150–155
Scarl E.A., Jamieson, J.R. and Delaune C.I. (1985). A fault detection
    and isolation method applied to liquid oxygen loading for the space
    shuttle. In *Proc. 9th Int. Joint Conf. on Artificial Intelligence*, Los
    Angeles, CA, pp. 414 416
Scarl, E.A., Jamieson J.R. and Delaune C.I. (1987). Diagnosis and
    sensor validation through knowledge of structure and function.
    IEEE Transactions on Systems, Man and Cybernetics, **17**(3),
    360–368
Shapiro S.C., Srihari S.N., Taie M.-R. and Geller J. (1986). VMES: A
    network-based versatile maintenance expert system. In *Proc. 1st
    Int. Conf. on Applications of Artificial Intelligence in Engineering
    Problems*. (Sriram D. and Adey R., eds.). pp. 925–936. Springer-
    Verlag
Strandberg C., Abromovich I., Mitchell D. and Prill K. (1985). Page-1: a
    troubleshooting aid for nonimpact page printing systems. In *Proc.
    2nd Conf. on Artificial Intelligence Applications*, Miami Beach, FL,
    pp. 68–74
Stuart J.D., Pardue S.D., Carr L.S. and Feldcamp D. (1985). *TITAN: An
    Expert System to Assist in Troubleshooting the Texas Instruments
    990 Minicomputer System*. Radian Technical Report ST-RS-00974.
    Also presented at the Expert Systems in Government Symposium,
    Virginia, 1985
Thandasseri M. (1986). Expert systems application for TXE4A exchanges.
    Electrical Communication, **60**(2), 154–161

Vesonder G.T., Stolfo S.J., Zielinski J.J., Miller F.D. and Copp D.H. (1983). ACE: An expert system for telephone cable maintenance. In *Proc. 8th Int. Joint Conf. on Artificial Intelligence*, Germany, pp. 116–121

Waterman D. (1986). *A Guide to Expert Systems*. Reading MA: Addison-Wesley

Williams T.L., Orgren P.J. and Smith C.L. (1983). Diagnosis of multiple faults in a nationwide communications network. In *Proc. 8th Int. Joint Conf. on Artificial Intelligence*, Germany, pp. 179–181

Winston P. (1984). *Artificial Intelligence*. Reading MA: Addison-Wesley

Young, M. (1987). A framework for describing troubleshooting behavior using default reasoning and functional abstraction. In *Proc. 3rd Conf. on Artificial Intelligence Applications*, Orlando, FL, pp. 260–265

17
Qualitative Plausible Reasoning and Assumptions

Anthony Grech
Claude Sammut
University of New South Wales

This paper describes an expert system shell which is intended for applications where conclusions must be made according to a set of assumptions. As conditions change over time, evidence for conclusions also changes and this will influence the decisions made. In order to deal with this dynamic situation, many aspects of an assumption-based truth maintenance system have been adopted. The shell has been used in a particular application, namely, the identification of radar emitters.

Introduction

Most expert systems that draw conclusions from uncertain evidence usually do so by assigning numerical degrees of belief to evidence and propagating these through to hypotheses. One problem with numerical representations of certainty is that they hide the reasons for believing a conclusion. Often certainties are assigned by guesswork, then through trial and error; the certainty factors or likelihoods are refined until the system behaves as intended. What is the meaning of these numbers? An expert does not weigh evidence by evaluating some complicated mathematical expression involving probabilities. There is usually some reason represented by a rule of thumb which helps to determine which evidence is more believable. Certainty factors hide these reasons. Therefore, when there is no sound statistical basis for probability measures, it seems reasonable that expert systems should use qualitative methods for dealing with uncertainty.

Apart from the technical argument against numerical representations, there is a practical one. One interpretation of a numerical degree of belief is that it, in some way, represents the probability of an outcome. However, in many problems, such as when an adversary is involved, the use of probabilities is highly questionable. What is the meaning of the prior probability of, say, a takeover bid in business or a surprise attack in warfare? In domains as dynamic as these, the statistical data either does not exist or is unobtainable.

A common problem when an adversary is involved is to determine exactly what is happening. For example, shares in a company many change hands but it may not be clear if there is one main buyer. If radar emissions are being received by a ship it is important to determine if the source is friendly or hostile. The evidence required to answer such questions may only become available over a period of time; however, it may be necessary to draw a tentative conclusion in case some guarding action must be taken. If there is the suspicion that the radar is from a hostile source then the crew should go on alert, that is, an assumption is made that the source is hostile in order to protect the ship. That assumption can be retracted later if further evidence shows that the platform (that is, the ship or aircraft carrying the radar) is friendly. Thus another useful feature of a plausible reasoning system is that it should be able to reason with and revise assumptions over time.

The original objective of the project described here was to develop a knowledge based system to assist in the identification of radar signals intercepted by electronic support measures (ESM) equipment. The approach taken was to build a general purpose shell which handles uncertainty qualitatively and also reasons with assumptions. Once the shell was completed, specific knowledge of radar emitters was added. In designing the shell, ideas have been borrowed from two previous pieces of work. To reason with incomplete or inaccurate evidence we use the Cohen and Grinberg (1983) method of endorsements. Reasoning with assumptions is based on the assumption-based truth maintenance system (ATMS) of de Kleer (1986a), which builds on the earlier truth maintenance system of Doyle (1979).

The program was written in UNSW-PROLOG running under UNIX. At the time of writing, the shell is complete and has been used on several trial knowledge bases. It has now been handed over to the Defence Research Centre, Salisbury, so that the knowledge base can be extended for practical use.

In this paper we will briefly describe the problem domain, then introduce the main concepts in truth maintenance. An overview of the implementation of the knowledge-based system, incorporating truth maintenance, is followed by an extended example.

The problem domain

On board ship, radar signals are intercepted by electronic support measures (ESM) equipment which an operator uses to try to identify the type of emission. The knowledge-based system is intended to aid in that identification. Radar emitters are carried by platforms such as ships and aircraft. The availability, certainty, precision, and cost of measurements vary depending on the context in which the system operates. For example, the interpretation of a signal received by ESM equipment may be completely different depending on whether the receiver is near land or on water, in what part of the world the receiver is located or the current level of hostilities. Thus, any conclusions drawn by the knowledge-based system depend on a set of assumptions which may change over time.

Initially, the identification system is provided with a description of the tactical situation and a set of signals which form an **emitter track**. An emitter track is the history of emissions assumed to originate from the same radar transmitter. Each signal is characterized by a set of parameters including the frequency of the signal, its pulse width, pulse repetition interval, scan type (that is, circular, conical, sector, steady) and scan period. In conventional radar identification these parameters are tested against ranges in an emitter parameter library (EPL). For numerical parameters, such as radio frequency (RF), the range is characterized by upper and lower bounds. For categorical parameters, such as scan type, subsets of an enumeration of possible values are used. If the measured values match those of a known emitter type recorded in the EPL then the matching emitter type is a **candidate** for the identification of the signal. In the case when no candidate is found, it is possible to fall back on trying to recognize the functional class of the radar rather than its specific type (O'Neill, 1987), that is, the function of the radar may be for navigation, search, fire control, etc. Alternatively, imperfect matches in the EPL may result in a list of candidates which may or may not contain the correct one. In current ESM systems, each of these situations must be resolved by a human operator.

The program described in this paper also begins by matching the incoming signal against records in an EPL. We assume that the EPL has been constructed so as to ensure, as far as possible, that the correct emitter type is among the list of candidates (Hood and Mason, 1987). Selecting the most likely candidates will be done by a knowledge-based system. Following the EPL match, each candidate is given an **endorsement**. This is an annotation which indicates how close the match is and if the occurrence of this type of emitter with these parameters is common or rare. It is left to the knowledge-based system to decide how much this endorsement should be believed. For example, if the emitter match is rare, this may still be considered strong support for a particular identification on special occasions, such as in times of hostility, otherwise, it will be considered weak support.

Since signals from emitters arrive over a period of time, evidence in support of a particular identification may become stronger or weaker depending on the nature of later signals or on new intelligence. These changes in support are represented by the addition of new endorsements. Sometimes endorsements will be negative in the sense that the new evidence suggests that the previous conclusion is doubtful. Since the EPL match may result in a number of candidates, evidence may support several, conflicting conclusions. Therefore, the system must be able to reason along several different lines until the conflicts are resolved. Sometimes it will not be possible to remove all conflicts. In this case, the most likely identification is chosen by weighing the evidence accumulated in the form of endorsements.

The following section describes the mechanism that permits the program to follow several lines of reasoning in parallel.

Assumptions and parallel chains of inference

By using different assumptions and following different lines of reasoning, it is possible to derive different conclusions from the same data. Uncertainty arises when there is no obvious best set of assumptions or best line of reasoning. However, as long as they are not too numerous, it is possible to follow several alternatives in parallel, the final outcome being a set of possible solutions, each supported by its own chain of inference. The strength of these chains will vary depending on how reliable the evidence is for each alternative. Therefore, the solutions may be ranked according to how well justified each one is. In our case ranking is done by user supplied rules. Thus, the goal of this shell is not to find a single, certain solution but a set of possibilities and the reasons for believing each one. De Kleer's assumption-based truth maintenance system was used as a basis for this work because it attempts to find all solutions and does so by treating disjoint beliefs in parallel. De Kleer (1986a, 1986b, 1986c) gives a detailed explanation of the ATMS. This section summarizes those parts of the ATMS system which are relevant to the present application.

The system consists of two parts:

- an ATMS whose task it is to determine what is and what is not believed, and
- a problem solver whose task it is to make inferences about the domain.

All inferences made by the problem solver are recorded and communicated to the ATMS as **assumptions**. The reason for describing a rule's

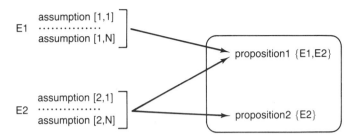

Figure 17.1   Environments and contexts.

conclusion as no more than an assumption is that the premises of the rule may themselves be assumptions, that is, there is insufficient evidence to confirm their truth absolutely.

A set of assumptions is called an **environment**. Figure 17.1 shows two propositions which can be derived from different sets of assumptions. These sets are called environments E1 and E2. Note that a proposition may be derived from more than one environment.

The set of all propositions derivable from the assumptions in an environment is the **context** of the environment. When we look at an example later, we will see that it is possible for a false proposition to be derived from an environment. In this case, the environment is defined to have no context because we cannot believe anything derived from it. Two propositions are derivable from E2, therefore these form the context of E2. Had further propositions been drawn using propositions 1 and 2, these would also be members of the context.

Every proposition has associated with it the minimal set of environments from which it can be derived. This set is called the **label** of the propositions. The label of proposition 1 is the set {E1, E2} since it can be derived from both environments.

In the example above, E1 and E2 represent two distinct sets of assumptions which support different lines of reasoning. It becomes necessary to separate assumptions into different environments when assumptions are found to conflict with each other.

Consider the following situation:

1.   a proposition has been derived identifying the scan type of the emitter as steady (unlike airport radar which is usually circular);

2.   a proposition has been derived suggesting that the emitter is in a particular geographic region, R, at sea;

3.   given (1), there is a rule which deduces that the function of the emitter is fire control;

4.   given (2), there is a rule which deduces that the emitter is on a hostile platform;

5.   given (1) and (2), there is a rule which deduces that the emitter is the specific type T; and

6.   some time later, we discover that there are no steady scan emitters in that region (that is, (1) and (2) are contradictory), so either the scan type or the region was incorrectly identified – we do not yet know which.

As mutually exclusive propositions are derived, a single chain of inference must be divided into separate chains with multiple solutions arising. This process of division of the problem space is called an **extension**. In an extension, results derived from the combination of contradictory assumptions are no longer believed. Results derived from assumptions which do not conflict are split into separate chains of inference since they are independent.

Thus, proposition (5) that the emitter is type T must be invalidated (possibly to be revalidated at some later time) and the other propositions remain unchanged. We now consider all data derived from (1) to be independent of those derived from (2) and belonging to different lines of reasoning.

All propositions, such as (5), with inconsistent environments are termed 'out' and remain out of any context until a consistent environment can be found for them. Thus, the belief, emitter type is T is sent out and the environment

scan_type of emitter is steady
position of emitter is R

is invalidated. Contradictory combinations of assumptions such as these are said to be nogood.

Before describing how these parallel chains of inference are maintained by the system, let us look next at the representation of knowledge in the knowledge base.

Structure of the knowledge base

The knowledge base is partitioned into three sections:

- antecedent–consequent rules,
- dependency characterization, and
- ranking rules.

Antecedent–consequent rules

These rules take the usual form:

if condition **then** action

where condition and action are simple conjunctive expressions. One important action in the system is the expression of belief in a proposition given a condition. For example:

if   type of emitter is T1
then endorse
        function of emitter is fire_control **and**
        scan_type **of** emitter **is** circular.

This rule states that we can be sure that the emitter is a fire control radar which has a circular scan provided that we believe that the emitter is type T1. Sometimes, a proposition is a necessary, but insufficient, condition for a belief. In this case we suggest a constraint, for example:

if   speed **of** platform in 0 .. 35
then maybe
        class **of** platform is ship.

This rule does not conclude that the platform is a ship. It merely notes that the speed is consistent with the constraints of a ship. At other times, we may have weak evidence to suggest a new hypothesis, for example:

if   strength **of** signal is weak
then **suggest** distant.

The difference between these last two forms is that the first makes a note of a constraint being satisfied but draws no conclusion whereas the second draws a tentative conclusion.

Dependency characterization

Dependency characterization predicates tell the system about the propositions which are mutually exclusive. They provide the information necessary to detect contradictions. For example, the predicate:

mutex([hostile, friendly, neutral]).

declares that a platform cannot be hostile, friendly and neutral at the same time. Internally, this mutual exclusion is achieved by creating nogood environments. Thus, the example above would be transformed to:

```
nogood([enemy, friendly]).
nogood([enemy, neutral]).
nogood([friendly, neutral]).
```

Nogood predicates inform the system that if an inference results in one of these pairs, that inference is inconsistent with previously derived propositions. Enumerating all such pairs can be quite inefficient; however, the shell uses some implementation tricks to remove this problem.

Domain constraints are similar to mutex predicates. For example:

```
domain(class of platform, [submarine, surface, airborne]).
```

declares that a platform may belong to one and only one of the classes in the associated list.

Ranking rules

These rules are required by the problem solver in order to indicate the likelihood of a candidate solution in the case that more than one line of reasoning has survived to reach a final conclusion. One advantage of numerical degrees of belief is that the best alternative can be chosen by a simple arithmetic comparison. However, when justifications are represented qualitatively by endorsements, rules must be supplied that will indicate when one rule has a better justification than another. In appearance, ranking rules are very similar to ordinary antecedent–consequent rules. The difference is that ranking rules do not attempt to add or remove conclusions. They merely annotate existing ones after the belief revision process has completed.

In the present application it has been found that once a set of consistent rules has been developed, it is rare to have more than one solution proposed even though there may have been several lines of reasoning at some point. When conflicts do arise, they are often due to uncertainty in the data. Suppose 90% of the readings taken for a particular emitter display a two level stagger PRI (pulse repetition interval) with the rest appearing gittered or fixed. This may indicate that it is an emitter which can change its PRI or it may simply be that 10% of the measurements are incorrect. A rule may suggest that the minority readings are due to noise and can be disregarded. Thus any conclusions drawn using this noisy data must be considered less reliable than conclusions which used the majority readings.

Ranking rules require the use of a new operation:

endorsement of X includes E

This checks to see if E is an expression which supports X. E can be any logical combination of propositions or assumptions. If E includes a conjunction, such as:

A and B

then both A and B must be true in a consistent environment of X. To implement the rule for disregarding noisy data we must be provided with the frequency of occurrence of a particular measured value. Thus:

```
if      endorsement of X includes E1
and     endorsement of Y includes E2
and     (occurrence of E1) − (occurrence of E2) > threshold
then    disregard X
```

where threshold indicates how infrequent a value must be before it is considered noise.

Implementation of the ATMS

Belief in a proposition depends on the assumptions from which it is derived. Beliefs are represented by nodes in a graph. If there are some reasons for believing a proposition and others for not believing it, then two nodes must be provided − one for the proposition and one for its negation. Negation is simply treated as a special case of two mutually exclusive beliefs. Each node contains four pieces of information:

- the proposition which is to be believed (simply called the belief),
- the consequents of the proposition,
- the endorsements for the proposition, and
- the minimal label for this proposition.

The last three fields in the node structure are described below.

The **consequents** of a node N are those nodes which contain propositions that were derived with the help of N, that is, the consequents list N as a **justification**. If the endorsements for N change, then the consequents of N must have their own endorsements reviewed. The list of consequents allows the system to track down the beliefs which have to be updated when assumptions are found to conflict.

The **endorsements** of a node are a list of compound terms, each having the following fields:

- **Type of endorsement** This field may have one of the values **suggestive** or **definite**. As the name implies, suggestive endorsements state that a proposition is possible but not yet confirmed. Definite endorsements confirm a belief in a proposition *provided that the endorsements of the justification are also definite.*

- **Justifications** This is a list of the nodes which directly imply the current node.

- **Label** This is the combination of all the labels from the justifications.

The label allows us to store the environments from which a proposition can be derived. For example, if the node N contains the label,

$\{\{a,b\}, \{c,d\}\}$

then N can be derived from either environment $\{a,b\}$ or $\{c,d\}$. Nodes derivable in the empty environment (that is, no assumptions are necessary) are known to be true. The label for a node is constructed by finding the union of the labels of its justifying assumptions.

The **minimal label** of a node is the minimization of the label of the same node. A label is termed minimal if no environment is a superset of any other in the label in that environment. For example:

$\{\{a,b\}, \{a\}, \{c\}\}$

is not minimal, whereas:

$\{\{a\}, \{c\}\}$

is. In this case $\{a, b\}$ is superfluous since it states that the current node can be derived from a & b; however, another environment says that the node can be derived from a alone. The original, unminimized form is also kept for convenience because it allows labels to be revised quickly when contradictory assumptions are found.

There is an important constraint to bear in mind when attempting to combine endorsements for a belief. Care must be taken to avoid combining bodies of evidence which may independently support the same conclusion but which rely on mutually exclusive propositions. Suppose the system has made two assumptions A and B and there are two rules:

if A then endorse C
if B then endorse C

We might be tempted to say that A and B together provide support for C. However, A and B might be mutually exclusive. A might assume that the emitter type is T1 and B might assume that the emitter type is T2. Suppose the rules are:

if type of emitter is T1 **then endorse** class of platform is ship.
if type of emitter is T2 **then endorse** class of platform is ship.

Since the emitter cannot be of both types, there is a conflict. However, it may not be clear at this stage which evidence should be believed. Therefore, the two sets of endorsements for the node are maintained separately.

Belief revision

When new evidence is obtained, endorsements are added to already existing beliefs. This involves adding a new justification to the set of justifications stored in the node representing a belief. Since a justification has a label (that is, the set of environments from which it can be derived) the label of the belief node must be augmented by the justification's label by finding the union of the two. The union may result in the same label for the belief if the justification contains evidence which is no different from that previously obtained. So a new justification does not necessarily change the evidence for a belief.

If the label in a node N changes, the endorsements of the consequents of N must be checked. So the consequents are marked as damaged and a breadth first algorithm individually updates damaged nodes. To do this, endorsements of damaged nodes are examined to identify those that have justifications mentioning a revised node; if so, new labels are calculated for these endorsements. This can cause changes to propagate throughout the whole graph. This revision is guaranteed to terminate even if circular supports exist; however, the process is time consuming.

Sometimes new evidence indicates that a belief can no longer be held true. This is discovered when there is no longer any environment which supports the belief (that is, the label is empty). In this case the node representing such a belief is 'sent out'. The node is removed from future processing and remains out as long as there are no justifications for it. Once a node (and possibly its consequents) is sent out, further processing may add new endorsements to a belief and cause it to be sent in again.

If a belief holds in the empty environment then it is known to be true. All nodes which conflict with something known to be true must be permanently sent out since, obviously, they are false. When these nodes are sent out, they affect more nodes in the graph. Any combination of justifications which *definitely* conclude a false node are inconsistent and are added to the nogood database. When a node is sent out because it no longer holds in a consistent environment, the same thing occurs. The difference is that if these nodes are ever sent in again, then the environments added to the nogood database at the time the node was sent out will have to be removed.

Maintaining the nogood database is not a trivial task. Suppose nogoods are kept in a minimal form, then any attempt to add an environment, which is subsumed by an existing minimal one, is unnecessary. However, if the minimal environment is later removed, those subsumed environments that would otherwise be present will need to be reintroduced. On the other hand, if minimality is not enforced, sending a node in is much simpler at the expense of exponentially increasing processing. The solution is to maintain two separate databases: one minimal, the other complete. The latter need only be consulted when a nogood is to be removed.

The final important aspect of belief revision is the ability to retract justifications. As an example, suppose two emitter tracks that are very close to each other are assumed to belong to the same platform. If the tracks suddenly diverge, that assumption is shown to be incorrect and must be retracted. This could result in other propositions also being sent out.

An example

A trace of operation of the radar identification system is helpful in bringing together the various concepts described above. We first present a small knowledge base in which the first four rules describe the characteristics of various emitters labelled 1, 2, 3 and 4.

```
r1
if      type of emitter is 1
then    endorse
        threat_level of platform is hostile and
        class of platform is submarine and
        function of emitter is search and
        scan_type of emitter is circular.

r2
if      type of emitter is 2
then    endorse
        threat_level of platform is neutral and
        class of platform is ship and
        function of emitter is search and
        scan_type of emitter is circular.
```

r3
if   type of emitter is 3
then   endorse
        threat_level of platform is friendly and
        class of platform is ship and
        function of emitter is track and
        scan_type of emitter is steady.

r4
if   type of emitter is 4
then   endorse
        threat_level of platform is hostile and
        class of platform is plane and
        function of emitter is search and
        scan_type of emitter is sector

The remaining rules are used when the system is trying to decide
between several candidates:

r5
if   location of platform is shipping_lane
then   suggest
        threat_level of platform is neutral.

r6
if   range of platform is close and
        scan_type of emitter is circular
then   endorse
        signal_level of emitter is strong.

r7
if   class of platform is submarine
then   endorse
        not duration of emitter is long.

r8
if   signal_level_variation of emitter is constant and
        angular_speed of platform is low
then   endorse
        speed of platform is slow.

r9
if   speed of platform is slow
then   endorse
        not class of platform is plane.

r10
if   class of platform is ship
then   endorse
        speed of platform is slow.

r11
if   class of platform is plane
then   endorse
         speed of platform is fast.

Operation begins when ESM measurements are entered into the system:

measurement	signal_level of emitter is weak
measurement	signal_level_variation of emitter is constant
measurement	angular_speed of platform is low
measurement	duration of emitter is long
measurement	location of platform is shipping_lane
measurement	range of platform is close

These measurements are matched against the Emitter Parameter Library resulting in a list of candidates being produced. The system then enters these candidates as assumptions. Now the task of the program is to use its knowledge to resolve the conflicting assumptions:

assume	type of emitter is 1
assume	type of emitter is 2
assume	type of emitter is 3
assume	type of emitter is 4

Both measurements and assumptions are handed over to the ATMS. Measurements are represented by belief nodes which have empty environments, that is, they are known to be true. The new assumptions are entered as nodes whose endorsements are the measurements. Note that, immediately, we have several lines of reasoning running in parallel since the assumptions conflict. The problem solver now attempts to fire rules using a forward chaining rule interpreter.

Rule 8 states that the speed of a platform is slow if it has a low angular speed and is carrying an emitter whose signal level variation is constant:

endorse	speed of platform is slow
because	signal_level_variation of emitter is constant and
	angular_speed of platform is low

Since the premises of this rule are known with complete certainty (they were measurements), the conclusion is known to be definitely true:

| definitely true | speed of platform is slow |

Each time a rule fires, the ATMS is called to update the graph by adding nodes and revising labels (that is, the reasons for believing a proposition). When the update is completed, control is returned to the problem solver which continues to look for rules to fire. For example, rule 9 can also draw a definite conclusion:

endorse	not class of platform is plane
because	speed of platform is slow
definitely true	not class of platform is plane

Sometimes rules, such as rule 5, are only suggestive. Usually, an emitter located in a shipping lane is on a neutral platform, but not always:

suggest	threat_level of platform is neutral
because	location of platform is shipping_lane

Rule 4 derives a conclusion which is known to be false since we have already concluded that the platform cannot be a plane. This is indicated by trying to fire the rule and then finding one of its conclusions blocked because it contradicts a previous, definite, conclusion:

endorse	threat_level of platform is hostile and
	class of platform is plane and
	function of emitter is search and
	scan_type of emitter is sector
because	type of emitter is 4
blocked	class of platform is plane

Since the assumption that the emitter is type 4 leads to an incorrect conclusion, the assumption is now known to be false. Furthermore, the propositions which have been endorsed cannot be assumed. These propositions are sent out but may be endorsed again later:

definitely false	class of platform is plane
definitely false	type of emitter is 4
cannot assume	threat_level of platform is hostile
cannot assume	function of emitter is search and
cannot assume	scan_type of emitter is sector

The problem solver continues to fire rules. Note that the conclusions drawn below can only be endorsed and are not found to be definitely true since there is no support from any proposition already known to be true. Rule 3 fires next:

endorse   threat_level of platform is friendly and
               class of platform is ship and
               function of emitter is track and
               scan_type of emitter is steady
because   type of emitter is 3

A proposition endorsed by rule 3 causes rule 10 to fire:

endorse   speed of platform is slow
because   class of platform is ship

Rule 2 endorses the characteristics of an emitter of type 2:

endorse   threat_level of platform is neutral and
               class of platform is ship and
               function of emitter is search and
               scan_type of emitter is circular
because   type of emitter is 2

Since rule 5 previously suggested that the platform was neutral, rule 2 now adds support to that proposition. Similarly, rule 2 adds to rule 3's support of the proposition that the platform is a ship:

add support to   threat_level of platform is neutral
add support to   class of platform is ship

Recall that rule 4 had derived a false conclusion and, therefore, none of its conclusions could be assumed true. Among these conclusions was the proposition that the function of the emitter is search. Rule 2 now supports this, and so it is 'unouted'.

unouting   function of emitter is search

Rule 6 states that if a platform is nearby and its emitter has a circular scan type then the signal level will be strong. Since the measured strength was weak, the conclusion is incorrect. This implies that at least one of the premises is false. Since the range is known to be close, the premise that the scan type is circular must be false. Thus the firing of rule 6 below is blocked by the ATMS and the conclusions are reviewed:

endorse   signal_level of emitter is strong
because   range of platform is close and
               scan_type of emitter is circular

blocked   signal_level of emitter is strong

The assumption that the emitter was of type 2 led to an assumption that the scan type was circular. This, in turn, led to an assumption that the signal level was strong. Since the last assumption is wrong, the assumptions along the chain of inference must also be wrong:

definitely false	signal_level of emitter is strong
definitely false	scan_type of emitter is circular
definitely false	type of emitter is 2

Because the incorrect assumptions supported other assumptions, support must be either removed or weakened for these:

cannot assume	function of emitter is search
remove support from	class of platform is ship
remove support from	threat_level of platform is neutral

Next, the problem solver uses rule 1 to endorse more propositions. Since some of these had previously appeared as assumptions from a rule which was blocked, the ATMS must 'unout' them:

endorse	threat_level of platform is hostile and
	class of platform is submarine and
	function of emitter is search and
	scan_type of emitter is circular
because	type of emitter is 1
unouting	threat_level of platform is hostile
unouting	function of emitter is search

One of the propositions endorsed by rule 1 is found to be blocked. Therefore, all the work done by this rule must be undone:

blocked	scan_type of emitter is circular
definitely false	type of emitter is 1
cannot assume	function of emitter is search
cannot assume	class of platform is submarine
cannot assume	threat_level of platform is hostile

At the end of this chain of inference only one of the assumptions about the emitters remains free of conflicts, namely, the emitter is of type 3. Thus the emitter has been successfully identified.

The inferences made by the firing of rules create a graph of belief nodes. This is shown in Figure 17.2. The white boxes contain propositions which are assumed to be true. Boxes with dark shading contain propositions which are known to be false, while the light shading

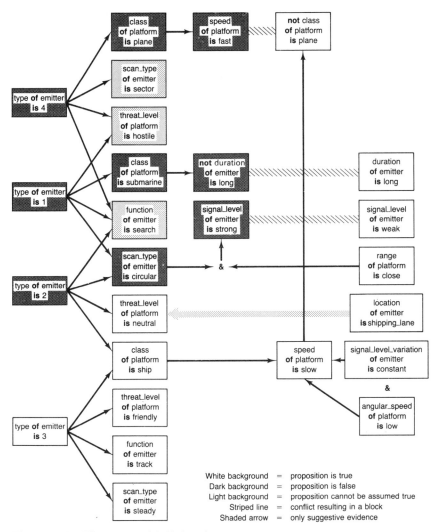

Figure 17.2 The graph of belief nodes.

indicates assumptions which have no support, one way or the other. The striped lines indicate a blocked assumption and the shaded arrows represent a suggestion rather than an endorsement.

This example works out well because the information provided by the measurements is sufficient to reduce the list of candidates to a single one. Therefore, there is no need to use ranking rules to decide among candidates. Let us now consider what would happen if we did not know either the signal level variation of the emitter or the angular speed of the platform. In this case, the assumptions of emitter 4 would not be blocked and, at the end of the inference, there would be two candidates, 3 and 4.

Two things can be done. Even without the missing information, the graph in Figure 17.2 can still indicate which nodes would result in a blockage. By working backwards, it is possible to suggest which additional measurements should be taken in order to resolve the conflict. Until these measurements are available, ranking rules can be used to suggest likely candidates. For example, a rule may use geographical information to suggest that the presence of hostile forces is unlikely, or that hostile forces are also unlikely to be seen in peacetime, etc. Ranking rules in this application will not produce a strict ordering of candidates, instead they will only give rough estimates of likelihood.

Conclusion

We have described a knowledge-based system for radar emitter identification which consists of two parts: a problem solver containing identification rules and an assumption-based truth maintenance system, which maintains consistency in the conclusions drawn by the problem solver. In particular, the ATMS enables problem solving to occur incrementally as new information concerning the state of the world is acquired.

Although this method of handling plausible reasoning is still under development, initial indications are that endorsements, combined with the ATMS, are a useful approach to the problem. In particular, the system provides a way of dealing with uncertainty which does not rely on numerical measures of belief.

Acknowledgements

This work has been supported by the Department of Defence. In particular we thank Dr Stephen Hood and Dr Keith Mason of the Electronics Research Laboratory, Defence Research Centre, Salisbury. They provided the domain knowledge and encouraged us in pursuing this approach to the problem. Stephen Hood suggested the large example used in the paper.

References

Cohen P.R. and Grinberg M.R. (1983). A theory of heuristic reasoning about uncertainty. *AI Magazine*, **4**(2), 17–24
Doyle J. (1979). A truth maintenance system. *Artificial Intelligence*, **12**(3), 231–272

Hood S.T. and Mason K.P. (1987). Knowledge-based systems for real-time applications. In *Applications of Expert Systems* (Quinlan J.R., ed.). Wokingham: Addison-Wesley

de Kleer J. (1986a). An assumption based TMS. *Artificial Intelligence*, **28**(1)

de Kleer J. (1986b). Extending the ATMS. *Artificial Intelligence*, **28**(1)

de Kleer J. (1986c). Problem solving with ATMS. *Artificial Intelligence*, **28**(1)

O'Neill J.L. (1987). Knowledge acquisition for radar classification. In *Applications of Expert Systems* (Quinlan J.R., ed.). Wokingham: Addison-Wesley

18

Problems of Computer-Aided Concept Formation

Donald Michie

The Turing Institute

Much activity in applied artificial intelligence centres around a new way of structuring information for storage in computer memory, the 'knowledge base'. The problems considered here are: (1) how machine-synthesized knowledge bases can be made to reflect the phenomenon of 'viewpoint' which characterizes human knowledge; (2) how to facilitate validation of synthetic knowledge bases; and (3) ways of extracting concept expressions from under-determined or unreliable training sets.

Introduction

Unlike a database, a knowledge base contains not only facts but rules, descriptions and hypotheses. Moreover, even a synthetic knowledge-based system can give the user reasoned justifications (Shapiro and Michie, 1986). To do this, its conceptualizations of the given problem must show a reasonable match with the way the human expert conceptualizes the same problem. What is stored must be validly describable as 'knowledge' rather than merely as 'information'. In this sense applied AI seeks to develop a scientific technology of concepts and allots a special place to the phenomenon of concept learning.

In computer-based industries the continued inability of most commercial systems, even so-called AI systems, to learn inductively from example data has posed a dilemma. On the one hand, to build really large knowledge bases, or even small knowledge bases for difficult problems, machine learning becomes a necessity. On the other hand, software technologists harbour suspicions concerning the 'soundness' of computer induction. Some of these suspicions are well grounded.

Inability to resolve the dilemma has frustrated large-scale plans. At the international meeting in Tokyo to review the 'initial stage' (1981–1984) of the Fifth Generation project the keynote speaker, Dr K. Kawanobe (1984), spoke of 'a number of techniques that have not yet been achieved'. They included 'the inductive inference function, which involves guesswork based on incomplete knowledge'. Turning to the coming 'intermediate stage' (1985–1989) Kawanobe pledged that 'attempts will be made to develop high level artificial intelligence including inductive inference, analogy and learning functions' and 'to develop techniques to make rules by inductive inference'.

The 'intermediate stage' of which Kawanobe spoke has now nearly passed, leaving little residue of these core themes. Reluctance about inductive learning is not to be explained by unfamiliarity with existing solutions. Software technologists in Japan, as elsewhere, may not be aware of this or that particular result, such as the milestone paper of Chilausky *et al.* (1976) recording the inductive construction of a complete above-expert system from historical data. But the availability of effective procedures is now widely known (Quinlan, 1979; Quinlan, 1983). Moreover, those industrial concerns which have made use of them are reaping rewards (Michie, 1987). So abstinence stems not so much from lack of feasibility. Rather, there is hesitation concerning the desirability of what is known to be feasible. The suspicion is that machine representations generated by induction necessarily lack structure. Moreover, bottom-up derivation from raw data seems to offend against the top-down style taught to programmers and systems analysts. There is also a feeling that validity checking is inherently incompatible with inductive procedures. These perceived gaps can be filled, as will appear.

A further weakness may be perceived in the inductive generation of concept expressions as practised today. Every human concept represents a bargain struck between perception and reality. The task of picking out the horses in a distant herd in which horses are intermingled with donkeys and mules cannot, of course, be entrusted to someone who has never seen an equid before. But the task can be carried out by obervers drawn from any number of horse-related milieus, for example, by cavalrymen, jockeys, polo players, huntsmen, farmers, etc. Yet the farmer's concept of a horse is different from that of the jockey. This becomes clear as soon as we consider the task of picking out racehorses and farm horses from a mixture of different kinds of horses. The jockey will easily identify racehorses while the farmer will easily identify farm horses. The two have different 'viewpoints'. The jockey's concept, in turn, differs from the cavalryman's, and so on. When used for defining concepts, contemporary induction algorithms ought to reckon with this question of viewpoint. We shall illustrate by reference to a concept of interest to those professionally concerned with the Space Shuttle (see Figure 18.1; also Michie, 1986).

	stab	errors	sign	wind	mag	vis	Class
1]	–	–	–	–	–	no	useauto
2]	no	–	–	–	–	yes	notauto
3]	yes	lx	–	–	–	yes	notauto
4]	yes	xl	–	–	–	yes	notauto
5]	yes	mm	negative	tail	–	yes	notauto
6]	–	–	–	–	out	yes	notauto
7]	yes	ss	–	–	light	yes	useauto
8]	yes	ss	–	–	med	yes	useauto
9]	yes	ss	–	–	strong	yes	useauto
10]	yes	mm	positive	head	light	yes	useauto
11]	yes	mm	positive	head	med	yes	useauto
12]	yes	mm	positive	tail	light	yes	useauto
13]	yes	mm	positive	tail	med	yes	useauto
14]	yes	mm	positive	head	strong	yes	notauto
15]	yes	mm	positive	tail	strong	yes	useauto
16]	yes	mm	negative	head	–	yes	notauto

```
[vis    ] :
    yes : [errors ] :
            ss : [stab   ] :
                    yes : [mag     ] :
                            light : useauto
                            med : useauto
                            strong : useauto
                            out : notauto
                    no : notauto
            mm : [stab  |  :    :
                    yes : [sign    ] :
                            negative : notauto
                            positive : [mag     ] :
                                    light : useauto
                                    med : useauto
                                    strong : [wind     ] :
                                            head : notauto
                                            tail : useauto
                                    out : notauto
                    no : notauto
            lx : notauto
            xl : notauto
    no : useauto
```

Figure 18.1 Example set and induced rule of the Shuttle autolander problem. The first 15 examples form the induction file built by the engineers. The 16th was supplied by validation-directed induction.

The autolander problem

During the last stage of the vehicle's descent a number of continuously monitored attributes are available to the pilot, such as aerodynamic stability (stab), deviations between earth-based estimates and vehicle-based estimates of altitude and velocity (errors), positive *versus* negative attitude of the vehicle (sign: nose-up *versus* nose-down), wind direction (wind: head *versus* tail), magnitude (mag) of atmospheric turbulence (light, medium, strong and out of range) and visibility (vis: can the pilot see the runway?). The pilot is expected in the light of this complex of information to decide from moment to moment whether he or she should be in manual control or whether to use the autolander.

Early in 1984, to address a NASA requirement, the autolander's chief designer, Mr Roger Burke, with engineering colleagues, attempted to construct a computer program to map the real-time values of monitored variables to the alternative decisions useauto and notauto. Such a program running on an on-board computer was needed to display continually updated advice to the pilot. After some months of (non-inductive) programming they concluded that further effort would not be rewarding. The trouble was later shown to have stemmed not from any intrinsic difficulty of the decision task but from the disability from which every expert suffers in articulating what he or she knows, whether about plant pathology, about medical diagnosis, about process control, about how to play lightning chess or about the movements of the stockmarket.

Mr Burke and his colleagues then attended a course in inductive programming given by Radian Corporation in Austin, Texas, based on the commercial induction software RuleMaster (Michie *et al.*, 1984). Relieved of the struggle to read the needed rules directly from inside their own heads, they were able, under the guidance of their instructor Mr Dick Shockett, to construct the solution shown in Figure 18.1 (translated for purposes of the present exposition from RuleMaster format into ExTran 7, a FORTRAN-based induction product (A-Razzak *et al.*, 1986)).

The upper half of Figure 18.1 shows a set of 15 example cases for generating the executable rule in the lower half. The character '–' denotes 'don't care'. The induced decision tree is read as follows: If vis is yes and errors is ss and stab is yes and mag is light then the decision is useauto, etc. The rule was subsequently validated on NASA's Space Shuttle simulator at Houston, Texas.

Problem definition:

rain
4

weather	logical	wet	dry	blustery
inside	logical	yes	no	
incar	logical	yes	no	
soaked	logical	yes	no	

2

| use | use an umbrella |
| dontuse | don't use an umbrella |

Cases:

	weather	inside	incar	soaked	decision
1	dry	–	–	–	dontuse
2	blustery	–	–	–	dontuse
3	–	yes	–	–	dontuse
4	–	–	yes	–	dontuse
5	–	–	–	yes	dontuse
6	wet	no	no	no	use

Rule:

```
weather
    wet : inside
            yes   : dontuse
            no    : incar
                    yes : dontuse
                    no: soaked
                            yes: dontuse
                            no: use

    dry      : dontuse
    blustery    : dontuse
```

Figure 18.2   The example set and induced rule of the umbrella problem.

Viewpoints and exceptions

At first sight, the set of 15 examples in the upper half of Figure 18.1 seems a satisfactory way of describing the operational concept which Burke and colleagues were tasked with capturing. Certainly the engineers themselves were satisfied, and we do not suggest that it is not a practical solution. But from an AI perspective it lacks something. *Whose* concept is it? The pilot's? The autolander designer's? NASA's? This returns us to the 'viewpoint' idea illustrated earlier with the task of identifying horses in a mixed herd. To clear the ground for machine treatment, let us consider the construction of a rule for advising a robot whether to use its umbrella.

Table 18.1   The umbrella example set using exception programming.

weather	inside	incar	soaked	Class
–	–	–	–	dontuse
>				
wet	no	no	no	use
<				

Figure 18.2 shows the umbrella problem as set up for the previously mentioned programming tool ExTran 7. We see a reasonably concise representation of the concept, first as a set of examples of what to do and second as an inductively derived executable decision rule. Again, though, whose concept is it? There must be at least two viewpoints, according to whether the robot lives in a land of rain or shine.

We can incorporate here the idea of viewpoints by use of a facility of ExTran 7 known as 'exception programming' (see Hassan and A-Razzak, 1988). The programming theorist Donald Knuth once said that to communicate a concept to a student you first have to tell him or her a lie. By subsequently working through the qualifications and exceptions, the original over-generalization is successively refined. Finally you confess: 'What I first said was not strictly true. But it got us started!'

Thus Table 18.1 begins with the general statement dontuse and then refines it (notice the bracket notation) with the single exceptional case, namely that *if* it is wet *and* the robot is not inside *nor* in the car *nor* already soaked, *then* use. The user's concept is fully documented in the upper half as a succinct two-line statement, one line of which sets a default class. This user is clearly a Mediterranean optimist. An inhabitant of Scotland will presumably proceed as in Table 18.2, with a different initial over-generalization, incrementally corrected by exceptions.

Table 18.2   The umbrella example set from a different viewpoint.

weather	inside	incar	soaked	Class
–	–	–	–	use
>				
dry	–	–	–	dontuse
blustery	–	–	–	dontuse
–	yes	–	–	dontuse
–	–	yes	–	dontuse
–	–	–	yes	dontuse
<				

Table 18.3   The autolander example set from two different viewpoints. A: The example set from the pilot's point of view. B: The example set from the designer's point of view.

A.	stab	errors	sign	wind	mag	vis	Class
	–	–	–	–	–	–	notauto
	>						
	–	–	–	–	–	no	useauto
	yes	ss	–	–	light	yes	useauto
	yes	ss	–	–	med	yes	useauto
	yes	ss	–	–	strong	yes	useauto
	yes	mm	positive	head	light	yes	useauto
	yes	mm	positive	head	med	yes	useauto
	yes	mm	positive	tail	light	yes	useauto
	yes	mm	positive	tail	med	yes	useauto
	yes	mm	positive	tail	strong	yes	useauto
	<						

B.							
	–	–	–	–	–	–	useauto
	>						
	no	–	–	–	–	yes	notauto
	yes	lx	–	–	–	yes	notauto
	yes	xl	–	–	–	yes	notauto
	yes	mm	negative	–	–	yes	notauto
	–	–	–	–	out	yes	notauto
	yes	mm	positive	head	strong	yes	notauto
	<						

With the autolander, as Table 18.3 makes clear, *both* viewpoints – the pilot's and the design engineer's – lead to economical concept expressions. These, moreover, are transformed by the induction algorithm into one and the same run-time form, the same decision tree expression that was first introduced in the lower half of Figure 18.1. We may say that the two different declarative forms of Table 18.3 have different **connotations** but the same **denotation**. The connotations correspond to mental descriptions. The denotation is procedural and embodies an executable prescription. This is essentially the same

Table 18.4 The autolander example set from the pilot's point of view using nested exceptions.

stab	errors	sign	wind	mag	vis	Class
–	–	–	–	–	–	notauto
>						
–	–	–	–	–	no	useauto
yes	ss	–	–	–	yes	useauto
>						
yes	ss	–	–	out	yes	notauto
<						
yes	mm	positive	head	light	yes	useauto
yes	mm	positive	head	med	yes	useauto
yes	mm	positive	tail	–	yes	useauto
>						
yes	mm	positive	tail	out	yes	notauto
<						
<						

distinction as is made in software between specification and implementation: what is perhaps surprising is that specifications can differ so much yet the implementation remains the same. Note that the exemplary compactness of the designer's concept could be matched in the pilot's if the syntax of the examples language included negation. Lines 3, 4 and 5 would collapse to yes ss – – (not out) yes useauto, and similarly for lines 8, 9 and 10, giving a total of 6 lines only. Negation can be achieved, not quite as neatly, by using nested exceptions as in Table 18.4.

These two forms, the pilot's and the designer's, both represent the culmination of a process of refinement. In each case, the author of the concept has interacted with successive versions of the declarative form, inspecting and testing, at each stage, the inductively-derived procedures. Use of defaults to express viewpoints in this way seems, at first sight, to demand interaction. Material developed by J.R. Quinlan (personal communication) suggests that this is not necessarily so. Quinlan applied a version of his C4 algorithm (Quinlan *et al.*, 1986) to historical records of the voting by American congressmen to yield a set of production-rules for classifying a given voting record as that of a Democrat or of a Republican. Figure 18.3 shows three rules which were collectively sufficient to classify correctly 128 out of 135 unseen cases, misclassifying 7. The algorithm extracts 10 C4 decision trees from a given training set, and distils from

---

Default class is democrat

Composite rule set:

Rule 1:

physician fee freeze in y
anti-satellite test ban in y u
synfuels corporation cutback in n u
$->$ class republican (96.8%)

Rule 2:

physician fee freeze in y
el salvador aid in y u
duty free exports in n u
export administration act south africa in y
$->$ class republican (98.3%)

Rule 3:

adoption of the budget resolution in n
physician fee freeze in y
education spending in y u
superfund right to sue in y u
$->$ class republican (97.7%)

7 errors / 135 unseen cases

Figure 18.3   Production-rule solution obtained with Quinlan's C4. (Per cent figures are confidence measures; in y u means 'one of {yes, undecided}' etc.)

these a compact set of productions by selectively eliminating conditions and rules from an initial pool of the leaf-to-root paths of all the trees (Quinlan, 1987). The algorithm chooses the commonest class as default, in this case class Democrat. As an experiment this was then manually reset to class Republican, whereupon a rerun generated the rules of Figure 18.4. In the absence of a critique from American politicians, it is an unverified speculation that the second result is more expressive of a Republican congressman's concept of characteristic voting patterns, and the first result more expressive of a Democrat's concept. It is interesting, however, that the Republican default yields a simpler and more accurate rule. Hence, even aside from the 'viewpoint' consideration, a purely statistical criterion for default setting should not be relied on as a substitute for empirical exploration of alternatives.

When using induction in the interactive mode, the statistical criterion is typically not applicable, so that choice of default according to user viewpoint seems natural. Successive refinement of a default classification by introduction of exceptions can be regarded as a form of interactive debugging, which leads stepwise from an initial null program

Default class is republican

Composite rule set:

Rule 2:

> physician fee freeze in n
> education spending in n y
> —>   class democrat (99.4%)

Rule 6:

> adoption of the budget resolution in y u
> physician fee freeze in n
> —>   class democrat (99.4%)

Rule 7:

> synfuels corporation cutback in y u
> education spending in n
> —>   class democrat (95.9%)

5 errors / 135 unseen cases

Figure 18.4   An alternative solution to the problem of Figure 18.3.

to the finished product. Such 'debugging' is carried on at a higher level of abstraction than the process of debugging familiar to us in the context of procedural programs. We now retrace the building of the autolander concept and show how a debugging step is facilitated by the exception programming method.

We first present the examples table as it was initially constructed by the NASA engineers (Table 18.5) and show how its incompleteness is pinpointed and corrected thus yielding the completed table of Figure 18.1 (upper half). It was because, and only because, this validated form of the example set was used for the default-based inductions that the run-time rule derived from the two viewpoints was the same. If the incomplete version shown in Table 18.5 had been used, two different rules would have resulted, representing the effects of 'subjective bias' – the pilot's and the engineer's, respectively. Before leaving the 'viewpoint' use of exception programming, note the strong top-down flavour imparted by such regimes of 'successive refinement'.

Validation directed induction

Most induction algorithms generate a decision rule consistent with the example set. When the example set does not fully specify all possible cases, the algorithm generalizes within the limit set by this consistency

Table 18.5   The incomplete example set of the autolander problem as built up by Burke and colleagues during the original rule-induction process. The missing case required to complete the set forms line 16 of Figure 18.1.

	stab	errors	sign	wind	mag	vis	Class
1]	–	–	–	–	–	no	useauto
2]	no	–	–	–	–	yes	notauto
3]	yes	lx	–	–	–	yes	notauto
4]	yes	xl	–	–	–	yes	notauto
5]	yes	mm	negative	tail	–	yes	notauto
6]	–	–	–	–	out	yes	notauto
7]	yes	ss	–	–	light	yes	useauto
8]	yes	ss	–	–	med	yes	useauto
9]	yes	ss	–	–	strong	yes	useauto
10]	yes	mm	positive	head	light	yes	useauto
11]	yes	mm	positive	head	med	yes	useauto
12]	yes	mm	positive	tail	light	yes	useauto
13]	yes	mm	positive	tail	med	yes	useauto
14]	yes	mm	positive	head	strong	yes	notauto
15]	yes	mm	positive	tail	strong	yes	useauto

and thereby fills gaps. This is the normal case when a human expert provides the example set, as was the case with the autolander problem. Without special facilities the developer may find it hard to check whether the set is logically complete, and hence whether generalization steps have occurred in building the executable rule. Facilities of the required kind are obtainable by use of the exception programming feature described earlier. We call these facilities collectively VDI (validation directed induction).

The input to an induction procedure of the type here discussed is a set of instances classified into decision classes. The output is a decision tree. VDI constitutes a form of **output validation**. Automated tools for **input validation**, to check that instances are logically consistent with one another, or with some user-supplied set of 'plausibility axioms', are the subject of separate study (Hassan, 1987).

VDI automatically discovers whether the examples specification is incomplete, that is, whether additional, currently non-specified examples would be needed to cover all cases. If it is incomplete then VDI identifies the non-specified set of examples and tests these against the decision rule produced by induction from the original (incomplete) example set. This gives the user the ability to see the effect of the generalization step. He or she may then endorse or reject that generalization. If the expert rejects

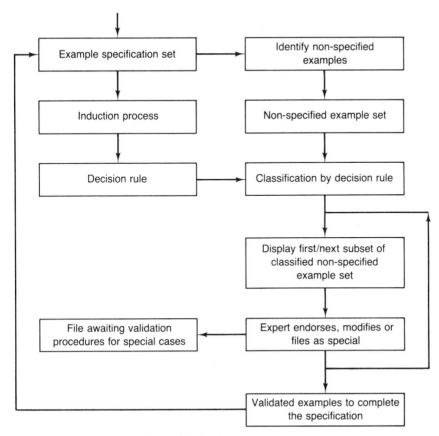

Figure 18.5   Validation-directed induction.

decision values given for the non-specified examples during this process of validation, he or she can enter new decision values. Figure 18.5 illustrates the validation process.

Validation of all non-specified cases finally yields a complete and validated examples set. This set now comprises a complete specification of the desired behaviour, and the induction algorithm produces from it a complete and validated decision rule. At each intermediate stage the induced rule can automatically be labelled on the screen according to whether each given decision point is:

1.   validated by derivation,
2.   validated by user endorsement, or
3.   awaiting validation.

No mechanism existed in RuleMaster to help the NASA engineers to identify the non-specified set of examples from the original set of examples which they had supplied. As is evident from Table 18.5, this set

Table 18.6

stab	errors	sign	wind	mag	vis	Class
yes	mm	negative	head	light	yes	UNSPEC
yes	mm	negative	head	med	yes	UNSPEC
yes	mm	negative	head	strong	yes	UNSPEC

is equal to the upper part of Figure 18.1 minus example 16. The non-specified cases are uncovered by application of ExTran's 'exception programming' after introducing a default class UNSPEC. The three cases corresponding to those leaves of the generated tree which retained the UNSPEC class label are shown in Table 18.6.

The rule originally obtained by the NASA engineers from their incomplete example set decided these cases on the basis of 'informed conjecture', that is, by generalization. If we highlight the decision branches for the above three cases on the decision tree induced from the

```
[vis     ] :
    yes : [errors  ] :
        ss : [stab    ] :
            yes : [mag    ] :
                light : useauto
                med : useauto
                strong : useauto
                out : notauto
            no : notauto
        mm : [stab    ] :
            yes : [sign     ] :
                negative : notauto
                positive : [mag     ] :
                    light : useauto
                    med : useauto
                    strong : [wind     ] :
                        head : notauto
                        tail : useauto
                    out : notauto
            no : notauto
        lx  : notauto
        xl  : notauto
    no : useauto
```

Figure 18.6 Decision tree with the cases decided by generalization highlighted.

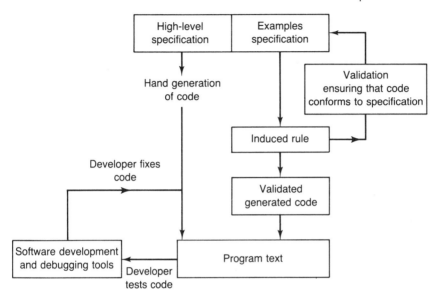

Figure 18.7   Programming in the VDI style with validation loop inserted.

original example set, we get Figure 18.6. The induced rule happens to be identical with the tree of Figure 18.2 because the decisions it gives for the above three cases conform with those of the complete example set as validated. The boxed items in Figure 18.6 highlight the generalization step. The reader can verify that the step consisted of dropping the wind and mag variables in lines 5 and 6 of the example set.

The described technique's practical use is as part of the kind of validation loop sketched in Figure 18.5. Note the provision for alternatives to user endorsement. These may include use of conventional simulators, as was done by NASA at Houston following the rule's discovery. In such a case 'pin-pointing' can enable the administrative authority to use simulation as a rifle rather than as a blunderbuss. Figure 18.7 summarizes the new approach.

The problem of under-determined classes

The above treatment of validation requires that a problem be specified in terms such that output consistency is attainable. In many real-life domains this consistency condition fails either because (1) the attribute set is not adequate, or (2) attribute values are subject to error. In (1) we speak of a problem domain as under-specified, implying the possibility of a fuller or better defined set of attributes. In (2) we speak of the domain as 'noisy', implying the presence of irreducible random variation. Either way, the training set reveals difficulty in the form of 'clashes'. A clash is said to occur whenever an instance (that is, an attribute vector) covers cases associated with different decision classes. A tree induced from a set containing clashes cannot show the desired one–one relation between leaves and classes. Moreover, the successive splitting used by contemporary induction algorithms results in ever-diminishing sample sizes as the wave of splitting travels from the root to more distant nodes. The splitting, therefore, is supported by weaker and weaker statistical estimates of the relative probabilities of the various alternative classes. Algorithms which do not take account of this rising level of estimation uncertainty generate trees which tend to be meaningful towards the root, but towards the leaves they increasingly 'track the noise'. Such trees show over-complex ramification. Also, as first noted by Breiman *et al.* (1984), they perform poorly when set to classify unseen cases (Figure 18.8, under 'old style induction' provides another instance of this phenomenon).

Faced with these circumstances Quinlan's C4 algorithm grows an initial over-complex tree, splitting according to 'gain ratio' (Quinlan, 1988), and then seeks to simplify it by a form of 'backward pruning'. Ascending from the leaves, the algorithm replaces subtrees by leaves whenever a defined error versus complexity trade-off so indicates. In tests on a number of practical problems the method has given excellent results.

In designing the CX algorithm for induction in the presence of indeterminacy, now incorporated in the ExTran inductive shell (A-Razzak *et al.*, 1986, revised 1988), a different approach was taken. The new idea is to subdivide the classification task stepwise into a **statistical description** step, producing what Carter and Catlett (1987) have termed 'class probability trees', and a **decision extraction** step to be effected by a separately defined decision function. If description and decision are kept distinct, we reason that a more correct treatment can be developed for each.

We shall illustrate with two case studies from the credit industry. In the first, after development of a class probability tree, the 'majority vote' principle proved adequate for extraction of decisions from the leaves. The second case study, however, suggests a more general class of decision functions. Trees are converted into tables, from which decisions can be generated by applying user-determined thresholds, or more complex functions if desired.

A credit card multinational

The problem submitted by this corporate client was that of classifying those applications for credit cards which their present methods of assessing credit-worthiness consign to a 'borderline zone'. The opera-

Experimental data

1014 'borderline' records from a multinational credit card company, post-classified into 483 GOOD and 531 BAD. Selection was from a file of about 10 000 records, on the criteria:

> *either*   marginally accepted on scorecard
> *or*   marginally rejected but manually reinstated

Numerical attributes, for example:

- years of age
- years of residence
- years with employer
- years with bank

were converted to logical (intervals) by domain specialists (18 attributes altogether).

Testing was done on one third of the data: other two-thirds were used for inducing the rules.

Old style induction gave trees of about **600 nodes**, about **55% accuracy**.
Client's existing treatment of borderliners, about **48% accuracy**.
ITL's CX algorithm ('forward pruning') gave trees of about **20 nodes** with **66% accuracy**.
This was later refined to over **70% accuracy**, by use of **Interactive CX**, and is now in routine testing.

Figure 18.8   Experiment by A-Razzak and Ahmad.

tional definition of 'borderline', accounting for some 10% of all applications, is given in Figure 18.8, which also summarizes other parameters and experimental findings. In the latter category was the discovery that the client's existing criteria for accepting borderliners gave less than 50% successful prediction of credit-worthiness, as judged by the verdict of history (that is, that the applicant subsequently paid, or that he or she subsequently defaulted). Hence any rule which could be substituted for these criteria with an improvement of prediction probability was regarded as desirable (see Carter and Catlett (1987) for a successful early application of rule induction in this area).

Figure 18.9 shows a class probability tree of the same general character as that obtained in execution of the commercial assignment. It is based on results presented in A-Razzak's 1988 adjunct to the ExTran 7 User Manual (A-Razzak *et al.*, 1986) which describes the interactive CX module. In the interests of proprietary discretion and also of clarity, a

```
464 \ 490
othrcard = A:    94 \ 68
                 bankyrs   =  0t3:    13 \ 32
                 bankyrs   =  4t9:    33 \ 16
                 bankyrs   =  gt10:   36 \  9
                 bankyrs   =  NA:     12 \ 11

othrcard = B:    2 \ 11

othrcard = C:    127 \ 77
                 bankyrs   =  0t3:    33 \ 42
                 bankyrs   =  4t9:    44 \ 20
                 bankyrs   =  gt10:   41 \ 10
                 bankyrs   =  NA:      9 \  5

othrcard = D:    112 \ 70

othrcard = NA:   129 \ 264
```

Key   othrcard means 'what other credit card does the applicant have?'
bankyrs means 'how many years has the applicant had an account with his bank?'
y \ z means 'y GOOD cases (applicant paid) and z BAD cases (applicant defaulted)'
NA means 'applicant failed to answer this question'

Figure 18.9   Class probability tree from 954 'borderline' credit-card applications on which the 'verdict of history' was available.

somewhat simpler tree has been derived from a somewhat larger training set than in the real-life case. The main features are that:

1.   two attributes only, out of the 18 supplied, were sufficient to extract most of the classification information which this attribute set was capable of yielding concerning the training set; and

2.   substantial improvement over the client's existing methods is attainable merely by labelling each leaf accept or reject according to whether the GOOD or the BAD historical verdict predominates among the cases associated with the given leaf.

As a comment on (2), credit industry professionals have pointed out to us that it is precisely these borderliners whose business would most eagerly be sought, if only their future paying behaviour could more reliably be assessed or influenced. Such applicants are likely to belong to that class of citizen whose finances tend to remain in a chronically volatile condition and, hence, who constitute the most active sector of any credit institution's market.

We now return to Figure 18.9 in order to comment on the rationale of CX's mode of generating class probability trees. This follows the 'forward pruning' paradigm of Kononenko *et al.* (1984) which has subsequently lost ground in competition with C4. Possibly, though, this is partly attributable to a greater investment of effort in tuning variants of the latter to high performance. In trials against CX of Wray Buntine's implementation of C4 in the XpertRule inductive shell (personal communication) on the same credit assessment history files as those here described, no clear superiority of performance of one algorithm over the other could be discerned.

The rationale of CX's splitting decisions is similar to the contingency table approach adopted by Quinlan (1987) in the different, but related, context of dropping conditions from the left-hand sides of production-rules. CX's use of contingency testing is made during the tree-building itself rather than being applied after the event to products of a tree built according to a different principle. Thus, to decide which of 18 attributes to use to split the initial set of 954 cases in Figure 18.9, CX examines 18 contingency tables each of the form:

	GOOD	BAD
othrcard = A	94	68
othrcard = B	2	11
othrcard = C	127	77
othrcard = D	112	70
othrcard = NA	129	264

There are several statistical tests that can be used to signal the presence of significant heterogeneity among the j frequency ratios occupying the right of the table (j is the number of subsets, that is, the size of the candidate attribute's value set – 5 in this case). CX uses χ^2 for $j-1$ degrees of freedom, with Yates' correction for continuity (see Snedecor and Cochran (1980) or similar textbook). If no attribute qualifies at $P < 0.01$ or other user-determined significance level, then the set is not split but labelled as a leaf. Otherwise, that attribute is selected for which P is least.

An interactive version of CX displays various derived properties of a candidate set including statistical and information–theoretic measurements. The user can weigh these and override the algorithm's attribute selection at will. As referenced in Figure 18.8, immediate improvement from 66% to 70% prediction accuracy on unseen cases was obtained in this style (a day or two's subsequent experimentation took the level to 75%). We would obviously like to automate as much as possible of this intuitive optimization. A first step might be to replace the χ^2 criterion with the $2 \times j$ variant of Fisher's 'exact test'.

Table 18.7   The leaves of the class probability tree shown in Figure 18.9 are here sorted according to the GOOD \ BAD frequencies of the associated cases. The cumulative ratios formed from these sorted frequencies can be used as the basis of a simple decision rule (see text).

subgroup number				GOOD \ BAD	cumulative ratios
1	othrcard = C	bankyrs	= gt10	41 \ 10	41 : 10
2	othrcard = A	bankyrs	= gt10	36 \ 9	77 : 19
3	othrcard = C	bankyrs	= 4t9	44 \ 20	121 : 39
4	othrcard = A	bankyrs	= 4t9	33 \ 16	154 : 55
5	othrcard = C	bankyrs	= NA	9 \ 5	163 : 60
6	othrcard = D	–		112 \ 70	275 : 130
7	othrcard = A	bankyrs	= NA	12 \ 11	287 : 141
8	othrcard = C	bankyrs	= 0t3	33 \ 42	320 : 183
9	othrcard = NA	–		129 \ 264	449 : 447
10	othrcard = A	bankyrs	= 0t3	13 \ 32	462 : 479
11	othrcard = B	–		2 \ 11	464 : 490

What if the client had regarded a 33% or 30% BAD rate, even in the borderline zone, as too high? He or she might have calculated that wholesale rejection of borderliners would be preferable to suffering such a rate. The original partitioning of the set of cases into a class probability tree would still remain valid. But we would need to supply a new procedure for harvesting decisions from the tree. A suitable procedure reorganizes the tree as shown in Table 18.7 – see Hassan (1988). The client is now invited to disclose his or her highest acceptable BAD rate. Let us suppose that the client settles for 28% for borderliners. Then a rule with an expected BAD rate of about 27% is indicated by the boxed cumulative ratio at the right-hand side of numbered line 5 of the tabulation. The corresponding rule is:

> **if** x is in the borderline file
> **and** x is in one of the leaves 1–5
> **then** accept x **otherwise** reject x.

A more exacting client might have demanded an expected BAD rate no worse than, say, 25%. We should then have had to redefine the rule so as to drop lines 4 and 5 of the table from the Class–accept conditions. The majority vote criterion, as can be seen from the right-hand box of numbered line 7, gives an expected BAD rate of about 33%. It can be

othrcard	bankyrs	Class
–	–	reject
>		
C or A	⩾ 4	accept
<		

Company accountant's
concept of credit
derived from Figure 18.9

othrcard	bankyrs	Class
–	–	accept
>		
B or NA	–	reject
–	⩽ 3	reject
<		

Sales executive's
concept of credit, also
derived from Figure 18.9

Figure 18.10   Two concept expressions responsive to the viewpoints of the accountant and the sales manager, respectively. Addition of one more production to each, namely if othrcard = (C or A] and bankyrs = NA then Class = undecided, could embody an agreed interim resolution of the resulting conflict (see text).

seen as a special case of the probability table procedure, obtained by adding line 6 and 7 to the Class–accept conditions.

A thresholded table in which subsets are ordered in this way according to frequency distributions over decision classes lends itself to restructuring into 'concept' form. To supply 'viewpoints' we postulate a company accountant, who dislikes bad debt, and a sales executive, who dislikes turning business away. Appropriate constructs are exhibited in Figure 18.10. We have allowed ourselves the convenience of recoding logical values such as 0t3 and of forming disjunctive value-subsets, such as B or D. We have also conceded to real life by allowing subjective shading of thresholds in the initial, pre-validation, phase of concept formation. Confrontation of the two concept expressions reveals a viewpoint-directed inconsistency between them at two points. The accountant rejects cases of othrcard = C and bankyrs = NA, to which the sales executive gives the benefit of the doubt. The sales executive accepts cases of othrcard = A and bankyrs = NA, from which the accountant witholds the benefit of the doubt. A more sophisticated basis for thresholding than raw cumulative ratios would be sensitive to the varying sampling errors associated with the GOOD/BAD frequencies of the different subsets. In the imagined case of confrontation, one supposes that discussion of the offending subgroups, comprising in all no more than 4% of all cases, might lead to agreed interim concept expressions pending new data on these subgroups (for example, as suggested in the legend for Figure 18.10).

Results

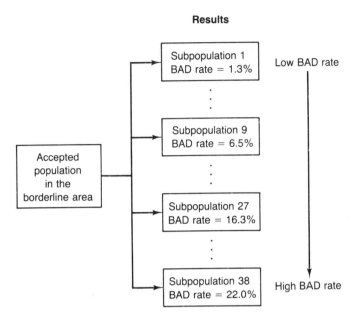

Figure 18.11 A fragmentary sample from a 38-subset probability table generated by CX from records sampled from the client's 'borderline zone'.

A large finance house

The above sales-oriented and savings-oriented descriptive forms were illustrative fancy. But the possibility is offered by probability-sorted tabulations of making computer-generated decisions intelligible and hence **discussable**, including in terms of 'viewpoints', by expert interested parties. This aspect played a key part in a subsequent study of several thousand records from the personal loan sector of a large finance house's business. As before, the client was accustomed to using a standard statistical 'scorecard' algorithm, and once again was dissatisfied with the poor discrimination which linear and additive models of this kind achieve in the region of the cutoff. The client was not prepared to tolerate *even in this region* a BAD rate in excess of 10%, and looked for considerably lower BAD rates than this overall. The combination of these severe requirements with the discriminatory weakness of purely statistical models had resulted in a credit assessment regime which rejected more than 80% of applicants, with unacceptable loss of business volume. Probability table analysis of this relatively small sample file indicated a threshold which, in larger-scale tests, more than doubled the acceptance rate, with a small *reduction* at the same time in BAD rate.

Example

Subpopulation 9   (100 GOODs, 7 BADs):

Loan:	$\leqslant 1000$
Years with bank:	$\leqslant 6$
Business source:	direct
Residential status:	owner
Age:	40–60
BAD rate:	6.5%

Figure 18.12   An entry selected arbitrarily from the class probability table on which Figure 18.11 was based.

The basis for the positive response of credit industry personnel can be summed up in the following terms:

- traditional methods treat loan applicants as a single population, and

- knowledge-based methods recognize that the population consists of subgroups.

An illustrative tabular fragment taken from the pilot phase of the work is shown in Figure 18.11, and Figure 18.12 shows the relevant attribute profile of one of the subgroups, selected arbitrarily. It cannot be too strongly emphasized that the most attractive feature to commercial staff of these tabular representations is that they are so eminently discussable, in contrast with the structureless linear combinations of weighted terms (discriminant functions, multiple regression, naïve Bayes, etc.) with which the industry has had to contend in the past.

Acknowledgements

I have been helped in this review by discussion and suggestions from Dr Mohammed A-Razzak and Mr Thamir Hassan, both of ITL-Knowledgelink, whose work with Mr Ahmad Ahmad on applications in the credit industry is discussed in the text. For exception programming and also the CX module, including its interactive use, see the newly revised version of the 1986 ExTran 7 User Manual by A-Razzak *et al*. I also wish to acknowledge provision by Mr Roger Burke of NASA of technical information concerning the Space Shuttle's autolander, and permission from J.R. Quinlan to refer to the unpublished results summarized in Figures 18.3 and 18.4.

References

A-Razzak M., Hassan T. and Ahmad A. (1986). *ExTran 7 User Manual*, Version 7.2. Glasgow: Intelligent Terminals Ltd (revised 1988). See also A-Razzak M. (1987). *Dealing with Noisy Data Using the CX Algorithm*. Working paper. Intelligent Terminals Ltd, Glasgow

Breiman L., Friedman J.H., Olshen R.A. and Stone C.J. (1984). *Classification and Regression Trees*. Belmont, CA: Wadsworth (Wadsworth's Statistics and Probability Series)

Carter C. and Catlett J. (1987). Assessing credit card applications using machine learning. *IEEE Expert*, **2**(3). 71–79

Chilausky R.L., Jacobsen B.J. and Michalski R.S. (1976). An application of variable-valued logic to inductive learning of plant disease diagnostic rules. In *Proc. 6th Annual Int. Symp. on Multiple-Valued Logic*, Utah State University

Hassan T. (1987). *Formal Validation of Induction Files*. Working paper, Intelligent Terminals Ltd, Glasgow

Hassan T. (1988). *Credit Assessment Using Decision Trees*. Working paper, Intelligent Terminals Ltd, Glasgow

Hassan T. and A-Razzak M. (1988). Exception programming: a new approach to defining specification examples. In *Proc. 4th Int. Expert Systems Conf.* Oxford: Learned Information (Europe) Ltd

Kawanobe K. (1984). *Current Status and Future Plans of the Fifth Generation Computer Systems Project*. (TR-083). Tokyo: ICOT

Kononenko I., Bratko I. and Roskar E. (1984). *Experiments in Automatic Learning of Medical Diagnostic Rules*. Technical Report, Josef Stefan Institute, Ljubljana

Kopec D. and Michie D. (1983). *Mismatch Between Machine Representation and Human Concepts; Dangers and Remedies*. Commission of the European Communities (Science and Technology Policy), FAST Series No 9

Michie D. (1986). The superarticulacy phenomenon in the context of software manufacture. *Proc. Royal Society (A)*, **405**, 185–212

Michie D. (1987). Current developments in expert systems. In *Applications of Expert Systems* (Quinlan J.R., ed.). Wokingham: Addison-Wesley, pp. 137–156

Michie D., Muggleton S., Riese C. and Zubrick S. (1984). RuleMaster: a second-generation knowledge engineering tool. In *Proc. 1st Conf. on Artificial Intelligence Applications, IEEE Computer Society*, pp. 591–597

Quinlan J.R. (1979). Discovering rules by induction from large numbers of examples: a case study. In *Expert Systems in the Micro-electronic Age* (Michie D., ed.). Edinburgh: Edinburgh University Press

Quinlan J.R. (1983). Learning efficient classification procedures and their application to chess endgames. In *Machine Learning: An AI Approach* (Michalski R.S., Carbonell J.G. and Mitchell T.M., eds.). Palo Alto: Tioga Publishing Co

Quinlan J.R. (1987). Generating production rules from decision trees. In *Proc. 10th Int. Joint Conf. on Artificial Intelligence*. Los Altos: Morgan Kaufmann

Quinlan J.R. (1988). Decision trees and multi-valued attributes. In *Machine Intelligence II* (Hayes J.E., Michie D. and Richard J., eds.). Oxford: Oxford University Press, pp. 305–318

Quinlan J.R., Compton P.J., Horn K.A. and Lazarus L. (1986). Inductive knowledge acquisition: a case study. In *Applications of Expert Systems* (Quinlan J.R., ed.). Wokingham: Addison-Wesley, pp. 157–173

Shapiro A. and Michie D. (1986). A self-commenting facility for inductively synthesised end-game expertise. In *Advances in Computer Chess 4* (Beal D.F., ed.). Oxford: Pergamon Press, pp. 147–165

Snedecor G.W. and Cochran W.G. (1980). *Statistical Methods*, 7th edn. Iowa: Iowa State University Press

19

Knowledge Acquisition: A Systematic Approach

John Debenham

University of Technology, Sydney

We present a basis for making the knowledge acquisition process rigorous; this then enables a team of knowledge engineers to work harmoniously together gathering knowledge for a large expert systems application. For simplicity we will illustrate our discussion using 'relations' and 'Horn clauses' as these two formalisms are very simple and are more widely understood than the language of more powerful expert systems shells. We will explore, in some detail, the notion of 'functional association' which underlies our approach; we also find that this notion enables us to clarify the distinction between 'data', 'information' and 'knowledge'. The goal of our knowledge acquisition procedure is the construction of a precise, but informal, 'application model'; the role of this application model will be discussed. Our approach to knowledge acquisition consists of two main components, the 'individual requirements', which are tests which are applied to each gathered fact, and 'knowledge elicitation', which is a procedure which guides the interview from one fact to the next in a systematic way. An important feature of our knowledge elicitation procedure is that the use of it is independent of whether the facts being gathered will eventually be classified as 'data', 'information' or 'knowledge'. Finally, we will show that conventional information diagrams can be employed to represent the different classifications of a given fact as 'data', 'information' and 'knowledge'.

Introduction

We are primarily interested in the construction of expert, knowledge-based systems which are fully integrated with corporate database systems. To date, few expert systems have been designed to interact fully with the organization's central database resource, although expert systems which are permitted to *access* databases are not rare. It is our belief that the coming age of 'knowledge processing' will not cause the 'centre of gravity' of computing activity to shift substantially in most organizations. The net effect of the advent of knowledge processing will largely be to extend and rigorize that part of current database applications which is referred to as the 'rules'. The developing discipline of knowledge engineering, which includes knowledge acquisition, will enable increasing numbers of rules of increasing complexity to be handled with comparative ease. Experience of plausible inference in current expert systems shells will equip knowledge engineers with the skills required to represent rules which include statements of probability. Thus, the so-called rules will then become known as the 'knowledge base' which will contain representations of greater numbers of rules of greater complexity than commonly seen today.

In our experience it is common for information analysts to feel inadequate to process rules. In practice, rules are often placed 'in the bottom drawer' to be dealt with later by *ad hoc* means. On the other hand, seminal works on knowledge acquisition have tended, to date, to ignore the systems architectural understanding of the information analyst (see Davis and Lenat, 1982; Eshelman *et al.*, 1986; Kahn *et al.*, 1985, 1986; Van De Brug *et al.*, 1986). Our approach to building knowledge bases attempts to draw together the architectural skills of the information analyst and the knowledge representation skills of the knowledge engineer – see Debenham (1986). We are primarily interested here with the first phase in the construction of a knowledge base, namely knowledge acquisition. The approach that we take to knowledge acquisition is largely independent of whether the fact being acquired will eventually be classified as 'data', 'information' or 'knowledge'. Thus our approach should be useful both to the information analyst wishing to develop skills in knowledge processing, and to the knowledge engineer wishing to develop skills in systems architecture. By developing the notion of 'functional associations' we show that facts may be acquired in a uniform way no matter whether those facts will eventually be classified as 'data', 'information' or 'knowledge'.

Clauses, groups and clusters

We use the following notation for Horn clauses:

```
employee-number/weekly-travel-loading:$'s( x, y ) ←
        employee-number/works-in( x , "factory" ),
        employee-number/address( x , z ),
        address/distance:km's( z, w ),
        y = w × 2.4
```

which could be used to represent that 'the weekly travel loading in dollars allocated to employees who work in the factory is 2.4 times the distance in kilometres from their home address to the factory'. We note that clauses are representations of associations between relations and (in general) populations. The single predicate to the left of the ← is called the **head**. The one or more predicates to the right of the ← are called collectively the **body**.

The clause in the above example tells us about the weekly travel loading for those employees who work in the factory. We may require additional clauses to specify the weekly travel loading for other employees who do not work in the factory. Such a collection of clauses is referred to as a **clause group**, or simply as a **group**. The unique predicate at the head of each clause in a clause group is called the **head predicate** of that group. The body predicates of all the clauses in a clause group are collectively called the **body predicates** of that group.

The Horn clause quoted above contains four relations; it enables us to deduce information about the head relation.

employee-number/weekly-travel-loading

from information in the other three body relations. Perhaps it is possible to deduce information about one of the body relations from the other three. For example, it might be possible to specify a rule which enabled us to deduce information about the relation

employee-number/works-in

from information in the other three relations. In this way we can construct groups, using the same set of relations, with a different relation as head. Such a collection of groups is called a **cluster**.

Functional associations

We think of an expert systems shell in general as consisting of the components shown in Figure 19.1, where:

- the **data base** supports a type hierarchy and contains a mechanism for representing an individual object in the application by a **label**. A set of similar labels may be grouped in a **population**. We distinguish between two types of population. A population which is associated with a particular set of labels (for example, the actual set of spare part numbers) is called a **name-population**. On the other hand, the population 'spare part' which just refers to the abstract thing 'spare part', and thus is *not* associated with any

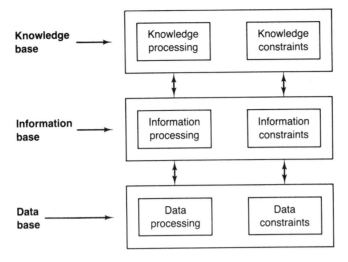

Figure 19.1

particular set of labels, is called a **thing-population**. Labels and populations are referred to by a name which consists of a text string in which the spaces are replaced by hyphens (-), units, if any, optionally shown separated from the string by a colon (:); for example, 24:$ and 36:% are two label names. In other words, our 'data base' is, in effect, what is commonly known as a 'data dictionary'.

- the **information base** consists of a mechanism for representing constant **tuples**. A set of similar tuples may be grouped in a **relation**. The component populations which make up the tuples in a particular relation are called the **domains** of that relation. We usually identify a relation by a list of its domain names where the domain names are separated by the slash character (/). For example:

  item-number/item-cost:$

  is the name of a dyadic relation. In other words, our 'information base' is what is commonly known as a 'database'. Note that our 'data base', discussed above, is written as two words to distinguish it from the conventional 'database' which is written as one word.

- the **knowledge base** contains a mechanism for representing Horn clauses. A set of clauses with the same head predicate can be grouped in a (clause) **group**.

We will refer to the fundamental, indivisible real objects in an application as the **data** in that application.

An important structural feature of many relations is the so-called 'functional dependency' *from* the key domains *to* the non-key domains. In a relation, domain A is said to be **functionally dependent** on the set of domains $\{B\}$ if to each value in the set of domains $\{B\}$ there corresponds precisely one value in domain A, at any given time. For example, in a shared medical practice in which, at most, one doctor was on duty at any time, the date and the time of day of an appointment could be sufficient to determine the doctor involved and the patient involved, that is:

date/time/doctor/patient(<u>dd-mm-yy, hr-min</u>, doc#, pat#)

The identification of the first two domains of this relation as the *key* implies that *if* we know the date *and* the time *then* we know the doctor and the patient. We say that the third and fourth domains of this relation are functionally dependent on a compound key consisting of both date and time taken together. Thus a relation can represent a functional dependency between items of data. However note that we cannot give a succinct definition of the above functional dependency; in fact the only way that we are likely to be able to specify the function is by listing all tuples concerning time, doctors and patients, which satisfy it.

Consider the simple rule: 'To convert from degrees Fahrenheit to degrees Celsius, subtract 32 and divide by 1.8'. This rule is also in functional form, in fact it is a function *from* degrees Fahrenheit *to* degrees Celsius. This function is also between two items of data which are 'degrees Fahrenheit' and 'degrees Celsius'. However, it differs from the relation just discussed in one important way; this time, we can actually define the function:

$$f : (\deg F) \rightarrow (\deg C)$$

by:

$$f(x) = (x - 32) \div 1.8$$

Both of the examples just considered concern functions between items of data. The first cannot be defined succinctly in the sense that a succinct definition that will 'work for all time' cannot be constructed; it is thus called an **implicit functional association**. The second can be defined succinctly and 'for all time'; it is thus called an **explicit functional association**. Note that we have used the word 'association' rather than 'dependency' to acknowledge that the context of our discussion is more general than functional dependencies in relations.

Consider the simple rule 'selling price is 1.25 times buying price' which might be represented by the clause:

item-no./item-sell:$(x, y) ← item-no./item-buy:$(x, z)
$$y = 1.25 \times z$$

This rule is also in functional form. In fact, it represents a function *from* the relation:

item-no./item-buy

to the relation:

item-no./item-sell

The nature of this function is quite explicit; it is succinct as it enables a large amount of information about the relation:

item-no./item-sell

to be deduced. Thus it is also an explicit functional association.

We are now in a position to define what we mean by the 'data', 'information' and 'knowledge' in an application:

- the **data** comprises the fundamental, indivisible real objects in that application;
- the **information** is the implicit functional associations between data in that application; and
- the **knowledge** is the explicit functional associations between items of information and/or data in that application.

Note that in this categorization there is no reference to implicit functional associations between items of information. This may appear to be an omission. Consider the following: *if* it is possible to specify a correspondence between all tuples that could belong to relation P and all tuples that could belong to relation R such that to each P-tuple there is a unique R-tuple, *and if*, at any time, to each tuple stored in P there is the (unique) corresponding tuple stored in R, *then* there is an implicit functional association from relation P to relation R. However, in this case, we would say that relation P was a candidate, compound key for relation R, thus giving rise to a new relation. In other words, there is little to be gained from considering implicit functional associations between items of information as being different from implicit functional associations between collections of items of data.

The distinction between implicit and explicit functional associations is hard to draw precisely. For example, consider the relation shown in Table 19.1, for which the general rule 'that if $a \leq 4$ then $b = 2 \times a$' always holds. Thus the first three lines of the current contents of the

Table 19.1

a	b
1	2
3	6
4	8
5	6
8	3
9	4

relation are instances of the general rule, and the other lines represent the exceptions to this general rule. Is this an implicit or an explicit functional association? After all, it can be represented in clausal logic as:

$$R(x, y) \leftarrow \leq(x, 4), y = 2 \times x$$
$$R(5, 6) \leftarrow$$
$$R(8, 3) \leftarrow$$
$$R(9, 4) \leftarrow$$

Thus no matter which way we consider it, this functional association is 'part implicit' and 'part explicit'. We will not try to resolve this apparent dilemma because it is our belief that, in practice, functional associations tend to be principally implicit or principally explicit. In other words, we suggest that if a functional association is under consideration which has both a substantial implicit part and a substantial explicit part then perhaps the functional association should be decomposed into two, or more, subassociations each of which is either clearly implicit or clearly explicit.

The application model

Knowledge acquisition is the first phase in the construction of an expert system. The goal of the knowledge acquisition phase is to construct a complete, consistent, correct and irredundant model of the application which is comprehensible to the domain expert, and which is in a sufficiently precise form to enable a trained person to translate it unambiguously into some implementable formalism. This model will be referred to as the **application model**. In contrast to our work, note the work of Diederich *et al.* (1986) which sees the generation of the knowledge base itself as the product of knowledge acquisition.

The role of the application model in the design of an expert system is crucial. The ultimate goal in building the application model is to construct a precise, concise and complete statement of 'all that is relevant in' the application. The application model should make perfect sense both to the knowledge engineer who knows little of the background to the application area, and to the domain expert from the application area who knows little about knowledge analysis. As far as the latter is concerned, the application model represents the most highly refined picture of the application that he or she is expected to understand; thereafter, the expert system building process will be in the hands of the knowledge engineer and a team of technical staff. Thus, for the knowledge engineer, the application model represents the final opportunity for the gathered facts to be checked for correctness, before they are represented in some formalism and eventually become an implemented expert system. The application model is not discarded once the expert system has been implemented, it is the kernel of the whole design *and maintenance* process; it forms the linchpin of the maintenance strategy.

There are many formalisms in use today which could be used to provide a language in which application models could be phrased. However, we have rejected them for two main reasons. The first reason is that we are not aware of a formalism which is disposed naturally and equally to data, information and knowledge. In other words, many formalisms tend at least to imply that a gathered fact, once represented in the formalism, should be classified either as data, as information or as knowledge. The second reason is that formalisms tend to complicate and retard communication between the knowledge engineer and the domain experts. Thus we prefer the 'in-formalism' of stylized natural language. Our 'in-formalism' is fixed (see Gruber and Cohen, 1986 for a description of an approach which provides representational primitives that are at the level of the expert's task).

The knowledge engineer is confronted with a complex problem of eliciting facts from the domain expert, whilst knowing that some of these facts may be used, and that those that will be used will eventually become either data, information, knowledge or constraints, but not knowing which of the four it will be. At the same time, the knowledge engineer is trying to ensure that the gathered facts satisfy the requirements of the data, information, knowledge and constraint representations! In other words, he or she must keep one eye on the business of constructing a good model quickly whilst the other eye is checking that the gathered facts are in a form which is suitable for representation. If these two goals are not pursued at the same time then this will inevitably lead to many frustrating, repeated interviews with the domain expert.

Knowledge acquisition: the individual requirements

Any individual fact that is gathered will be phrased in the language of the application model and is required to satisfy the 'individual requirements' if the fact is to become an acceptable statement in the application model.

The **individual requirements** are the 'uniqueness requirement', the 'type of identification requirement' and the 'atomic requirement'. These individual requirements are deliberately pragmatic (see Gaines, 1986, for an interesting taxonomy of the objects involved in the knowledge transfer process; see also Hayward *et al.*, 1986, for a discussion of different 'levels' of knowledge). The individual requirements apply equally to statements which are destined to become either data, information or knowledge. The uniqueness requirement is concerned with the clarification of the *wording* of a fact. The type identification requirement is concerned with the clarification of the *structure* of the data in a fact. The atomic requirement is concerned with the scope of the *meaning* of a fact.

The **uniqueness requirement** is concerned with the standardization of jargon. This requirement insists that the words, phrases and technical jargon used should be correct and there should be no 'duplication of reference'. By 'duplication of reference' we mean that each word and phrase in the application model should refer to, at most, one thing of interest in the application, and each thing of interest in the application should be referred to by, at most, one phrase. This applies both to words, phrases and technical jargon used to describe objects in the application and to words, phrases and technical jargon used to describe processes in the application. For example, there is an ambiguity in 'savings accounts' which could refer to an individual object in a set of objects called 'account types', or to the 'set of all accounts which are savings accounts'. We avoid this ambiguity by rejecting the phrase 'savings accounts' and using instead the predicate is-a[savings-account-no.](...) which is satisfied by the set of savings account numbers, and savings-account-type to represent the object. Note that these two forms may be linked by the 'if and only if' statement:

$$\text{is-a[savings-account-no.]}(\,x\,) \longleftrightarrow$$
$$\text{account-no./account-type}(\,x,\,\text{"savings-account-type"}\,)$$

An example of jargon used to describe a process is the use of the phrases 'crate up', 'prepare for despatch' and 'parcel' to describe what happens to goods after they have been delivered to the Despatch Department and before they have actually been despatched.

The **type identification requirement** is concerned with the development of the data dictionary including a type hierarchy. This requirement insists that all phrases referring to fundamental, indivisible, real objects in the application should be identified as such, and should be recorded as either a population or a label in a data dictionary which supports a type hierarchy. Each new label will be attached to any name-population of which it is a member. For each new thing-population, any subtype or supertype relationships between it and other thing-populations will be recorded in the type hierarchy. The type identification requirement insists that the data in the application should be accurately identified; the knowledge engineer will classify each fundamental, indivisible object as either a population name, a label name or both. If a fundamental, indivisible object can be classified as both a population name and a label name then, to satisfy the uniqueness requirement, that object will be given two separate names, one for the population name and one for the label name.

In a sense, the type identification requirement forces the knowledge engineer to take a 'top down' approach to the analysis of data during knowledge acquisition, that is, the knowledge engineer should be persistently checking the extent to which each real concept in the presented facts should be decomposed. The strategy that we prescribe is for the knowledge engineer *to decompose concepts as much as is necessary and no more*. By 'necessary' we mean that the decomposition should prove, in the context of the application, to be sufficient for the foreseeable future.

The **atomic requirement** insists that the fact is 'atomic'. An **atomic fact** is one which can be expressed as a statement in the language of the application model and which *can be interpreted* as having one of the following forms:

1.   The definition of a new population. For example, 'We are interested in part numbers' or 'The day of the week is of fundamental importance'.

2.   Specification of a constraint on a known name-population. For example, 'Part numbers all lie between 100 and 999'.

3.   The identification of a label for a known name-population. For example '456 is a valid part number' or 'Today's date is 8th August 1988'.

4.   The definition of a relation for two or more populations. For example, 'The cost of a spare part may be determined by knowing its spare part number'.

5.   Specification of a constraint on a known relation. For example, 'The cost of any spare part is greater than $1 and less than $100', or 'The cost of any spare part will never change by more than 20%'.

6.   The identification of a tuple for a known relation. For example, 'The cost of spare part number 456 is $23'.

7.   The definition of a group for two or more populations and/or relations. For example, 'The selling price for a spare part item is determined by the cost price of that item, the customer discount rate and, if appropriate, a factor for slow moving stock'.

8.   The specification of a constraint on a known group. For example, 'The selling price of a spare parts item will always depend on the cost price of that item'.

9.   The identification of a clause for a known group. For example,
     'The selling price for fast moving spare part items is the cost price
     of that item plus 35%, and then less the customer discount rate'.

In the above definition we have used the adjective 'known', for example
in 'known population'. By 'known' we mean that the population, or
whatever, has already been defined; in particular, a 'known population'
will have been recorded in the data dictionary and, if it is a thing-
population, entered in the type hierarchy. Note that the examples given
above are examples of facts that *could be interpreted* as having the form
which they illustrate. In addition, many of these examples could, in fact,
illustrate more than one of the nine forms quoted. Note that the
description of a subtype relationship between two known thing-
populations is not an atomic fact. In a sense, subtype relationships are
knowledge. For example, suppose that two thing-populations 'employees'
and 'engineers' have been defined, and that the statement is made that 'all
engineers are employees' then this establishes a subtype relationship
between the two thing-populations 'employees' and 'engineers'. This subtype relationship could be expressed as the clause:

is-a[employee](x) ← is-a[engineer](x)

and hence thought of as an explicit functional association; in other words,
it is knowledge.

    In contrast with an atomic fact, a **divisible fact** is one that contains
two or more atomic facts. Recall that all facts will have satisfied both the
uniqueness requirement and the type identification requirement, and thus
the data (that is, the populations and labels) will have been identified.
This greatly simplifies the business of checking that the atomic
requirement is satisfied. For example, consider the given fact '#234 is a
spare part number; these are the part numbers which lie between #100
and #999'. Suppose that in the satisfaction of the uniqueness and type
identification requirements for this, and previously presented, facts the
following decisions have been made:

● 'parts' is a thing-population,
● 'part number' is the identifying population of the population
  'parts',
● 'spare parts' is a thing-population,
● 'spare part number' is the identifying population for the population
  'spare parts', and
● '#234' is a label which belongs to the population 'part number'.

In the satisfaction of the atomic requirement we now identify the
following atomic facts:

- '#234' belongs to the population 'spare part number', and
- all spare spare part numbers lie between 100 and 999.

Thus we see that the given fact is a divisible fact comprising two atomic facts; in addition, the given fact establishes the subtype relation between the populations 'spare parts' and 'parts'.

The atomic requirement may seem premature; after all, during knowledge acquisition newly gathered facts are yet to be classified as knowledge, information or data. On the contrary, the atomic requirement attempts to detect divisible facts before the classification stage because, if this can be achieved, then the principle of 'each real object being represented in one place and in one place only' will have been substantially satisfied. In addition, it can help to reduce the amount of re-interviewing of the domain expert and hence it should help to reduce the amount of work on subsequent visits to the knowledge acquisition phase.

Satisfaction of the atomic requirement entails both that the sample fact be expressible as a statement in the language of the application model and that the fact be classifiable as a member of one of the nine categories, as listed in the definition of an atomic fact. In our exper-ience, neither of these requirements consitutes any real restriction. Consider the first of these two requirements which insists that the sample fact either be representable as a simple statement or as a compound statement in the language of the application model. If the sample fact can be represented as a simple statement then this is equivalent to satisfying requirements (1), (3), (4) or (6) in the definition of an atomic fact. If the sample fact can be represented as a compound statement then this will restrict the syntax in which statements of forms (2), (5), (7), (8) and (9), in the definition of an atomic fact, can be expressed. In the second of these two requirements, note the wording of this requirement 'that *can* be interpreted . . .' As we shall see, this preliminary classification is of great assistance in guiding the knowledge elicitation process. We stress that this preliminary classification should not in any way influence the classification of objects; this takes place during the following phase, namely, knowledge analysis.

The definition of an atomic fact refers to facts that 'can be interpreted' as 'the specification of a constraint'. In practice, when facts are presented it is often not possible to decide whether they will be classified eventually as constraints or as knowledge. We will see later that this decision is often made in the fourth phase, namely 'knowledge implementation'. Thus, as far as knowledge acquisition is concerned, we choose not to refer to constraints explicitly, and to view tentatively any fact, which could be seen as a potential constraint, as knowledge.

The satisfaction of the individual requirements, in particular the type identification requirement, will have identified labels and populations and thus will have identified those facts which are destined to become data. It is, however, premature to conclude that the remaining facts will have been classified as information or knowledge. It is also undesirable for the knowledge engineer to even contemplate this, as, during knowledge acquisition, the knowledge engineer should concentrate on the data and on getting the data correct. However, one useful division of facts can be made. Some facts will have the property that they can be interpreted as having form (1), (4) or (7) in the definition of an atomic fact; such a fact is called a **general fact** or **GEF**. Other facts will not have this property; such facts are called **particular facts** or **PAF**.

Knowledge acquisition: knowledge elicitation

Thus far we have discussed the extraction and representation of single facts in the language of the application model. During this operation, the knowledge engineer should have meticulously dissected the components of each fact when identifying the data in that fact. We have not yet addressed the issue of how the knowledge engineer should systematically lead the domain expert to enunciate atomic facts and then to develop these facts in an orderly and directed sequence. The technique for doing this is called **knowledge elicitation**. The work reported here is designed principally for application to a traditional interview. There are, of course, other sources of knowledge, including machine-generated knowledge (see Arbab and Michie, 1985; Quinlan, 1987; Neves, 1985).

Knowledge acquisition in general, which includes knowledge elicitation in particular, is a procedure that is performed by the knowledge engineer 'on the fly'. Knowledge acquisition should make efficient use of the domain expert's time. The procedure that we describe for knowledge elicitation is simple and directed. The procedure gives the knowledge engineer some · simple tools that enable knowledge to be gathered in a uniform way, thus the procedure is suitable for team work. In our view, knowledge elicitation should proceed at a reasonable pace to prevent the expert (and the knowledge engineer) from becoming bored and losing concentration. Thus knowledge elicitation is not a procedure which permits a thorough analysis of what is going on; the domain expert's time is usually too precious for that. Our strategy is to gather as much knowledge as we can, in a sufficiently ordered way for it to form useful 'blocks', in the time available.

Suppose that the domain expert has just enunciated the sample fact 'the interest rate on savings accounts is 5%'; what should the knowledge engineer do next? There are many choices as this fact has established directly, or by implication, a number of concepts including: accounts, account type, savings, interest, interest rate and the value 5%. Having

Figure 19.2

ascertained that this fact satisfied the individual requirements, the knowledge engineer could ask any of the following questions:

- What other things are there of interest beside accounts?
- What other things are associated with accounts beside account type and interest rate?
- What other sorts of accounts are there beside savings accounts?
- What other interest rates apply beside 5%?
- Are the concepts 'account type' or 'interest type' associated with any other things beside accounts?
- Is 'savings' associated with anything other than an account, as in a 'savings account'?
- Is 5% associated with anything other than the interest rate on savings accounts?

It is easy to see that any of these questions could lead the discussion well away from the fact under consideration. Our approach to knowledge elicitation determines a specific sequence of questions which the knowledge engineer should ask. It is interesting to note that this sequence is quite independent of whether the fact will eventually be classified as data, information or knowledge. It is also interesting to note that this sequence of questions should prevent the discussion from moving away from the fact under consideration until everything about that fact has been gleaned.

When checking that a sample fact satisfies the atomic requirement, the knowledge engineer is required to form a tentative, or subconscious, view as to how that fact could be classified. No matter whether this view classifies the sample fact as data, information or knowledge, the fact 'the interest rate on savings accounts is 5%' is basically about a functional association between 'an account of type savings' and 'an interest rate of value 5%', as illustrated in Figure 19.2. The knowledge engineer should first confirm that this functional association is well defined by asking 'Do you mean that *all* savings accounts have an interest rate of 5%?' Assuming that the answer is affirmative, the knowledge engineer now knows that an account of type savings always has an interest rate of 5%; in other words, the functional association recorded is 'well defined'.

In the next step, the knowledge engineer decides whether the fact is a GEF or a PAF. Note that it cannot be interpreted as both because

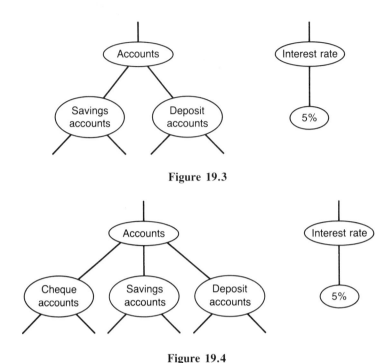

Figure 19.3

Figure 19.4

such ambiguities have been removed in the satisfaction of the individual requirements by the identification of the populations and the establishment of the data dictionary.

If the knowledge engineer regards a fact as a GEF then the fact is recorded. In particular, if the GEF is the definition of a new thing-population then the knowledge engineer should immediately inquire what the identifying name-population is. No matter what the GEF states, the knowledge engineer should then attempt to identify sufficient PAFs to define fully that GEF. We might describe this process as **particularization**. When the knowledge engineer is advised by the domain expert that sufficient PAFs have been presented to specify the given GEF fully, then the GEF is called a **complete GEF**.

If the knowledge engineer regards a fact as a PAF then the fact is recorded and the knowledge engineer will then attempt to 'generalize' the PAF as we now describe. The **generalization** of a PAF is a particular GEF to which the given PAF belongs. To illustrate 'generalization' we consider the business of generalizing the fact 'The interest rate on savings accounts is 5%'. Suppose that 'savings accounts' is interpreted as a label and that the fact is seen as being of class (6) in the definition of an atomic fact, that is, the fact is a PAF. As we have seen, a crude analysis of this fact is as a premise 'account of type savings' and a conclusion 'interest of value 5%'. To generalize this PAF we generalize these two items; to do this we

Figure 19.5

need to know what is 'particular' about these items as they are. In this example, it seems reasonable to suspect that what is particular about the premise is that the account is a *savings* account, and what is particular about the conclusion is that the interest rate is 5%. However, some of this information may already be recorded in the type hierarchy. Suppose that segments of the type hierarchy are as shown in Figure 19.3. Then to generalize the given functional association between 'savings accounts' and '5%' the knowledge engineer will look for associations, first between all associated concepts, and second between the immediately superior concepts, in the type hierarchy. Thus the next two questions should be 'Do all deposit accounts have a certain interest rate?' and 'Are there any other sorts of accounts?' Suppose that the answers to these questions are 'Yes, 4%' and 'Yes, cheque accounts', respectively. The knowledge engineer will then enter 'cheque accounts' in the type hierarchy as shown in Figure 19.4. Then the knowledge engineer should ask 'Do all cheque accounts have a certain interest rate?' Suppose that the answer is 'Yes, 3%'. The knowledge engineer should now confirm these observations by checking the immediately superior concept in the type hierarchy; the knowledge engineer should ask 'So all accounts have an interest rate of some value associated with them?' Suppose that the answer is 'Yes', then the GEF of Figure 19.5 is the generalization of the original PAF because it is 'just superior' to the original PAF in the type hierarchy.

The knowledge engineer may consider it prudent to develop this generalization process further. To do this, the knowledge engineer should focus on the 'conclusion' of this newly found GEF and should ask 'Are there any other objects which have an interest rate?' Suppose that the answer is 'Yes, fixed bonds attract 7% interest.' Once again, the knowledge engineer should inspect the type hierarchy to discover the situation shown in Figure 19.6. The next two questions should be 'Do all variable bonds have an interest rate?' and 'Are there any other objects which have an interest rate?' Suppose that the answers to these questions are 'Yes 6%' and 'No, that is all.' By now, the knowledge engineer has identified two more GEFs, making three in total, as illustrated in Figure 19.7. The knowledge engineer should confirm that these are correct. This completes the description of our technique for generalizing a PAF to its natural GEF. Having constructed this GEF the knowledge engineer should then check that it is complete in the sense described earlier.

By this stage in the knowledge elicitation process we have hopefully obtained a complete GEF. In practice this GEF may well be incomplete. This hopefully complete GEF has either been constructed by

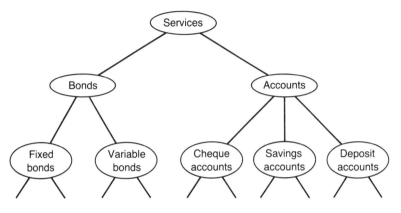

Figure 19.6

completing a given GEF or by generalizing and completing a given PAF. Supposing that we have a GEF, the general idea now is to try to extract any knowledge from the domain expert that would enable us to calculate, or deduce, the PAFs in this GEF *from* other facts.

For example, suppose that we have the complete GEF referred to above, that is, 'The type of an account determines the interest rate on that account'. Associated with this GEF we have the three PAFs: 'account of type savings has an interest rate of 5%', 'account of type cheque has an interest rate of 3%' and 'account of type deposit has an interest rate of 4%'. It is quite reasonable to think of this GEF as information, that is, this GEF could be represented by a relation in which the three PAFs could then be represented. The next question for this example should be 'Can the interest rate on the various account types be deduced from anything else?' If the knowledge engineer is told that 'No, the interest rates are set by the Chief Manager each morning and sometimes fluctuate from day to day with the Chief Manager's mood' then this line of questioning can be abandoned, unless it is considered relevant to investigate the Chief Manager's moods. However, if the knowledge engineer is told that 'The interest rate for each account type can be derived from a formula based on the security factor of the account

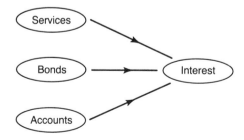

Figure 19.7

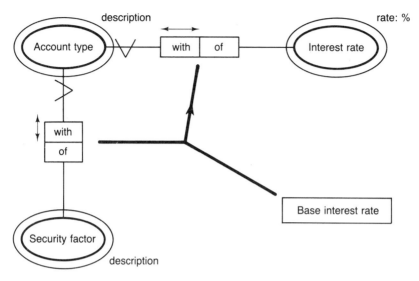

Figure 19.8

type and the base interest rate' then the knowledge engineer has discovered both a new object 'base interest rate' and a new functional association between 'account type' and 'security factor'. The knowledge engineer has also discovered a new GEF linking these together. It may be represented by the heavy arrow in Figure 19.8. This new functional association must be subjected to the basic test to determine whether it is well defined. Thus the knowledge engineer should ask 'Do you mean that the interest rate associated with *all* account types can be deduced from the security factor associated with the account and the base interest rate?' If the answer is affirmative, the knowledge engineer will either abandon this line of questioning, or seek other ways in which the relation account-type/interest-rate could be deduced from the contents of other relations. Note that once again our strategy is to seek more facts by working back from the conclusion of a given functional association. This strategy helps to prevent the question sequence from drifting aimlessly away from incomplete 'bundles' of facts.

Our method has brought us a long way from the original fact 'the interest rate on savings accounts is 5%'. We summarize the method so far. Given a fact:

1.   Confirm that it satisfies the individual requirements; if it fails to satisfy these requirements then it should be rejected and recon-structed.
2.   Confirm that any functional association in the fact is well defined.
3.   Note whether the fact is a PAF, a GEF, or both.

4.   4.1   If the fact is a GEF and, in particular, defines a new thing-population then find the identifying name-population; then, no matter what form the GEF has, complete it.

      4.2   If the fact is a PAF, construct the natural GRF to which it belongs and complete this GEF. Note that all new facts introduced in this step, or elsewhere, must satisfy the individual requirements.

5.   The knowledge engineer may choose to generalize the complete GEF just constructed by focusing on the 'conclusion' of the GEF.

6.   The knowledge engineer then looks for knowledge which enables the PAFs in this GEF to be deduced from other facts.

In short, this procedure has led us from a single fact to a set of statements; this set of statements is called a **bundle** generated by the original fact. Note the conservative introverted nature of the strategy which continues to seek facts which lead 'into' and not 'away from' the initial fact. Thus the strategy seeks to find out all it can about one thing before moving on to another. This should help to minimize unnecessary to-ing and fro-ing. See LaFrance (1986) for a different approach to completing knowledge.

As a means of remembering this method, the following may be useful. For any fact presented:

- **check** that it satisfies the individual requirements,
- **confirm** that any functional association in the fact is well defined, and
- **classify** it as a PAF or a GEF.

Given a GEF:

- **identify** the name-population of a new thing-population, and
- **complete** that GEF.

Given a PAF:

- **explore** other similar PAFs, and
- **generalize** to a complete GEF.

Given a complete GEF, note its 'premise' and 'conclusion':

- **deduce** the PAFs in this GEF from knowledge involving other GEFs, and
- **associate** this given GEF with other GEFs whose conclusion is either the 'premise' or the 'conclusion' of this given GEF.

Having completed the enquiry indicated by the above method, what should the knowledge engineer do next? This will depend on the purpose of the enquiry. After all, the knowledge engineer may be pursuing a long chain of reasoning to unravel the way in which the domain expert comes to some complex conclusion, in which case the knowledge engineer will be guided, to a great extent, by an understanding of the logical structure which supports this complex conclusion. On the other hand, the knowledge engineer may simply be 'fishing for facts' and attempting to build up a picture of the domain expert's world, in which case the knowledge engineer should then focus on one of the new functional associations and explore associations between it and other functional associations, etc. etc. (See Hickman (1986) for a discussion of four different strategies for knowledge elicitation; also see Marcus and McDermott (1986) for a discussion of a system which identifies cases when additional knowledge is required.) One major concern of any approach to knowledge elicitation is that the same fact may be gathered, recorded and represented in the expert system more than once. This can be dangerous if one of the representations of such a fact is changed later on. However, note that the chances of this happening should be substantially reduced by the development and maintenance of the data dictionary and the type hierarchy. When a new fact is presented, the data in it will be compared with, and checked against, the data in the data dictionary; if duplications are not recognized at this stage then they should be detected when an attempt is made to enter the data in the type hierarchy. Once duplications in the data have been correctly identified, duplications in any information or knowledge built with that data should be easy to determine. We presume that the storage and processing of knowledge is supported by a computerized system (see Abrett and Burstein, 1986; Hayward, 1986).

The description of our approach to knowledge elicitation may seem simple; it is intended to be. In our view the knowledge elicitation procedure should restrict the style of the knowledge engineer as little as possible, while trying to satisfy the goals of being a procedure which:

- gathers knowledge in a uniform way that is suitable for team work;
- gathers knowledge quickly and without fuss, thus respecting the domain expert's time;
- groups the gathered knowledge into small blocks which will be useful in the expert system building process;
- gathers knowledge in such a way that the gathered knowledge can realistically be described as 'complete';
- gathers knowledge in a way that is quite comprehensible to the domain expert; and
- may be performed 'on the fly' and will not intrude unnecessarily on the interview.

Representing functional associations

We have discussed the problem of object classification. Once an object has been classified, the next step is to represent that object. The **object representation problem** is the problem of determining *how* an object will be represented in the expert systems shell. The representation of data is fairly simple. However, the representation of information and knowledge, that is, the representation of functional associations, is of some interest. In this section we consider the properties of 'relations' as a formalism for representing information, and the properties of 'groups' as a formalism for representing knowledge. We will propose that the 'cluster' is the appropriate basic unit for knowledge acquisition.

The representation of implicit functional associations

The **information** items in an application are the implicit functional associations between items of data. These functional associations can be of essentially two different kinds. The distinction between these two kinds of functional association is determined by whether or not the functional association represents an association between two or more tangible, physical objects. For example, 'spare parts have a cost' may be interpreted as a functional association from the abstract notion of a 'spare part' to the abstract notion of 'cost'; on the other hand, 'spare part number 1234 costs \$12' may be interpreted as a functional association *from* a label associated with a real spare part *to* a label associated with a real cost. Items of information which are functional associations between labels, which are associated with real objects, are represented by tuples in the information language. The functional associations which are between populations, which are *not* associated with particular real objects, are represented by relations in the information language.

One important feature of the relation as a formalism is that it is 'non-information-goal-dependent' in a sense which we now explain. In practice, relations often have a natural 'key' domain. For example, in a finance house application the relation

account-no./interest-rate($\neq$, x:%)

could be used to store the daily interest rate payable on each account. Note that account number determines the interest rate, but not vice versa. The account number is then the **key domain**. The key domain of a relation identifies an **information-(functional-) dependency** between the domains; this functional dependency is *from* the key domain(s) *to* the non-key domain(s).

Assuming that the information-base management system provides a modest level of query processing, the relation above could be used to satisfy the following forms of query:

1.   to find the daily interest rate payable on a given account,

2.   to find one (or all) account numbers whose daily interest rate payable is some given value, and

3.   to find those account numbers whose daily interest rate payable differs from that of 6 months ago.

In queries of form (1), the first argument of the relation will be used as the 'input' and the second argument as the 'output'. In queries of form (2), the second argument of the relation will be used as the 'input' and the first argument as the 'output'. In queries of form (3) both arguments are used in a pattern matching process and thus play both 'input' and 'output' roles. Thus we conclude that relations, together with a modest information-base management system, provide a 'non-(information-) goal dependent' formalism in the following sense. A formalism is said to be **information-goal-dependent** if the data items occurring in expressions represented in the formalism are assigned either 'input' or 'output' roles. The relation, which represents functional associations between data objects, has no *a priori* assignment of the roles 'input' and 'output' to its arguments.

The representation of explicit functional associations

We now discuss the ability of the language of Horn clause logic to represent information and knowledge goal dependencies. Knowledge has been defined as the explicit functional associations between items of data and/or information. As we have already noted, these functional associations are of two kinds. Items of knowledge which are functional associations which enable a particular set of labels or tuples to be derived are represented by clauses in the knowledge language. The functional associations which do *not* enable a particular set of labels or tuples to be derived are represented by groups in the knowledge language. For example, 'the sale price of an item is determined by the cost price of that item' may be interpreted as a functional association from the relation

item-no./cost-price

to the relation

item-no./sale-price

However, this functional association does not enable a particular set of labels or tuples to be derived. Thus this functional association could be represented by a group. Also, for example, 'the sale price of an item costing less than \$10 is the cost price of that item marked up by 20%' may be interpreted as a functional association just as the previous example. However, unlike the previous example, this functional association *does* enable a particular set of tuples to be derived. Thus this functional association could be represented by a clause:

$$\text{item-no./sale-price:\$(x, y)} \leftarrow \text{item-no./cost-price:\$(x, z),}$$
$$z < 10\text{:\$, } y = z \times 1.2$$

Consider the following example: if, in a finance house, 'interest on accounts is determined by multiplying the account balance by the account interest rate (per cent)' then this functional association may be represented by the (single clause) clause group:

$$\text{account-no./interest-pay(\#, x:\$)} \leftarrow$$
$$\text{account-no./interest-rate(\#, y:\%),}$$
$$\text{account-no./balance(\#, z:\$),}$$
$$x = z \times (y - 100) \qquad\qquad\qquad\qquad [A]$$

This clause could be used to satisfy the following forms of query:

1. to find the daily interest payable on a given account,
2. to find one (or all) account numbers whose daily interest payable is some given value, and
3. to find the accounts whose daily interest payable is less than that of 6 months ago.

As for relations, in queries of form (1) the first argument of the predicate

account-no./interest-pay

will be used as the 'input' and the second argument as the 'output'. In queries of form (2) the second argument of the predicate will be used as the 'input' and the first argument as the 'output'. In queries of form (3) both arguments are used in a pattern matching process and thus both play 'input' and 'output' roles. Thus we conclude that, like relations, clausal logic provides a non-(information-) goal-dependent formalism.

However, the above clause contains a 'knowledge-(functional-) dependency'. A Horn clause identifies a **knowledge-(functional) dependency** between the predicates in the clause; this functional dependency is *from* the body predicates *to* the head predicate. For example, in clause [A], note that the information in

account-no./interest-pay

depends on the information in

account-no./interest-rate

and in

account-no./balance

as well as on rules for simple arithmetic. Note that the above clause was constructed as a response to the business rule 'interest on accounts is determined by multiplying the account balance by the account interest rate (per cent)'. Note also that this business rule contains no knowledge functional dependency; it does *not* contain any explicit implication that clause [A] represents *all* that the business rule has to say. For example, perhaps the business rule also implies that

account-no./interest-rate($\underline{\#}$, y:%) ←
    account-no./interest-pay($\underline{\#}$, x:$),
    account-no./balance($\underline{\#}$, z:$),
    x = z × (y − 100)   [B]

and that

account-no./balance($\underline{\#}$, z:$)←
    account-no./interest-pay($\underline{\#}$, x:$),
    account-no./interest-rate($\underline{\#}$, y:%),
    x = z × (y − 100)   [C]

A formalism for knowledge is said to be **knowledge-goal-dependent** if the data and information items occurring in expressions represented in the formalism are assigned 'input' and 'output' roles. We have already noted that clausal logic provides a non-(information-) goal-dependent formalism. However note that in clause [A] above the predicates

account-no./interest-rate
account-no./balance

are, in a very real sense, the 'input' predicates whose values are used by the clause to calculate the values of the 'output' predicate

account-no./interest-pay

Thus we conclude that clausal logic is a knowledge-goal-dependent formalism. In particular, we have seen how clausal logic is incapable of representing directly a sentence which contains no knowledge-functional dependency.

Table 19.2

Formalism	Information-goal-dependent	Knowledge-goal-dependent
Trad. prog.	Yes	Yes
Groups	No	Yes
Clusters	No	No

In summary we have seen that, unlike the traditional programming languages employed by conventional database management systems to represent rules, the language of Horn clause logic is *not* an information-goal-dependent formalism. However, the language of Horn clause logic is a knowledge-goal-dependent formalism.

Knowledge dependencies (in clauses) differ from information dependencies (in relations) in two important ways. First, it is usually far from obvious from the 'raw facts' as to which (knowledge) dependency is actually intended. Second, it is usually far from obvious as to which of the intended knowledge dependencies will subsequently be required as an operational component of the overall expert system. These two observations together, in effect, imply that analysing knowledge as an activity is substantially more complex than analysing information and data. Furthermore, they imply that we should not see the 'clause group' as a satisfactory fundamental unit for knowledge acquisition. We propose that the 'cluster' is the appropriate basic unit for gathering knowledge. We will see that, in general, 'clusters' are *not* a knowledge-goal-dependent formalism.

Table 19.2 summarizes the goal-dependency properties of three formalisms. These three formalisms are traditional programming languages ('trad. prog.'), the language of Horn clause logic which is based on groups ('groups') and the language of 'clusters' which will be introduced later in this paper.

Modelling functional associations

When constructing the application model, the knowledge engineer's task is to gather facts in a form that will facilitate representation as either data, information, knowledge or constraints. Each gathered fact will be required to satisfy our 'individual requirements'. To satisfy the 'atomic requirement' the knowledge engineer must bear in mind the way in which a gathered fact *may* subsequently be represented, and should ensure that the fact is in a form which is suitable for representation. Setting constraints aside for the moment, the alternatives could be shown as in

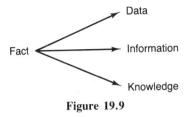

Figure 19.9

Figure 19.9. One might hope that if a certain gathered fact had the property that it could be represented correctly in any of these three forms then it should be possible to convert any one of these representations to the other two. We now indicate, in the context of an example, how this might be achieved.

Let us consider again the sample fact 'The interest rate on savings accounts is 5%'. As a starting point let us subject this fact to a 'B-R-like' analysis – see Verheijen and Van Bekkum (1982). We might well construct the diagram in Figure 19.10, where we have extended the notation to include the particular LOTs 'savings' and '5%' in rectangular boxes at the bottom of the diagram. The heavy arrow indicates functionality in the logical sense of 'if savings then 5%'. We could interpret this diagram by isolating the 5% box, interpreting the rest of the diagram as the population name 'the interest rate on savings accounts' whose *only* label is named '5%'. Alternatively, we could have isolated 'savings' and used the rest of the diagram to define the population name 'account types whose interest rate are equal to 5%', *one of whose* labels is named 'savings'.

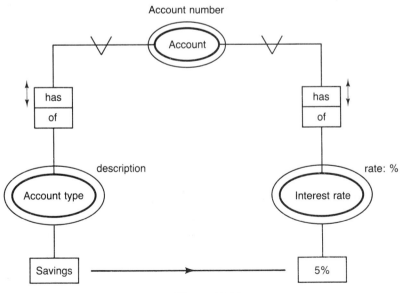

Figure 19.10

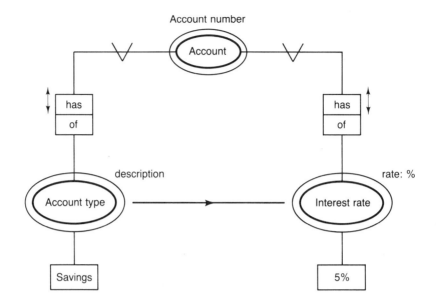

Figure 19.11

Suppose now that the knowledge engineer decides to introduce a relation 'account-type/interest-rate'. Then this could be represented by Figure 19.11, which can be interpreted as defining a relation into which tuples, such as (savings,5%) may be placed.

Alternatively, because account is a total role in, and is the primary key of, the two relations with which it is connected in Figure 19.11, we can draw the arrow between these two relations (as shown in Figure 19.12) which indicates that the sample fact is to be interpreted as a functional association between two relations. In other words, it is knowledge. It could be expressed in logic as a group. One member of this group would be the clause for savings accounts. That clause could be expressed in logic as:

account-no./interest-rate(x, 5) ← account-no./account-type(x, 'savings')

What is emerging here is a calculus of B-R diagrams which may allow us to move freely between a data, information or knowledge representation of a fact. The principle that we have 'discovered' may be stated as follows. In a diagram of the form shown in Figure 19.13, for which the fact 'if the value of A is a then the corresponding value of B is b' is true, this may be represented as:

- data *either* by establishing a population name derived from the whole diagram excluding b, and a unique, single label named b, *or*

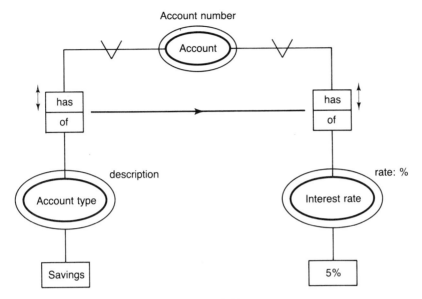

Figure 19.12

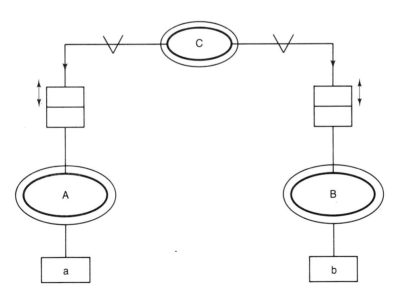

Figure 19.13

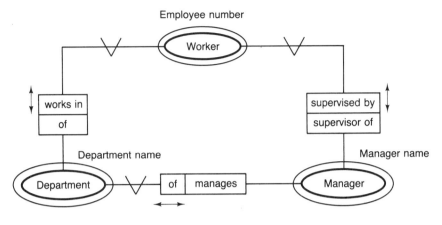

Figure 19.14

by similarly excluding a to establish a population name one of whose labels is named a;

- information by storing the tuple (a,b) in an A/B relation; and
- knowledge by the clause:

C/B(x, b) ← C/A(x, a)

We have just seen how a B-R diagram for a fact can be interpreted in three different ways thereby classifying the fact as data, information and knowledge, respectively. It is interesting to see that this classification can be pre-empted by considering three different representations of a sample fact in the language of the application model. These are respectively:

```
['account-interest-rate' such that
   ( the account has ('account-type' = 'savings') ) ] = 5%
      if 'account-type' = 'savings' then 'account-interest-rate' = '5%'
      if an account has ( 'account-type' = 'savings' ) then that account has
         ( 'account-interest-rate' = 5% )
```

It is not difficult to see that we have found an example of a rule for manipulating statements in the language of the application model. This rule will convert a statement which pre-empts one of the three different classifications (that is, data, information and knowledge) to a statement which pre-empts another classification. We will not pursue this here.

As another example, consider the sample fact 'workers are supervised by the manager of the department in which they work'. The information in this fact could be represented by Figure 19.14. Note that this diagram is of the general form just described. Thus suppose the second sample fact 'The Hardware Department is managed by Jones' is

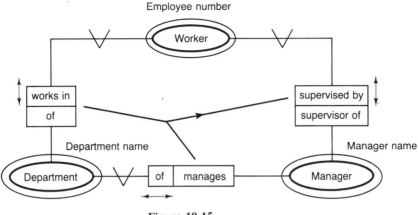

Figure 19.15

true. Then this second fact may be represented as:

- data *either* by establishing a population 'The Hardware Department Manager' whose only label is 'Jones', *or* by establishing a population 'The Departments which are managed by Jones' one of whose labels is 'Hardware';

- information by inserting the tuple ('hardware','Jones') in a relation:

  Department-name/Manager-name(,)

- knowledge by the clause:

  Employee-no./Supervisor-name(x, 'Jones') ←
      Employee-no./Department-name(x, 'Hardware')

The first sample fact 'workers are supervised by the managers of the department in which they work' also contains some knowledge. This knowledge may be represented in Figure 19.14 by noting that the diagram is 'commutative'. A **commutative diagram** is one in which if there are two paths from one node to another then following either path for any particular initial object leads to the same object at the end of the path. In this example, if we follow the dependencies from worker to manager by the two different routes we arrive at the *same* particular manager for any particular worker. The commutativity of this diagram may be represented by the following 'if and only if' statement:

Employee-no./Supervisor(x, y) ⟷
    Employee-no./Department(x, z),
    Department/Manager(z, y)

The 'if' part of this statement could be represented by the heavy arrows in Figure 19.15.

Summary

We have explored the notion of functional associations, which has enabled us to clarify the distinction between information and knowledge. The role of the application model has been described. We have presented our approach to knowledge acquisition which is based on an understanding of functional associations. Our approach to knowledge acquisition, in general, is systematic and is suitable for teamwork. Our approach to knowledge elicitation, in particular, remains independent of the eventual classification of the facts being gathered as either data, information or knowledge. Finally we have shown how a given functional association may be analysed correctly as data, information and knowledge, and how these three options can be represented on a conventional information analysis diagram.

References

Abrett G. and Burstein M.H. (1986). The KREME knowledge editing environment. In *Proc. Knowledge Acquisition for Knowledge-Based Systems Workshop*, Banff, Alberta, Canada, 2–7 Nov, 1986

Arbab B. and Michie D. (1985). Generating rules from examples. In *Proc. 9th Int. Conf. on Artificial Intelligence*. Los Angeles CA

Davis R. and Lenat D. (1982). *Knowledge-Based Systems in Artificial Intelligence*. McGraw-Hill

Debenham J.K. (1986). Expert systems: an information processing perspective. In *Proc. 2nd Australian Conf. on Applications of Expert Systems*, Sydney

Diederich J., Ruhmann I. and May M. (1986). KRITON: A knowledge acquisition tool for expert systems. In *Proc. Knowledge Acquisition for Knowledge-Based Systems Workshop*, Banff, Alberta, Canada, 2–7 Nov, 1986

Eshelman L., Ehret D., McDermott J. and Tan M. (1986). MOLE: A tenacious knowledge acquisition tool. In *Proc. Knowledge Acquisition for Knowledge-Based Systems Workshop*, Banff, Alberta, Canada, 2–7 Nov, 1986

Gaines B.R. (1986). An overview of knowledge acquisition and transfer. In *Proc. Knowledge Acquisition for Knowledge-Based Systems Workshop*, Banff, Alberta, Canada, 2-7 Nov, 1986

Gruber T. and Cohen P. (1986). Design for acquisition: principles of knowledge system design to facilitate knowledge acquisition. In *Proc. Knowledge Acquisition for Knowledge-Based Systems Workshop*, Banff, Alberta, Canada, 2–7 Nov, 1986

Hayward S. (1986). A structured development methodology for expert systems. In *Proc. Knowledge-Based Systems 1986*, London, July 1986

Hayward S.A., Wielinga B.J. and Breuker J.A. (1986). Structured analysis of knowledge. In *Proc. Knowledge Acquisition for Knowledge-Based Systems Workshop*, Banff, Alberta, Canada, 2–7 Nov, 1986

Hickman F. (1986). Knowledge acquisition: the key to success for commercial expert systems. In *Proc. Knowledge-Based Systems 1986*, London, July

Kahn G., Breaux E.H., Joseph R.L. and DeKlerk P. (1986). An intelligent mixed-initiative workbench for knowledge acquisition. In *Proc. Knowledge Acquisition for Knowledge-Based Systems Workshop*, Banff, Alberta, Canada, 2–7 Nov, 1986

Kahn G., Nowlan S. and McDermott J. (1985). MORE: an intelligent knowledge acquisition tool. In *Proc. 9th Conf. on Artificial Intelligence*, Los Angeles CA

Kelly B.A. (1986). System development methodology. In *Proc. Knowledge-Based Systems 1986*, London, July 1986

LaFrance M. (1986). The knowledge acquisition grid: a method for training knowledge engineers. In *Proc. Knowledge Acquisition for Knowledge-Based Systems Workshop*, Banff, Alberta, Canada, 2–7 Nov, 1986

Marcus S. and McDermott J. (1986). SALT: A Knowledge Acquisition Tool for Propose and Revise Systems. Carnegie-Mellon University Technical Report

Neves D.M. (1985). Learning procedures from examples and by doing. In *Proc. 9th Int. Conf. on Artificial Intelligence*, Los Angeles CA

Quinlan J.R. (1987). Generating production rules from decision trees. In *Proc. 10th Int. Joint Conf. on Artificial Intelligence*, Milan, Italy

Van De Brug A., Bachant J. and McDermott J. (1986). The taming of R1. In *IEEE Expert*, **1**(3)

Verheijen G.M.A. and Van Bekkum J. (1982). NIAM: an information analysis method. In *Information Systems Design Methodologies: A Comparative Review* (Olle T.W. and Verrijn-Stuart A.A., eds.). IFIP North-Holland

20
Maintaining an Expert System

P. Compton
Garvan Institute of Medical Research

K. Horn
Telectronics Pty Ltd

J.R. Quinlan
University of Sydney

L. Lazarus

K. Ho
Garvan Institute of Medical Research

GARVAN-ES1 is a medical expert system which has been in routine use since mid-1984. It provides clinical interpretations for diagnostic reports issued by a clinical laboratory assay service carrying out thyroid assays. There has been a program of ongoing knowledge maintenance since the system's installation. This paper documents this maintenance experience and some of the hypotheses it has suggested.

1   Introduction

In traditional software development the maintenance phase of a project is of major importance. It might be necessary to add further functionality to the programs not envisioned in the original system specification and there may be errors and omissions in the code. Expert systems and knowledge engineering have been introduced precisely for situations where it is difficult to identify the knowledge required for a task or judgement, so one would expect that the maintenance phase of an expert system project will be of even more importance than for traditional programs. In their report on the long-term maintenance of R1 (XCON), a system which configures computers, Bachant and McDermott (1984) argue, in fact, that an expert system will never have all the knowledge it needs and that it is essential to introduce a system into routine use in order to uncover the inadequacies in its knowledge. In fact, the size of the technical group responsible for maintaining R1 increased rather than decreased over the four years' experience described. This report seems to be the only significant account of long-term maintenance of an expert system, so the aim of this present paper is to recount our experience in maintaining an expert system, GARVAN-ES1.

GARVAN-ES1 has been used to interpret some 20 000 thyroid hormone assay reports since its introduction into routine use in mid-1984. All interpretations have been checked by experts and the system's knowledge upgraded when inadequacies have been found. In contrast to R1 the system has not been required to encompass new tasks during this period and there have been only minor changes in the type of data requiring interpretation. The changes have been essentially minor corrections and additions to the system's knowledge base. The aim of this paper then is to document this process of incremental knowledge acquistion and the hypotheses this experience has suggested.

2   The domain of GARVAN-ES1

To understand an expert system it is perhaps more important to understand the duties and responsibility of the expert system than the knowledge it contains.

Medical diagnostic testing is meant to assist the referring clinician with either diagnosis or management of a patient's illness. Such testing is now widely used, and there is an ever increasing variety of diagnostic tests which can be requested. It has been traditional for the pathologist or other relevant expert to provide some sort of clinical interpretation of the laboratory results, which is added to the report to assist the referring clinician. As the range of diagnostic tests increases, making a clinical comment more necessary, so has the laboratory workload, making provision of the comment more difficult; these days, many reports are issued without comments. This is an ideal domain for expert systems, firstly in that the knowledge domain is bounded; an expert uses only the laboratory data and related information, such as the patient age and the referring doctor's brief notes. This is quite different to other medical applications where the expert being emulated has direct contact with the patient, with all the open-ended possibilities that this implies. Secondly, use of a clinical interpretation expert system does not require the cooperation of some human agent; it can be automated as part of report generation (which these days is normally computerized) and, in fact, all of the data used in report interpretation is likely to be stored in the existing laboratory database. We hypothesize that this suitability of the report interpretation domain for expert systems is the reason why three of the four medical expert systems, including GARVAN-ES1, which Buchanan

(1986) reviewed as being in routine use in 1986, provide clinical interpretation of laboratory reports. GARVAN-ES1 itself provides interpretative comments for thyroid laboratory reports (Horn et al., 1985; Compton, 1987).

A basic requirement of the domain is that no misinterpretations be made. Hence all reports issued by GARVAN-ES1 are checked by an expert and signed. This has not been difficult to arrange since the Garvan Institute has always had a policy of experts providing comments for, and signing the reports issued by, the Institute's assay service and still provides this service for the other knowledge domains covered by the assay service. The experts are happy to have their work, at least for thyroid report interpretation, reduced to checking and signing. This long-term checking of reports and the consequent detection of errors and omissions in GARVAN-ES1 has provided the basis for the ongoing maintenance described in this paper.

It is important to note that it is the actual referring clinician who has the responsibility for diagnosing and treating the patient. Ideally, the clinician does not rely exclusively on laboratory data to make his diagnosis. There is noise in any measurement; laboratory error is possible; there is always the possibility of physiological variation which is not pathological and, finally, so-called *normal* ranges or *reference* ranges are intended to cover only 95% of the normal population and are themselves subject to error. The experienced clinician makes his diagnosis in the context of a whole range of clinical signs and symptoms and other data, of which laboratory data and its suggested clinical interpretation form just one (albeit important) component, while the tyro clinician, with less experience of the exceptions, may be more inclined to take laboratory data as absolute. These are the reasons why the diagnostic comments that the expert may add to a report cannot be an actual diagnosis, only an interpretation of results, although this should generally correspond to the diagnosis. For these reasons there is no default interpretation in GARVAN-ES1, there is no interpretation called 'normal'. If an abnormal pattern in the results is not identified by the expert system, no comment is made, in conformity with the clinical practice of 'no abnormality detected'.

It is important to note also that experts do not necessarily know how to interpret every profile of laboratory data observed. They rarely misinterpret reports in that the interpretation they provide would be diagnostically erroneous and would mislead the referring clinician. But there are some data profiles that are simply not well understood. The expert may provide no comment or may outline some hypothetical mechanism that could cause the profile observed while indicating that, with current clinical knowledge, this hypothetical interpretation is not diagnostically important. In fact, the availability of GARVAN-ES1 has assisted in identifying some data profiles of minor interest whose existence would not otherwise have been documented.

The domain of GARVAN-ES1 is thyroid disease. The analytes measured by the laboratory are not of themselves of interest in this paper and will be referred to by their normal abbreviations of T3 for triiodothyronine, TSH for thyrotropin, etc. Similarly, other technical terms describing different types of interpretations are not of interest in this paper, and will not be expanded upon.

3   The GARVAN-ES1 program

Details of the system have been described previously (Horn *et al.*, 1985). It is written in C and a preprocessor translates English-like production rules into C code. The program is restricted to a 64 K job space on a PDP 11/73 under TSC Plus and, in contrast to when it was first introduced, now requires overlaying. This is not a problem as each case is still run in about one second on this multiuser system and is a minor addition to the report generation process.

3.1   Inference engine and knowledge base

Knowledge is expressed as production rules (Winston, 1984; Davis and King, 1984; see also Figures 20.3–20.5, 20.7, 20.9) and since all relevant data are available before running the system only forward chaining is required. The system proceeds through all rules only once and rules which fire assert or retract further facts or produce an interpretation. Any facts that are asserted because a rule fires are immediately available to later rules. Since all rules are allowed to fire, multiple interpretations are possible. However, the design aim is a single interpretation for a given case so that the knowledge base is changed if multiple interpretations, even if appropriate, are produced. The resulting shallow knowledge is an advantage since all interpretations are then explicit and problems in the final wording of an interpretation on an issued report are avoided. Conflict resolution is explicit, in that the conditions which would exclude rules in a conflict resolution strategy are included in the rules to prevent them from firing, resulting in highly modular knowledge.

Since rules are fired once only, some domain knowledge is implicit in the rule ordering. For example, the rules which categorize the actual assay results and classify the referring doctor's comment come before the rules which use this categorized data to assert further facts relating to hormonal profiles or assign clinical interpretations. The system also has explicit interpretations for cases with missing data. Since the system was designed to produce interim reports, as well as complete reports, it was essential that rules were explicitly encoded for missing data. The 20 000-

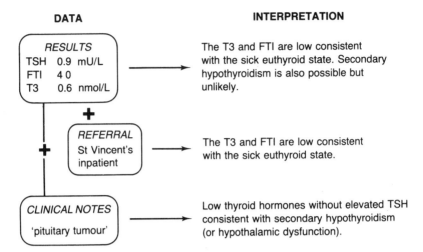

DATA   **INTERPRETATION**

RESULTS
TSH   0.9 mU/L
FTI   4 0
T3   0.6 nmol/L

The T3 and FTI are low consistent with the sick euthyroid state. Secondary hypothyroidism is also possible but unlikely.

REFERRAL
St Vincent's inpatient

The T3 and FTI are low consistent with the sick euthyroid state.

CLINICAL NOTES
'pituitary tumour'

Low thyroid hormones without elevated TSH consistent with secondary hypothyroidism (or hypothalamic dysfunction).

Figure 20.1   Probability is indicated in the wording of interpretations. The first interpretation, which depends only on laboratory data, indicates two possibilities of different likelihood. The extra data that the patient is sick enough to be an inpatient, or has a pituitary abnormality, provides information to discriminate between the two interpretations.

odd cases on which the expert system has been run include both these complete and incomplete reports.

The system does not use probabilistic reasoning. When it was introduced, we did not know whether probability would eventually be required, but it has not been. If every interpretation is explicit then probability can be included in the wording of the interpretation rather than as part of the inference mechanism (Figure 20.1). This approach seems consistent with the way experts state the conclusion probabilistically, rather than indicating a probabilistic connection between data and conclusion. Also it allows an expert's verbal statement of probability to be included directly rather than requesting a numerical equivalent.

Similarly, at the start of the project we were uncertain how experts really dealt with numerical laboratory results. Did they use the continuous nature of the numeric information in some probabilistic fashion or was it possible to capture their expertise by classifying results into broad categories? We have found that it has been sufficient to classify assay results for each analyte into seven broad categories. There is a primary classification of whether results are undetectable, low, normal or high, and a secondary classification of whether the results are borderline (Horn *et al.*, 1985). In some instances experts have put results into further categories of extremely high or extremely low, but it has not been necessary to use such categories because it has been possible to produce rules to reach the same conclusion, dependent on other aspects of the data set which have been acceptable to the experts. We will argue below that these fairly coarse categories are adequate because experts identify the correct interpretation by using a hypothetico-deductive reasoning method of excluding alternatives (Popper, 1963).

4 Knowledge maintenance

4.1 Tools

The fundamental knowledge maintenance tool is a database of 'cornerstone cases'. These are cases which, at some stage, have required a change in the system's knowledge, either because the system failed to interpret the case, interpreted it wrongly or because more than one interpretation was produced. Every time the system's knowledge is changed the interpretations for all the cornerstone cases are checked to see that the additions to the system's knowledge have been incremental and have not corrupted the knowledge. Other systems such as EXPERT and EMYCIN provide for a similar testing of changes to a knowledge base with a database of cases (Buchanan *et al.*, 1983).

The key tool for understanding why the system arrived at a certain interpretation is a facility which allows for manual entry and manipulation of data, and allows examination of the rules which have fired in arriving at the interpretation and the further facts which have been asserted in the process. This module also allows data to be passed straight to the cornerstone case database. The rule base can, of course, be searched for text strings to identify rules that may be of interest.

4.2 Procedures

The experts who sign the reports put aside reports with missing, incorrect or multiple interpretations and pencil in the correct interpretation. A clerk will immediately arrange for a report to be sent out with the appropriate interpretation manually entered. The report requiring a change to the rules is put aside for the knowledge engineer. Many of the errors are obvious and the knowledge engineer will not need to consult an expert, otherwise the expert who rejected the report will be consulted as to why the interpretation was inappropriate. Occasionally, the knowledge engineer will seek a second expert opinion or will consult the Director of the Institute as the ultimate arbiter of GARVAN-ES1's knowledge. The rules are then changed or added to while ensuring that the interpretations in the database remain the same. The examples below indicate the steps in this process.

An important facet of the maintenance process is that it proceeds on a case by case basis. In the initial phase of a knowledge engineering

LABORATORY REPORT   Mary Citizen
                           1 The Avenue
                           Smalltown

Date 11/5/87   Medicare No   007
Ref: Dr. A. Doctor   Sex   female
The Surgery   D.O.B.   15/5/32
Smalltown   Request ID   870511.042

ASSAY	RESULT	REF RANGE
FTI	136	65–155
T4U	1.20	0.6–1.25
TT4	163 nmol/L	60–150
T3	3.5 nmol/L	1.2–2.8 nmol/L
TSH	<0.13 mU/L	0.2–6.0 mU/L

COMMENT: Elevated T3 and T4
          consistent with increased binding protein.

Figure 20.2   This is a copy of a report from mid-1987 with personal information changed. Laboratory results are given with the normal reference range. Assay results can be judged as high or low, etc., by comparison with the reference range information. The comment shown was generated by GARVAN-ES1; according to the expert it was obviously incorrect and the report was issued with a different comment.

project the expert and knowledge engineer work in close collaboration and apply a concentrated effort across the whole knowledge domain. In this development phase, when a system misinterprets or fails to interpret a case, the expert can remember in broad terms the knowledge he has communicated before and knows how the knowledge relating to this new case fits with the existing knowledge. In contrast, in the maintenance phase the expert may no longer remember what knowledge has been previously included or may, in fact, be a different expert. A number of experts have been involved with GARVAN-ES1 since the start of the project.

Knowledge engineering has been reasonably consistent in that only two knowledge engineers have been involved. K. Horn was responsible for much of the initial development while P. Compton has been responsible for most of the maintenance. However, the project was a learning experience for both knowledge engineers and the maintenance strategies evolved over time. One of us (PC) has had considerable experience in laboratory endocrinology, which has simplified communication with the experts.

RULE(10580)
IF   FT4 is missing and
        (T4U is high or FTI is normal)
        and TT4 is high
THEN discthy NOW TRUE

RULE(32301.28)
IF   discthy and not hithy
        and not e2_ntsh
        and T3 is high
        and not pregnant and not on_t4 and not query_t4 and not ovulatory
THEN INTERPRETATION(*"Elevated T3 and T4 consistent with increased binding protein"*)

Figure 20.3   A partial rule trace for the case shown in Figure 20.2. The case causes rule 10580 to fire which asserts discthy. Since discthy is true and the T3 is high, but none of the other facts which would exclude rule 32301.28 have been asserted, this rule then fires, producing an interpretation.

4.3   Knowledge maintenance example

Figure 20.2 provides an example of a case which occurred in mid-1987 where the interpretation given by GARVAN-ES1 was clearly incorrect. When the case was discussed with an expert, the expert was highly critical of GARVAN-ES1 for making such a poor interpretation. The expert said that the interpretation was clearly T3-toxicosis rather than increased binding protein, because the TSH was undetectable and the T3 was elevated. On the basis of these comments the knowledge base was modified. Despite this obvious error in GARVAN-ES1's knowledge, evidently no cases which showed up this inadequacy in the system's knowledge had occurred previously.

4.3.1   Simple correction of a wrong rule

The case in Figure 20.2 was run through the manual data entry system and the rules which fired inappropriately were identified. A partial rule trace is shown in Figure 20.3. The laboratory data was first classified by the system, with the relevant classifications being that the FTI was normal, the TT4 and T3 were elevated and the TSH was undetectable. The elevated TT4 and normal FTI then caused rule 10580 to fire. (Note, the rule numbers suggest far more rules than the actual 300-odd in the system. The rule number is used to encode information as to the other rules from which the rule under consideration may have been derived and to indicate to which categories the interpretation belongs.) The firing of rule 10580 asserted the intermediate fact discthy. (It should be noted that

RULE(32301.28)
IF   discthy and not hithy
        and not e2_ntsh
        and T3 is high
        and TSH isnt low and TSH isnt undetect
        and not pregnant and not on_t4 and not query_t4 and not ovulatory
THEN INTERPRETATION(*"Elevated T3 and T4 consistent with increased binding protein"*)

Figure 20.4   The rule in Figure 20.3 is now excluded from firing when TSH is low or undetectable (additions in italics).

intermediate facts are used to summarize hormonal profiles. They simplify later rules while helping to capture the expert's apparent grouping of results into profiles. discthy indicates that the measures of free and bound thyroxine (FTI and TT4) are discordant while e2_ntsh indicates that T3 and the FTI are elevated but the TSH is normal.) Rule 32301.28 then fired because discthy was true and the T3 was elevated but none of the other facts which could prevent this rule from firing had been asserted. According to the expert the undetectable TSH should have indicated an interpretation of T3-toxicosis and so should have excluded 32301.28 from firing. In fact, if the TSH had been normal, a less categorical exclusion of the increased binding interpretation, rule 17310 would have fired and asserted the intermediate fact e2_ntsh[2] which would have then excluded 32301.28 from firing. This failure of GARVAN-ES1 to encompass a very obvious reason why a rule should not fire is a classical type of error in the system's knowledge. It is obvious that an undetectable TSH should exclude rule 32301.28 from firing, but this knowledge is not included until the system comes across such a case and misinterprets it. An extra condition to exclude undetectable TSH was then inserted (Figure 20.4).

The cornerstone cases in the database were then tested and no cases were missed by the exclusion of undetectable TSH. The reason why no cases were misinterpreted is not because a perfect change was made to the rule, but that there are no cases in the database which cause 32301.28 to fire. It is not unusual to find rules without related cases in the database. Such rules may exist because they were very successful rules introduced early on in the development and have successfully interpreted all relevant cases. Such a rule may also exist because it arises from some earlier break-up of a rule into two or more rules. Not all the resulting rules will necessarily be associated with cases in the databases. In fact, some such rules may never be used since, although they arose from a widely used rule, the particular profile they now detect almost never occurs. This particular rule has arisen from an earlier split in the rules.

In all rule modification the principle has been followed of making the rule as broad as possible, on the assumption that it is more efficient to have general rules which can be corrected if necessary, rather than endless highly-specific rules. In many cases, undetectable TSH leads to the same interpretation as low TSH, so the exclusion of undetectable TSH in this particular rule (Figure 20.4) was expanded to exclude low as well as undetectable TSH and again no cases in the database were affected. This broadening was not checked with the experts because, from experience, experts do not perform well when asked about hypothetical cases and are liable to give advice which complicates the whole knowledge engineering process. The hypothetical cases may appear reasonable but, in fact, never occur in practice. This is a particularly simple example of rule narrowing. In more complex examples, the first attempt at narrowing the rule will miss cases in the database. The rule might be restored and an earlier rule in the knowledge base, which asserted some fact used by the final rule, may be narrowed, or the narrowing made more specific until no cases in the database are missed.

4.3.2   Adding new knowledge

The next stage was to provide a rule or rules to interpret this case correctly. Such a new rule could have been derived from rule 32301.28 but the latter does not have a case in the database, and has been inappropriately fired by one T3-toxic case in three years. (It is interesting to note that although this rule had not caused problems in three years, the very next correction to the knowledge base was to the same rule, which this time fired inappropriately for a patient whom the referring clinician had noted was hyperthyroid.) Alternatively, it is highly likely that there is a suitable rule in the knowledge base which could be broadened to cover the case, since GARVAN-ES1 already successfully interprets many cases of T3-toxicosis. It is easy to find the rules in a knowledge base which have fired, but not so easy to find rules that, with minor changes, might have fired. The version of the GARVAN-ES1 system used provides for a simple search for rules which contain a specific text string. This can be made more sophisticated by allowing the union and intersection of various searches to be easily examined (Horn, 1988) or the knowledge can be stored using a relational model (Jansen, 1987) and a maintenance version of GARVAN-ES1 is being developed using this approach. At present, however, the simplest way to identify likely candidate rules for alteration is to develop a very broad rule or rules for the case in hand and then to test the database of cornerstone cases. If any cases cause the new rules to fire then the rules which these cases normally cause to fire can be compared to the new rule. The knowledge engineer is then in a position to broaden a suitable existing rule or narrow the new rule so that it does not pick up any cases from the database. The new case is, of course, added to the database.

IF   (TSH is undetect or TSH is low)
         and T3 is high
THEN INTERPRETATION ("...T3 toxicosis...")

Figure 20.5 A rule for T3-toxicosis which is only appropriate in the context of the case in Figure 20.2.

The new rule that was tested is shown in Figure 20.5. The expert stated that the interpretation for the case in Figure 20.2 should have been T3-toxicosis because the T3 was elevated and the TSH was undetectable. This statement was taken literally to provide this example; the knowledge engineer would normally narrow such a rule since his own domain knowledge and experience of how GARVAN-ES1's knowledge is structured would suggest that the rule is much too broad.

The rule in this form was hit by 18 cases in the database (Figure 20.6). These 18 cases covered ten interpretations. The ten interpretations covered eight different classes of interpretation, as three of the rules gave essentially the same interpretation. It is also interesting to note, however, that the rule was not general enough to pick up all cases of T3-toxicosis; one of the five T3-toxicosis cases in the database was missed.

The only interpretation related to T3-toxicosis was provided by

---

Rule no	Interpretation
21200.45	Elevated thyroid hormones consistent with over-replacement
22100.01	Elevated thyroid hormones consistent with thyrotoxicosis
30000.28	Elevated T3 consistent with increased binding protein
32820.05	Elevated T3 and normal FTI & T4 with suppressed TSH is consistent with T3-toxicosis
32000.29	Elevated T3 consistent with oestrogen effect. Query increased binding protein
32010.28	Elevated T3 consistent with increased binding protein
32321.28	Elevated T4 and T3 consitent with increased binding protein
32910.07	Elevated T3 and normal FTI & T4 is consistent with a goitre but is more likely due to increased binding protein
32900.06	Elevated and normal FTI & T4 is consistent with a goitre
———	(no thyroid disease)

Figure 20.6 The 18 cases in the database which caused the new rule in Figure 20.5 to fire also caused the indicated rules to fire and produce the interpretations shown.

RULE(32820.05)
IF   e2_utsh

> and northy and T4U isnt high
> *replaced by and not lothy and T4U isnt high*

and
((T3_BORD isnt high and not ovulatory and not pregnant)
or
(not pregnant and hyperthyroid))
and not goitre
THEN DIAGNOSIS (*"Elevated T3 and normal THY with suppressed TSH is consistent with T3-toxicosis"*)

Figure 20.7   The rule which was altered so that it would fire on the data in Figure 20.2. The rule was changed by replacing the second line with the alternative line shown in italics.

rule 32820, shown in Figure 20.7. An examination of this rule suggested that the reason it did not fire for the case in Figure 20.2 was because it required northy to be true. Rather than northy being true, the trace in Figure 20.3 shows that the case had caused the contrary fact of discthy to be asserted by rule 10580. Although not shown in the rule trace in Figure 20.3, the case had caused all the other facts required by rule 32820.05 to be asserted.

It did not seem essential to the rule that northy be asserted so this condition was removed. However, when this constraint was removed, the rule was fired by a cornerstone case for which a quite different interpretation relating to antithyroid treatment was appropriate. This outcome of the rule change was in no way intuitively obvious. So that the rule did not fire on the 'antithyroid treatment' case, the condition was changed so that the rule would not fire if the fact lothy was asserted. The endocrinological details are not of particular importance but the case provides an example of the iterative process involved in maintenance knowledge engineering. The iterative process was fairly simple in this particular case, as initial narrowing of the rule did not result in any cases in the database being missed.

5   Hypotheses

The reason that the rule in Figure 20.5 was hit by so many cases is that it is far too broad. In the context of the particular case, this rule identifies the key features which accurately determine that the interpretation is T3-toxicosis, but these features occur in many other cases as Figure 20.6 indicates. The rule provides an example for conflict resolution but, more importantly, provides a classic example of the type of knowledge available in the knowledge maintenance phase of a project. The rules that an expert provides to interpret a case are only adequate *in the context of that particular case*. The expert is usually very reliable in interpreting the set of data correctly, but when the same rule is applied elsewhere it is quite inadequate or even ridiculous. To explain these observations we hypothesize that the expert uses two types of reasoning. Firstly, he identifies the correct interpretation for the case, and secondly he *justifies* this interpretation. The justification – the reasons why he is correct – is what the expert communicates. The insight – the actual process by which he reached that particular interpretation – is not available. In the expert's justification, he identifies the features in the data which distinguish the correct interpretation from other likely interpretations. This would appear to be an example of the proposal by Karl Popper (1963) that we never prove a hypothesis correct, we only disprove the alternatives. That is, the expert does not identify the data which truly identifies the case as T3-toxic because, as Figure 20.6 shows, his identification of the relevant data is quite inadequate. What he does is identify the data which *exclude* the other *likely* hypotheses. In the expert's justification, he is essentially disproving hypotheses rather than proving a hypothesis. Something the expert will provide fairly complex reasons which effectively exclude a number of hypotheses, but never all. For example, if the patient is male and the data profile is unusual suggesting some atypical interpretation, the expert may provide some quite sophisticated and complex rule, but this rule will fail to include the condition that the patient not be pregnant (pregnancy leading to some other interpretation). His insight and initial examination of the data so obviously exclude an interpretation related to pregnancy, that he does not consider it in the justification.

We hypothesize that when experts provide rules, they only identify data which distinguish between a small set of hypotheses, but the expert system is meant to use the resulting rules in the real world to distinguish between all possible hypotheses. The net effect is that expert systems, regardless of their knowledge formalism, must make errors and must be run in an environment where they can gradually be refined as a result of their mistakes. This is not to say that expert systems cannot become truly expert, for humans have precisely the same limitation. Popper (1963) has proposed that we can never be certain that what we hypothesize is true, we can only disprove earlier hypotheses and replace them with an unproven refinement or new hypothesis. Our present state of knowledge is an unproven hypothesis, but one that is less wrong than its predecessor. It seems that this is a fair description of a knowledge base at any stage of its development.

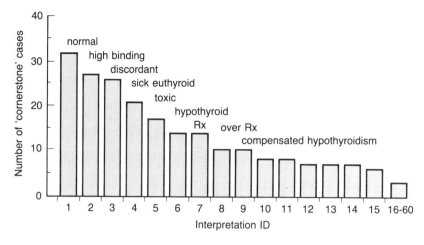

Figure 20.8   The number of cases in the database of 'cornerstone cases' for each interpretation. Only the first nine are named and the number of cases for interpretations 16 to 60 has been averaged.

6   Growth of the system

Support for this Popper hypothesis of knowledge maintenance is found in the growth of GARVAN-ES1. Figure 20.8 indicates the composition of the database of cornerstone cases, showing the number of cases for each interpretation. Not only have some 300 cases had to be added to the database since mid-1984, but there are clearly many cases for each interpretation. The figure names only some of the 15 interpretations which have a sizeable number of cases. Many interpretations have only one or two cases in the database. However, those interpretations which have a numbers of cases are very common, and represent interpretations for which an expert would assume that it would be easy to generate rules; examples are toxicosis (a different interpretation from T3-toxicosis above), hypothyroidism, etc. In fact, it has been necessary for the experts to see a whole range of cases for each interpretation before they provided adequate rules. Although an expert knows perfectly well when to interpret a case as thyrotoxic, he is unable to communicate this knowledge until the cases that require it arise. The large numbers of cases suggest again that experts do not provide global rules; they provide rules in the context of the data in hand. They are able themselves to interpret cases easily when they arise, but not to anticipate their appearance and provide appropriately general rules.

   Some of the cases in Figure 20.8 are due to the laboratory changing from measuring FT4 to measuring FTI (and the related measure of T4U) which give similar, but slightly different, information. Generally, however, the data represent cases which simply failed the rules and for

| 1984 | 1987 |

RULE(22310.01)
IF   (bhthy or utsh_bhft4 or vhthy)
      and not on_t4
      and not surgery
      and (antithyroid or hyperthyroid)
THEN DIAGNOSIS("... thyrotoxicosis")

RULE(22310.01)
IF   ((((T3 is missing)
      or(T3 is low and T3_BORD is low))
      and TSH is missing
      and vhthy
      and not (query_t4 or on_t4 or surgery or tumour
      or antithyroid or hypothyroid or hyperthyroid))
      or(
      (((utsh_bhft4 or
      (hithy and T3 is missing and TSH is missing))
      and (antithyroid or hyperthyroid))
      or
      utsh_vhft4
      or
      ((hithy or borthy)
      and T3 is missing
      and (TSH is undetect or TSH is low)))
      and
      not on_t4 and not (tumour or surgery)))
      and (TT4 isnt low or T4U isnt low)
THEN DIAGNOSIS("... thyrotoxicosis")

Figure 20.9   The same rule in 1984 when the system was first introduced and its current state in 1987. The details of the knowledge expressed by the rule are irrelevant; the figure is meant only to illustrate the expansion of knowledge.

which the rules had to be modified. Some of the cases relate to 'borderline results' from the various analyte measurements. The expert does not generally consider borderline results in his or her initial rule, but when borderline results occur, they may be accepted as either 'normal' or 'abnormal' depending on the context. The expert is best able to make this assessment in a context of real data. It has been suggested elsewhere that context-based reasoning explains the ability of expert clinicians to cope with errors and noise in laboratory data, when they occur (Compton *et al.*, 1986). Of the cases in Figure 20.8, 32 have been grouped under the interpretation normal, that is, they did not require an interpretation. These cases are included in the database because, at one stage, they were misinterpreted in some way.

The effect of the incremental changes to a rule can be seen in Figure 20.9. Clearly the rule has grown considerably. If the current rule is replaced by the earlier rule and all the cases in the 1987 database tested, three cases cause either version of the rule to fire and produce the appropriate interpretation, six cases are missed by the 1984 rule and four cases cause the 1984 rule to fire inappropriately giving the wrong interpretation. In the changes from 1984 to 1987, these four cases wrongly interpreted by this rule would have also required additions to the knowledge base to ensure their correct interpretation. The net effect of the change since 1984 is that the knowledge base has increased in size by about 80%. Half of the expansion has been due to the addition of new rules and half to the modification of existing rules. This expansion of the knowledge base has brought about an increase in accuracy of the system from 96% (Horn *et al.*, 1985) to 99.7%. (Accuracy of the system is taken as the percentage of reports generated which are accepted by the experts. We suspect that this should be viewed not as its absolute accuracy, but as accuracy with respect to **diagnostically important** interpretations. In a recent study with the C4 inductive learning program (Quinlan *et al.*, 1987) using 10 000 cases analysed by GARVAN-ES1, it emerged that, in up to 2% of reports, experts may formulate a more sophisticated interpretation if challenged to provide their most comprehensive analysis. Since the experts have to go to a little trouble to put aside a case, it seems that sometimes they do not do so if a more refined interpretation will not be of diagnostic importance to the referring clinician.) This data would suggest that a law of diminishing returns applies to knowledge maintenance. Number of rules is not a good indicator of knowledge base size, because of the different ways rules can be organized. The figures above show a range of sizes for rules and also some examples of disjunctions; if the disjunctions are removed and the numbers of rules expanded accordingly the system currently has over 600 rules. It currently provides some 60 different interpretations (not including the varying description of the analyte profile which is included as part of the interpretation). There are some millions of possible data configurations but we have not estimated how many of these are likely to occur in practice.

7 Knowledge engineering strategies for the future

Feigenbaum (1977) has emphasized that knowledge engineering – getting knowledge from experts into expert systems – is a major bottleneck in the widespread deployment of expert systems. This bottleneck has many causes: problems of communication between experts and knowledge engineers, the difficulty of adding knowledge to a knowledge base (note the complexity of some of the rules shown), etc. However we hypothesize that the dichotomy between insight and justification that we have emphasized here is the basic problem with all knowledge engineering, not just the maintenance phase we have described. Popper (1963) considers that hypotheticodeductive reasoning applies to all knowledge and, following him, we suggest that it definitely applies to all knowledge engineering. We never prove things, we only disprove alternatives and are left with the current best hypothesis. The essential problem in knowledge engineering is that the expert does not provide us with the information on his 'insight' or how he reached the correct interpretation; he provides us with his 'justification' for excluding the other hypotheses that perhaps could be considered. If we are to use knowledge engineering based on dialogue with experts to build expert systems it must take into account that an expert's rule is essentially a justification of a hypothesis within a context.

One approach to this would be to set up the expert system so that the context in which an expert provided a rule is part of the knowledge base and is used to help determine which rules can fire. For example, in the case discussed above, if the very broad rule in Figure 20.5 that the expert provided was added to the knowledge base, then it would also be part of the knowledge base that this rule was added because rule 32301.28 (Figure 20.2) had fired inappropriately. For future cases then, the new rule would be used to determine the interpretation *only when both it and 32301.28 were able to fire*. This would preserve the context in which knowledge had been acquired from the expert and minimize the knowledge engineering problems described above. For a totally new rule, for a case the expert system previously failed to interpret, we know nothing about the expert's context and the new rule is likely to subsume existing rules. However, the hidden context for this rule is that the expert system knew nothing about this sort of case for which the expert has generated a new rule, so the new rule should only be used in this context, when none of the other rules can fire. These conflict resolution strategies may well exist in many expert system shells. However, here they are based on a hypothesis of how knowledge is communicated and it is proposed that they should not be included as heuristic inferencing strategies but as part of the knowledge base.

A second strategy is based on the recognition that, essentially, all verbal expression of reasoning is a form of debate. A debate is won, not by proving a hypothesis is correct, but by demonstrating it is the preferable alternative within the context. In more free form argument, we are all familiar with the phenomenon that most of the argument is spent in defining the context in which the argument is to take place and then redefining the context when we start to lose. Knowledge addition to an expert system should take place as if the expert is trying to convince the expert system that it is wrong. This suggests that the basic knowledge maintenance tool should be a means of looking at the knowledge that a system has, within a context which can be changed at will. Again, elements of this approach are found within many knowledge engineering tools, but it seems that perhaps the most general approach to this would be to use a relational model to describe the knowledge (Jansen, 1987), thereby allowing complete flexibility to changing the context. GARVAN-ES1 is currently being redeveloped along these lines (Jansen and Compton, 1988).

The other alternative is to use inductive techniques to learn from data sets (Quinlan *et al.*, 1987). Not only are these techniques attractive for pragmatic reasons but they are based on the implicit recognition that the best source of expert knowledge is based on actual expert analysis of real data. The inductive learning algorithms are intended to find the features in the data which best distinguish between the hypotheses covered by the data set. They thus have strong similarities with the expert's justification of an hypothesis within a context. Perhaps, ultimately, the two approaches will converge.

8 Summary

GARVAN-ES1 has been maintained since mid-1984, with its knowledge upgraded whenever it misinterpreted a case. Although it appears to be highly accurate, it can still make mistakes with potentially serious consequences, suggesting that the system must be used under supervision and maintenance must be continued.

We hypothesize that the essential problem with knowledge engineering is that, when experts provide rules, they only identify data which distinguishes among a small set of 'likely' hypotheses. Using this knowledge the expert system must then try to distinguish between all possible hypotheses in the real world. To facilitate knowledge engineering, this fundamental feature of how an expert communicates his knowledge must be taken into account.

Despite this problem, we are optimistic about the future of expert systems because the same problem underlies human acquisition of knowledge. We never know that what we hypothesize about the world is true, we only disprove earlier hypotheses. Our present state of knowledge is not correct – it is a set of unproven hypotheses – but a set of hypotheses that are less wrong than their predecessors. This hypothesis of Popper's seems to be not only a good description of human knowledge but a fair description of a knowledge base at any stage of its development.

Acknowledgements

Our thanks to Bob Jansen and Ian Jenssen for their helpful comments on this manuscript.

References

Bachant J. and McDermott J. (1984). R1 revisited: four years in the trenches. *AI Magazine*, **5**(3), 21–32

Buchanan B. (1986). Expert systems: working systems and the research
     literature. *Expert Systems*, **3**(1), 32–51
Buchanan B.G., Barstow D., Bechtel R., Bennet J., Clancey W.,
     Kulikowski C., Mitchell T. and Waterman D.A. (1983).
     Constructing an expert system. In *Building Expert Systems* (Hayes-
     Roth F., Waterman D.A., Lenat D.B., eds.). pp. 127–167.
     Reading MA: Addison-Wesley
Compton P. (1987). Expert systems for the clinical interpretation of
     laboratory reports. In *Clinical Chemistry – Proceedings of the XIII
     International Congress of Clinical Chemistry* (Van der Heiden O.,
     den Boer N.C. and Souverijn J.H.M., eds.). Plenum Press, in
     press
Compton P.J., Stuart M.C. and Lazarus L. (1986). Error in laboratory
     reference limits as shown in a collaborative quality assurance
     program. *Clin Chem*, **32**, 845–849
Davis R. and King J.J. (1984). The origin of rule-based systems in AI. In
     *Rule-Based Expert Systems, the MYCIN Experiments of the Stanford
     Heuristic Programming Project*. (Buchanan B.G. and Shortliffe
     E.H., eds.), pp. 20–54. Reading MA: Addison-Wesley
Feigenbaum E.A. (1977). The art of artificial intelligence: themes and
     case studies in knowledge engineering. In *Proc. IJCAI-5*,
     1014–1029
Horn K. (1988). Thesis, in preparation
Horn K., Compton P., Lazarus L. and Quinlan J. (1985). An expert
     computer system for the interpretation of thyroid assays in a
     clinical laboratory. *Aust. Comp. J.*, **17**(1), 7–11
Jansen R. (1987). A data dictionary approach to the software engineering
     of rule-based expert systems. In *Proc. AI 87 Conference*, Sydney,
     101–124
Jansen R. and Compton P. (1988). *The Knowledge Dictionary: A
     Relational Tool for the Maintenance of Expert Systems*. Technical
     Report TR-FC-88-01, CSIRO Division of Information Technology
Popper K.R. (1963). Conjectures and Refutations. London: Routledge
     and Kegan Paul Ltd
Quinlan J.R., Compton P.J., Horn K.A. and Lazarus L. (1987).
     Inductive knowledge acquisition: a case study. In: *Applications of
     Expert Systems* (Quinlan J.R., ed.). Reading MA: Addison-Wesley
Winston P. (1984). *Artificial Intelligence* 2nd edn. Reading MA: Addison-
     Wesley

Index